SCOTLAND: A LITERARY GUIDE

Poetry

Society Inebrious
The Voyage
To Find the New
A Perpetual Motion Machine
Penguin Modern Poets 15 (with E.
  Brathwaite and E. Morgan)
The State of the Nation
The Auld Symie
He Will Be Greatly Missed
A Century of People
A Pint of Bitter
A Lunar Event
Scotland, Yes
This Fine Day
A Celtic Quintet (with J. Bellany)
In This Corner: Selected Poems
  1963–83
Haven (with J. Bellany)
Summoned by Knox
Homage to MacDiarmid (with J.
  Bellany)
Bright Lights Blaze Out (with Owen
  and O'Callaghan)

Stories

Hammer and Thistle (with D.
  Morrison)
The Edge of the Wood

Non-fiction

Thom Gunn & Ted Hughes
George Mackay Brown
The Ballad
The Sensual Scot
Modern Scottish Literature
MacDiarmid: The Terrible Crystal
True Characters (with R. Giddings)
The Book of Rotters (with R.
  Giddings)

Longman Dictionary of Poets
Muriel Spark
Who Was Really Who in Fiction (with
  R. Giddings)
MacDiarmid: A Critical Biography

As Editor

The Penguin Book of Socialist Verse
The Martial Muse: Seven Centuries of
  War Poetry
Cambridge Book of English Verse
  1939–75
Making Love: The Picador Book of
  Erotic Verse
The Bawdy Beautiful: The Sphere
  Book of Improper Verse
Mounts of Venus: The Picador Book
  of Erotic Prose
Drink To Me Only: The Prose (and
  Cons) of Drinking
Smollett: Author of the First
  Distinction
The Sexual Dimension in Literature
A Scottish Poetry Book
Scott: The Long Forgotten Melody
Byron: Wrath and Rhyme
The Thistle Rises: A MacDiarmid
  Miscellany
MacDiarmid: Aesthetics in Scotland
The Letters of Hugh MacDiarmid
The Poetry of Motion
Muriel Spark: An Odd Capacity for
  Vision
Harold Pinter: You Never Heard Such
  Silence
Auden: The Far Interior
A Second Scottish Poetry Book
Scottish Quotations
The Quest for Le Carré

SCOTLAND: A LITERARY GUIDE

Alan Bold

ROUTLEDGE

First published in 1989 by
Routledge
11 New Fetter Lane, London EC4P 4EE
© 1989 Alan Bold

Printed in Great Britain by
T. J. Press (Padstow) Ltd
Padstow, Cornwall

British Library Cataloguing in Publication Data

Bold, Alan, *1943—*
Scotland: a literary guide.
1.   Scotland. Literary associations, to 1986
I.   Title
941.1

ISBN 0–415–00731–3

CONTENTS

PREFACE

This guide examines, in alphabetical order, most of the significant literary locations in Scotland. Counties have been indicated more prominently than regions, which are given in parentheses. Distances are, generally, as the crow flies, and road numbers emphasise destinations rather than routes.

Although a small country in terms of size and population Scotland has produced many writers internationally acknowledged as truly great; for example, David Hume, Adam Smith, Burns, Scott, Carlyle, Stevenson, and MacDiarmid. I have, of course, covered all the obvious names as well as providing information on writers whose work may be unfamiliar to the reader. In an attempt to give the book character, I have made use of local colour and illustrative quotations. It should be noted that the amount of space given to an author may depend, to some degree, on the amount of information available. By any reckoning William Dunbar is a writer of genius yet little is known about his life. By contrast, the career of A. J. Cronin is well documented. Though there is more Cronin then Dunbar in this book it is by chance, therefore, rather than choice.

Instead of fixing an arbitrary shut-out date I have included modern writers who seem to me to have particular topographical relevance. The inclusion of a living author does not necessarily imply a value judgment on his or her work.

ACKNOWLEDGMENTS

For financial assistance while researching and writing this book I am grateful to the Scottish Arts Council. The living authors whose work is cited in the following pages generously gave me permission to quote copyright work. Much of the modern material is based on correspondence and conversation with the authors involved and to them I extend my thanks. I would also like to thank the following individuals for supplying information: J. M. Allan; A. F. Bryce; Isabel Couperwhite; Isabel Crawford; Loudon Craig; Konrad Hopkins; Graham Hopner; W. M. Howard; Moira Innes; Tom Leonard; Hugh Mackay; Amelia Macleod; H. Moore; A. D. Reid; Bill Shannon; Isabel Walker; the Earl of Wemyss and March.

For permission to quote poems, as specified in the text, acknowledgment is made as follows: W. H. Auden (from *Collected Poems*) to Faber and Faber and Random House; Alan Bold (from *In this Corner*: Macdonald Publishers) to the author; George Bruce (from *Collected Poems*) to the author and Edinburgh University Press; John Buchan ('By a Scholar') to the Rt Hon. The Lord Tweedsmuir, CBE; Helen B. Cruickshank (from *Collected Poems*) to Gordon Wright; Douglas Dunn (from *Barbarians*: Faber and Faber) to the author; Robert Garioch (from *Complete Poetical Works*) to Macdonald Publishers, Edinburgh; W. S. Graham (from *Collected Poems*: Faber and Faber) to Mrs Nessie Graham; George Campbell Hay (from 'The Old Fisherman') to the Trustees of the W. L. Lorimer Memorial Trust Fund; Henry Henderson (from 'The Sands of Reay') to John Humphries; Maurice Lindsay (from *Collected Poems*: Paul Harris) to the author; Norman MacCaig (from *Collected Poems*: Chatto and Windus) to the author; Hugh MacDiarmid (from *The Complete Poems of Hugh MacDiarmid*, *The Letters of Hugh MacDiarmid*, *Lucky Poet*) to the estate of Hugh MacDiarmid; Sorley MacLean (from *Spring Tide and Neap Tide*: Canongate) to the author; Edwin Morgan (from *Poems of Thirty Years*: Carcanet Press) to the author; Edwin Muir (from *Collected Poems*) to Faber and Faber and Oxford University Press, New York; Charles Murray (from *Hamewith*) to Aberdeen University Press for Charles Murray Trust; Wilfred Owen (from *The Collected Poems of*

ACKNOWLEDGMENTS

Wilfred Owen) to the estate of Wilfred Owen and Chatto and Windus; Walter Perrie (from *A Lamentation for the Children*: Canongate) to the author; Tom Scott (from *Brand the Builder*: Ember Press) to the author; Iain Crichton Smith (from *Selected Poems*: Macdonald Publishers) to the author; Sydney Goodsir Smith (from *Collected Poems*) to Mrs Hazel Smith and John Calder (Publishers); William Soutar ('Autobiography') to the Trustees of the National Library of Scotland; W. J. Tait (from *Collected Poems*: Paul Harris) to the author; Vagaland (from *The Collected Poems of Vagaland*: Shetland Times) to M. Robertson.

ABBOTSFORD, Roxburghshire (Border) 2½m SE of Galashiels, off A7

Sir Walter Scott

Abbotsford, the home of Sir Walter Scott (1771–1832), is maintained by the author's descendants and open to the public (24 March–31 Oct. 10am–5pm, Sun. 2–5pm). Visitors are shown the study (containing Scott's writing desk and chair); the library (with some 9,000 books collected by Scott); the drawing room (hung with Chinese hand-painted paper given to Scott by his cousin, Hugh Scott of Draycott); the armoury (with Scott's blunderbuss, yeomanry sword and pistols); the entrance hall (with walls showing oak panelling from the Auld Kirk of Dunfermline); the dining room where Scott died on 21 September 1832.

Throughout his life Scott's literary success was accompanied by giant steps up the social ladder. In 1804 he inherited his late uncle's property of Rosebank in Kelso, sold it for £5,000 and took a seven-year lease on Ashestiel, a superbly situated farmhouse in Ettrick Forest, six miles from Selkirk. When in 1811, the lease on Ashestiel ran out Scott decided to buy – from Dr Robert Douglas, parish minister of Galashiels – Cartley Hole farmhouse and farm on the right bank of the Tweed. He knew he would have to 'have recourse to my pen to make the matter easy'. Half the 4,000-guinea puchase price (for around 110 acres) was raised by John Ballantyne & Co. on the promise of a new narrative poem. Scott completed the purchase of his property, moved into it on 28 May 1812, 'resumed the pen in my old Cossack manner', and, completed *Rokeby* (1813), a poem in six cantos. Since the land he had acquired had once belonged to the monks of Melrose who had used a ford below the house, Scott renamed his property Abbotsford.

When *Rokeby* was published it started well enough and then sales faltered and failed to live up to expectations. The reason was that a rival had entered the field: Lord Byron who 'awoke one morning and found myself famous' after the publication of the first two cantos of *Childe Harold's Pilgrimage* in 1812. Scott acknowledged Byron's brilliance and realised he would never again have a monopoly of the market for narrative verse. It must be remembered that Scott did not overrate the artistic merit of his own poetry and when he was offered the Laureateship in 1813 he turned it down and suggested that Robert Southey was a more suitable man for the job.

As if the blow to his commercial viability as a poet was not enough to cope with, Scott's publisher, John Ballantyne & Co., was in serious difficulty (largely through its unwanted stock of Scott's antiquarian projects). With the generous help of a £4,000 loan from the fourth Duke of Buccleuch, Scott was able to avoid bankruptcy but he had to wind up John Ballantyne & Co. and put himself in the hands of Archibald Constable to whom he promised a new narrative poem by November. The poem planned was *The Lord of the Isles* and Scott had an opportunity to do some research on the geographical background. Will Erskine, Sheriff of Orkney and Shetland, invited Scott to tour the Scottish islands. Before Scott left, however, he arranged for Archibald Constable to publish, anonymously, his first novel.

Back in 1805, encouraged by the success of his verse, Scott had thought of attempting a prose narrative. Accordingly he 'threw together about one-third part of the first volume of *Waverley*' and had it advertised under the imprint of John Ballantyne. Somehow, a 'critical friend' discouraged Scott from issuing the novel and, rather than risk his prestige as a poet by an impetuous adventure into prose, he abandoned the idea and put the manuscript into an old writing-desk which was eventually stored in a lumber garret at Abbotsford.

Now, in 1813, while looking in the desk for fishing-tackle for a friend, he came across the lost manuscript and quickly completed it. Scott said that 'the tale of Waverley was put together with so little care that I cannot boast of having sketched any distinct plan of the work'. Because of this, and still sensitive about his poetic reputation, Scott decided against putting his name to a work which might well fail to impress a public already partly won over by Byron.

Waverley was published, in three volumes, on 7 July 1814 and so indifferent was Scott to his impact as a novelist that he, literally, left the book behind him. In the company of Will Erskine and the Northern Lighthouse Commissioners, Scott left Fraserburgh on 1 August 1814 for a two-month tour of the Scottish islands. In his absence *Waverley* took off on its own astonishing journey to international celebrity and by the end of the year 5,000 copies had been sold at a profit of more than £2,000. 'I have seldom,' said Scott, 'felt more satisfaction than when, returning from a pleasure voyage, I found *Waverley* in the zenith of popularity, and public curiosity in full cry after the name of the author.'

He had every reason to be satisfied. Here was a way in which he could finance his increasingly ambitious plans for Abbotsford – and this at a time when his fears about the selling power of his poetry were being justified. *The Lord of the Isles* was published in January 1815, his second novel *Guy Mannering* the month after. By his own standards the sales of *The Lord of the Isles* were disappointing and he told James Ballantyne: 'Since one line has failed, we must just stick to something else.' The 'something else' was novel-writing. *Guy Mannering*, written in six weeks, was an instant success. The first edition of 2,000 sold out in a day. Scott therefore decided to abandon poetry and stick to prose. The acquisition of Abbotsford coincides with Scott's career as a novelist.

There can be little doubt that the creation of Abbotsford meant more to Scott than his reputation as a poet or novelist. We have it on Lockhart's authority that 'at the highest elevation of his literary renown – when princes bowed to his name, and nations thrilled at it – he would have considered losing all that at a change of the wind, as nothing, compared to parting with his place as the Cadet of Harden and Clansman of Buccleuch'. And it was at Abbotsford that he could play to perfection the part of well-connected landed gentleman. The novels he wrote at Abbotsford financed his social status as a laird though the mercenary motivation does not detract from the quality of Scott's art.

Abbotsford, transformed from a farmhouse to a magnificent mansion, was completed in 1824. Scott took great joy in settling the estate on his son Walter in 1825 on the occasion of his marriage to Jane Jobson of Lochore, the heiress niece of Scott's friend Sir Adam Ferguson. Scott's words on settling Abbotsford on his son were: 'I have now parted with my lands with more pleasure than I ever derived from the acquaintance or possession of them; and if I be spared for ten years I think I may promise to settle as much more again upon these young folks.' He was, in fact, to be spared seven more years – but as a debtor, not a benefactor.

What happened in 1826 was that the chain of credit that Scott (as a partner in James Ballantyne & Co.) and Archibald Constable depended on broke loose. The secure anchor which the chain clung to, Constable's London agent Hurst, Robinson & Co., was suddenly exposed as a thing of speculative sand, not solid cash. The London firm had gambled their assets and collapsed. This in turn ruined Constable, whose numerous bills and promises were now rendered worthless. And the ruin of Constable inevitably meant the ruin of James Ballantyne & Co., which Scott had established. He knew he was faced with 'the prospect of absolute ruin'. However he turned down offers of financial help from the Duke of Buccleuch and other friends and said defiantly: 'No! this right hand shall work it all off!' Indeed it did, but at a terrible cost to his health.

To settle his debts of almost £117,000 (including private debts of around £20,000) Scott agreed to pay the money made from his writing into a trust.

He was allowed to remain in Abbotsford but had to sell 39 North Castle Street, his Edinburgh home of twenty-five years standing. Yet he himself remained a valuable property. With Constable no longer in business there was a rush of publishers anxious to secure the services of Scott. Longman paid over £8,000 for *Woodstock* (1826) and Scott, delighted at this 'matchless sale for less than three months work', increased his efforts. However, human tragedy followed hard on the heels of his earlier financial catastrophe. On 16 May 1826 Charlotte, Lady Scott, died at Abbotsford. Scott, already shaken by the collapse of his commercial affairs, wrote in his *Journal*:

> I think my heart will break. Lonely, aged, deprived of my family . . . an impoverished and embarrassed man, deprived of the sharer of my thoughts and counsels, who could always talk down my sense of the calamitous apprehensions which must break the heart which must bear them alone. Even her foibles were of service to me, by giving me things to think of beyond my weary self-reflections.

However, typical of his strength of character was his determination not 'to blaze cambric and crape in the public eye like a disconsolate widower, that most affected of all characters'.

Scott continued to make money and by the end of 1828, according to his son-in-law, had earned around £40,000 for his creditors since his financial crash. 'No literary biographer,' wrote Lockhart, 'in all likelihood, will ever have such another fact to record.' The wand of the Wizard of the North was still intact. By 1831 he had cleared all his debts and admitted that 'I could never have slept straight in my coffin till I had satisfied every claim against me'. After a Mediterranean cruise, Scott came back to Abbotsford to observe, 'I have seen much but nothing like my ain house'. In this house he died, in the presence of his children.

ABERDEEN, Aberdeenshire   (Grampian)

John Barbour

Aberdeen, on the Don and Dee, was a royal burgh under David I; King's College was founded in 1495, Marischal College in 1593. John Barbour (*c.* 1320–95) was born in Aberdeen a few years after Robert the Bruce's great victory over the English at Bannockburn (1314). By 1357 he was Archdeacon of Aberdeen, a position he retained for the rest of his life. He was made a member of the Scottish royal household by Robert II, founder of the Stewart dynasty. Robert II commissioned Barbour to write *The Bruce*, a narrative poem in octosyllabic couplets comprising twenty books and 13,550 lines. Part of it was printed in 1571, the full text in 1616.

In celebrating a Scottish hero Barbour expressed, in powerful vernacular verse, the notion of independence, as in the celebrated lines on freedom:

> A! Freedom is a noble thing!
> Freedom makis man to have liking;   *choice*
> Freedom all solace to man givis:
> He livis at ease that freely livis!
> A noble hart may have nane ease,
> Na ellis nocht that may him please,   *nor*
> Gif freedom failye; for free liking
> Is yarnit owre all othir thing.   *yearned for*

Lord Byron

Captain John 'Mad Jack' Byron took, as his second wife, Catherine Gordon of Gight (in the parish of Fyvie). As she was the last laird of Gight, Mad Jack probably made the match for her money – which he quickly squandered. George Gordon Noel Byron (1788–1824) was born in London on 22 January 1788 and some two years later his father, pursued by creditors, took the family to Aberdeen. Mad Jack died in 1791 and Byron lived with his mother in Broad Street. According to an article by Dr Gorden Blaikie in *Harper's Magazine* (August 1891), Byron was sent at the age of five to the school of 'Bodsy' Bower in Longacre. His mother withdrew him from this school and after being taught by two private tutors (subsequently ministers of the Church of Scotland) Byron attended Aberdeen Grammar School, then situated in Schoolhill. The school registers show his name entered quarterly from 29 January 1796 to 18 June 1798 – the month after he succeeded his grand uncle as Lord Byron. As the school registers before 1796 do not exist, it is probable that Byron entered the school in November 1794. There is a Byron statue in Skene Street, in the gardens of the grammar school. When the novelist Eric Linklater (1899–1974) attended Aberdeen Grammar School from 1913 to 1916 he felt that the statue of 'Byron, through the window, undid the schoolroom teaching that literature must be a solemn thing' (*The Man on My Back*, 1941).

On inheriting the family title in 1798, Byron and his mother moved to England but the poet never forgot the formative years he spent in Scotland. *Hours of Idleness* (1807) contains 'Lachin Y Gair' and 'When I Roved a Young Highlander' but, more significantly, Byron's masterpiece *Don Juan* (1819–24) affirms his Scottish origins (X, 17–18):

> But I am half a Scot by birth, and bred
> A whole one, and my heart flies to my head. . . .
> As 'Auld Lang Syne' brings Scotland, one and all,
>   Scotch plaids, Scotch snoods, the blue hills, and clear streams,

The Dee, the Don, Balgounie's brig's *black wall*,
   All my boy feelings, all my gentler dreams
Of what I *then dreamt*, clothed in their own pall,
   Like Banquo's offspring; – floating past me seems
My childhood in this childishness of mine:
I care not – 'tis a glimpse of *'Auld Lang Syne'*.

Alexander Scott

Alexander Scott, poet and critic, was born on 28 November 1920 at 13 Western Road, a two-room cottage in Woodside on the northern outskirts of Aberdeen. He moved, in 1922, to top flat in tenement at 22 Jamaica Street, near Kittybrewster Railway Station and attended Kittybrewster primary school from 1926 to 1932. In 1929 Scott settled in his grandfather's newly built bungalow at 55 Cattofield Place on the edge of the then developing Hilton estate; he was at Hilton Intermediate School (Jan- June 1933), Central Secondary School, Schoolhill (Sept. 1933–June 1939) and a student at Aberdeen University from 1939 to 1941 and 1945 to 1947. While he was absent on war service – from 1941 to 1945 during which time he was awarded the Military Cross for leading a company attack on a German regimental headquarters at the battle of the Reichswald (1945) – the house in Cattofield Place was destroyed in Aberdeen's worst bombing raid (spring 1943). On demobilisation Scott lived (1945–6) in his mother-in-law's hotel, Woodside House Hotel, on the south bank of the River Don at Woodside and then in his parents' flat at 64 Hilton Terrace, on a corporation housing estate.

After teaching (from October 1947 to September 1948) at Edinburgh University, Scott became the lecturer in Scottish literature (the first appointment of its kind in Scotland) at Glasgow University. In 1971 he was appointed Head of Department of Scottish Literature (again, the first appointment of its kind in Scotland) at Glasgow University. His books include a biography of William Soutar, *Still Life* (1958) and *Selected Poems 1943–74* (1975). His most sustained poem on Aberdeen, 'Heart of Stone', was written for television and collected in *Cantrips* (1968). It evokes, in Scots verse, the essential character of Aberdeen:

The sea-gray toun, the stane-gray sea,
The cushat's croudle mells wi the sea-maw's skirl   *pigeon's coo, mingles*
Whaur bath gae skaichan fish-guts doun the quays *scavenging*
Or scrannan crumbs in cracks o the thrang causeys,*scraping, busy*
A lichthous plays the lamp-post owre a close,
The traffic clappers through a fisher's clachan   *village*
Whaur aa the vennels spulyie names frae the sea, *alleys, plunder*
And kirks and crans clamjamfrie,   *crowd*

| Heaven and haven mixter-maxtered heave | *confused* |

To the sweel o the same saut tide.

David Toulmin

David Toulmin (born John Reid in 1913) settled in a flat at 7 Pittodrie Place in 1971, a year before the publication of his first book *Hard Shining Corn* (1972). After a lifetime working as a 'fee'd loon' on various farms, Toulmin was suddenly acclaimed as a literary celebrity and an authentic voice of Buchan. Toulmin's highly regarded novel *Blown Seed* (1976) was written at 7 Pittodrie Place.

ABERFELDY, Perthshire (Tayside) 10m SW of Pitlochry on A826

Robert Burns

A signposted footpath leads to the Falls of Moness (one mile south-west) where Robert Burns (1759–96) is said to have written 'The Birks of Aberfeldie' which begins:

> Now simmer blinks on flow'ry braes,   *shines, slopes*
> And o'er the crystal streamlets plays.
> Come, let us spend the lightsome days
>   In the birks of Aberfeldie!   *birches*

> *Bonie lassie, will ye go,*
> *Will ye go, will ye go?*
> *Bonie lassie, will ye go*
>   *To the birks of Aberfeldie?*

From 25 August to 16 September 1787, Burns toured the Scottish Highlands with his irascible friend William Nicol. According to James Barke's *The Wonder of All the Gay World* (1949, the fourth novel in his sequence on the life of the poet) Burns and Nicol:

> crossed the River Tay to see for themselves the famous birch-trees of Aberfeldy.
>   They clambered up to the Falls of Moness and there and then the Bard took pencil and paper and wrote his first draft of 'The Birks of Aberfeldy'.
>   Here even the prosaic Nicol was somewhat moved.

ABERLADY, East Lothian   (Lothian)   5m NW of Haddington

Nigel Tranter

At the mouth of the Peffer Burn on the coast, Aberlady has been the home of the novelist Nigel Tranter (born in Glasgow on 23 November 1909) since 1938. After training as an accountant, Tranter became a full-time writer and settled in Aberlady. Initially he rented Cross Cottage, an eighteenth-century cottage beside the ancient market-cross and lived there while writing the novels *Mammon's Daughter* (1939), *Harsh Heritage* (1940), *Eagles' Feathers* (1941), and *Watershed* (1941). From 1941 to 1946, while a serving soldier, Tranter wrote five novels, and on his return to Aberlady wrote a series of eighteen novels beginning with *Island Twilight* (1947).

In 1950 Tranter moved from the village to Quarry House, an eighteenth-century house on Luffness estate, on the shore of Aberlady Bay. His novel *Ducks and Drakes* (1953) was prompted by the controversy over the setting up of a Nature Reserve at Aberlady Bay. Tranter, who was much involved in this dispute (even to the extent of appearing in court), eventually became a member of the Committee of Management. Tranter is a prolific novelist perhaps best known for his trilogy on the life of Robert the Bruce: *The Steps to the Empty Throne* (1969), *The Path of the Hero King* (1970), and *The Price of the King's Peace* (1971).

ABERUTHVEN, Perthshire   (Tayside)   11m SW of Perth on A9

Robin Bell

The village of Aberuthven becomes the fictional village of *Strathinver* (1984) in the book of that name by Robin Bell (born 4 January 1945 in Dundee). Bell's father was a minister of the parishes of Aberuthven and Gask, and Bell grew up in the Manse of Aberuthven in the years after the Second World War. *Strathinver* is a sequence of sixty poems covering the period 1945–53 and introducing a fictionalised cast of local characters. Bell himself appears in the book as 'a slim, shy youth,/a fourth person singular to the town'.

AILSA CRAIG

Robert Burns

This islet, off the coast of Ayrshire, informs a simile Robert Burns (1759–96) used in his song 'Duncan Gray':

> Duncan fleech'd, and Duncan pray'd   *wheedled*
> (Ha, ha, the wooing o't!)
> Meg was deaf as Ailsa Craig
> (Ha, ha, the wooing o't!)

The granite rock from Ailsa Craig is used in the manufacture of curling stones.

ALEXANDRIA, Dunbartonshire   (Strathclyde)   Vale of Leven 3m N of Dumbarton

Tobias Smollett

A Smollett Museum (open Easter–September, daily 11am–6pm) is housed in Castle Cameron, near Cameron House, at the south end of Loch Lomond. It contains the papers of Lewis M. Knapp, author of *Tobias Smollett* (1949) as well as portraits of Smollett (1721–71) and first editions of his works. There is also a photograph of the plane tree at Dalquhurn House under which Smollett was supposedly born; and a painting of the first design of the Smollett Monument at Renton. Castle Cameron is still in the possession of the Smollett family who sold Cameron House in 1983. Formerly the Smollett Museum comprised a room in Cameron House.

In *Humphry Clinker* (1771) Smollett mentions Cameron House, for Jerry Melford explains:

> We have fixed our headquarters at Cameron, a very neat country-house belonging to commissary Smollett, where we found every sort of accommodation we could desire. . . . It is situated like a Druid's temple, in a grove of oak, close by the side of Lough-Lomond, which is a surprising body of pure transparent water, unfathomably deep in many places, six or seven miles broad, four and twenty miles in length, displaying above twenty green islands, covered with wood; some of them cultivated for corn, and many of them stocked with red deer.

Cameron House was the family home of the Smolletts from 1763. The present house (a baronial mansion of the Victorian period) is built on the house Smollett knew (and which was destroyed by fire).

James Boswell, Samuel Johnson

Boswell and Johnson visited Cameron House in 1773. The entry for Wednesday 27 October in Boswell's *Journal of a Tour to the Hebrides* (1785) describes the visit to see Smollett's cousin James who purchased the Cameron Estates in 1763 (the Smolletts previously staying at the Place of Bonhill nearby):

> We were favoured with Sir James Colquhoun's coach to convey us in the evening to Cameron, the seat of Commissary Smollett . . . Mr Smollett was a man of considerable learning, with abundance of animal spirits; so that he was a very good companion for Dr Johnson, who said to me, 'We have had more solid talk here than at any place where we have been.'
>
> I remember Dr Johnson gave us this evening an able and eloquent discourse on the *Origin of Evil*, and on the consistency of moral evil with the power and goodness of God. He shewed us how it arose from our free agency, an extinction of which would be a still greater evil than any we experience. . . . Mrs Smollett whispered me, that it was the best sermon she had ever heard. Much do I upbraid myself for having neglected to preserve it.

ALFORD, Aberdeenshire   (Grampian)   29½m W of Aberdeen on
A944

Charles Murray

Charles Murray (1864–1941), born in Alford on 28 September 1864, was educated locally at Gallowhill School. The Charles Murray Memorial Trust was founded in 1942 and on 24 August 1956 the **Murray Park** was officially opened in Alford. Centenary celebrations were held in Murray Park on 26 September 1964.

In 1881 Murray was apprenticed to a firm of civil engineers in Aberdeen and in 1888 he emigrated to South Africa where he worked as an engineer with a gold-mining company. His break with his native land led him to dote on it and in a speech, of 25 October 1925 in Aberdeen, he described himself as 'having, during many years in a new country, kept warm my affection for the old, and retained my interest in its simple life, its old-fashioned characters and customs, and its expressive language'. Murray's verse was nostalgic in tone as he acknowledged by calling his first collection *Hamewith* (1900). 'Hamewith' means 'homewards' and Murray looked back to Scotland with an intense longing.

In 'The Whistle', from *Hamewith*, he produced a poem that seemed to encapsulate the experience of the Scottish child. There is a splendid evocation of place and weather and a narrative about youthful high spirits being dismissed by the grim schoolteacher who 'lickit' the boy and 'brunt the whistle that the wee herd made'. The first stanza is a brilliant display of dialect Scots:

He cut a sappy sucker from the muckle rodden-tree,	*rowan-tree*
He trimmed it, an' he wet it, an' he thumped it on his knee;	
He never heard the teuchat when the harrow broke her eggs,	*lapwing*
He missed the craggit heron nabbin' puddocks in the seggs,	*frogs*
He forgot to hound the collie at the cattle when they strayed,	
But you should hae seen the whistle that the wee herd made!	

Hamewith also reprinted 'Spring in the Howe o' Alford' which first appeared in *A Handful of Heather* (1893, printed for private circulation). It begins:

There's burstin' buds on the larick now,	*larch*
A' the birds are paired an' biggin';	*building*
Saft soughin' win's dry the dubby howe,	*sighing, winds, muddy*
An' the eildit puir are thiggin'.	*elderly, borrowing*

Murray's war-time volume *A Sough o' War* (1917) confirmed his stature as an outstanding writer of vernacular verse. 'Dockens Afore His Peers' is a little masterpiece, a self-portrait of the Scot who is canny to the point of low cunning. Dockens wishes to secure exemption from military service for his youngest son and when he is unsuccessful at appealing to the conscience he unscrupulously appeals to the pocket.

Murray was a genuinely popular poet, one revered by the people who do not normally respond to contemporary poetry. His poems demonstrated the appeal of Scots so convincingly that when 'There's aye a something' appeared in the Aberdeen *Press and Journal* in 1933 the first edition of the paper sold out by 9am and two extra editions had to be printed. In a speech in Aberdeen on 2 December 1912 Murray said of his Scots poems:

That these things should be written in the vernacular was neither accidental not intentional. It was simply inevitable. If I had been forced to or tried to write in English I certainly could have done nothing.

Murray's strength was that he drew on the oral currency coined in his native Aberdeenshire.

Murray retired in 1924, returned to Scotland and died in Banchory, Kincardineshire, on 12 April 1941.

ALLOWAY, Ayrshire   (Strathclyde)   1½m S of Ayr on B7024

Robert Burns

Burns Cottage, the birthplace of Robert Burns (1759–96), is open to the public (summer 9am–7pm, Sun. 2–7pm; winter 9am–5pm, Sun. 2–5pm). It was bought in 1884 (when in use as an alehouse) by the Alloway Burns Monument Trustees who built a museum at the rear to house papers and relics of the poet – including the Burns family bible, a Kilmarnock edition of *Poems, Chiefly in the Scottish Dialect* (1786), and a plaster mask of the poet's skull. The cottage contains the bed in which Burns was born.

The poet's father William Burnes (the 'e' was dropped after his death) was born in 1721, the son of a tenant-farmer. William trained as a gardener and became a 'very well-inclined lad'. At least the certificates which said so protected him from his father's reputation as a Jacobite sympathiser and helped him move south to Edinburgh where he landscaped private gardens and worked on the city's recreation park, the Meadows.

In 1750 William Burnes accepted an offer of gardening in Ayrshire and earned enough to lease seven acres of nurseryland at Alloway, a tiny village outside the county town of Ayr. Though he still had to work as head gardener on the Doonholm estate of the Provost of Ayr, Burnes hoped to become an independent market-gardener. At a fair in 1756 Burnes met and fell in love with Agnes Broun, a tenant-farmer's daughter with red hair, clear skin, dark eyes and a good singing voice. With Agnes in mind he spent the summer and autumn evenings of 1757 building, with his own hands on his own seven acres, the clay thatched cottage of two rooms with adjoining stable and byre. By winter this 'but and ben' – or 'auld clay biggin' as Robert Burns called it in 'The Vision' – was white-washed and ready, so on 15 December 1757, William Burnes married Agnes Broun, eleven years his junior, and took her back to the cottage.

Robert Burns – the first of seven children to William and Agnes – was born in the cottage on 25 January 1759 (an anniversary celebrated annually in Scotland and abroad). Ten days later a storm blew out the gable above the fireplace. Mrs Burnes and her baby had to shelter in a neighbour's house. Burns later made a song from the incident, in 'There was a Lad':

> Our monarch's hindmost year but ane
> Was five-and-twenty days begun,
> 'Twas then a blast o' Janwar' win'
>   Blew hansel in on Robin.

> The gossip keekit in his loof,   *glanced, face*
> Qho' scho – 'Wha lives will see the proof,
> This waly boy will be nae coof: *thumping, dolt*
>   I think we'll ca' him Robin.

12

'He'll hae misfortunes great an' sma',
But ay a heart aboon them a'.   *above*
He'll be a credit till us a':
   We'll a' be proud o' Robin!'

Burns's childhood, within a closely knit family group, was a happy one.
His industrious, intelligent father used his little leisure to improve the
penmanship he had learned at school and Mrs Burnes sang old Scottish
songs to her children. There were stories told by Mrs Burnes's cousin Betty
Davidson, 'remarkable for her ignorance, credulity and superstition'. She
had, Robert remembered,

> the largest collection in the county of tales and songs concerning
> devils, ghosts, fairies, and brownies, witches, warlocks, spunkies,
> kelpies, elf-candles, dead-lights, wraiths, apparitions, cantraips,
> giants, inchanted towers, dragons and other trumpery.

As if to reinforce these tales of the supernatural, there was the close
proximity (half a mile from the cottage) of **Kirk Alloway**. This early-
sixteenth-century church was last used in 1756 and was already roofless
during the childhood of Robert Burns. Kirk Alloway features in 'Tam O'
Shanter', Burns's best-known narrative poem, originally written in 1790
to accompany the illustration of Kirk Alloway in Francis Grose's *Antiquities of Scotland*:

> The lightnings flash from pole to pole;
> Near and more near the thunders roll;
> When, glimmering thro' the groaning trees,
> Kirk-Alloway seem'd in a bleeze,
> Thro' ilka bore the beams were glancing,   *every chink*
> And loud resounded mirth and dancing. . . .

> Warlocks and witches in a dance:
> Nae cotillion, brent new frae France,   *brand*
> But hornpipes, jigs, strathspeys, and reels,
> Put life and mettle in their heels.
> A winnock-bunker in the east,   *window-seat*
> There sat Auld Nick, in shape o' beast;
> A tousie tyke, black, grim, and large,   *shaggy dog*
> To gie them music was his charge:
> He screw'd the pipes and gart them skirl,
> Till roof and rafters a' did dirl.
> Coffins stood round, like open presses,   *cupboards*
> That shaw'd the dead in their last dresses;

> And, by some devilish cantraip sleight,   *magic device*
> Each in its cauld hand held a light . . .

The poet's father is buried in the churchyard in front of Kirk Alloway though the gravestone, with epitaph composed by Burns, is a replacement since the original was removed by souvenir hunters.

Just beyond the kirk is the old **Brig O' Doon** which plays a crucial part in 'Tam O' Shanter' as the bridge enables Tam and his grey mare Meg to shake off the witches hot on their heels:

> Now, do thy speedy utmost, Meg,
> And win the key-stane of the brig;
> There, at them thou thy tail may toss,
> A running stream they dare na cross!

Opposite the Brig O' Doon is the **Burns Monument**, built by public subscription. The project, started in 1814, was supported by Sir Alexander Boswell of Auchinleck, son of James Boswell. Completed in 1823 at a cost of £3,000, it is a Grecian structure complete with fluted Corinthian columns. In the Burns Monument museum are various important items: the wedding ring of Jean Armour, the woman Burns married in 1788; the bible he gave to Highland Mary Campbell; a lock of Highland Mary's hair; drinking glasses given by Burns to Agnes 'Clarinda' McLehose; the poet's snuffbox and personal seal. Statues of Tam O' Shanter and his drinking friend Souter Johnnie, by James Thom, are in the garden that surrounds the Burns Monument. The money to buy Burns Cottage in 1884 was raised from the admission charges to the Burns Monument.

Mount Oliphant farm, two miles from Burns Cottage and still farmed, was the poet's home for eleven years. By 1766 William Burnes had four children and rather than see them become 'little underlings' in someone else's household he rented the seventy-acre hilltop farm of Mount Oliphant and stocked it on the strength of a £100 loan. Unfortunately the farm had, in the opinion of the poet's brother Gilbert, 'almost the very poorest soil I know of in a state of cultivation'. Distance and pressure of work virtually isolated the Burns family from John Murdoch's little school in Alloway though William Burnes did not neglect the education of his children. He used his evenings, at Mount Oliphant, to instruct the boys from a rather forbidding collection of books on grammar and theology, a diet spiced by the fortuitous acquisition of a book teaching letter-writing by example from stylists such as Pope and Bolingbroke. In 1772 Burnes sent Robert and Gilbert on alternate weeks to study at the village school in Dalrymple, four miles from Ayr, and the following summer sent Robert to Ayr itself to lodge for three weeks with Murdoch, now an English master at the burgh school. The fourteen-year-old Burns studied English and began to study French.

With the benefit of his new sophistication Burns returned to Mount Oliphant and 'first committed the sin of *rhyme*' in response to an amorous impulse linked to social indignation. He was gathering the harvest sheaves with his partner, Nellie Kilpatrick, a 'bonie, sweet, sonsie lass' of thirteen (a year younger than him) and wondered – so he recorded in his Commonplace Book – 'why my pulse beat such a furious rattan when I looked and fingered over her hand, to pick out the nettle stings and thistles'. When he discovered that the words of Nellie's favourite song were composed by 'a small country laird's son' he knew he could improve on it. 'My Handsome Nell'; which Burns later thought of as 'very puerile and silly' remains a tender and accomplished impression of his adolescent infatuation:

> But Nelly's looks are blithe and sweet.
>   And what is best of a'.
> Her reputation is complete,
>   And fair without a flaw.
>
> She dresses aye sae clean and neat,
>   Both decent and genteel;
> And then there's something in her gait
>   Gars ony dress look weel.
>
> A gaudy dress and gentle air
>   May slightly touch the heart.
> Buts it's innocence and modesty
>   That polishes the dart.
>
> 'Tis this in Nelly pleases me,
>   'Tis this enchants my soul!
> For absolutely in my breast
>   She reigns without control.

In 1769, on the death of the landlord, a factor took over the affairs of Mount Oliphant and hounded William Burnes for payments. 'My indignation,' Burns wrote eight years later, 'yet boils at the recollection of the scoundrel tyrant's insolent, threatening epistles, which used to set us all in tears.'

These distressing circumstances inform an important pasage in 'The Twa Dogs', spoken by Caesar:

> I've noticed, on our laird's court-day
> (An' monie a time my heart's been wae),
> Poor tenant bodies, scant o' cash,
> How they maun thole a factor's snash: *endure, abuse*
> He'll stamp an' threaten, curse an' swear

He'll apprehend them, poind their gear;   *seize*
While they maun staun', wi' aspect humble,
An' hear it a', an' fear an' tremble!
   I see how folk live that hae riches;
But surely poor-folk maun be wretches.

Unable to engage outside help William Burnes was forced to rely on the efforts of his eldest son, who, at fifteen, became the farm's principal labourer and experienced 'the chearless gloom of a hermit with the unceasing moil of a galley-slave'. Driving a team of oxen through the rough ground of Mount Oliphant to manoeuvre the plough over the mounds and hollows was a formidable physical burden. Undoubtedly, the strain of these years contributed to the rheumatic heart condition that resulted in the poet's premature death. Release from Mount Oliphant came in 1777 when William Burnes made an oral agreement with one David McLure to rent the 130 swampy acres of Lochlea farm in the parish of Tarbolton.

ALTRIVE LAKE, Selkirkshire (Border)   By Yarrow Water,
off B709

James Hogg

Altrive Lake, the valley of a drained loch, is associated with James Hogg (1770–1835), the Ettrick Shepherd. Having failed as a farmer in Dumfriesshire and lost money trying to buy a sheep farm in Harris, Hogg at last achieved success in 1813 with the publication of his poetic sequence *The Queen's Wake*, containing (for example) the supernatural tale of Kilmeny:

> Kilmeny had been where the cock never crew,
> Where the rain never fell, and the wind never blew;
> But it seemed as the harp of the sky had rung,
> And the airs of heaven played round her tongue,
> When she spake of the lovely forms she had seen,
> And a land where sin had never been;
> A land of love, and a land of light,
> Withouten sun, or moon, or night.

In 1815 the Duke of Buccleuch, greatly impressed by Hogg's art, gave him Moss End farm (now called Eldinhope) at Altrive for a nominal rent. After marrying Margaret Phillips in 1820, Hogg took a lease on the nearby farm of Mount Benger (slightly to the north) which turned out to be a disaster. Sir Walter Scott noted, in his *Journal* of 3 February 1827, 'James Hogg writes that he is to lose his farm, on which he laid out, or rather threw away, the profit of all his publications.' Hogg was bankrupted in 1830 but returned to Altrive where he spent his remaining years.

ANNAN, Dumfriesshire (Dumfries and Galloway) 5m S of Ecclefechan, on A75

Thomas Blacklock, Robert Burns

Annan, the small town at the mouth of the river Annan, was the birthplace of Thomas Blacklock (1721–91), the blind minister and man of letters. It was Blacklock's letter praising Robert Burns's *Poems, Chiefly in the Scottish Dialect* (1786) that convinced the poet he should stay in Scotland instead of going to Jamaica. Burns acknowledged that

> a letter from Dr Blacklock to a friend of mine overthrew all my schemes [of settling in Jamaica] by rousing poetic ambition. The doctor belonged to a set of critics for whose applause I had not even dared to hope.

Dr Blacklock's letter, delivered via the Rev. George Lawrie and Gavin Hamilton, expressed 'astonishment' at the quality of Burns's poems. Blacklock had lost his sight as an infant, as a result of smallpox, and subsequently studied in Edinburgh where he became friendly with the philosopher David Hume. His *A Collection of Original Poems* appeared in 1760 and in 1764 he settled in Edinburgh (after a period as minister of Kircudbright) where he supported himself by tutoring.

Thomas Carlyle

According to his *Reminiscences* (1881), Thomas Carlyle (1795–1881) regarded Annan as 'a fine, bright, self-confident little town'. It was a subject he could speak on with authority. In 1806 Carlyle was taken by his father to Annan Academy (now the Old Grammar School) which he attended until 1809. The Academy was the original of the Hinterschlag Gymnasium in *Sartor Resartus* (1833–4) which describes the career and philosophy of a German philosopher Diogenes Teufelsdröckh ('Devil's Dung'). In *Sartor Resartus* ('The Tailor Re-Patched') Teufelsdröckh claims his 'evil days' dawned at the Hinterschlag Gymnasium as he was among strangers 'harshly, at best indifferently disposed towards me; the young heart felt, for the first time, quite orphaned and alone'. Carlyle too was, initially at least, unhappy at school, being a sensitive boy vulnerable to bullying. However, as *Sartor* makes clear, there were times when he rebelled:

Only at rare intervals did the young soul burst forth into fire-eyed rage, and with a stormfulness (*Ungestüm*) under which the boldest quailed, assert that he too had Rights of Man, or at least of Mankind.

Carlyle excelled at mathematics and appreciated the teaching of Adam Hope who (he wrote in *Reminiscences*) was 'a praise and glory to well-doing boys, a beneficent terror to the ill-doing or dishonest blockhead sort'.

At the age of thirteen, Carlyle the schoolboy first saw Edward Irving (1792–1834) when Adam Hope introduced this former pupil, then a brilliant student at Edinburgh University, to the Rector of Annan Academy. Born in Annan on 4 August 1792, Irving was to become famous – then infamous – as a millenialist preacher eventually deprived of his Church of Scotland ministry in 1833 because of supposed heresy. It was in Annan Parish Church that Irving was baptised, ordained to the ministry and deposed. His connection with Carlyle was considerable. Irving graduated from Edinburgh University in 1809 and became a schoolteacher in Haddington where he taught, and fell in love with, Jane Baillie Welsh. Carlyle met Irving in Edinburgh in 1815 and again in Annan the following year. When Carlyle went to Kirkcaldy in 1816 as a schoolmaster, Irving was teaching in the same town and the two men became close friends. It was Irving who introduced Carlyle to Jane Welsh's household in 1821 at a time when he, Irving, might have married Jane had he not been engaged to another. In 1892 a statue of Irving was unveiled in front of Annan's Town Hall.

When Carlyle was a pupil at Annan Academy he stayed in the town for four nights every week, going back to Ecclefechan at the weekends. During this time he lodged with a local shoemaker named Waugh. In 1814 Carlyle returned to Annan Academy as a teacher of mathematics, boarding with the Rev. Glen, a minister of a Burgher-Secessionist Congregation in Annan. Of his teaching post at Annan Academy, Carlyle wrote (in *Reminiscences*) that it was 'not a gracious destiny, nor by any means a joyful, indeed a hateful, sorrowing and imprisoning one'.

ANSTRUTHER, Fife   (Fife)   4m SW of Crail on A917

William Tennant

A plaque in the High Street marks the birthplace of William Tennant (1784–1848) who was born in Anstruther Easter on 15 May 1784. Lame from childhood, Tennant mastered various languages and was appointed, in 1834, Professor of Oriental Languages at St Andrews University. His poetic masterpiece is the mock-heroic *Anster Fair* (1812), a poem whose narrative panache and occasional eccentricity of rhyme probably influenced Lord Byron's *Don Juan*, also written in *ottava rima*. The poem, based on the song 'Maggie Lauder' (composed around 1642 and attributed to Francis Sempill of Beltrees), describes the games held to find a Scot worthy of marrying Maggie Lauder, who supposedly lived in Anstruther's East Green in the sixteenth century. In the seventh stanza of Canto III, Tennant writes (using the local name Anster for Anstruther):

> And, from our steeple's pinnacle outspread,
>   The town's long colours flare and flap on high,
> Whose anchor, blazon'd fair in green and red,
>   Curls, pliant to each breeze that whistles by;
> Whilst, on the boltsprit, stern, and topmast-head,
>   Of brig and sloop that in the harbour lie,
> Streams the red gaudery of flags in air,
> All to salute and grace the morn of *Anster Fair*.

Tennant is buried in the churchyard, near the north-east corner of the church.

Robert Louis Stevenson

In 1848 Robert Louis Stevenson (1850–94) spent part of his summer holidays, from Edinburgh University, studying the harbour works at Anstruther. He lived at Cunzie House (plaque), Crail Road, and wrote to his mother:

> I am utterly sick of this grey, grim, sea-beaten hole. I have a little cold in my head, which makes my eyes sore; and you can't tell how utterly sick I am, and how anxious to get back among trees and flowers and something less meaningless than this bleak fertility.

Alastair Mackie

The poet Alastair Mackie (born in Aberdeen in 1925) settled in Anstruther in 1959 as a schoolteacher.

ARBROATH, Angus   (Tayside)   17m NE of Dundee on A92

Bernard de Linton

Arbroath Abbey, a magnificent red sandstone ruin, was founded in 1178 by William the Lion and dedicated to St Thomas of Canterbury. In 1309 Bernard de Linton, Chancellor of Scotland since 1307, became Abbot of

Arbroath. It was Bernard who drafted the Declaration of Arbroath, the classic statement of Scottish independence.

Since his sacrilegious murder of 'Red' John Comyn in the Franciscan church of Greyfriars, Dumfries, in 1306, Bruce's name had been anathema to the papacy and Pope John XXII followed Clement V in regarding the Scottish king as an unrepentant sinner. When four Scottish bishops ignored a papal summons they were therefore excommunicated along with their king. However, the Scots, having fought so hard for their independence, were ready to confront an unsympathetic Pope.

At a meeting at Arbroath Abbey in April 1320 the Scottish nobility, the *communitas*, unanimously agreed to endorse a letter of protest which was composed in memorable Latin prose by Bernard de Linton. It is likely that the letter was discussed and drafted in the chapter-house and written out in the scriptorium of the monastery and that Bruce was, at the time, a guest of Bernard's. The celebrated Declaration of Arbroath, dated 6 April 1320, was sent to Pope John XXII in Avignon, and though he acknowledged receipt of the letter he waited until 1329, when Bruce was on his deathbed, to acknowledge Bruce and his successors as kings of an independent Scotland.

Bernard de Linton's statement (as translated by Lord Cooper of Culross) remains an inspirational text in Scotland:

> For so long as one hundred men remain alive, we shall never under any conditions submit to the domination of the English. It is not for glory or riches or honours that we fight, but only for liberty, which no good man will consent to lose but with his life.

Sir Walter Scott

Sir Walter Scott, in *The Antiquary* (1816) – the third Waverley novel and Scott's own favourite Scott novel – gave Arbroath the name Fairport 'for various reasons'. After meeting the antiquary – Johnathan Oldbuck, the Laird of Monkbarns – on the Edinburgh-Queensferry coach, young Mr Lovel takes up residence in Fairport, a situation that provokes much speculation. Described as a 'thriving seaport town', Fairport is nevertheless not the kind of place Oldbuck would immediately associate with a man such as Lovel. Scott explains:

> it remained a high and doubtful question, what a well-informed young man, without friends, connexions, or employment of any kind could have to do as a resident of Fairport. Neither port wine nor whist had apparently any charms for him. He declined dining with the mess of the volunteer cohort, which had been lately embodied, and shunned joining the convivialities of either of the two parties which then divided Fairport as they did more important places. He was too little

of an aristocrat to join the club of Royal True Blues, and too little of a democrat to fraternise with an affiliated society of the *soi-disant* Friends of the People, which the borough had also the happiness of possessing.

Fortunately for all concerned, Mr Lovel turns out to be Lord William Geraldin, heir to the Earl of Glenallen, and thus a suitable husband for Isabella Wardour.

In one of his conversations with Lovel, the inquisitive antiquary is astonished to learn that his young friend is entirely satisfied with his lot in life, having financial independence as well as few ambitions. Oldbuck responds:

And how came Fairport to be the selected abode of so much self-denying philosophy? It is as if a worshipper of the true religion had set up his staff by choice among the multifarious idolaters of the land of Egypt. There is not a man in Fairport who is not a devoted worshipper of the Golden Calf – the Mammon of unrighteousness. Why, even I, man, am so infected by the bad neighbourhood, that I feel inclined occasionally to become an idolater myself.

Lovel explains that he has chosen to stay in Fairport because it has so few distractions.

Marion Angus

Born in Aberdeen (where she spent most of her adult life), Marion Angus (1866–1946) was brought up in Arbroath in the manse of her father, a United Presbyterian minister. She returned to Arbroath in her final years and after her death her ashes were scattered in the sea off Elliot's Point. Her poems, using the Angus dialect, have a metrical solidity and an emotional appeal, as in 'In a Little Old Town', which begins:

> The haar creeps landward from the sea,   *cold mist*
> The laigh sun's settin' reid.
> Wha's are the bairns that dance fu' late
> On the auld shore-heid?

ARBUTHNOTT, Kincardineshire (Grampian) 10m S of Stonehaven
on B967

John Arbuthnott

John Arbuthnott (1667–1735) was born on 29 April 1667 at Arbuthnott where (from 1665) his father was minister of **Arbuthnott Church**

21

(consecrated in 1242, original chancel still extant). He studied at the universities of Aberdeen, Oxford and St Andrews and settled in London where he was physician to Queen Anne and friend to such as Swift and Pope. He is best-known as the creator of John Bull, featured in *The History of John Bull* (1712), *A Review of the State of John Bull's Family* (1713) and *A Postscript to John Bull* (1714). In *A Sermon Preached to the People at the Mercat Cross, Edinburgh* (1706) he expressed his approval of the parliamentary union of Scotland and England.

Lewis Grassic Gibbon

Lewis Grassic Gibbon, whose trilogy *A Scots Quair* (1932–4) unfolds in the Mearns (as that part of Kincardineshire south of the Grampians is called, supposedly after Mernas who was given the area by his brother Kenneth II), was buried in the south-west corner of **Arbuthnott Churchyard** in February 1935. Born James Leslie Mitchell on 13 February 1901 at Hillhead of Segget, Auchterless, Aberdeenshire, he moved with his family to Bloomfield farm (house now a modernised cottage) high on the Reisk road north of Arbuthnott Church. Mitchell's parents were tied to this unproductive land until the death of Mitchell's father in 1937 and Bloomfield was Mitchell's home until he left school. His love-hate relationship with the land developed on Bloomfield farm.

Arbuthnott shaped Mitchell's young life. He was educated at **Arbuthnott School** (north of Arbuthnott Church) where he impressed the village schoolmaster, Alexander Gray, with his expertise as an essayist and Gray preserved the 'Essay Book Kept by James Leslie Mitchell, Arbuthnott School, 1914'. These schoolboy essays are remarkably accomplished for a boy of thirteen as the following extract demonstrates:

> Everything around seemed to acclaim harvest. The wide fields of waving corn, gleaming yellow in the morning sunshine, the sharp click! click! of the binder, the voice of the driver calling his horses, who seem greatly to relish a few mouthfulls of ripe grain and the busy workmen rapidly 'stooking' (I think that's the way you spell it) the sheaves – all of them acclaim the same thing.

In *Sunset Song* (1932), the first volume of the trilogy Mitchell published under his pseudonym Lewis Grassic Gibbon (derived from his mother's maiden name, Lilias Grassic Gibbon), Bloomfield farm becomes Blawearie and Arbuthnott becomes Kinraddie. Gibbon begins *Sunset Song* by tracing the history of Kinraddie back to the reign of William the Lion (1165–1214) when a Norman, Cospatric de Gondeshil, was knighted for slaying a gryphon. This takes the reader into the world of folklore where gossip is as sacred as holy writ and rumours become legends by virtue of their longevity. Kinraddie is a cluster of croft-farms though by 1911, when the action of the novel begins, there are only nine left. Blawearie farm – consisting of 'coarse, coarse, land, wet, raw, and red clay' – is leased by John Guthrie, a bigoted, brutal, insensitive, ignorant man. His daughter, Chris, is the central figure in the trilogy and she and her brothers live in fear of Guthrie whose general attitude is one of negativity. Chris loves the Standing Stones (now gone) of Blawearie but Guthrie says they are 'coarse, foul, things'. Life itself, to Guthrie, is coarse. 'Coarse' is, indeed, the essential epithet of abuse through the novel.

Chris, however, is a thinker and therefore a rare, rather than a coarse, creature. She goes to college in Duncairn to acquire some experience of events outside Kinraddie. Her life is dramatically altered by three events (and, as befitting a trilogist, Gibbon arranges everything in triplicate). First, her mother poisons herself and her twins rather than face another pregnancy and the concomitant heartache; then Guthrie dies a broken man (and Chris weeps for him at his funeral, remembering that his spirit had been crushed by the unequal challenge of making a living from the land); then Chris marries Ewan Tavandale and makes him the master of Blawearie.

As the novel approaches its end (which is the beginning of the second part of the trilogy) the mood becomes increasingly bleak. War breaks out and destroys what was left of Kinraddie's communal identity. Chris's husband Ewan enlists and comes back on leave, before going to France, a changed man. Whereas once he had been caring and tender, now he is indifferent and crude. Chris and Ewan part as bitter enemies in a domestic war and later Chris learns that Ewan has been shot as a coward and deserter for attempting to quit the conflict and go back to Blawearie. Chris understands this romantic gesture, cherishes the memory of Ewan and the promise of young Ewan, their son. As the novel closes she prepares for a new way of life as the wife of the new minister of Kinraddie. Chris is both a convincingly realised character and a symbolic figure who feels:

> Scotland lived, she could never die, the land would outlast them all, their wars and their Argentines, and the winds come sailing over the Grampians still with their storms and rain and the dew that ripened the crops – long and long after all their little vexings in the evening light were dead and done.

ARDOCH, Dunbartonshire   (Strathclyde)   1m E of Cardross

Robert Bontine Cunninghame Graham

Robert Graham (1735–97), who was born at Gartmore House, left Scotland at the age of seventeen to live in Jamaica as a plantation-owner. In 1772 he returned to Scotland on inheriting Ardoch estate and built the present Ardoch House, where he lived until 1777 when he returned to Gartmore House (there writing his well-known lyric 'If doughty deeds my lady please'). In 1903 his grandson Robert Bontine Cunninghame Graham (1852–1936), having sold Gartmore House in 1883, bought back Ardoch (which had been sold in 1887). Ardoch House (which has a plaque given by Graham's South American admirers) served as Graham's Scottish base from September 1904 onwards. As well as travelling and pursuing his political interests (as MP for north-west Lanarkshire from 1886 to 1892 and one of the founders of the National Party of Scotland in 1928) he wrote such books as *Faith* (1909), *Hope* (1910) and *Charity* (1912).

ARISAIG, Inverness-shire   (Highland)   8m S of Mallaig on A830

Alasdair MacMhaighstir Alasdair

A clock in the tower of Arisaig Catholic Church commemorates Alasdair MacMhaigstir Alasdair (Alexander Macdonald, *c.* 1695–*c.* 1770), the great Gaelic poet. Son of the minister of Islandfinnan, in Moidart, he was first cousin of the famous Flora MacDonald. He studied at Glasgow University and became a teacher at a Charity School at Islandfinnan. In 1741 he produced a Gaelic-English dictionary for the SPCK and in 1745 abandoned teaching to take up a commission in Bonnie Prince Charlie's Jacobite army, serving in the Clanranald Regiment and (so tradition says) teaching Gaelic to the Prince. After the defeat of the clans at Culloden, in 1746, Alasdair became bailie to the Clanranalds on the island of Canna. He returned to Moidart around 1752 and lived near Arisaig for the remainder of his life. A Gaelic nationalist, he wrote satirical and political poems promoting the Jacobite cause and also produced outstanding nature poems. His greatest work *Birlinn Chlann Ragnahill* ('The Birlinn of Clanranald') was written after 1751 when his collection *Ais-eridh na Sean Chánain* ('Resurrection of the Ancient Scottish Tongue') appeared. The poem describes a voyage made by Clanranald's galley from South Uist to Carrickfergus in Ireland. The translation of *The Birlinn of Clanranald* (1935) by Hugh MacDiarmid (1892–1978) begins:

God bless the craft of Clanranald

When brangled first with the brine
Himself and his heroes hurling;
The pick of the human line!

ARRAN, Bute   Island in Firth of Clyde

Robert McLellan

The dramatist Robert McLellan (1907–85) went to live in Arran in 1938, with his wife Kathleen. When he left for the army in 1940, his wife remained on Arran which became McLellan's home for the rest of his life. He died at his home, High Corrie, on 30 January 1985.

More than any of his contemporaries, McLellan was able to write effective plays in Scots and about Scotland. He delved into Scottish folklore for *Jeddart Justice* (1934) and *Toom Byres* (1936); produced a satirical comedy on clerical standards in *The Hypocrite* (1967); and revitalised Scottish history in his finest play, *Jamie the Saxt*, which was first performed in Glasgow's Lyric Theatre, by the Curtain Theatre Company, in 1937. *Jamie the Saxt* is one of the classics of the modern Scottish theatre and was revived, with great success, by the Scottish Theatre Company in 1982.

Though Arran featured very little in McLellan's work for the theatre it provided the setting for two poetic works: *Sweet Largie Bay*, a dramatic poem for seven voices, was broadcast in 1956; the television poem *Arran Burn* (1965) was transmitted in 1965.

ASHESTIEL, Selkirkshire   (Border)   4m W of Galashiels

Sir Walter Scott

Visible from Caddonfoot, Ashestiel was the home of Sir Walter Scott (1771–1832) at a crucial creative period in his life. As he recalled, in his *Journal* (4 April 1826): 'Ashestiel . . . is a beautiful place in summer, where I passed nine happy years'. Scott's stay in Ashestiel (from 1804 to 1812) coincided with his most productive period as a poet, as witness *The Lay of the Last Minstrel* (1805), *Marmion* (1808), and *The Lady of the Lake* (1810).

In 1799, thanks to the influence of the third Duke of Buccleuch, whose territory it largely concerned, Scott was appointed Sheriff-Depute of Selkirkshire at £300 a year. His judicial duties were undemanding and he spent much of his time in the Borders collecting the ballads that appeared in *The Minstrelsy of the Scottish Border* (1802–3). On the first edition, which sold out in three months, Scott made £100 profit and then sold his copyright for a further £500. In 1804 Scott inherited his late uncle's property of Rosebank, in Kelso, and sold it for £5,000. He then took a seven-year lease of Ashestiel, a superbly situated farmhouse in the Ettrick Forest. He was now well placed to advance his literary career.

Encouraged by the attention paid to the *Minstrelsy* Scott thought he might attempt something similar of his own and, borrowing Coleridge's 'Christabel' metre for the purpose, accepted the suggestion of the Countess of Dalkeith (later Duchess of Buccleuch) that he use the legend of Gilpen Horner. Scott's first major poetic work, *The Lay of the Last Minstrel*, was published in 1805 in an instantly consumed first edition of 750 which brought the author £169. Scott then sold his copyright for £500.

Marmion begins with a description of Ashestiel in November:

> November's sky is chill and drear,
> November's life is red and sear:
> Late, gazing down the steepy linn,
> That hems our little garden in,
> Low in its dark and narrow glen
> You scarce the rivulet might ken,
> So thick the tangled greenwood grew,
> So feeble trill'd the streamlet through:
> Now, murmuring hoarse, and frequent seen
> Through bush and brier, no longer green,
> An angry brook, it sweeps the glade,
> Brawls over rock and wild cascade,
> And, foaming brown with doubled speed,
> Hurries its waters to the Tweed.

When, in 1811, Scott was nearing the end of the lease on Ashestiel, he bought Cartley Hole, on the Tweed, and subsequently transformed it into Abbotsford.

ASSYNT, Sutherland   (Highland)   33m WNW of Lairg

Norman MacCaig

The coastal parish of Assynt is one of the main topographical subjects in the poetry of Norman MacCaig (born 1910) who spent his summer holidays in Achmelvich (two miles west of Lochinver, the main village in the parish) then Inverkirkaig (two-and-a-half miles south-south-west of Lochinver). An enthusiastic angler, MacCaig has featured the rocky landscape and lochs of Assynt in such poems as 'Midnight, Lochinver' (from *A Round of Applause*, 1972), 'Sheep Dipping, Achmelvich' (from *Measures*, 1965), 'Above Inverkirkaig' (from *Surroundings*, 1966) and 'A Man in Assynt' (from *A Man in My Position*, 1969). Originally written for television, 'A Man in Assynt' begins:

> Glaciers, grinding West, gouged out
> these valleys, rasping the brown sandstone,
> and left, on the hard rock below – the
> ruffled foreland –
> this frieze of mountains, filed
> on the blue air – Stac Polly
> Cul Beag, Cul Mor, Suilven,
> Canisp – a frieze and
> a litany.

ATHELSTANEFORD, East Lothian   (Lothian)   3m NE of Haddington

Sir David Lyndsay

A memorial (of 1965) in the churchyard commemorates the legend that Athelstaneford takes its name from the defeat of the English leader Athelstan in the tenth century by the Scots who were inspired by the sight of a St Andrews cross in the sky, hence the origin of the Scottish national flag. Sir David Lyndsay (*c.* 1490–1555), author of *Ane Pleasant Satire of the Thrie Estaitis* (1540), lived for a while in the castle of Garleton, at the foot of Byres Hill (ruins still visible at East Garleton Farm).

Robert Blair

Robert Blair (1699–1746) was minister at Athelstaneford from 1731 to 1746 and is buried in the churchyard of the present church (built 1780, extended 1867). A **Blair Monument** (of 1857) stands in front of the village hall. Blair's long poem *The Grave* (1743) is a long metrical discussion of death. Though it has fallen out of favour, sections of it still impress as the following quotation shows:

> Oft in the lone churchyard at night I've seen,
> By glimpse of moonshine chequering through the trees,
> The schoolboy with his satchel in his hand,
> Whistling aloud to bear his courage up,
> And lightly tripping o'er the long flat stones
> (With nettles skirted and with moss o'ergrown),
> That tell in homely phrase who lie below.
> Sudden he starts, and hears, or thinks he hears,
> The sound of something purring at his heels;

Full fast he flies, and dares not look behind him,
Till out of breath he overtakes his fellows;
Who gather round, and wonder at the tale
Of horrid apparition, tall and ghastly,
That walks at dead of night, or takes his stand
O'er some new-opened grave, and (strange to tell!)
Evanishes at crowing of the cock.

A posthumous edition of *The Grave* was illustrated with engravings by William Blake.

John Home

Blair's successor as minister of Athelstaneford was John Home (1722–1808) who lived at Home House, thought to be the oldest house in the village. A plaque in the porch of the present church commemorates Home though he had to resign his ministry in 1757 after becoming a literary celebrity with his verse drama *Douglas*. When the play was premiered at the Canongate Theatre, Edinburgh, on 14 December 1756 an enchanted member of the audience shouted out 'Whaur's yer Wully Shakespeare noo?'. After the sensational success of the play, Home was criticised by the Church of Scotland who feared that worshippers might transfer their allegiance from the pulpit to the stage.

AUCHINLECK, Ayrshire (Strathclyde) 13m E of Ayr on A76

James Boswell

Auchinleck House, completed in 1762, was built by Lord Auchinleck, father of James Boswell (1740–95): there is no admission to the house but visitors interested in exploring **Auchinleck Estate** should contact the owner, James Boswell; or the Auchinleck Boswell Society at 131 Main Street, Auchinleck. After his marriage to Margaret Montgomerie in 1769 Boswell stayed for a while in Auchinleck House (or Place Affleck as it was also called).

Born in Edinburgh on 29 October 1740, Boswell was educated privately and at Edinburgh University. After an argument with his father, who disapproved of his interest in wine and women, Boswell studied law at Glasgow University from 1759 to 1760, eventually qualifying and practising in Edinburgh. He first met Dr Samuel Johnson on 16 May 1763 in Thomas Davies's Bookshop in Russell Street, London, and overcame Johnson's initial antagonism. After Johnson and Boswell toured Scotland in 1773, Boswell brought his friend to Auchinleck as Johnson states in *A Journey to the Western Islands of Scotland* (1774):

28

From *Glasgow* we directed our course to *Auchinleck*, an estate devolved through a long series of ancestors, to Mr *Boswell's* father, the present possessor. . . . *Auchinleck*, which signifies a *stony field*, seems not now to have any particular claim to its denomination. It is a district generally level, and sufficiently fertile, but like all the *Western* side of *Scotland*, incommoded by very frequent rain. It was, with the rest of the country, generally naked, till the present possessor finding, by the growth of some stately trees near his old castle, that the ground was favourable enough to timber, adorned it very diligently with annual plantations.

Lord *Auchinleck*, who is one of the Judges of *Scotland*, and therefore not wholly at leisure for domestick business or pleasure, has yet found time to make improvements in his patrimony. He has built a house of hewn stone, very stately, and durable, and has advanced the value of his lands with great tenderness to his tenants.

Boswell, in his entry for 4 November 1773 in his *Journal of a Tour to the Hebrides* (1785), writes:

I was glad to have at length a very fine day, on which I could shew Dr Johnson the *Place* of my family, which he has honoured with so much attention in his 'Journey'. He is, however, mistaken in thinking that the Celtick name, *Auchinleck*, has no relation to the natural appearance of it. . . . *Auchinleck* does not signify a *stony field*, as he has said, but a *field of flag stones*; and this place has a number of rocks, which abound in strata of that kind.

Boswell's *Life of Samuel Johnson* appeared in 1791 and quickly assumed the status of a classic. Boswell, who scrutinised the personality of Johnson, was an extraordinary character in his own right as witness the Yale Editions of *The Private Papers of James Boswell*. In *Boswell: Laird of Auchinleck* (1977), edited by Joseph W. Reed and Frederick A. Pottle, the great biographer agonises over his own weakness for drink and debauchery, writing on 1 September 1779, 'I was at this time conscious of what is the state of a man who has a craving for strong drink; and I dreaded being perhaps at some future period of my life a wretched sot.' However he was happy at the notion of succeeding his father as Laird of Auchinleck, as he writes in his entry for 11 May 1782:

After breakfast Mr Millar walked with me to Auchinleck. My heart warmed as I viewed the scenes of my early years. But I declare I am happier now than when I was a boy. I felt a kind of exultation in the consciousness of a line of ancestors, and in the prospect of being *laird* myself, and ruling over such a fine Place and such an extent of country.

Boswell's last years in London were disfigured by depression and drunkenness: he died in London on 19 May 1795, his remains being moved to the family Mausoleum built by Lord Auchinleck in 1753.

The Auchinleck Boswell Society, founded in 1970, restored the old parish church (in which the Boswell family worshipped) as the **Boswell Museum** and renovated the adjoining **Mausoleum**. Both museum and mausoleum are open to the public.

Sir Alexander Boswell

James Boswell's son, Sir Alexander Boswell (1775–1882) was born in Edinburgh and educated at Eton and Oxford. He succeeded to Auchinleck Estate in 1795 and married Grace Cummings three years later. A minor poet and energetic antiquarian, Boswell established a private printing press in Auchinleck, in 1815, and produced editions of his own poetic and antiquarian writings as well as reprints of Scottish historical material. Influenced, inevitably, by the verse of Robert Burns (1759–96), Boswell was largely responsible for raising funds for the Burns Monument at Alloway; as deputy Grand Master of the Mother Lodge of Kilwinning he laid the foundation stone in 1820.

In 1816 Boswell became a Tory MP for Ayrshire and served as Lieutenant-Colonel of the Ayrshire yeomanry during the period of unrest leading up to the Reform Act of 1832. For his efforts in this capacity he was made a baronet in 1821.

The publication of a satirical 'Whig Song' in the *Glasgow Sentinel* offended his neighbour James Stuart of Dunearn who attributed the piece to Boswell and challenged him to a duel which took place at Auchtertool, Fife, on 26 March 1822. Boswell was mortally wounded and died the next day; he is buried in the family vault in Auchinleck church. Stuart was acquitted after a murder trial and Sir Walter Scott (1771–1832) drew on the duel in his novel *St Ronan's Well* (1824).

AUCHMITHIE, Angus   (Tayside)   4m NE of Arbroath

Sir Walter Scott

As well as being credited with the creation of the Arbroath Smokie, Auchmithie contributed to Scottish literature through the work of Sir Walter Scott. In the third Waverley novel, *The Antiquary* (1816), Arbroath becomes Fairport and Auchmithie becomes the tiny fishing community of Mussel Crag. Jonathan Oldbuck, the Antiquary, visits Mussel Crag after the death, by drowning, of Steenie, the eldest son of Saunders and Maggie Mucklebackit:

The Antiquary . . . soon arrived before the half-dozen cottages at Mussel Crag. They now had, in addition to their usual squalid and uncomfortable appearance, the melancholy attributes of the house of mourning. The boats were all drawn up on the beach; and, though the day was fine, and the season favourable, the chant, which is used by the fishers when at sea, was silent, as well as the prattle of the children, and the shrill song of the mother, as she sits mending her nets by the door. A few of the neighbours, some in their antique and well-saved suits of black, others in their ordinary clothes, but all bearing an expression of mournful sympathy with distress so sudden and unexpected, stood gathered around the door of Mucklebackit's cottage, waiting till 'the body was lifted'.

Charles MacLean

By 1840 Auchmithie boasted twelve boats and by 1855 there were thirty-three boats. The fishing community declined, though, after the First World War and as Charles MacLean writes, in *The Fringe of Gold* (1985), 'by 1929 there were only ten boats and eleven fishermen, most of them old men'. In the Second World War, a German mine blew a hole in the harbour wall 'and started a decay which has continued ever since'.

Alexander Lowson

Alexander Lowson described Auchmithie in *Tales, Legends and Traditions of Forfarshire* (1891):

Were it not for the fine breeze, laden with ozone, which is nearly always blowing upon it from the ocean, this village, instead of being what it is, a remarkably healthy place, would certainly be a hot-bed of disease.

Lowson took exception to the middens in front of the doors of the cottages and regarded the place as 'an indescribable scene of dirt and disorder'.

AUCHTERARDER, Strathearn, Perthshire (Tayside) 15m SW of Perth on A9

James Kennaway

James Kennaway (1928–68), the novelist, was born at Kenwood Park, Auchterarder, on 5 June 1928. The stone house, set in more than four acres of ground facing south-east to the Ochil Hills, was built for the Kennaway family in 1912. Kennaway's grandfather, a lawyer and factor, set up the family business in Auchterarder and when he died, in 1921, Charles Gray Kennaway (1894–1941) – James Kennaway's father – settled in Auchterarder. During Charles Gray Kennaway's last lingering illness (in a sanitorium near Aberdeen) he wrote *Gentleman Adventurer* (posthumously published in 1951), a novel about the life and times of Charles Hay of Auchterarder between the Jacobite uprisings of 1715 and 1746. The novel opens, on New Year's Day 1700, with a glimpse of old Auchterarder:

> A blustering gale, half sleet, half snow, chill with the tempestuous northerly blast blowing straight from the snow-clad heights of Ben-y-Gloe and the Cairngorms, swept across the vale of Earn to lash its fury against the northern spurs of the Ochils, driving (it would almost seem) before it the dust and ashes of the passing year, for it wanted now but an hour till midnight on this last night of the year of grace 1699. In gusts, now strengthening now dying away, it swirled the swift-falling snow and sleet straight up the long causeway following the only ridge between the Earn River and the hills; that causeway which forms the one street of the wind-swept straggling village of Auchterarder, its cottages hidden in the solid blackness, save where an occasional light showed through a half-shuttered window or ill-fitting door.

James Kennaway's novel *Household Ghosts* (1961) is set in Strathearn, the valley that surrounds Auchterarder (ancient capital of Strathearn).

AUCHTERMUCHTY, Fife   (Fife)   9m E of Cupar on A91

Anonymous

An anonymous satirical poem 'The Wyf of Auchtermuchty' – from the Bannantyne Manuscript (1568) – cites the disasters that befall a man who decides to reverse the domestic routine and become a housewife while his wife goes out to work in the fields. The marital battle is resolved in the final stanza with the husband submitting to the domestic superiority of his wife:

> Than up scho gat ane mekle rung   *large cudgel*
> And the gudeman maid to the dur.   *door*
> Quoth he, dame I sall hald my tung
> For and we fecht I'll gett the woir;   *fight, worse*
> Quoth he, quhen I forsuk my pluche   *plough*
> I trow I bot fursuk my seill   *happiness*
> For I and this hows will nevir do weill.

James Hogg

Auchtermuchty features in a supernatural tale which forms part of James Hogg's prose masterpiece *The Private Memoirs and Confessions of a Justifed Sinner* (1824). Towards the end of his confessions, the sinner Wringhim is treated to a story passed from one Lucky Shaw to the servant William of Penpunt. In the context of the novel (which deals with diabolic possession) it comes as light relief and begins:

> It was but the year afore the last, that the people o' the town o'
> Auchtermuchty grew so rigidly righteous, that the meanest hind
> among them became a shining light in ither towns an' parishes. There
> was nought to be heard, neither night nor day, but preaching,
> praying, argumentation, an' catechising in a' the famous town o'
> Auchtermuchty.

Fortunately for the folk of Auchtermuchty (it transpires) an old man called Robin Ruthven hears crows, from 'some ither warld than this', conspiring how to trap the townspeople with their own bait.

When the congregation meet next day, in the kirk of Auchtermuchty, the regular minister is missing. His replacement is 'a strange divine' who convinces the people that their town should be given to the devil 'if there was not forthwith a radical change made in all their opinions and modes of worship'. The inhabitants of Auchtermuchty are delighted since 'Nothing in the world delights a truly religious people so much, as consigning them to eternal damnation'.

Next time the 'strange divine' comes to Auchtermuchty the kirk is packed with people 'from the East Nook of Fife to the foot of the Grampian hills'. Robin Ruthven comes to the rescue by lifting the gown of the preacher and revealing a pair of cloven feet. There is consternation and the devil flees, leaving Auchtermuchty to its own devices:

> A' the auld wives an' weavers o' Auchtermuchty fell down flat wi'
> affright, an' betook them to their prayers aince again, for they saw
> the dreadfu' danger they had escapit, an' frae that day to this it is a
> hard matter to gar an Auchtermuchty man listen to a sermon at a', an'
> a harder ane still to gar him applaud ane, for he thinks aye that he
> sees the cloven foot peepin out frae aneath ilka sentence.

James Allan Ford

James Allan Ford, the respected novelist, was born on 10 June 1920 in Rose Cottage, Bow Road, Auchtermuchty, the home of his paternal grandparents Douglas and Margaret Ford (who are buried in Auchtermuchty Cemetery). Soon after his birth he was taken to a smallholding called The Howe, in the hills north of Auchtermuchty, where his maternal grandfather James Allan lived. After a brief recuperative holiday there, his mother brought him back to Edinburgh where he was educated (at the High School and University). He served with the Royal Scots during World War Two and, after the fall of Hong Kong, was interned by the Japanese. Until he retired in 1979, Ford worked as a Civil Servant (eventually as Principal Establishment Officer for Scotland). His novels include *A Statue for a Public Place* (1965), *A Judge of Men* (1968), and *The Mouth of Truth* (1972).

AYR, Ayrshire   (Strathclyde)   12m S of Kilmarnock on A79

Robert Burns

Ayr (which received its charter from William the Lion in 1202) is a county and market town associated with Robert Burns (1759–96) who was born in nearby Alloway (1½ m south of Ayr). In 'Tam O' Shanter' Burns praises Ayr parenthetically:

> This truth fand honest Tam O' Shanter,
> As he frae Ayr ae night did canter:
> (Auld Ayr, wham ne'er a town surpasses,
> For honest men and bonie lasses.)

Burns worshipped in the old parish church in whose churchyard stands the **Martyrs' Monument** (honouring seven Covenanters put to death for asserting their religious rights).

Burns's poem 'The Brigs of Ayr' was written in 1786 and inscribed to John Ballantine the banker who, as Provost of Ayr, was then having a new bridge built across the River Ayr. In the poem the **Auld Brig** (a thirteenth-century structure) has angry exchanges with the New Brig:

NEW BRIG
   Auld Vandal! ye but show your little mense,   *direction*
Just much about it wi' your scanty sense:
Will your poor, narrow foot-path of a street,
Where twa wheel-barrows tremble when they meet,
Your ruin'd, formless bulk o' stane an' lime.
Compare wi' bonie brigs o' modern time?
There's men of taste would tak the Ducat stream.
Tho' they should cast the vera sark and swim,
E'er they would grate their feelings wi' the view
O' sic an ugly, Gothic hulk as you.

AULD BRIG
   Conceited gowk! puff'd up wi' windy pride!

34

This monie a year I've stood the flood an' tide;
And tho' wi' crazy eild I'm sair forfairn,   *age, worn out*
I'll be a brig when ye're a shapeless cairn!

The Auld Brig had the last laugh for, in a storm, the New Brig was swept away and replaced by the present bridge in 1877.

The Tam O' Shanter Inn, High Street, is open to the public (April–Sept., Mon.–Sat. 9.30am–5.30pm; Oct.–March, noon–4pm). It was formerly a brewhouse frequented by Douglas Graham (1738–1811) who supplied it with malt on market days. When Burns composed 'Tam O' Shanter' in the autumn of 1790 for Francis Grose's *Antiquities of Scotland* he provided a prose version of the story which begins:

On a market day, in the town of Ayr, a farmer from Carrick, and
consequently whose way lay by the very gate of Alloway Kirk-yard,
in order to cross the River Doon at the old bridge, which is about two
or three hundred yards farther on than the said gate, had been
detained by his business, till by the time he reached Alloway it was
the wizard hour, between night and morning.

This should be compared with the poetic version on p. 204, depicting Tam and Souter Johnnie drinking. There is a **Burns Statue** in the centre of Ayr, erected by the people of Ayrshire.

BALAVIL, Inverness-shire   (Highland)   2½m NE of Kingussie

James Macpherson

Balavil (formerly Belleville) was built, on the site of Raits Castle, for James Macpherson (1736–96) whose Ossianic poems *Fingal* (1761) and *Temora* (1763) were the literary sensations of their time, appealing equally to shrewd Scots and sophisticated Europeans such as Napoleon and Goethe.It is generally accepted that Macpherson built, on the basis of a few Gaelic originals, the imposing Ossianic edifice he presented to the world. As Dr Johnson and others realised, the poems were not scholarly translations of Ossian but fanciful fabrications. Nevertheless, the rhetoric of Macpherson's Ossianic poems influenced the Romantic movement. *Fingal* begins with a fine flourish:

Cuthullin sat by Tura's wall; by the tree of the rustling sound.
His spear leaned against a rock. His shield lay on grass, by his side.
Amid his thoughts of mighty Carbar, a hero slain by the chief in war;
The scout of ocean comes, Moran the son of Fithil!

Following the Ossianic affair, Macpherson lived in London before and after an interlude (1763–6) as secretary to the Governor of Florida. He accumulated wealth and purchased, towards the end of his life, the Badenoch estate on which Balavil stands. He died at Balavil on 17 February 1796 and was buried, at his own expense, in Westminster Abbey, London.

BALBIRNIE PARK, Glenrothes   (Fife)   6m N of Kirkcaldy

Adjacent to the small town of Markinch and at the north-east corner of the new town of Glenrothes, Balbirnie Park comprises 416 acres and contains a late neolithic stone circle (moved 125 metres south-east of its original site by Glenrothes Development Corporation who bought the park in 1969) as well as a medieval stob cross (originally located at the entrance to St Drostan's Church, Markinch) and a modern craft centre (established in 1972). Originally landscaped to a plan prepared by Robert Robinson in 1779, the estate was developed to a design made by the younger Thomas White in 1815. Balbirnie House, the home of the Balfours of Balbirnie for over 300 years, was remodelled from plans submitted by the architect Robert Crichton in 1815.

Duncan Glen

In *The Autobiography of a Poet* (1986) Duncan Glen describes his days as apprentice to a printer in Fife. Margaret, the woman he eventually married, lived at the end of the High Street in Markinch and Glen recalls walks with her to see 'the houlets and squirrels in Balbirnie woods'. Glen (born in Cambuslang in 1933) lived for a period in a farm cottage near Star of Markinch, a small village once the home ofthe popular novelist Annie S. Swan (1859–1943) who lived with her schoolmaster husband, James Burnett Smith, in the schoolhouse from 1883 to 1885.

Alan Bold

In 1975 the poet Alan Bold (born in Edinburgh in 1943) moved to a cottage in Balbirnie Park. Glenrothes Development Corporation (who have poems on paving stones by Hugh MacDiarmid, Sydney Goodsir Smith and Joe Corrie in the town centre) commissioned three public poems from Bold for installation in Glenrothes New Town. Bold's work changed dramatically as he responded to the natural environment of Balbirnie. Having previously written many political poems, complete with urban images, he began to explore the landscape of Balbirnie, as in 'One April Day' from *In This Corner: Selected Poems 1963–83* (1983):

> A glorious sun-soaked day sprang out of nowhere
> To spread itself over the marshy fields where bullocks

Strolled in line and where breeding puddocks
Spawned among slime and sizzled in the torrid air.

It was Spring becoming Summer, a day among days,
When a field graced by chickweed and molehills
Looked seethingly alive, when the low stone walls
Shone and bouquets of birds flowered on trees.

At night, at full moon, trails of frogspawn
Sparkled like a string of black beads, shook
With the blind faith of life – little black
Dots alive beneath the brilliant sterile moon.

With the artist John Bellany, Bold produced three limited editions of etchings and poems under the imprint of Balbirnie Editions: *A Celtic Quintet* (1983), *Haven* (1984), and *Homage to MacDiarmid* (1985).

BALLACHULISH, Argyllshire   (Highland)   12m S of Fort William
on A82

Robert Louis Stevenson

On 8 November 1752 James Stewart of the Glens was hanged on a wooded hillock two miles south-west of Ballachulish after being wrongly accused of the 'Appin Murder'; a memorial tablet stands beside the ruined Kirk of Veil. The 'Appin Murder' resulted in the death of Colin Campbell of Glenure – the 'Red Fox' who had been awarding forfeited Stewart and Cameron lands to the Campbells – and local tradition attributes the murder to a Stewart of Ballachulish. However both James Stewart and his foster-brother Alan Breck Stewart were wrongly accused of the murder which is described in Robert Louis Stevenson's *Kidnapped* (1886). After Glenure has been shot, David Balfour comes across his friend Alan Breck in the Wood of Lettermore:

> Just inside the shelter of the trees I found Alan Breck standing, with a fishing-rod. He gave me no salutation; indeed it was no time for civilities; only 'Come!' says he, and set off running along the side of the mountain towards Balachulish; and I, like a sheep, to follow him.

The aftermath of the murder is evoked in *Catriona* (1893), the sequel to *Kidnapped*.

BALMACLELLAN, Kirkcudbrightshire (Dumfries and Galloway)
20m E of Dumfries on A712

Sir Walter Scott

Robert Paterson (1715–1801), the original of Sir Walter Scott's Old Mortality, moved to this village around 1768 though soon afterwards he was on the roads about his self-appointed business. As *Old Mortality* (1816) indicates, Paterson dedicated his life to repairing the tombs of the Covenanters. His wife Lizzie Gray stayed on in Balmaclellan, supporting her family by running a small school until her death in 1785. A statue and tombstone were erected in Balmaclellan, to the memory of Old Mortality. The tombstone, in Balmaclellan churchyard, was inscribed in 1855, the text beginning:

> To the Memory of Robert Paterson, Stone-engraver, well known as 'Old Mortality,' who died at Bankend of Caerlaverock, 14th February, 1801, aged 88; also of Elizabeth, his spouse, who died at Balmaclellan village, 5th May, 1785, aged 59.

There is also a headstone commemorating Paterson at Caerlaverock Churchyard, as his exact place of burial is a matter of speculation.

BALNAKEIL BAY, Sutherland (Highland)

Rob Donn MacAoidh

By the ruin of Durness kirk (near the north-west tip of Scotland, reached by A838) an obelisk commemorates Rob Donn MacAoidh (Robert MacKay) who was born in Strathmore around 1715 and died in 1778. He grew up on the lands of the MacKay chief, Lord Reay, who supported the Hanoverian side during the 1745 Jacobite rising. Rob Donn, however, shared with other Gaelic poets a sympathy for Bonnie Prince Charlie and wrote several Jacobite poems. When Lord Reay died in 1761, Rob Donn wrote a moving elegy for his patron. Rob Donn's poems circulated orally in his lifetime; after his death they were collected by local ministers and a first collection, *Songs and Poems in the Gaelic Language by Robert MacKay*, appeared in 1829.

BALQUHIDDER, Perthshire   (Central)

Sir Walter Scott

At the east end of Loch Voil, Balquhidder has a church of 1855, the ruins of two earlier churches, and – in the churchyard – the family tomb of Rob Roy MacGregor (1671–1734), the outlaw featured in Sir Walter Scott's *Rob Roy* (1817). In Scott's fiction Rob Roy ('as gude as Robin Hood or William Wallace') supports Frank Osbaldistone against his treacherous cousin Rashleigh ('A detestable villain'). In fact Rob Roy MacGregor (1671–1734) farmed at Balquhidder and operated as a cattle-dealer but also stole cattle and levied blackmail. Imprisoned at Newgate, he was saved from transportation by a pardon and died in bed at Inverlochlarig (in his house, which once stood six miles west of Balquhidder). In an introduction to his novel Scott says:

> He owed his fame in a great measure to his residing on the very verge of the Highlands, and playing such pranks in the beginning of the 18th century, as are usually ascribed to Robin Hood in the middle ages, – and that within forty miles of Glasgow, a great commercial city, the seat of a learned university. Thus a character like his, blending the wild virtues, the subtle policy, and the unrestrained licence of an American Indian, was flourishing in Scotland during the Augustan age of Queen Anne and George I.

The Rob Roy country, popularised by Scott, stretches from Loch Ard and the River Forth on the south to Strathfillan and Glen Dochart on the north; and from Loch Lubnaig on the east to Loch Lomond on the west. Or, as Frank Osbaldistone observes, in *Rob Roy*, 'that mountainous and desolate territory, which, lying between the lakes of Loch-Lomond, Loch-Katrine, and Loch-Ard, was at this time currently called Rob Roy's, or the MacGregor, country'.

William Wordsworth

Wordsworth's ballad, 'Rob Roy's Grave', from *Memorials of a Tour in Scotland* (1801), was composed under the erroneous impression that 'generous Rob' – compared to Robin Hood by Wordsworth – was buried at the head of Loch Katrine.

Robert Louis Stevenson

Rob Roy's son Robin Oig, who was executed for the abduction of Jean Kay in 1754, is supposed to lie under the stone beside his father's slate slab (the stones dating from centuries before Rob Roy's era). He appears in Robert Louis Stevenson's *Kidnapped* (1886) as Alan Breck's opponent in a piping contest. In *Catriona* (1893), the sequel to *Kidnapped*, David Balfour meets the eponymous heroine in Edinburgh; when he tells her that he was recently 'on the braes of Balwhidder' she says 'The name of it makes all there is of me rejoice . . . I am loving the smell of that place and the roots that grow there.' Alasdair Alpin MacGregor (1889–1970), an authority on the Highlands and Islands, is cited on his father's tombstone which notes that his ashes were scattered in the Hebrides.

BARNS HOUSE, Peeblesshire   (Border)   3m SW of Peebles

John Buchan

John Buchan's first full-length novel, *John Burnet of Barns* (1898), is set in the seventeenth century and features, as narrator, a hero who shares characteristics in common with the author, Burnet being (like Buchan) a Glasgow University man fond of fishing and hillwalking and possessing an appetite for adventure. Here is Burnet's first-personal description of his square stone house at Barns:

> The house of Barns stands on a green knoll above the Tweed, half-away between the village of Stobo and the town of Peebles. Tweed here is no great rolling river, but a shallow, prattling stream, and just below the house it winds around a small islet, where I loved to go and fish; for it was an adventure to reach the place, since a treacherous pool lay not a yard below it. The swelling was white and square, with a beacon tower on the top, which once flashed the light from Neidpath to Drochil when the English came over the Border. It had not been used for half a hundred years, but a brazier still stood there, and a pile of rotten logs, grim mementoes of elder feuds.

The heroine of the novel, Marjory Veitch, comes from Dawyck, further up the river.

Clearly Burnet's house is based on the old Barns Tower, built by the Burnets towards the end of the sixteenth century and now a roofed ruin a short distance from the present Barns House, which is a mansion built in 1778.

BARRA, Outer Hebrides   (Western Isles)

Sir Compton Mackenzie

In 1934 Sir Compton Mackenzie (1883–1972) made his decision to build a bungalow, Suidheachan, on the Isle of Barra. He describes the situation in the seventh volume of his autobiography *My Life and Times* (10 vols, 1963–71):

> The site chosen by me . . . was an acre of the sandy machair close to Tràigh Mhòr, the great cockle-beach, and about 300 yards from the long beach called Tràigh Iais which faced the Atlantic. According to Father John Macmillan this was where Macneil of Barra used to eat his lunch when out snipe-shooting and was called Suidheachan – the sitting down place. So we decided to call the three-sided bungalow I proposed to build Suidheachan. . . . The 27 crofters of Ardvore, the township on whose common grazing I proposed to build, had all given their assent to my feu.

During his period on Barra (he settled in Edinburgh in 1953) Mackenzie wrote his novel-sequence *The Four Winds of Love* (6 vols, 1937–45) as well as immensely popular comic novels such as *Whisky Galore* (1947). In *The North Wind of Love* (1944) Mackenzie's partly autobiographical hero, John Ogilvie, retires to Castle Island, in the Outer Hebrides, and from his home – Tigh nan Ròn (the House of the Seals) – encourages others to take up the cause of Scottish Nationalism. In *Whisky Galore* the two islands of Great and Little Todday are modelled, respectively, on Barra and Eriskay (which lies to the north-east of Barra). After Mackenzie's death, on 30 November 1972, his body was taken to Barra for burial at the ruined church and chapel of St Barr, Eoligarry.

Hugh MacDiarmid

In 1937 the poet Hugh MacDiarmid (1892–1978) visited Barra, in connection with his research for his book on *The Islands of Scotland* (1939).

Fionn Mac Colla

After studying Gaelic at Glasgow University, the novelist Fionn Mac Colla – pseudonym of Tom MacDonald (1906–75) – earned his living by teaching. From 1946 to 1959 he lived at the Schoolhouse, Northbay, Barra, where he wrote *The Ministers*, posthumously published in 1979. Though acclaimed by Hugh MacDiarmid as a 'definite literary genius' and appealing greatly to readers interested in a distinctively Scottish literature, Mac Colla was neglected most of his life. While on Barra, for example, he also wrote 'The Tsar's White Hell' (the first volume of a book about the Russian prison system) and a big Russian-Scottish novel 'Facing the Muzhik'. These books were rejected at the time and remain unpublished.

BELL ROCK, North Sea   Reef 11m SE of Arbroath

Robert Southey

Originally known as Inchcape Rock, the Bell Rock was so called (according to tradition) because of a bell placed there by an Abbot of Arboath. This bell was removed by a pirate who was wrecked on the rock one year later. Robert Southey (1774–1834) used this story as the basis of his ballad 'The Inchcape Rock' (1802) which contains these quatrains:

> Without either sign or sound of their shock
> The waves flow'd over the Inchcape Rock;
> So little they rose, so little they fell,
> They did not move the Inchcape Bell.
>
> The Abbot of Aberbrothok
> Had placed that bell on the Inchcape Rock;
> On a buoy in the storm it floated and swung,
> And over the waves its warning rung.

Sir Walter Scott

The rock is covered by water at high tide and in a gale of 1799 seventy ships were wrecked on the reef. The lighthouse was built 1807–11 by John Rennie and Robert Stevenson, grandfather of Robert Louis Stevenson (1850–94). In 1814 Sir Walter Scott made a six-week voyage round Scotland with the Commissioners of the Northern Lights and Robert Stevenson, their Surveyor-Viceroy. In his journal entry for 30 July 1814 Scott writes:

> Waked at six by the steward: summoned to visit the Bell-Rock, where the beacon is well worthy attention. Its dimensions are well known; but no description can give the idea of this slight, solitary, round tower, trembling amid the billows, and fifteen miles from Arbroath, the nearest shore. The fitting up within is not only handsome, but elegant. All work of wood (almost) is wainscot; all hammer-work brass; in short, exquisitely fitted up.

In his 'Reminiscences of Sir Walter Scott, Baronet', Robert Stevenson describes the landing on the Bell Rock and Scott's response to a request to write something in the Lighthouse album. After some time Scott wrote 'Pharos Loquitur' in the album:

> Far in the bosom of the deep,
> O'er these wild shelves my watch I keep,
> A ruddy gem of changeful light
> Bound on the dusky brow of night.
> The seaman bids my lustre hail
> And scorns to strike his timorous sail.

R. M. Ballantyne

R. M. Ballantyne (1825–94) stayed on the reef for a fortnight before writing his adventure *The Lighthouse* (1865).

BENBECULA, Outer Hebrides   (Western Isles)

Fionn Mac Colla

After studying Gaelic at Glasgow University, the novelist Fionn Mac Colla – pseudonym of Tom MacDonald (1906–75) – earned his living by teaching. From 1940 to 1946 he lived at the Schoolhouse, Torlum, Benbecula where he wrote most of 'Move Up, John' (a still-unpublished novel) and conceived *The Ministers*, a novel posthumously published in 1979.

BEN DORAN, Argyllshire   (Highland)   3m SE of Loch Tulla

Duncan Ban MacIntyre, Hugh MacDiarmid

The mountain (3,523 ft) features in the poem 'Moladh Beinn Dòbhrainn' by the Gaelic poet Duncan Ban MacIntyre (1724–1812). Both Hugh MacDiarmid (1892–1978) and Iain Crichton Smith (born 1928) have translated the poem into English. MacDiarmid's version - 'The Praise of Ben Dorain' from his anthology *The Golden Treasury of Scottish Poetry* (1940) – begins:

> Over mountains, pride
> Of place to Ben Dorain!
> I've nowhere espied
> A finer to reign.
> In her moorbacks wide
> Hosts of shy deer bide;
> While light comes pouring
> Diamond-wise from her side.

Grassy glades are there
With boughs light-springing,
Where the wild herds fare
(Of these my singing!),
Like lightning flinging
Their heels on the air
Should the wind be bringing
Any hint to beware.

BIGGAR, Lanarkshire   (Strathclyde)   18m SW of Peebles on A702

Dr John Brown

Dr John Brown (1810–82) was born on 22 September 1810 at the manse in Biggar where his father was minister. Brown's most entertaining essays, including 'Rab and his Friends', appeared in the first two volumes of his *Horae subsecivae* (1858, 1861).

Hugh MacDiarmid

From 1951 until his death in 1978, the poet Hugh MacDiarmid (Christopher Murray Grieve, 1892–1978) lived, with his wife Valda, at Brownsbank Cottage, Candymill, by Biggar. In a letter of 26 January 1951, to Francis George Scott, MacDiarmid writes:

> We finally migrated to this new abode about three weeks ago. . . . It is a very nice place, away up in a fold in the hills – yet handy for the main bus route. . . . The cottage is too small unfortunately, we had to store a good deal of our stuff. But we've got dug in fairly comfortably now and will be all right when we've everything finally settled and the right routine devised.

MacDiarmid entertained many writers at Brownsbank, including most of the modern Scottish poets (Norman MacCaig, Sydney Goodsir Smith, etc.) as well as distinguished visitors such as the Russian poet Yevgeny Yevtushenko.

BIRNAM, Perthshire (Tayside) ¾m SE of Dunkeld

William Shakespeare

Birnam, built on the river Tay in the nineteenth century, has Shakespearean associations. In *Macbeth* (IV.i) the third Apparition assures the tragic hero:

> Macbeth shall never vanquish'd be until
> Great Birnam wood to high Dunsinane Hill
> Shall come against him.

Macbeth exclaims 'That will never be', but in the final act of the drama Malcolm orders his soldiers to conceal their numbers by cutting and carrying boughs from Birnam Wood, thus bringing Birnam Wood to Dunsinane Hill with catastrophic consequences for Macbeth. From Birnam Hill (1,324 ft), behind the village, there is a fine view of Dunsinane Hill, twelve miles south-east. The ruined fort at Birnam is known as Duncan's Castle and beside the Inchewan Burn is the old Birnam Oak.

BORGUE, Kirkcudbrightshire (Dumfries and Galloway) 4m S of Kircudbright on B727

William Nicholson

William Nicholson (1782–1849) was born in Borgue on 15 August 1782 and is commemorated in his old school by a relief portrait of him playing the pipes. Known as 'Wandering Wull' and the 'Galloway Poet' he became a travelling packman. Nicholson, who suffered from bad eyesight, drank to excess and on 16 May 1849 he died in poverty. His best-remembered poems are 'Aiken Drum' and 'The Brownie of Bludnock.' He is buried in the old churchyard at Kirkandrews, two miles west of Borgue.

BOTHWELL, Lanarkshire (Strathclyde) 8m SE of Glasgow on A74

Joanna Baillie

Joanna Baillie (1762–1851), daughter of the minister of Bothwell, was born on 11 September 1762 in the old thatched manse of Bothwell. Though her birthplace no longer exists, a **Joanna Baillie Monument** was unveiled, in the grounds of Bothwell parish church, on 12 January 1899.

Joanna Baillie's father became Professor of Divinity at Glasgow

University in 1776. In 1784, six years after his death, the family moved to London where Joanna remained for the rest of her life.

Her dramatic gifts – as displayed in *Plays of Passion* (1798) – impressed Sir Walter Scott who paid tribute to her in the Introduction to the third canto of *Marmion* (1808). Although her plays have dated she is remembered for lyrics and songs such as 'Goodnight, Goodnight', 'Saw Ye Johnnie Comin'', 'It Fell on a Morning', and 'Wooed and Married And 'A'. In 'Lines to Agnes Baillie on Her Birthday' she recalled her early years in Bothwell:

> Dear Agnes, gleamed with joy and dashed with tears,
> O'er us have glided almost sixty years
> Since we on Bothwell's bonnie braes were seen,
> By those whose eyes long closed in death have been –
> Two tiny imps, who scarcely stooped to gather
> The slender harebell or the purple heather;
> No taller than the foxglove's spikey stem,
> That dew of morning studs with silvery gem.
> Then every butterfly that crossed our view
> With joyful shout was greeted as it flew,
> And moth and lady-bird and beetle bright
> In sheeny gold were each a wondrous sight.
> Then, as we paddled barefoot, side by side,
> Among the sunny shallows of the Clyde,
> Minnows, or spotted par with twinkling fin,
> Swimming in mazy rings the pool within,
> A thrill of gladness through our bosoms sent,
> Seen in the power of early wonderment.

BRAEMAR, Aberdeenshire   (Grampian)   29m NE of Pitlochry on A93

Robert Louis Stevenson

Opposite the Invercauld Festival Theatre (once a church) is the house where Robert Louis Stevenson (1850–94) wrote *Treasure Island* (1883) in circumstances described in 'My First Book' (meaning first novel) in the *Idler*, August 1894 (reprinted in *Essays in the Art of Writing*, 1912):

> In the fated year [1880] I came to live with my father and mother at Kinnaird [where the story 'Thrawn Janet' was written], above Pitlochry. . . . I love my native air, but it does not love me; and the end of this delightful period was a cold, a fly-blister, and a migration to the Castleton of Braemar. There it blew a good deal and rained in

a proportion; my native air was more unkind than man's ingratitude, and I must consent to pass a good deal of my time between four walls in a house lugubriously known as the Late Miss McGregor's Cottage. And now admire the finger of predestination. There was a schoolboy [Lloyd Osbourne, Stevenson's stepson to whom *Treasure Island* is dedicated] in the Late Miss McGregor's Cottage, home for the holidays, and much in want of 'something craggy to break his mind upon'. He had not thought of literature [but] with the aid of pen and ink and a shilling box of water-colours, he had soon turned one of the rooms into a picture gallery . . . I would sometimes join the artist (so to speak) at the easel, and pass the afternoon with him in a generous emulation, making coloured drawings.

On one of these occasions I made the map of an island; it was elaborately and (I thought) beautifully coloured; the shape of it took my fancy beyond expression; it contained harbours that pleased me like sonnets; and with the unconsciousness of the predestined, I ticketed my performance 'Treasure Island'. . . . As I paused upon my map of 'Treasure Island' the future characters of the book began to appear there visibly among imaginary woods; and their brown faces and bright weapons peeped out upon me from unexpected quarters, as they passed to and fro, fighting and hunting treasures, on these few square inches of a flat projection. The next thing I knew I had some papers in front of me and was writing out a list of chapters. . . . On a chill September morning, by the cheek of a brisk fire, and the rain drumming on the window, I began *The Sea Cook*, for that was the original title. I have begun (and finished) a number of other books, but I cannot remember to have sat down to one of them with more complacency.

BRANXHOLM TOWER, Roxburghshire   (Border)   3m SE of Hawick off A7

Sir Walter Scott

Branxholm Tower, standing on lands belonging to the Scotts of Buccleuch from the reign of James I, was burned by the Earl of Northumberland in 1532 and blown up by Surrey in 1570. Sir Walter Scott of Buccleuch began to rebuild it in 1571 and the repairs were completed by his widow. it is still a private residence. In *The Lay of the Last Minstrel* (1805) by Sir Walter Scott (1771–1832) the old minstrel comes to Newark Castle where the Duchess of Buccleuch encourages him to tell his tale of the sixteenth-century feud between the Buccleuchs and the Cranstouns. The first stanza of Canto I runs:

The feast was over in Branksome tower,
And the lady had gone to her secret bower;
Her bower that was guarded by word and by spell,
Deadly to hear, and deadly to tell –
Jesu Maria, shield us well!
No living wight, save the lady alone,
Had dared to cross the threshold stone.

BRIG O' TURK, Perthshire   (Central)   7m W of Callander on A821

Sir Walter Scott

Brig o' Turk, in the Trossachs, has both verbal and visual artistic associations. North of the hamlet is **Glen Finglas**, the setting of Sir Walter Scott's ballad 'Glenfinlas; or, Lord Ronald's Coronach':

O so it fell, that on a day,
   To rouse the red deer from their den,
The Chiefs have ta'en their distant way,
   And scour'd the deep Glenfinlas Glen.

John Ruskin

The celebrated portrait of John Ruskin (1819–1900) by John Everett Millais (1829–96) shows the great cultural critic standing by a waterfall in Glen Finglas. Brig o' Turk itself was the scene of a famous triangular relationship involving Millais, Ruskin and Ruskin's Scottish wife Effie (Euphemia) Chalmers Gray. Millais and the Ruskins took a Highland holiday together and arrived on 2 July 1853 at Brig o' Turk where they stayed for almost four months: first at Trossachs New Hotel (burned down around 1900), then (after a week) at the cottage (first on the right when entering Brig o' Turk) of a local schoolmaster Alex Stewart. The Ruskins' marriage had not been consummated and Effie was greatly attracted to Millais (and vice versa). A year later Effie was granted a decree of nullity on the grounds of Ruskin's 'incurable impotency'; she married Millais in July 1855.

BROUGHTON

BROUGHTON, Peeblesshire   (Border)   5m E of Biggar on A701

John and Anna Buchan

Broughton Green, the farmhouse (formerly an inn), at the north end of the village on the Edinburgh-Carlisle road was the summer holiday home of John Buchan (1875–1940) and his sister Anna Buchan ('O. Douglas', 1877–1948). In 1851 John Buchan's maternal grandfather John Masterton became tenant of Broughton Green. Masterton's daughter Helen, well-known locally for her yellow hair, met the twenty-six-year-old minister John Buchan – the novelist's father – when he preached at Broughton Free Church during the winter of 1873–4 when the regular minister was abroad for the sake of his health. Helen was seventeen in 1874 when she married the Rev. John Buchan; and a week older than eighteen when she gave birth to the writer John Buchan (in Perth, on 26 August 1875, as the Rev. John Buchan had been called to the Knox Church, Perth). When John and Anna Buchan were growing up in Fife and Glasgow they spent their summers at Broughton Green with the Mastertons. Buchan loved exploring the ruined kirk, the trout pool and the high hills hunched around Broughton village. Janet Adam Smith, in her *John Buchan* (1965), notes:

> John Buchan developed into a hardy walker and ranged the hills in search of new burns to fish, until the ranging became an end in itself, and with his catch in his pockets he would drop down again to Broughton for tea – new-baked scones, and apple-and-rowanberry jelly – having charted yet another corner of his world. . . . [The Masterton] home at Broughton Green was a mixture of order and freedom: the order of a well-run farm as well as the order of a well-run, godly household.

Buchan participated in family prayers, went to two services on Sunday; but also heard ballads and listened to stories of the Covenanters who had sheltered in the peat-hags between Tweed and Clyde. When his grandmother died in 1901, Buchan said 'Since ever I was a very little boy I have liked Broughton better than any other place in the world'.

Witch Wood (1927), John Buchan's own favourite Buchan novel, is set in Woodilee which is an imaginative recreation of Broughton as it might have been in the seventeenth century. David Sempill, an intellectually astute young minister, comes to Woodilee kirk, actually the ruined kirk at Broughton in whose graveyard Buchan's little sister Violet is buried. (To the despair of the Buchan family, Violet died at Broughton in the summer of 1893 when she was only five.) In the novel Buchan gives the witch wood the presence of a protagonist as he contrasts the restraints of Calvinism with the emotive power of paganism. Woodilee, in the novel, exists in the shadow of the wood:

Everywhere, muffling the lower glen of the Woodilee burn and the immediate vale of the Aller, and climbing far up the hillside, was the gloom of trees. In the Rood glen there was darkness only at the foot, for higher up the woods thinned into scrub of oak and hazel, with the knees of the uplands showing through it. The sight powerfully impressed his fancy. Woodilee was a mere clearing in a forest. This was the *Silva Caledonis* of which old writers spoke, the wood which once covered all the land and in whose glades King Arthur had dwelt.

Anna Buchan, whose *Penny Plain* (1913), was written at Broughton, adored the village. In her essay 'An Upland Village' – included in *Farewell to Priorsford* (1950) – she describes Broughton as 'a village that wins and holds deep affection' then adds:

> In our early childhood it was the quietest of villages. If we did not reckon time by 'the day the chaise ga'ed through Elsrickle', at least we could easily have counted all the vehicles that passed in a week. An infrequent carriage and pair, some gigs and slow-moving farm-carts, a baker's van or two, and – great excitement – the pigman's cart. The 'pigman', let it be explained, had no connection with swine, but gave 'pigs' or dishes in exchange for old clothes.

Anna Buchan mentions a neighbour called Peggy Leithen, a surname Buchan gave to his Edward Leithen – first seen in the story 'Space' in *The Moon Endureth* (1912), then in *The Power-House* (1913), *John Macnab* (1925), *The Dancing Floor* (1926), *The Gap in the Curtain* (1932), and *Sick Heart River* (1941). Another local surname – Hannay – is commemorated in a stained glass window to the left of the pulpit in Broughton Free Church, now the **John Buchan Centre**. Richard Hannay, Buchan's most famous hero, is encountered in the following books: *The Thirty-Nine Steps* (1915), *Greenmantle* (1916), *Mr Standfast* (1919), *The Three Hostages* (1924), and *The Island of Sheep* (1936). When Buchan was appointed Governor-General of Canada in 1935 and created a Baron, he took for his title the name of the village of Tweedsmuir, south of Broughton.

Opened in August 1983, the John Buchan Centre is situated in the kirk where Buchan's parents first met. The building dates from the Disruption of 1843 and was refurbished in the 1890s. When Broughton Free Church closed in 1978, the Biggar Museum Trust – subsequently supported by the John Buchan Society (founded 1979) – began to plan the John Buchan Centre. As well as photographs and books relating to the careers of John and Anna Buchan, the centre contains the uniform Buchan wore in 1933 as Lord High Commissioner to the General Assembly of the Church of Scotland; and the khaki uniform he wore when signing Canada's Declaration of War against Germany in September 1939.

BROUGHTY FERRY, Angus   (Tayside)   1m E of Dundee on A930

Mary Shelley

Broughty Ferry, with the fifteenth-century Broughty Castle standing by the sea, is indirectly associated with the story of Frankenstein. Mary (Wollstonecraft Godwin) Shelley (1797–1851), wife of the poet, and author of *Frankenstein* (1818), spent the years 1812–14 with the Baxter family in Broughty Ferry. She recalled her time in the house near Peep o' Day Lane in her Introduction to the 1831 edition of *Frankenstein*:

> I lived principally in the country as a girl, and passed a considerable time in Scotland. I made occasional visits to the more picturesque parts; but my habitual residence was on the blank and dreary northern shores of the Tay, near Dundee. Blank and dreary on retrospection I call them; they were not so to me then. They were the eyry of freedom, and the pleasant region where unheeded I could commune with the creatures of my fancy. I wrote then – but in a most common-place style. It was beneath the trees of the grounds belonging to our house, or on the bleak sides of the woodless mountains near, that my true composition, the airy flights of my imagination, were born and fostered. I did not make myself the heroine of my tales. Life appeared to me too common-place an affair as regarded myself. I could not figure to myself that romantic woes or wonderful events would ever be my lot; but I was not confined to my own identity, and I could people the hours with creations far more interesting to me at that age, than my own sensations.

Broughty Ferry, then, played an important part in the imaginative development of the aspiring author though it is unlikely that Frankenstein and his monster were the creatures of Mary's fancy at that time.

In 1814 Mary eloped with Shelley and in February of the following year their daughter was born, though she lived for only a few days. It has been argued that the creation of the Frankenstein monster was a literary recreation of Mary's unfortunate experience of childbirth. In his book *A Chiel Among Them* (1982) David Toulmin speculates:

> Because of the traumatic state of her mind, Mary Shelley became so engrossed in her novel that her thoughts went haywire. Her fictional child was created beyond the bounds of reason . . . behind the monster's eloquence is Mary's grief. But it is a brooding grief . . . likely to be the result of her own maternal loss.

Mary herself, in the 1831 Introduction, refers to the novel as both a 'hideous progeny' and 'the offspring of happy days, when death and grief were but words'. What Mary omits to say is that when she eloped with

Shelley in 1814 the couple sailed down the Rhine and probably spent the night somewhere near Castle Frankenstein near Darmstadt. Mary would have heard tales of the alchemist Konrad Dippel (1673–1734) who was born in Castle Frankenstein and believed in the possibility of isolating the spirit of life. Dippel, not a Broughty Ferry fantasy, is the true original of Victor Frankenstein.

BROW WELL, Dumfriesshire (Dumfries and Galloway) 10m SE of Dumfries, off B725

Robert Burns

Outside the village of Ruthwell a signpost indicates **Brow Well** which has the inscription 'The Brow Well visited by the poet Burns, July 1796'. In 1796 Burns was seriously ill with a rheumatic heart condition. However, his friend Dr William Maxwell diagnosed 'flying gout' and prescribed riding and bathing as a cure. So Burns went to the health spa at Brow to drink the chalybeate waters from Brow Well and immerse himself up to his armpits in the Solway Firth (take road to the right from Brow Well, through a gate to the Solway). Maxwell's treatment was to prove fatal to a man with a serious heart condition.

When he was at Brow (3–16 July 1796) Burns realised he was dying and the word spread. Maria Riddell, with whom Burns had quarrelled, was ill herself and recovering near Brow. She sent her carriage for the poet whose deathly appearance horrified her. With 'the stamp of death' on his features he asked her: 'Well, Madam, have you any commands for the other world?' The comfort he received from his reconciliation with Maria prompted him to write to Mrs Frances Anna Dunlop who had stopped writing to the poet in 1795 as a protest against his enthusiastic attitude towards the French Revolution. His pathetic letter did bring a reply which he read on his death-bed in Dumfries.

Burns was not only ill at Brow, but anguished. When he got a tailor's demand for money for his Volunteer uniform he was seized with a hysterical panic and wrote to George Thomson, for whose *Select Scottish Airs* he had written more than a hundred song lyrics, asking for £12:

A cruel scoundrel of a haberdasher to whom I owe an account, taking it into his head that I am dying, has commenced a process, and will infallibly put me into jail. Do, for God's sake, send me that sum, and that by return of post.

Burns enclosed with the letter his last poem, 'Fairest Maid on Devon Banks', completed at Brow Well. It comprises a chorus and two stanzas, the last of which runs:

Then come, thou fairest of the fair,
Those wonted smiles, O let me share,
And by thy beauteous self I swear
No love but thine my heart shall know!

On 18 July a cart was borrowed to take Burns back to Dumfries where he died three days later.

CAERLAVEROCK CASTLE, Dumfriesshire   (Dumfries and Galloway)   9m S of Dumfries, off B725

Sir Walter Scott

Caerlaverock Castle dates back to 1220. In 1300 the castle was besieged by Edward I with a force of 3,000 men and from the fourteenth century onwards it was a seat of the Maxwell family whose motto 'I bid ye fair' is over the entrance. In 1640 the castle surrendered to the Covenanters. Lord Maxwell's Dainty Fabrick, a Renaissance mansion built within the castle around 1620, is the Ellangowan of Sir Walter Scott's *Guy Mannering* (1815).

Slightly further inland from the castle, at Caerlaverock Church, is a headstone to Robert Paterson (1715–1801) in the churchyard. Paterson was the original Old Mortality and, as Scott's novel *Old Mortality* (1816) indicates, dedicated his life to repairing the tombs of the Covenanters. Tradition states that Paterson died at Bankend (two miles north of Caerlaverock Castle). In 1855 his name was inscribed on the family tombstone at Balmaclellan but a few years after this the publishing firm of Adam and Charles Black felt it was more likely that he lay in Caerlaverock churchyard. They erected a headstone, with mallet and chisel over the following inscription:

Erected to the Memory of Robert Paterson the Old Mortality of
Sir Walter Scott Who was buried here February, 1801.
Why seeks he with unwearied toil,
    Through Death's dim walks to urge his way,
Reclaim his long-asserted spoil,
    And lead oblivion into day?

CAPE WRATH, Sutherland (Highland)

Sir Walter Scott

Cape Wrath is the 523ft high north-west extremity of mainland Scotland. In the summer of 1814 Sir Walter Scott (1771–1832) embarked on a six-week voyage round Scotland with the Commissioners of the Northern Lights and their Surveyor-Viceroy Robert Stevenson, grandfather of Robert Louis Stevenson. In his journal entry for Saturday 20 August 1814 Scott writes:

> Sail by four in the morning and by half-past six are off Cape Wrath. . . . On this dread Cape, so fatal to mariners, it is proposed to build a lighthouse and Mr Stevenson has fixed on an advantageous situation. It is a high promontory, with steep sides that go sheer down to the breakers, which lash its feet. There is no landing, except in a small creek about a mile and a half to the eastward. There the foam of the sea plays at long bowls with a huge collection of large stones, some of them a ton in weight, but which these fearful billows chuck up and down as a child tosses a ball.

The lighthouse, built in 1828, can be seen for twenty-seven miles.

Neil Gunn

The Silver Darlings (1941), by Neil Gunn (1891–1973), takes the hero Finn on a voyage with Roddie Sinclair, the most courageous captain in Dunster (actually Dunbeath where Gunn was born). It is an epic voyage, the first time a Dunster boat has attempted to go beyond the Moray Firth. Bound for Stornoway, the boat goes round Cape Wrath:

> Finn had often heard of Cape Wrath and now had plenty of time to gaze on its towering crags against which white sea-birds floated like blown feathers, their high cries sounding afar off and inward, in echo of rock and cavern. It inspired the crew with awe and held them to silence . . .

Cape Wrath is reached by the Kyle of Durness ferry (no cars) at Keoldale; in summer the ferry connects with a minibus service to the cape.

CARDROSS, Dunbartonshire   (Strathclyde)   3m NW of Dumbarton
on A814

A. J. Cronin

Cardross, where Robert the Bruce died in 1329, is the birthplace of A. J. Cronin (1896–1981). He was born on 19 July 1896 at Rosebank Cottage: his father was an Irish Catholic who worked as an insurance agent and travelling salesman for margarine; his mother, a Scottish Protestant, became a travelling saleswoman and eventually the first woman public health visitor with Glasgow Corporation. Cronin was a child when his father died and he moved, with his mother, to live with her parents in Dumbarton. After studying medicine and practising as a general practitioner, he began to write following a breakdown in his health in 1930. Encouraged by the success of *Hatter's Castle* (1931) he became one of the most successful writers of his time; the television series *Dr Finlay's Casebook* (based on his work and set in the fictional town of Tannochbrae) made him a household name in his later years.

CARRADALE, Argyllshire   (Strathclyde)   13m NE of Campbeltown
on B842

Naomi Mitchison

Born in Edinburgh (10 Randolph Crescent) on 1 November 1897, daughter of the Oxford physiologist J. S. Haldane, Naomi Mitchison (whose brother was J. B. S. Haldane, the controversial geneticist) married, in 1916, the Labour barrister and politician G. R. (later Lord) Mitchison. Since 1937 she has lived mainly at Carradale House. During the 1960s she was adopted as adviser and Mmarona (mother) by the Bagkatha tribe of Botswana which she visits annually. She has written more than seventy books including the historical novels *The Conquered* (1923), *Cloud Cuckoo Land* (1925), *The Corn King and the Spring Queen* (1930), and *The Bull Calves* (1947).

CASTLE DOUGLAS, Kirkcudbrightshire   (Dumfries and Galloway)
13m SW of Dumfries on A75

Sir Walter Scott

Castle Douglas is a market town at the north end of Carlingwark Loch. Sir Walter Scott's friend Joseph Train lived in Castle Douglas and supplied the 'author of *Waverley*' with material for his novels. For instance, Train told Scott the story, used as the basis of *Guy Mannering* (1815), of an astrologer who predicted the future of a child born in a house he stayed at; Train encouraged Scott to build his fictional portrait of John Graham of Claverhouse around tales told by Robert Paterson, the original of *Old Mortality* (1816); Train gathered information about the original of Madge Wildfire in Scott's *The Heart of Midlothian* (1818). Train died in a house in St Andrew Street and is commemorated by a plaque in the town hall. He was buried at Kirton, two miles south of Castle Douglas, in 1852.

CHANONRY POINT, Ross-shire   (Highland)

Kenneth Mackenzie

According to tradition Kenneth Mackenzie, the Brahan Seer, was tipped head first into a spiked barrel of boiling tar (in the 1660s) on Chanonry Point, a low promontory of the Black Isle opposite Fort George. A memorial marks the place of the execution, ordered by Isabella, Countess of Seaforth. Mackenzie, who worked as a labourer on the Brahan estates of the Earls of Seaforth, attracted attention on account of the prophecies he gave in Gaelic. When the third Earl of Seaforth visited Paris he left his wife, Elizabeth, Countess of Seaforth, at home in Brahan Castle. Concerned about Seaforth's well-being abroad, she summoned the Seer and demanded information about her absent husband. The Seer was reluctant to give details but, when ordered to be explicit by the Countess, painted a verbal picture of Seaforth 'on his knees before a fair lady, his arm round her waist, and her hand pressed to his lips'. Furious at this embarrassing information, delivered before her own servants, the Countess condemned the Seer to death. Before he died the Seer is said to have predicted the doom of the Seaforth family, a prophesy that was fulfilled. Among other prophecies attributed to the Seer are the catastrophe of Culloden, the Highland Clearances and the building of the Caledonian Canal. Andrew Lang (1844–1912), the poet who took a special interest in paranormal phenomena, was sceptical about the Seer: 'We can scarcely ever . . . find any evidence that the prophecies were recorded before the event. . . . We are, in fact, dealing with poetic legend, not with evidence.'

CLUNY'S CAGE

CHAPEL OF GARIOCH, Aberdeenshire   (Grampian)   18m NW of
Aberdeen, off A96

William Alexander

William Alexander (1826–94) was born at Rescivet, Chapel of Garioch, and educated at the parish school. He worked as a ploughman until an accident led to the loss of a leg when he was in his early twenties. Moving to Aberdeen, he worked as a journalist and his novel *Johnny Gibb of Gushetneuk* (1871) was first serialised in the *Aberdeen Free Press* (1869–70), a newspaper he later edited. Set in the imaginary Aberdeenshire parish of Pyketillim, it comprises forty-nine scenes giving (to quote the subtitle) 'Glimpses of the Parish Politics about AD 1843'. The Disruption of 1843 brings Johnny Gibb, a farmer, to the fore as a supporter of the Free Church of Scotland: 'It was not Johnny Gibb's intention to be a Disruption leader, yet he had become so *de facto*'.

In his study of *The Scottish Novel* (1978) Francis Russell Hart praises *Johnny Gibb of Gushetneuk* as 'the masterpiece of Scottish Victorian fiction' and 'Victorian Scotland's most impressive single novel'. Alexander's strength is his ability to contrast an English narrative with dialogue displaying the vitality of the Aberdeenshire vernacular. The same method is used in *Sketches of Life Among my Ain Folk* (1875):

> He knew Baubie Huie, moreover, and his estimate of Baubie was expressed in the words – 'Sang, she's a richt quine yon, min; there's nae a deem i' the pairt'll haud 'er nain wi' ye better nor she'll dee; an' she's a fell ticht gweed-leukin hizzie tee,' which, no doubt, was a perfectly accurate description according to the notions entertained by the speaker of the qualities desirable in the female sex.

quine young girl; *deem* dame; *fell* extremely; *ticht* plump; *gweed* good.

CLUNY'S CAGE, Inverness-shire   (Highland)

Robert Louis Stevenson

On the southern slope of Ben Alder, on Loch Ericht's west shore, is 'Cluny's Cage' where, in September 1746 'Bonnie Prince Charlie' (Charles Edward Stuart, the Young Pretender) hid when a fugitive following the defeat of the Scottish clans at Culloden (16 April 1746). The prince stayed here until 13 September when the news of two French privateers in Loch nan Uamh shifted him. Covering the 100 miles to the coast within a week he boarded *l'Heureux* at Borrodale and on 20 September 1746 left Scotland. Ewen Macpherson of Cluny joined the Jacobites in 1745,

57

retreated to 'Cluny's Cage' after Culloden and died in exile in France in 1756. In Robert Louis Stevenson's *Kidnapped* (1886) Alan Breck and David Balfour visit Cluny's Cage (Chapter 23):

> Quite at the top, and just before the rocky face of the cliff sprang above the foliage, we found that strange house which was known in the country as 'Cluny's Cage'. The trunks of several trees had been wattled across, the intervals strengthened with stakes, and the ground behind this barricade levelled up with earth to make the floor. A tree, which grew out from the hillside, was the living centre-beam of the roof. The walls were of wattle and covered with moss. The whole house had something of an egg shape; and it half hung, half stood in that steep, hillside thicket, like a wasps' nest in a green hawthorn.

CLYTH, Caithness   (Highland)   2m E of Lybster

Donald Campbell

The Widows of Clyth (1979), a play by Donald Campbell (born in Wick on 25 February 1940), explores the aftermath of a tragedy of 1876 when a fishing boat went under and five widows were left to cope with twenty-six children. The lighthouse on Clyth Ness is visible for eighteen miles.

COLINTON, Midlothian   (Lothian)   3m W of Swanston

Robert Louis Stevenson

Colinton Village is associated with Robert Louis Stevenson (1850–94) whose maternal grandfather, the Rev. Lewis Balfour (1777–1860) was minister of **Colinton Parish Church** from 1823–1860. Stevenson's mother Margaret grew up in **Colinton Manse** and Stevenson often stayed in his maternal grandfather's home. Colinton Parish Church and Manse are situated beside the Water of Leith to the left over Dell Road bridge. In *Memories and Portraits* (1887) Stevenson describes the place thus:

> I have named, among many rivers that make music in my memory, the dirty Water of Leith. Often and often I desire to look upon it again, and the choice of a point of view is easy to me. It should be at a certain water-door, embowered in shrubbery. . . . It was a place in that time like no other: the garden cut into provinces by a great hedge of beech, and overlooked by the church and the terrace of the churchyard, where the tombstones were thick, and after nightfall 'spunkies' might be seen to dance at least by children; flower-pots

lying warm in sunshine; laurels and the great yew making elsewhere a pleasing horror of shade; the smell of water rising from all round, with an added tang of paper-mills; the sound of water everywhere, and the sound of mills – the wheel and the dam singing their alternate strain; the birds on every bush and from every corner of the overhanging woods pealing out their notes until the air throbbed with them; and in the midst of this, the manse.

The mills mentioned by Stevenson have been demolished.

On the church wall beside the gate is an Interpretation Point on the Robert Louis Stevenson Heritage Trail. In the churchyard is a memorial to the Rev. Lewis Balfour. Stevenson described his maternal grandfather, in *Memories and Portraits*, as a 'man of singular simplicity of nature; unemotional, and hating the display of what he felt; a lover of his life and innocent habits to the end'.

CRAIGENPUTTOCK, Dumfriesshire   (Dumfries and Galloway)   7m
W of Dunscore

Thomas Carlyle

As Thomas Carlyle (1795–1881) said in a document of June 1867, Craigenputtock is a moorland farm 'at the head of the Parish of Dunscore, in Nithsdale, Dumfriesshire'. In May 1828 Carlyle and his wife Jane Welsh Carlyle (1801–42) – who had married on 17 October 1826 – left their house at 21 Comely Bank, Edinburgh, to live in the remote farmhouse of Craigenputtock. Jane, who inherited the house, disliked its distance from what she regarded as civilised life, and when Carlyle first proposed marriage and settlement at Craigenputtock she ridiculed the idea; 'You and I keeping house at Craigenputtock! I would as soon think of building myself a nest on the Bass Rock . . . I could not spend a month at it with an angel.' Nevertheless she lived there for six years with Carlyle.

It was the financial insecurity they had experienced in Edinburgh and Carlyle's determination to find a solitude suitable for serious work that persuaded Jane to move to Craigenputtock. She and her husband lived on the farm while Carlyle's brother Alick farmed the land. Carlyle wrote to Goethe in 1828 about his purpose in coming to the bleak moor: 'I came hither purely for this one reason: that I might not have to write for bread, might not be tempted to tell lies for money'.

When Carlyle lived at Craigenputtock there were eight rooms and a kitchen at his disposal; in the study, a room off the ground-floor drawing-room, he wrote *Sartor Resartus* (1833–4). He also addressed to Jane, in 1830, some stanzas setting their lonely home in a cosmic context:

Lone stands our home amid the sullen moor.
　　Its threshold by few friendly feet betrod;
Yet *we* are here, we two, still true, though poor:
　　And this, too, is the world – the city of God!

O'erhangs us not the infinitude of sky,
　　Where all the starry lights revolve and shine?
Does not that universe within us lie
　　And move – its Maker or itself divine?

Jane felt no affection for Craigenputtock, however, though she cherished
its association with her father (as she wrote in a letter of 24 May 1833):
'I wish its improvement had not been my Father's work; and then I should
not care though it were let on a nineteen years lease to the Devil himself'.

Carlyle saw it differently. In *Reminiscences* (1881) he writes warmly of
his life with Jane at the farmhouse:

> In fact, the saving charm of [Jane's] life at Craigenputtock, which to
> another young lady of her years might have been so gloomy and
> vacant, was that of conquering the innumerable Practical Problems
> that had arisen for her there – all of which, I think all, she
> triumphantly mastered. . . . Perfection of housekeeping was her clear
> and speedy attainment in that new scene. Strange how she made the
> Desert blossom for herself and me there; what a fairy palace she had
> made of that wild moorland home of the poor man! . . . We were
> not unhappy at Craigenputtock; perhaps these were our happiest days.
> Useful, continual labour, essentially successful; that makes even the
> moor green. I found I could do fully *twice* as much work in a given
> time there, as with my best effort was possible in London – such the
> interruptions, etc. Once, in the winter time, I remember counting that
> for three months, there had not any stranger, not even a beggar,
> called at Craigenputtock door.

Though few called on the Carlyles at Craigenputtock, visitors included
Lord Jeffrey, editor of the *Edinburgh Review*; and Ralph Waldo Emerson.

After Jane's death in 1866 Carlyle inherited Craigenputtock and decided
to bequeath it to Edinburgh University (whose Rector he was in 1865 to
1866). Carlyle's document of June 1867 stipulates that the annual revenue
of the estate should be divided into ten John Welsh Bursaries (John Welsh
being Jane's father). Craigenputtock was subsequently sold.

CROMARTY, Ross and Cromarty   (Highland)   20m NE of Inverness
on A832

Sir Thomas Urquhart

A memorial plaque (erected by the Saltire Society) in the Old Kirk of
Cromarty (dating from 1700) commemorates Sir Thomas Urquhart (*c.*
1611–60) who was born in Cromarty Tower, a site now occupied by
Cromartie House. Urquhart, a fervent Royalist, fought at the battle of
Turriff in 1639. In 1642, while living at Cromarty Tower, he wrote *Trissote-*
tras (1645), an account of trigonometry. After the battle of Worcester
(1651) he was imprisoned in the Tower of London but returned to
Cromarty on parole before moving to Europe where he died, supposedly
from an uncontrollable fit of hilarity on hearing of the Restoration of
Charles II in 1660.

His works deal, obsessively as well as brilliantly, with favourite themes.
Pantochronochanon (1652) reaches back to Urquhart's family roots in the
third century; *The Discoverie of a Most Exquisite Jewel* (1652) describes
the Admirable Crichton (James Crichton of Cluny) and features an essay
on the necessity of a universal language; *Logopandecteison* (1653) has
further observations on the universal language. Urquhart is best known,
though, for his translation of the first three books of Rabelais's *Gargantua*
and Pantagruel (1653 and 1693). This Rabelaisian recreation subsequently
inspired at least two novels produced in Scotland: Sydney Goodsir Smith's
Carotid Cornucopius (1947) and Robert Nye's *Falstaff* (1976). Here is
Urquhart's version (Book 1, Chapter 10) of the childhood of Gargantua:

> Gargantua, from three years upwards unto five, was brought up and
> instructed in all convenient discipline, by the commandment of his
> father; and spent that time like the other little children of the country,
> that is, in drinking, eating and sleeping: in eating, sleeping and
> drinking: and in sleeping, drinking and eating. Still he wallowed and
> rolled himself up and down in the mire and dirt: he blurred and sullied
> his nose with filth; he blotted and smutched his face with any kind of
> scurvy stuff; he trod down his shoes in the heel; at the flies he did
> often times yawn, and ran very heartily after the butterflies, the empire
> whereof belonged to his father.

Hugh Miller

Hugh Miller's Cottage, Church Street – the last remaining thatched cottage
in Cromarty – was built in 1711 for John Fiddes (who paid for it in gold
gained by buccaneering) and his wife Jean Gallie. Their initials can be
seen on the mantle of one of the lower rooms. In the cottage, in the room

on the right at the head of the stairs, Hugh Miller (1802–56) was born on 10 October 1802. A sea-captain's son – and great-grandson of John Fiddes – Miller achieved fame as a geologist and author. The cottage was opened to the public in 1900 and in 1938 the National Trust for Scotland acquired it from Cromarty Town Council. Open April–October (10am–5pm; also Sun. 2–5pm from June–Sept.) it charts the career of the 'Cromarty Stonemason'. The Birthroom contains a scrubbed-wood nursing chair, Miller's stonemason's mallet, and the shepherd tartan plaid he wore in Edinburgh as editor of the *Witness* (the evangelical weekly he ran from 1840 until his death). An adjoining 'Man of Letters Room' displays papers relating to Miller's literary activities along with letters from such as Darwin and Thomas Carlyle. The Geology Room has fossils of the ancient armoured fishes from Miller's collection (with his descriptions of the specimens). In the garden the visitor can look up to the imposing monument erected to Miller and examine the stone sundial Miller hewed for his uncles:

> During my period of convalescence, I amused myself in hewing for
> my uncles, from an original design, an ornate dial-stone; and the
> dial-stone still exists, to show that my skill as a stone-cutter rose
> somewhat above the average of the profession in those parts of the
> country in which it ranks highest.

Miller, who became a stonemason at the age of seventeen, combined his trade with a study of natural history and a devotion to literature. He published *Poems Written in the Leisure Hours of a Journeyman Mason* in 1829 but concentrated on prose after the poor reception of this first volume. Working at the rock face of the Old Red Sandstone quarries he unearthed evidence of the life of the period and included his essays on the subject in the *Witness*. These essays were collected as *The Old Red Sandstone* (1841), Miller's most celebrated book. His ability to combine information with imagery is remarkable, as in the following remarks on the fin structure of Cheiracanthus:

> In the Chimaera Borealis, a cartilaginous fish of the Northern Ocean,
> the spine seems placed in front of the weaker rays, just if I may be
> allowed the comparison, as in a line of mountaineers engaged in
> crossing a swollen torrent, the strongest man in the party is placed
> on the upper side of the line, to break off the force of the current
> from the rest. In the Cheiracanthus, however, each fin seems to
> consist of but a single spine, with an angular membrane fixed to it by
> one of its sides, and attached to the creature's body on the other.
> Its fins are masts and sails – the spine representing the mast, and the
> membrane the sail.

The Old Red Sandstone went through twenty-one editions in thirty-six years and is now valued as a work of literature as well as a landmark in natural history. Miller's evangelical outlook and his determination to reconcile religion and geology led him to adhere to the successive creation hypothesis at a time when it was discredited. Towards the end of his life Miller was still struggling to synthesise his biblical faith with his geological knowledge and in a mood of depression – while working on *The Testimony of the Rocks* (1857) – shot himself in Edinburgh.

CRUDEN BAY, Aberdeenshire (Grampian) 6½m SW of Peterhead on A975

Bram Stoker

Bram Stoker (1847–1912) stayed at the local hotel in Cruden Bay when working on his supernatural masterpiece *Dracula* (1897) in which he describes 'a vast ruined castle, from whose tall black windows came no ray of light, and whose broken battlements showed a jagged line against the moonlit sky'. Local tradition identifies Count Dracula's Castle with Slains Castle, now a ruin but built in 1664 and extended in 1836. An earlier Slains Castle was destroyed in 1594 by James VI because the Earl of Errol of the time plotted with Spain.

CULLEN, Banffshire (Grampian) 20m E of Elgin on A98

James Boswell, Dr Samuel Johnson

Cullen is an historic sea-town where, in 1327, Robert the Bruce's queen, Elizabeth de Burgh, died. In *The Journal of a Tour to the Hebrides* (1785) James Boswell describes a visit he and Dr Johnson made to Cullen on 26 August 1773:

> We breakfasted at Cullen. They set down dried haddocks broiled, along with our tea. I ate one; but Dr Johnson was disgusted by the sight of them, so they were removed. Cullen has a comfortable appearance, though but a very small town, and the houses mostly poor buildings.

The sea-town subsequently prospered and the harbour (begun in 1817) thrived in the great days of the herring industry.

George MacDonald

A century after Boswell's visit, George MacDonald (1824–1905) – the poet and novelist whose literary world of fantasy influenced J. R. R.

Tolkien and C. S. Lewis – lived in a house (later a tea room) in Grant Street. In his novels *Malcolm* (1875) and *The Marquis of Lossie* (1877) the setting is Cullen, renamed Portlossie by MacDonald.

CUPAR, Fife   (Fife)   8m W of St Andrews on A91.

Sir David Lyndsay

Cupar has been a royal burgh since 1328. Sir David Lyndsay (*c.* 1490–1555) was the eldest son of David Lyndsay of the Mount, three-and-a-half miles north-west of Cupar. He was probably educated at Cupar (which had a grammar school in 1357, later amalgamated with English School to form Cupar Academy in 1822). By 1511 Lyndsay was at the court of James IV; James IV's son was a little over a year old when he was crowned James V in 1513 and, due to the domination of the Douglas family at the child-king's court, Lyndsay was banished to his East Lothian estate. When, in 1528, James V finally hounded his Douglas stepfather out of Scotland and asserted his authority, Lyndsay was recalled to the court and knighted. Lyndsay's masterpiece, *Ane Pleasant Satyre of the Thrie Estaitis*, had a royal premiere before the court at Linlithgow in 1540, and a revised version was performed on 7 June 1552 at Castle Hill, Cupar (site occupied by Castlehill School). *The Thrie Estaitis* is recognised as Scotland's greatest dramatic work and is regularly revived at the Edinburgh International Festival.

Sir John Scot

Scotstarvit Tower, two miles south-west of Cupar, dates from the sixteenth century; from 1611 it was the home of Sir John Scot (1585–1670). Scot edited (with Arthur Johnston) the *Delitiae Poetarum Scotorum* (1637), an anthology of Latin verse by thirty-seven Scottish poets. When Cromwell occupied Scotland in 1652, Sir John Scot of Scotstarvit lost his posts as Privy Councillor, Lord of Session and circuit judge. A scholar who encouraged the map-maker Timothy Pont, Scot criticised the Scottish nobility in *The Staggering State of the Scots Statesmen* (posthumously published in 1754).

Henrietta Keddie

Henrietta Keddie (1827–1914) was a lawyer's daughter born in Cupar, though as a child she moved to Elie where the family's coal-mine was located. She was educated in Edinburgh, returned to Fife to stay in St Andrews, then – on the death of her father – set up a private school in

Cupar which she and her sister ran from 1848–70. Her literary success enabled her to leave the school and she moved to London in 1884. On 8 June 1914 she died in Oxford. Her best-remembered work is the novel *Logie Town* (1887), a novel (published under the pseudonym Sarah Tytler) about a Fife town apparently modelled on Cupar.

Hugh MacDiarmid

In 1913 C. M. Grieve (1892–1978) – the poet Hugh MacDiarmid – secured a job in Cupar as assistant editor on the Innes newspapers *Fife Coast Chronicle, St Andrews Citizen*, and *Fife Herald*. In a letter of 20 August 1916 to George Ogilvie, Grieve wrote:

> Unfortunately in the eyes of my well-wishing relatives Cupar happens to be a boozy little hole . . . I enjoyed Cupar immensely – worked harder than I should have believed it possible for me to do and simultaneously drank like a fish, acquiring in time the art . . . of accurately transcribing and telephonically transmitting while wildly intoxicated reports from the shorthand of brother-journalists, who collapsing under the strain of work and wine, had passed into hopeless conditions which left it up to the unbowled-over one of the party to see that their papers were not 'let down'.
>
> Unfortunately or fortunately, I did not get on well with one of the bosses. We were mutually incompatible. A rupture beyond repair at last sent me to a new sphere in Forfar.

It was in Cupar that Grieve met Margaret 'Peggy' Skinner, a copyholder with the Innes papers, who became his first wife in 1918.

Fred Urquhart

From October 1939 to December 1940 novelist and storyteller Fred Urquhart (born 1912) lived at 29 South Road, a house owned by Peggy Grieve, the first wife of Hugh MacDiarmid. Towards the end of 1938 Peggy Grieve rented the house to Mary H. Litchfield, a schoolteacher who lived there until her death in the spring of 1947. Litchfield admired Urquhart's work and in the spring of 1939 invited him to stay a weekend at 29 South Road. He returned as a paying guest in October and subsequently used the character of Mary Litchfield for his fictional Mrs Poppy Chiltern in 'Once a Schoolmissy', collected in *The Last Sister* (1950).

In the summer of 1940 a regiment of Polish soldiers arrived in Cupar and Urquhart had many opportunities to study them and the local girls. The result was the novella *Namietnosc* (Polish for 'passion'), or 'The Laundry Girl and the Pole' which he wrote in the period October–

December 1940. It was translated into Polish and appeared as a serial in *Dziennik Zolnierza*, the Polish soldiers' daily. It is included in Urquhart's collection *The Clouds Are Big With Mercy* (1946).

During the time he lived at 29 South Road, Urquhart remembers various literary visitors including Willa and Edwin Muir (the latter had been engaged to Mary Litchfield when they were both resident in Glasgow); and Douglas Young (1913–73).

DALKEITH, Midlothian   (Lothian)   6m SE of Edinburgh, on A68

Edwin Muir

In the South Esk valley, near Dalkeith, stands Newbattle Abbey which was founded by Cistercian monks in 1140 under the patronage of David I. In 1936 the 11th Marquess of Lothian gave this, his former family home, to the nation as a residential adult education college. From 1950 to 1955 the poet Edwin Muir (1887–1959) was Warden of Newbattle Abbey College and enjoyed his contact with mature students from a variety of backgrounds. In *An Autobiography* (1954) he wrote of the students:

> They were eager, and more intelligent than I had ever dreamed they could be, and to watch over them and see their minds unfolding was an experience I am glad not to have missed.

Though he got on well with staff and students, Muir disliked the necessity of dealing with committees and was relieved when an offer to deliver the 1955–6 Charles Eliot Norton lectures at Harvard (published as *The Estate of Poetry* in 1962) gave him the opportunity to retire from Newbattle.

Tom Scott, George Mackay Brown, Archie Hind

From all accounts Muir was a wonderfully sympathetic teacher and during his time at Newbattle he encouraged the literary aspirations of such students as Tom Scott (born 1918), George Mackay Brown (born 1921), and Archie Hind (born 1928). Brown described his first period (beginning October 1951) at Newbattle as 'probably the happiest year of my life'. Brown returned for a second spell at Newbattle in summer 1956 to prepare himself for entry to an English course at Edinburgh University.

DALMALLY, Argyllshire   (Strathclyde)   24m E of Oban on A85

Duncan Ban MacIntyre

Monument Hill, two miles south-west on the old Inverary road (a dead-end) has a granite temple commemorating Duncan Ban MacIntyre (Donnchadh Ban Mac an t-Saoir, 1724–1812), the Gaelic poet. From the temple there are magnificent views of Kilchurn Castle and Loch Awe. Dalmally lies at the foot of Glen Orchy where MacIntyre was born on 20 March 1724 and where he worked as a gamekeeper and forester employed by the Campbells. He was non-literate and his poems were written down and edited, in 1768, by John, son of the Rev. James Stuart of Killin. A year before the publication of his poems MacIntyre moved to Edinburgh where he became a member of the City Guard and later served as a soldier in the Breadalbane Fencibles.

His greatest poems were composed in the period before he moved to Edinburgh. He wrote various praise-poems for his Campbell employers, such as 'A Song to Lord Glenorchy' and 'Lament for Colin of Glenure' (the Campbell killed in the Appin murder of 1752). His best-known poem 'The Praise of Ben Dorain' ('Moladh Beinn Dòbhrainn') has been translated by both Hugh MacDiarmid (1892–1978) and Iain Crichton Smith (born 1928).

Derick Thomson

MacIntyre is revered as a great nature poet and his 'Summer Song' (as translated by Derick Thomson) conveys the sensuous quality of his observation:

> The rising sap beneath the bark
> moistens the birch's veins,
> till shoot and wand, and branch and bough
> are clothed with leaves again;
> the sultry heat sucks from the mould
> the fecund birch-top's food,
> no snuff's aroma can excel
> this flowering of the wood.

DENHOLM, Roxburghshire   (Border)   5m NE of Hawick on A698

John Leyden, Sir Walter Scott

John Leyden (1775–1811), the poet and linguist, was born in Denholm on 8 September 1775: there is a memorial in the village green and his thatched cottage birthplace, nearby, is marked with a plaque. Leyden was educated at home (to the age of nine) before going to village school at Kirktown and then Edinburgh University. A brilliant linguist who could eventually speak thirty languages, he worked as a private tutor in St Andrews from 1796 to 1798. Licensed as a preacher he returned to Edinburgh and published *A Historical and Philosophical Sketch of the Discoveries and Settlements of the Europeans in Northern and Western Africa at the Close of the Eighteenth Century* (1799). He also assisted Sir Walter Scott with his *Minstrelsy of the Scottish Border* (1802–3) and himself edited *Scottish Descriptive Poems* (1802). In 1803 he became an assistant surgeon in Madras, India; on 28 August 1811 he died in Java. In *The Lord of the Isles* (1815) Scott mourns (IV, xi) Leyden's death after citing Scottish scenes:

> – Scenes sung by him who sings no more!
> His bright and brief career is o'er,
>   And mute his tuneful strains;
> Quench'd is his lamp of varied lore
> That loved the light of song to pour;
> A distant and a deadly shore
>   Has *Leyden*'s cold remains!

In a note, Scott explains that Leyden composed 'Macphail of Colonsay, and the Mermaid of Corrievrekin' for the *Minstrelsy*' in 1801:

> soon before his fatal departure for India, where, after having made farther progress in Oriental literature than any man of letters who had embraced those studies, he died a martyr to his zeal for knowledge, in the island of Java, immediately after the landing of our forces near Batavia, in August 1811.

Sir James Murray

Sir James Murray (1837–1915), author of *The Dialect of the Southern Counties of Scotland* (1873) and editor of the *Oxford English Dictionary* (from 1879), was born in Denholm on 7 February 1837. For his authoritative work as a lexicographer he was knighted in 1908.

DEVIL'S BEEF TUB, Dumfriesshire   (Dumfries and Galloway)   4m N of Moffat

Sir Walter Scott

A deep hollow in the hillside near the source of the River Annan, the Devil's Beef Tub is mentioned in *Redgauntlet* (1824) by Sir Walter Scott.

Mr. Maxwell (the Laird of Summertrees, also known as 'Pate-in-Peril') tells Alan Fairford how he escaped when handcuffed to Sir Henry Redgauntlet. The two men were being taken to Carlisle to be tried for their part in the Jacobite rising of 1745:

'We were to halt for breakfast at Moffat. Well did I know the moors we were marching over, having hunted and hawked on every acre of ground in very different times. So I waited, you see, till I was on the edge of Errickstane brae – Ye ken the place they call the Marquis's Beef-stand, because the Annandale loons used to put their stolen cattle in there?. . . . Ye must have seen it as ye came this way; it looks as if four hills were laying their heads together, to shut out daylight from the dark hollow space between them. A d——d deep, black, blackguard-looking abyss of a hole it is, and goes straight down from the roadside, as perpendicular as it can do, to be a heathery brae. At the bottom, there is a small bit of a brook, that you would think could hardly find its way out from the hills that are so closely jammed round it. . . . And so, just when we came on the edge of this Beef-stand of the Johnstones, I slipped out my hand from the handcuff, cried to Harry Gauntlet, "Follow me!" – whisked under the belly of the dragoon horse – flung my plaid round me with the speed of lightning – threw myself on my side, for there was no keeping my feet, and down the brae hurled I, over heather and fern, and blackberries, like a barrel down Chalmers' Close, in Auld Reekie. G—, sir, I never could help laughing when I think how the scoundrel redcoats must have been bumbazed; for the mist being, as I said, thick, they had little notion, I take it, that they were on the verge of such a dilemma. . . . And so off I set, and never buck went faster ower the braes than I did; and I never stopped till I had put three waters, reasonably deep, as the season was rainy, half a dozen mountains, and a few thousand acres of the worst moss and ling in Scotland, betwixt me and my friends the redcoats.

Sir Henry Redgauntlet, however, is recaptured and executed in Carlisle.

DINGWALL, Ross-shire   (Highland)   18½m NW of Inverness on A9

Neil Gunn

From 1937 to 1949 the novelist Neil Gunn (1891–1973) rented Braefarm House, three miles along the road from Dingwall to Strathpeffer. Here he wrote eleven of his twenty novels, including *Wild Geese Overhead* (1939), *The Silver Darlings* (1941), *The Green Isle of the Great Deep* (1944), and *The Lost Chart* (1949). Braefarm House is described by Nan, the heroine of *The Shadow* (1948), as 'really quite a decent farmhouse. All of five bedrooms and an enormous bathroom which may have been another bedroom once'. In their biography of *Neil M. Gunn* (1981) Francis Russell Hart and John Pick note that 'At Brae [Gunn] had reached a peak of popular success and esteem. Now a decline began.' He moved to Kincraig, near the busy Dingwall-Invergordon Road and in 1951 went to Kerrow, in Glen Cannich. He sold Kerrow in 1959, settling in Dalcraig, which Gunn described as 'A neat compact cottage . . . facing south over the Beauly Firth, about two miles by the shore road (quiet) from Kessock Ferry and Inverness.' After the death of Daisy in 1963 Gunn went into a decline. He died on 15 January 1973 and was buried in the cemetery above Dingwall.

DRUMLITHIE, Kincardineshire   (Grampian)   6m SW of Stonehaven, off A94

Lewis Grassic Gibbon

Drumlithie has an eighteenth-century steeple whose bell was tolled, during the days of handloom weaving, to regulate the weavers' mealtimes. As part of the Howe of the Mearns, it comes in for comment in Lewis Grassic Gibbon's trilogy *A Scots Quair* (1932–4). In *Sunset Song*, the first volume of the trilogy, the heroine Chris approaches Drumlithie:

> some called it Skite to torment the folk and they'd get fell angry at that in Skite. No more than a rickle of houses it was, white with sunshine below its steeple that made of Skite the laugh of the Howe, for feint the kirk was near it. Folk said for a joke that every time it came on to rain the Drumlithie folk ran out and took in their steeple, that proud they were of the thing, it came from the weaver days of the village when damn the clock was there in the place and its tolling told the hour.

DRYBURGH ABBEY, Berwickshire   (Border)   6m SE of Melrose, off A68

Sir Walter Scott

Founded in 1150 by Hugh de Morville, Constable of Scotland, Dryburgh Abbey is an imposing ruin standing in a setting of lawns and specimen trees in a bend of the Tweed. As the abbey lands belonged to his great-grandfather, Sir Walter Scott (1771–1832) was buried, as was his right, in

St Mary's Aisle – with his wife, who predeceased him in 1826. Scott's son-in-law and biographer, John Gibson Lockhart (1794–1854) died (like Scott) at Abbotsford and was buried at the foot of Sir Walter''s tomb.

Scott's View, looking across the Tweed to the Eildon Hills, is near Bemersyde (two miles north on the B6356), the Haig family home since the twelfth century.

DUMBARTON, Dunbartonshire   (Strathclyde)   16m NW of Glasgow
on A82

Tobias Smollett

Tobias Smollett (1721–71) was educated at Dumbarton Grammar School. In Smollett's day the school was situated in the old Parish Church, on the site of the present parish church (of 1811), the 'Riverside', at the bottom of Church Street. When Smollett went to the school, his father dead and his mother moving to Edinburgh, it was a vaulted apartment under the steeple of the old parish church. Though Smollett's first novel *Roderick Random* (1748) contains a horrific account of a Scottish schooling – complete with sadistic monster in charge of children – Smollett was taught at Dumbarton by John Love, a gifted and progressive man who practised, as well as preaching, the abolition of corporal punishment. In *The Present State of All Nations*, which he completed in 1768, Smollett describes Dumbarton thus:

> Dumbarton, the county town, which bestows its name upon the shire, is a small inconsiderable royal borough, situated near the conflux of the Clyde and Leven; and at present remarkable for nothing but its castle, which has been described by the pens of Buchanan and Camden. It is a steep rock, rising up in two points, and everywhere inaccessible except by a very narrow passage or entry, fortified with a strong wall and rampart.

A. J. Cronin

After the death of his Irish Catholic father, A. J. Cronin (1896–1981) came, with his mother, to live with her strongly Presbyterian parents at Willowbrook, next to Miller's farm in what is now Roundriding Road. Divided between the Roman Catholic faith of his father and the Protestant creed of his mother's family, Cronin was known as the 'Wee Pope' when he attended Dumbarton Academy (at the eastern foot of Church Street). He studied medicine at Glasgow University, married fellow student Agnes Mary Gibson (in 1925), and practised medicine in Harley Street from 1926 to 1930 when a duodenal ulcer forced him to recuperate for six months at Dalchenna Farm, near Inveraray, Argyll. On 15 August 1930 he wrote to Dumbarton Library:

I am an old Dumbarton Academy boy and enclose my card. At present I am on holiday at the above address [Dalchenna Farm]. I am engaged at the moment on a piece of writing and require some information regarding conditions in the Dumbarton shipyards fifty years ago. Would it be possible to get any details from books in your library? If so, I would come down and consult them if you would be kind enough to let me know a suitable time.

The result of his research was *Hatter's Castle* (1931), a novel set in Levenford (that is, Dumbarton). Obviously influenced by George Douglas Brown's *The House with the Green Shutters* (1901), it tells a grim tale of family life dominated by a domestic tyrant – James Brodie, the hatter. Cronin's maternal grandfather, Archibald Montgomerie, owned a hatter's shop at 145 High Street and is thought to be the original of the appalling Brodie. The book finally destroyed Cronin's relationship with his mother's family.

After the publication of *Hatter's Castle*, Cronin became a prolific and immensely popular novelist, as witness *The Citadel* (1937), *The Stars Look Down* (1941), and *The Spanish Gardener* (1950). The television series *Dr Finlay's Casebook* brought his name to the attention of millions of viewers and he died (6 January 1981) as a tax exile in Switzerland.

Maurice Lindsay

In 1976 the poet Maurice Lindsay (born 1918) left Glasgow and settled at 7 Milton Hill, Milton (two miles east of Dumbarton). His house is a wooden box on stilts looking over the Clyde and Renfrew hills to the front; and (at the back) up to the Kilpatrick hills. Lindsay's *Collected Poems* (1979) contains a poem 'On Milton Hill' beginning:

Since I moved up to live among the birds,
gathering round my house their shawl of woods,
trees have turned staves where notes and dotted wings
measure the movements each new season brings,
phrasing the round of fields and sky, the moods
that seas and clouds whip up, or fleck to curds.

DUMFRIES, Dumfriesshire   (Dumfries and Galloway)   On A75

Robert Burns

Tired of farming and determined to devote himself professionally to Excise work, Robert Burns (1759–96) signed, on 10 September 1791, the formal renunciation of the seventy-seven-year lease on Ellisland farm. On 11 November he moved into a flat in Stinking Vennel, now **Bank Street**: the house is now gone but a plaque marks the site. Burns had good friends in Dumfries, such as Dr William Maxwell, an armchair French revolutionary, and John Syme, Distributor of Stamps in Dumfries. In February 1792 he was promoted to the Dumfries Port Division and thus earned an extra £20 a year.

Increased leisure time gave Burns the opportunity to increase his literary output and William Creech contacted him about a new edition of the poems. However, most of Burns's energy was concentrated on writing songs, not only for James Johnson's *Scots Musical Museum* (1787–1803), of which he was now, in fact, if not in name, editor; but for George Thomson's *Select Scottish Airs* (1793–1841). Burns contributed 114 songs, including 'Scots Wha hae', to Thomson's collection.

Nevertheless, the songwriting Exciseman could not avoid conflict. He was now openly expressing his enthusiasm for developments in revolutionary France. When, with other Excisemen, Burns captured the smuggling schooner *Rosamond* he obtained four carronades and donated them to the French Convention. This was provocative enough, but when he made a public gesture of approval for the French Revolution at the theatre (apparently joining in a chorus of *Ça Ira*) he was reported to the Excise who made an official enquiry into his loyalty. Burns defended himself to Graham of Fintry, protesting that he prized the British Constitution 'next after my God' and stating that, though once an 'enthusiastic votary' of France, he had become disillusioned when 'she came to show her old avidity for conquest'. Graham of Fintry saw to it that he kept his job but he was advised to hold his tongue in future.

Respectability, certainly, could have been his. In May 1793 he moved into a fine red sandstone house in Millbrae Vennell – now a museum, open to the public (April–Sept. 10am–5pm, Sun. 2–7pm; Oct.–March 10am–5pm, excluding Suns) in the renamed **Burns Street**. Here Burns wrote some of his greatest songs. A letter to Thomson explained that 'untill I am compleat master of a tune, in my own singing, (such as it is) I can never compose for it'. Using this method to compose new words and repair old ones Burns wrote some 370 lyrics in the last ten years of his life. The sheer volume of work from Dumfries alone is evidence enough to refute the charges that he degenerated, in his last years, into a habitual drunk.

Apart from inclination, Burns's health did not permit daily alcoholic indulgence, yet because of his fame every misdemeanour (and there were several) spread from Dumfries back to Edinburgh and Ayrshire. When in the mood for drinking, Burns frequented the **Globe Inn**, off the High Street, which still has the chair used by the bard.

Because Burns was expansive in his cups rumours still circulated about his revolutionary sympathies. As if to prove his loyalty – and protect his recent promotion to Acting Supervisor of the Dumfries Excise – Burns joined the Dumfries Volunteers in 1795. He also composed a patriotic anti-French song, 'Does haughty Gaul invasion threat'. In 1795 he lost his 'only daughter and darling child' and, ironically, realised that the war with France – leading to a ban on imports – was cutting into his income. He told Mrs Frances Anna Dunlop that he was 'the victim of a most severe Rheumatic fever' and that because of the food shortage in Dumfries (which eventually provoked riots) his 'family, and hundreds of other families, are absolutely without one grain of meal'.

By April 1796 Burns was emaciated through illness and seriously worried about the state of his finances. Nevertheless he had to give up work and, because Jean was pregnant again, an eighteen-year-old neighbour Jessie Lewars was brought in to nurse the poet and help with the housework. Hearing Jessie sing 'The Robin Cam' to the Wren's Nest' he composed new words for it to express his feelings for her:

> O, wert thou in the cauld blast
>   On yonder lea, on yonder lea,
> My plaidie to the angry airt,   *quarter*
>   I'd shelter thee, I'd shelter thee.
> Or did Misfortune's bitter storms
>   Around thee blaw, around thee blaw,
> Thy bield should be my bosom,   *shelter*
>   To share it a', to share it a'.
>
> Or were I in the wildest waste,
>   Sae black and bare, sae black and bare,
> The desert were a Paradise,
>   If thou wert there, if thou wert there.
> Or were I monarch of the globe,
>   Wi' thee to reign, wi' thee to reign,
> The brightest jewel in my crown
>   Wad be my queen, wad be my queen.

However it was Burns himself who was badly in need of help. His friend Dr Maxwell diagnosed 'flying gout' and prescribed riding and bathing as a cure. So Burns went to the health spa at Brow to drink the chalybeate waters from Brow Well and immerse himself up to his armpits in the sea, the Solway Firth. It was to prove fatal for a man with a serious heart condition.

On 18 July Burns returned to Dumfries and wrote to James Armour asking him to come and help Jean. On 21 July, three days after his return to Dumfries, he died. His body lay in state for a day at the town hall and for his military funeral two regiments accompanied the coffin to the Dead March from Handel's *Saul*. More appropriately, ten thousand people came to join in the funeral procession that took the poet's body from the **Mid Steeple** in High Street to **Saint Michael's Church**. He was buried in the north-east corner of St Michaels **churchyard**.

William and Dorothy Wordsworth, John Keats

Wordsworth visited the grave in 1803 and reflected on the death of a fellow poet in 'At the Grave of Burns':

> The tear will start, and let it flow;
> That 'poor Inhabitant below,'
> At this dread moment – even so –
>   Might we together
> Have sate and talked where gowans blow,
>   Or on wild heather.
>
> What treasures would have then been placed
> Within my reach; of knowledge graced
> By fancy what a rich repast!
>   But why go on? –
> Oh! spare to sweep, thou mournful blast,
>   His grave grass-grown.

Wordsworth's sister observed, in her *Journal*, 'The churchyard is full of . . . expensive monuments in all sorts of fantastic shapes – obelisk wise, pillar wise'. These are still in evidence, as is the site of Burns's grave. On one of the pillars in the church a brass plaque marks the pew used by Burns when he worshipped in St Michael's.

In 1815 Burns was reinterred in the mausoleum, near the grave. The domed temple has a relief showing the Muse discovering Burns at the plough then throwing her mantle round him. Keats, who wrote a sonnet 'On Visiting the Tomb of Burns' thought the mausoleum 'not very much to my taste'. The **Burns Statue** in Dumfries was erected in 1882.

Thomas Aird

Thomas Aird (1802–76), author of *Orthuriel and Other Poems* (1840) was appointed editor of the *Dumfries and Galloway Herald* in 1835 and died on 25 April 1876 in Dumfries. Carlyle, who met Aird in Edinburgh, said his poetry had 'a healthy breath as of mountain breezes'. He is buried near Burns's tomb.

J. M. Barrie

J. M. Barrie (1860–1937) was educated at **Dumfries Academy**, a building made of local red stone in 1801. The regional museum for the Solway area – Dumfries Museum – is housed in the **Observatory** which contains papers relating to Burns and Barrie.

DUNBEATH, Caithness   (Highland)   18m SW of Wick on A9

Neil Gunn

In this village, overlooking Dunbeath Bay, the novelist Neil M. Gunn (1891–1973) was born on 8 November 1891. His birthplace is located in the biography *Neil M. Gunn* (1981) by F. R. Hart and J. B. Pick:

> Coming down the steep brae into Dunbeath, you see the wide coastal fields of the big farm, Dunbeath Mains, and glimpse Dunbeath Castle on its headland. On the left is the Free Kirk, on the right the Kirk of Scotland, the post office, the old school (built in the 1870s) with its modern addition, and then a hairpin loop. As the road curves inland you see the old stone bridge, Dunbeath Water reaching up the wooded strath, and across the bridge a terrace of two-storey stone houses. A garage, a hotel, a shop – and the red stone house with slate roof and orange drainpipes, built by his father in the 1880s – the house where Neil was born.

Gunn attended the village school until he was twelve, when he went to live with his married sister Mary in St John's Town of Dalry, Kircudbrightshire. Inevitably, Dunbeath provided Gunn – an Edenic novelist fascinated by the childhood idyll – with the background for some of his best books.

Morning Tide (1930) evokes 'The loneliness of the bouldered beach. . . . The dark undulating water . . . the sea's edge' as Hugh, a fisherman's son like Gunn, establishes his relationship with the environment. *Highland River* (1937) – whose commercial success enabled Gunn to give up his excise work in Inverness and concentrate on writing – describes the life of another autobiographical character, Kenn, as he gradually comes to self-knowledge ('ken' being idiomatic Scots for 'know'). Up the strath that runs by Dunbeath Water is the river that becomes the spiritual source of life for nine-year-old Kenn:

In this mood he arrived at the well, which was at the foot of a steep
bank by the side of the river. Carelessly he bumped the pail down
on the flat stone, and at the sound, as at a signal in a weird fairy tale,
the whole world changed. . . . For from his very feet a great fish had
started ploughing its way across the river, the king of fish, the living
salmon.

Kenn's encounter with the salmon (which he catches) is the first real
challenge of his life 'for of all that befell Kenn afterwards, of war and
horror and love and scientific triumphs, nothing ever had quite the splendour and glory of that struggle by the Well Pool'.

The Silver Darlings (1941) opens with a background of 'the end of the
Napoleonic era' and the clearance of crofters from Caithness. Young
Finn's adventure unfolds against the success of Dunbeath's fishing
industry, for the herrings are the silver darlings of the title and their
presence promises wealth for Dunster (that is, Dunbeath):

Never had Dunster known such talk, such expectation, such secret
groupings and meetings. Where husbands or sons were shy or
backward their womenfolk encouraged them. Women who knew how
to spin hemp taught others. In the meeting- or ceilidh-houses at night
nothing was talked about but the coming fishing. 'Creels of silver
herring will turn into creels of silver crowns' became the joke that
never lost its gleam. There were two creel-makers in Dunster, and
they worked all day and far into the night. . . . Along the cliff-heads,
from every cottage door within sight, eyes watched the fleet of boats
as in the later afternoon they put out to sea.

The Silver Darlings is dedicated to the memory of Gunn's father James,
a fishing skipper whose way of life is vividly conveyed in the novel.

DUNDEE, Angus   (Tayside)   34m NNE of Edinburgh

Sir Walter Scott

Dundee, Scotland's fourth city (since 1889), lies on the north shore of the
Firth of Tay. It was made a royal burgh by William the Lion around 1190
and was the first Scottish town to fully accept the Reformation. John
Graham of Claverhouse (1648-9) was born at Old Claverhouse Castle
three miles north-east of Dundee (site marked by a dovecot, monument
to the celebrated soldier at Claverhouse) and became infamous as 'Bloody
Clavers' for ruthlessly suppressing the Covenanting conventicles. He was
made hereditary constable of Dundee in 1683 and supported James VII
when William of Orange came to the throne. Created Viscount Dundee

on 12 November 1688 he was, as Sir Walter Scott notes in *Old Mortality* (1816), killed during his 'great and decisive victory' at the battle of Killie-crankie on 27 July 1689. He is featured in the song, from Scott's play *The Doom of Devorgoil* (1830), beginning:

> To the Lords of Convention 'twas Claver'se who spoke,
> 'Ere the King's crown shall fall there are crowns to be broke;
> So let each Cavalier who loves honour and me,
> Come follow the bonnet of Bonny Dundee.'

Robert Fergusson

At the age of twelve Robert Fergusson (1750–74) went to Dundee Grammar School (where Sir William Wallace was once a pupil) on a bursary obtained for him through an uncle. He remained in Dundee for two years and in 1765 matriculated at St Andrews University.

Thomas Hood

Thomas Hood (1799–1845) was sixteen when, ill from an early attack of rheumatic fever which left him with a weak heart, he came to stay at his aunt's house in Nethergate. Hood established himself in England as a consummate master of light verse and also as the author of the indignant and influential 'Song of the Shirt'.

William Thom

In the last year of his life William Thom (1798–1848), the 'Inverurie poet', lived in two rooms in the Hawkhill district of Dundee. He died in Croft Lane on 29 February 1848 and was buried in the Western Cemetery, Perth Road, Dundee, on 3 March. In January 1858 a headstone was erected 'by admirers of the poet, over the spot where his remains are interred'.

George Gilfillan

George Gilfillan (1813–78), a Secessionist minister's son, was born on 30 January 1813 in Comrie, Perthshire, and became minister of School Wynd Church, Dundee. He lived at 5 Paradise Road, Dundee, from around 1840 until his death on 13 August 1878. There is a memorial church named after him in Whitehall Crescent.

Gilfillan was a minor poet and energetic man of letters. He produced a three-volume *Gallery of Literary Portraits* (1845, 1849, 1854) and theological works such as *The Christian Bearings of Astronomy* (1848) and *The Apocalypse of Jesus Christ* (1851). His *Life of Robert Burns* appeared in

1856 and his *Life of Sir Walter Scott* in 1870. A year before he died, William McGonagall (see below) produced 'Lines in Praise of the Rev. George Gilfillan' and McGonagall subsequently wrote a poem on 'The Burial of the Rev. George Gilfillan':

> On the Gilfillan burial day,
> In the Hill o' Balgay,
> It was a most solemn sight to see,
> Not fewer than thirty thousand people assembled in Dundee,
> All watching the funeral procession of Gilfillan that day,
> That death had suddenly taken away,
> And was going to be buried in the Hill o' Balgay.

(The hill of Balgay is on the north side of Dundee.)

William McGonagall

Although he was born and died in Edinburgh, William McGonagall (*c.* 1825–1902) is always associated with Dundee where he lived at numbers 19 and 32 Paton's Lane and also at Step Row (from which he was evicted in 1894). He spent three of his childhood years on the Orkney island of South Ronaldsay and was eleven when his father settled in Dundee. McGonagall married Jean King on 11 July 1846, worked (like his father) as a handloom weaver, and pursued his ambitions as an amateur Shakespearean actor in Dundee's Theatre Royal in Castle Street. (Opened in 1810, the building is still in use as a store, and can be identified by a bust of Shakespeare in a niche high up.) His absolute faith in his own histrionic and literary abilities enabled him to persevere despite being exploited as an object of ridicule. By 1877 the cards he distributed carried the legend 'William McGonagall, Poet & Tragedian'.

In his 'Brief Autobiography', introducing *Poetic Gems* (1890), McGonagall describes how he was first inspired to write verse. During the Dundee holiday week of 1877 he heard a voice crying 'Write! Write!' so composed four metrically crude quatrains 'about my best friend . . . Reverend George Gilfillan'. The publication of this in the Dundee *Weekly News* greatly encouraged McGonagall who regarded himself as a gifted poet although he relied on doggerel, was totally indifferent to euphony, was absolutely ignorant of imagery, was unaware of the possibilities of verbal texture, and was unconcerned with the seductive power of rhythm. Nevertheless he believed in himself as the bard of Dundee and his greatest strength was his uncritical admiration of his own metrical powers.

His second poetic effort was 'The Railway Bridge of the Silvery Tay', written while sitting on a wooden seat at the end of the Magdalen Green 'in view of the beautiful structure' (opened on 31 May 1878). The first stanza runs:

Beautiful Railway Bridge of the Silvery Tay!
With your numerous arches and pillars in so grand array,
And your central girders, which seem to the eye
To be almost towering to the sky.
The greatest wonder of the day,
And a great beautification to the River Tay,
Most beautiful to be seen,
Near by Dundee and the Magdalen Green.

On 28 December 1879 this bridge was blown down in a gale while a train was crossing. Seventy lives were lost and twenty-nine bodies were never recovered. McGonagall mourned the tragedy in 'The Tay Bridge Disaster' which ends:

It must have been an awful sight,
To witness in the dusky moonlight,
While the Storm Fiend did laugh, and angry did bray,
Along the Railway Bridge of the Silv'ry Tay.
Oh! ill-fated Bridge of the silv'ry Tay,
I must now conclude my lay
By telling the world fearlessly without the least dismay,
That your central girders would not have given way,
At least many sensible men do say,
Had they been supported on each side with buttresses,
At least many sensible men confesses,
For the stronger we our houses do build,
The less chance we have of being killed.

McGonagall's 'The Famous Tay Whale' is, like his other poems, a piece of metrical journalism recording an actual event:

'Twas in the month of December, and in the year 1883,
That a monster whale came to Dundee,
Resolved for a few days to sport and play,
And devour the small fishes in the silvery Tay.

The 'monster whale' managed to avoid the Dundee harpoonists but was found floating near Stonehaven, towed ashore and sold to John Wood, a Dundee showman:

So Mr John Wood has bought it for two hundred and twenty-six pound,
And has brought it to Dundee all safe and all sound;
Which measures 40 feet in length from the snout to the tail,
So I advise the people far and near to see it without fail.

The bones are now in the museum in the Albert Institute, McGonagall's poem being displayed beside them. When the **Burns Statue** was unveiled outside the Albert Institute in 1884, McGonagall was turned away by the police.

In his lifetime McGonagall, a staunch teetotaller, contrived to make himself a figure of fun by performing to abusive audiences in pubs and by (for example) travelling to Balmoral (in the summer of 1878) in the vain hope of being received by Queen Victoria. He was the victim of various hoaxes yet his posthumous popularity has been astonishing and he has been the subject of one-man shows by several entertainers (including Spike Milligan). Judging by the enduring appeal of his personality and invariably banal poetry it seems safe to assume that McGonagall was not so much an appallingly bad poet as a genuine poetic primitive.

DUNFERMLINE, Fife   (Fife)   17m NW of Edinburgh on A283

'Sir Patrick Spence'

Dunfermline, dominated by the great Abbey Church (Norman nave of 1150, Gothic choir of 1817–22), is mentioned in the first line of the famous ballad 'Sir Patrick Spence':

> The king sits in Dunfermline toun,
>   Drinking the blood-red wine:
> 'O whar will I get guid sailor,
>   To sail this ship of mine?'

The king was Alexander III (1241–86). As his daughter Margaret (1261–83) was to marry King Erik of Norway in 1281, Alexander sent courtiers to attend the ceremony scheduled for August. It is an historical fact that courtiers who went with Margaret to Norway were drowned on the return voyage; Sir Patrick's name does not appear in the chronicles but survives in the oral tradition which underlines the contrast that distinguishes the ballad – the king drinks wine, Sir Patrick swallows salt water and dies. Margaret, incidentally, died giving birth to the Maid of Norway who herself died of seasickness on a voyage from Norway to Scotland in 1290.

Robert Henryson, William Dunbar

Little is known of the poet Robert Henryson (c. 1420–c. 1490), one of the great Scottish makars of the fifteenth century, apart from the certainty that he was a schoolmaster in Dunfermline. William Dunbar's 'Lament for the Makaris' notes that death has done for Henryson:

> In Dunfermline he hes done roun

With Maister Robert Henrysoun

Henryson's work ranges from 'The Abbey Walk' (which mentions 'ane abbey . . . fair to see') to his sustained Scots masterpiece *The Testament of Cresseid*.

Dorothy Dunnett

Dorothy Dunnett was born Dorothy Halliday on 25 August 1923 in the Davaar Nursing Home, Dunfermline, while her parents were living in Glencraig, east of Dunfermline and near her grandparents' home at Ballingry. At the age of three she moved to Edinburgh and in 1946 she married Alastair Dunnett, editor of *The Scotsman*. She is best known for her sequence of historical novels featuring the fictional Scots mercenary Francis Crawford of Lymond and Sevigny. Six novels comprise his story: *The Game of Kings* (1961), *Queen's Play* (1964), *The Disorderly Knights* (1966), *Pawn in Frankincense* (1969), *The Ringed Castle* (1971) and *Checkmate* (1975).

DUNGAVEL HOUSE, Lanarkshire (Strathclyde) 5m SW of Strathaven

Hugh MacDiarmid

Towards the end of 1949 the fourteenth Duke of Hamilton (encouraged by his brother the tenth Earl of Elkirk) offered the poet Hugh MacDiarmid (C. M. Grieve, 1892–1978) a five-apartment outhouse adjacent to his Lanarkshire mansion, Dungavel House, near Strathaven. MacDiarmid was in the house by October 1949 and in a letter of 23 March 1950 to Neil Gunn describes his new home as 'a fine commodious house in the middle of a pine wood, where for once I have room to dispose even all my books and papers in a reasonably orderly and get-at-able way'. During the period MacDiarmid lived at Dungavel, he wrote *Aesthetics in Scotland* (an essay, posthumously published in 1984). When the National Coal Board bought the estate, in 1950, they decided to establish a School for Miners in the mansion and adjoining lodges and MacDiarmid was requested to leave by August 1950; he subsequently moved to Brownsbank Cottage, Candymill, Biggar, his home for the rest of his life. In 1969 the Scottish Prison Service acquired Dungavel House which has been in operation as a prison from 1975.

DUNNOTTAR CASTLE, Kincardineshire (Grampian) 1½m S of Stonehaven, off A982

Standing on a rocky cliff 160 feet above the sea, Dunnottar Castle is one of the most impressive ruins in Scotland. It was a stronghold of the Keith family, the Earls Marischal of Scotland, from the fourteenth century. In 1297 it was stormed by Sir William Wallace who put the English garrison to the sword; in 1645 it was besieged by Montrose. During the Commonwealth wars the Honours of Scotland (the Scottish regalia comprising crown, sword and sceptre) were hidden in the castle and smuggled out in 1652, past Cromwell's troops, by Mrs Grainger, wife of the Kinneff Church minister, and her woman servant. The Honours were then hidden under a flagstone in **old Kinneff Church**, five miles to the south. In July 1685, 167 Covenanters were imprisoned in the 'Whig's Vault', most of them subsequently destroyed by torture and ill-treatment.

Sir Walter Scott

In **Dunnottar Churchyard**, where the **Covenanters' Stone** commemorates those who died in the 'Whig's Vault', Sir Walter Scott (1771–1832) met Robert Paterson (1715–1801), the Old Mortality of Scott's novel. In his introduction to the 1830 'Magnum Opus' edition of *Old Mortality* (1816) Scott describes the meeting:

> It is about thirty years since, or more, that the author met this singular person [Robert Paterson] in the churchyard of Dunnottar, when spending a day or two with the late learned and excellent clergyman, Mr Walker, the minister of that parish, for the purpose of a close examination of the ruins of the Castle of Dunnottar, and other subjects of antiquarian research in that neighbourhood. Old Mortality chanced to be at the same place, on the usual business of his pilgrimage; for the castle of Dunnottar, though lying in the anti-covenanting district of the Mearns, was, with the parish churchyard, celebrated for the oppressions sustained there by the Cameronians [the Covenanting sect formed by Richard Cameron after the Battle of Bothwell Bridge, 1679] in the time of James II. . . .
>
> It was whilst I was listening to this story [of the Whig's Vault], and looking at the monument [to the Covenanters] that I saw Old Mortality engaged in his daily task of cleaning and repairing the ornaments and epitaphs upon the tomb. [Unfortunately] he would not speak frankly upon the subject of his occupation. He was in a bad humour, and had, according to his phrase, no freedom for conversation with us.

DUNOON

Lewis Grassic Gibbon

Lewis Grassic Gibbon – James Leslie Mitchell (1901–35) who went to school in Stonehaven – mentions Dunnottar Castle in the Prelude ('The Unfurrowed Field') to *Sunset Song* (1932): 'Dunnottar Castle that stands out in the sea beyond Kinneff, well-builded and strong, and the sea splashes about it in the high tides and there the din of the gulls is a yammer night and day'.

DUNOON, Argyllshire (Strathclyde) A885

Robert Burns

A holiday resort on the west shore of the Firth of Clyde, Dunoon has, at the foot of Castle Hill, a statue of Robert Burns's Highland Mary who was born on the site of Auchnamore farm, behind the town. In 1786 Burns (1759–96) accepted a job as a plantation book-keeper in Jamaica and turned his attentions to Mary Campbell (1763–86). They apparently intended to marry and emigrate to Jamaica together; Burns arranged to meet Mary in Greenock in September so they could sail for Kingston. When he heard the news of her death he was devastated and abandoned his plans to emigrate. Instead, he headed for Edinburgh which embraced him as the author of *Poems, Chiefly in the Scottish Dialect* (31 July 1786). In his 'Highland Mary' Burns laments the loss of his love:

> O, pale, pale now, those rosy lips
> I aft hae kiss'd sae fondly;
> And clos'd for ay, the sparkling glance
> That dwalt on me sae kindly . . .

Robin Jenkins

Robin Jenkins (born on 11 September 1912 in Cambuslang, Lanarkshire) taught at Dunoon Grammar School and resides in the town. His novel *A Toast to the Lord* (1972) was partly prompted by the presence of the American Polaris submarine base on the Holy Loch which bisects the united parish of Dunoon and Kilmun. The novel is set in Ardhallow, a small resort on the Clyde, where the community lives with the threat of destruction as the USS Perseus is anchored in Loch Hallow with Polaris submarines in attendance. Against this background Jenkins tells a tale that ends in 'murder, suicide and cancerous death'.

DUNSINANE, Perthshire   (Tayside)   8m NE of Perth

William Shakespeare

In Shakespeare's *Macbeth* (IV.i.) the Third Apparition assures the tragic hero:

> Macbeth shall never vanquish'd be until
> Great Birnam wood to high Dunsinane Hill
> Shall come against him.

Macbeth is satisfied but, in the final act of the drama, Malcolm orders his soldiers to conceal their numbers by cutting and carrying boughs from Birnam Wood, thus bringing the wood to Dunsinane Hill (1,012 ft) with disastrous consequences for Macbeth. The ancient fort at Dunsinane is known locally as Macbeth's Castle.

DUNSYRE, Lanarkshire   (Strathclyde)   6½m E of Carnwarth

Ian Hamilton Finlay

Stonypath, the home of the poet Ian Hamilton Finlay (born 28 October 1925 in Nassau, Bahamas), is situated on a hillside, near Dunsyre village, up a track signposted (by the poet) 'The way up and the way down is one and the same (Heraclitus)'. Since moving to Stonypath in 1967, Finlay and his wife Sue have transformed it from a neglected farmhouse and farm (on the estate of Sue Finlay's father) into a literary-philosophical garden complex. Finlay's ambition was to create a neoclassical garden on a cottage scale and he has designed Stonypath (or Little Sparta as he calls it in a characteristically pugnacious gesture) as a place where nature and culture coalesce: a pink stone, for example, is engraved with the motto 'Sea Pink' thus giving the image a three-dimensional form. Finlay is fond of heroic figures and his garden pays tribute to some of his own heroes. In the front garden are two juxtapositions which metaphorically transform trees into columns by placing stone column-bases against them: on the left (looking from the sunken garden) is a tribute to Fabre d'Eglantine, who composed the French Revolutionary calendar; on the right is a similar salute to Saint-Just. Near the top pond in Little Sparta the notion is expanded into a hillside Pantheon celebrating Jules Michelet (whose *History of the Revolution* is a favourite of Finlay's), Robespierre, Jean Jacques Rousseau, Corot and the fantastic landscape painter Caspar David Friedrich. As Finlay writes in his *Unconnected Sentences on Gardening* 'certain gardens are described as retreats when they are really attacks'. Finlay works with a talented team of craftsmen who translate his poetic concepts into physical form. In his courtyard he has a temple (dedicated 'To Apollo/His Music/His Muses/His Missiles') where many of his works are exhibited. Visitors wishing to visit Stonypath should write, in the first instance, to Finlay.

ECCLEFECHAN, Dumfriesshire   (Dumfries and Galloway)   9m NW
of Gretna Green, off A74

Thomas Carlyle

Thomas Carlyle (1795–1818) was born on 4 December 1795 in the first-floor bedroom of the north wing of the **Arched House** on the main street of Ecclefechan. The house – now a museum open to the public from March to October (10am–6pm, excepting Sundays) – was built around 1791 by Carlyle's father and uncle, both master-masons working in south-west Scotland. Carlyle was devoted to his father and extracted from James Carlyle's example his own work ethic. In *Reminiscences* (edited by James Anthony Froude and published in 1881 within weeks of Carlyle's death) Carlyle writes:

> It must have been about [1791] that my Father and his Brothers, already Master-masons, established themselves in Ecclefechan. They all henceforth began to take on a civic existence, to 'accumulate' in all senses; to grow. They were among the best and truest men of their craft (perhaps the very best) in that whole district; and recompensed accordingly. Their gains, the honest wages of Industry, their savings were slow but constant; and in my Father's case continued (from one source or other) to the end. He was born and brought up by the poorest; by his own right hand he had become wealthy, as he accounted wealth, and in all ways plentifully supplied. His household goods valued in money may perhaps somewhat exceed £1,000; in real inward worth, their value was greater than that of most kingdoms, – than all Napoleon's conquests, which did not endure. He saw his children grow up round him to guard him and do him honour; he had (ultimately) a healthy respect from *all*, could look forward from the verge of this Earth, rich and increased in goods, into an Everlasting Country where through the immeasurable Deeps shone a solemn sober Hope. I must reckon my Father one of the most *prosperous* men I have ever in my life known.

Carlyle attended the village school at Ecclefechan before going to the grammar school at Annan (where he later taught) and it was from Ecclefechan that, on the eve of his fourteenth birthday in November 1809, he walked the hundred miles to Edinburgh in three days. While studying at

Edinburgh University he sent his washing back to Ecclefechan by the local carrier, receiving in return a steady supply of oatmeal. Though he encountered difficulties in his intellectual and emotional life (with his wife Jane Carlyle) he persevered and at the time of his death (5 February 1881) was regarded as one of the greatest of all Victorians. Books such as *Sartor Resartus* (1833–4), *The French Revolution* (1837), *On Heroes, Hero Worship and the Heroic in History* (1841) and *Past and Present* (1843) established him as not only a philosopher who preached a message of 'Natural Supernaturalism' but a prophet who promised salvation through endless effort. For Carlyle the supreme reality was spiritual rather than material and before his death he indicated that he did not want to be honoured in Westminster Abbey but to be buried, beside his parents, in Hoddam Churchyard, a few hundred yards from his birthplace. In 1927 a Carlyle Statue was erected in Ecclefechan and in 1935 the National Trust for Scotland assumed the responsibility of maintaining Carlyle's birthplace. The Arched House contains various items associated with Carlyle, including a sofa from the Carlyles' Chelsea home at Cheyne Row, Chelsea; a wall clock used by Jane Carlyle's father at Haddington before hanging in the kitchen at Cheyne Row; pieces from Jane Carlyle's dinner service; relics (such as hats worn by Carlyle); and copies of Carlyle manuscripts from Register House, Edinburgh.

EDINBURGH, Midlothian   (Lothian)

Edinburgh – capital of Scotland, Athens of the North, home of the Scottish Enlightenment, setting for the world's largest annual arts festival – is the most literary place in Scotland. Space permits only a selective list of the many writers who have lived here and some of the characters who have affected authors.

Gavin Douglas

In 1501 Gavin Douglas (1474–1522) was appointed provost of St Giles and lived in his episcopal palace in the Cowgate. His *Eneados* (1513, printed 1553), a translation of Virgil's *Aeneid* into Middle Scots, contains (in the Prologue to Book VII) a vivid impression of an Edinburgh winter:

> The plane street is, and every hie way
> Full of floshis, dubbis, mire and clay.   *bogs, puddles*

After the battle of Flodden (1513) Douglas was made a burgess of Edinburgh. In 1515, the year he was appointed Bishop of Dunkeld, the Duke of Albany had him imprisoned in 'the wyndy and richt unpleasant castell and royk of Edinburgh'.

William Drummond

William Drummond of Hawthorden (1585–1649) – born on 13 December 1585 in the family house of Hawthorden near Roslin, Midlothian – was educated at the high school which was built in 1567 in the garden of Blackfriars monastery, at the end of Infirmary Street, near the end of High School Wynd (school demolished 1777 to make way for the second high school). Drummond also attended Edinburgh University in buildings built over by the present complex.

Allan Ramsay

Allan Ramsay (1686–1758), one of Scotland's most influential men of letters, came to Edinburgh in 1701, rising from apprentice to master wigmaker, operating from a shop in the Grassmarket. He formed the conversational Easy Club in 1712, opened a bookshop in 1718 and in 1720 was publishing books 'sold at the sign of the Mercury, opposite the head of Niddry's Wynd' – now Niddry Street – where he lived and worked on *The Tea Table Miscellany* (five volumes, 1724–32) and *The Gentle Shepherd* (1725), his pastoral drama. In 1726 he moved to the Luckenbooths (gone) – a group of buildings in the High Street 'alongside St Giles's church' – and changed his sign from the Mercury to the twin heads of Ben Jonson and William Drummond of Hawthorden. Ramsay expanded his business by establishing, in 1728, the first circulating library in Scotland; as the bookseller William Creech took the ground floor below Ramsay's business the place acquired the name Creech's Land.

In 1736 Ramsay opened Edinburgh's first regular theatre, the New Theatre, at the foot of Carrubber's Close, 135 High Street (plaque). Ramsay was appalled when a parliamentary act of 1737 prevented theatre performances outside London, thus closing his theatre. He drank with John Gay (1685–1732) at Jenny Ha's Change-house (gone), which stood in front of Queensberry House (now a home for the elderly), 64 Canongate, the mansion of the Duchess of Queensberry, Gay's patroness. Ramsay also drank at Lucky Wood's tavern, in the Canongate, and wrote an 'Elegy on Lucky Wood in the Canongate, May 1717'. Another convivial Edinburgh character celebrated by Ramsay was Lucky Spence who ran a brothel near Holyrood Palace. 'Lucky Spence's Last Advice' includes the following practical stanza:

> Whan e'er ye meet a Fool that's fow,　　*full*
> That ye're a Maiden gar him trow,
> Seem nice, but stick to him like Glew;
> 　And whan set down,
> Drive at the Jango till he spew,　　*drink*
> 　Syn he'll sleep soun　　*then, sound*

Around 1740 Ramsay designed Ramsay Lodge, now at the heart of Ramsay Gardens (built as a student hall of residence and block of flats for Sir Patrick Geddes in 1893). It was, to Ramsay's annoyance, ridiculed as Goose Pie House because of its startling octagonal appearance. Ramsay is commemorated by a tablet on the south wall of Greyfriars Church; and by the Allan Ramsay Monument (north-east corner of West Princes Street Gardens) sculpted from Carrara marble by John Steel.

Dr Samuel Johnson, James Boswell

In 1773 Dr Samuel Johnson (1709–84) arrived in Edinburgh to begin his Scottish tour with James Boswell (1740–95). Boswell describes the circumstances in his *Journal of a Tour to the Hebrides* (1785):

On Saturday the fourteenth of August, 1773, late in the evening, I received a note from him, that he was arrived at Boyd's inn [The White Horse Inn, Boyd's Close, St Mary's Wynd – gone but plaque on site], at the Canongate. I went to him directly. He embraced me cordially; and I exulted in the thought, that I now had him actually in Caledonia. . . . Mr Johnson and I walked arm-in-arm up the High-street, to my house [gone] in James's court: it was a dusky night: I could not prevent his being assailed by the evening effluvia of Edinburgh. . . . A zealous Scotsman would have wished Mr Johnson to be without one of his five senses upon this occasion. As we marched slowly along, he grumbled in my ear, 'I smell you in the dark!' But he acknowledged that the breadth of the street, and the loftiness of the buildings on each side, made a noble appearance.

Johnson spent four days at Boyd's and when the two men returned from their tour (arriving in Edinburgh on 9 November) stayed with Boswell who noted in his journal:

We arrived this night [9 November] at Edinburgh, after an absence of eighty-three days. For five weeks together, of the tempestuous season, there had been no account received of us. I cannot express how happy I was on finding myself again at home.

David Hume

David Hume (1711–76), one of the great figures of the Scottish Enlightenment and still one of the most readable of philosophers, was regarded in his lifetime as a wayward son of Edinburgh. His rejection of religion, his scepticism ('In all the incidents of life we ought still to preserve our scepticism'), his contempt for superstitions, his praise of passion above reason – all these made him a formidable enemy of established religion and metaphysical fancy. Yet contemporaries agreed that Hume was a most lovable and affable individual. After his death, Adam Smith wrote:

upon the whole, I have always considered him, both in his lifetime and since his death, as approaching as nearly to the idea of a perfectly wise and virtuous man, as perhaps the nature of human frailty will permit.

In his brief autobiography, *My Own Life* (18 April 1776) Hume wrote:

I was born the 26th of April 1711, old style, at Edinburgh. I was of a good family, both by father and mother; my father's family is a branch of the Earl of Home's or Hume's; and my ancestors had been proprietors of the estate, which my brother possesses, for several generations. My mother was Daughter of Sir David Falconer, President of the College of Justice: the title of Lord Halkerton came by succession to her brother.

Hume studied law, then philosophy, at Edinburgh University. His works *A Treatise on Human Nature* (1739) and *Essays Moral and Political* (1741), however, offended his old university which in 1744 turned down his application for the Chair of Ethics and Pneumatical Philosophy. Hume's scepticism was unacceptable to Edinburgh, at that time, and after a period away from the city he settled in Riddle's Court, 322 High Street, where he wrote *Political Discourses* (1752) and started work on his *History of England* (1763). He was forty when he 'arrived at the dignity of being a householder' in Riddle's Court and forty-one when appointed librarian of the Faculty of Advocates.

In 1753 Hume moved to Jack's Land, (renumbered 229) Canongate. In 1762 he took apartments in James Court (destroyed by fire), off the Lawnmarket. Hume enjoyed the convivial atmosphere of the old town, liked to eat and imbibe in Johnny Dowie's tavern in Libberton's Wynd. His last house was in the New Town, at the corner of St Andrew Square and St David Street, where he died – 'as fast as my enemies, if I have any, could wish, and as easily and cheerfully as my best friends could desire' – on 25 August 1776. The **David Hume Monument**, in Old Calton Burying Ground, was designed by Robert Adam in 1777: it is an imposing Roman cylinder with a large urn in a niche above the doorpiece. The **David Hume Tower** (1960–3) was built as part of Edinburgh University's George Square redevelopment.

Tobias Smollett

In 1766 Tobias Smollett (1721–71) stayed with his sister, Mrs Telfer, in the second flat of 182 Canongate, above the archway leading into St John Street. The apartments are now entered up circular steps in the house now numbered 22 St John Street (where there is a plaque). Smollett painted a memorable verbal picture of Edinburgh in *Humphry Clinker* (1771). In the words of Matthew Bramble, the Welsh squire,

> The city stands upon two hills, and the bottom between them; and, with all its defects, may very well pass for the capital of a moderate kingdom – It is full of people, and continually resounds with the noise of coaches and other carriages, for luxury as well as commerce. . . . You are no stranger to their method of discharging all their impurities from their windows, at a certain hour of the night [this being a] practice to which I can by no means be reconciled; for notwithstanding all the care that is taken by their scavengers to remove this nuisance every morning by break of day, enough still remains to offend the eyes, as well as other organs of those whom use has not hardened against all delicacy of sensation . . . Edinburgh is hot-bed of genius. – I have had the good fortune to be made acquainted with many authors of the first distinction; such as the two Humes [the philosopher David Hume, and the Rev. John Home, author of the tragedy *Douglas*, 1757], Robertson [the historian Dr William Robertson], Smith [the economist Adam Smith], Wallace [the economist Rev. Robert Wallace], Blair [Rev. Hugh Blair, first professor of rhetoric and belles-lettres at Edinburgh University], Ferguson [the philosopher Rev. Adam Ferguson], Wilkie [Rev. William Wilkie, author of *The Epigoniad*, 1757], etc. and I have found them all as agreeable in conversation as they are instructive and entertaining in their writings.

John Home

John Home (1722–1808) was born on the east side of Quality Street, near Bernard Street, Leith (house demolished) and was educated at the grammar school and Edinburgh University. Home became minister of Athelstaneford in 1746. On 14 December 1756 his verse drama *Douglas* was first produced at the Canongate Theatre (gone) in **Playhouse Close**, 200 Canongate (where there is a plaque). The first night was a sensational success, prompting a member of the audience to shout out 'Whaur's yer Wully Shakespeare noo?' Home's involvement in the theatre offended the Church of Scotland authorities who persuaded him to resign from his ministry on 7 June 1757. In 1778 he returned to Edinburgh where he died on 5 September 1808. He was buried in the churchyard of South Leith parish church: a tablet, on the south side of the outer wall of the church, is visible from Kirkgate Street.

Robert Louis Stevenson, W. E. Henley, Muriel Spark

Brodie's Close, in the Lawnmarket, takes its name from Francis Brodie, father of Deacon Brodie (1741–88) whose name is commemorated in the title of a public house on the opposite side of Lawnmarket (corner of Bank Street). Burgher by day, burglar by night: Brodie has been scrutinised as a classic case of the Scottish split personality. Robert Louis Stevenson collaborated with W. E. Henley on a play, Deacon Brodie, which was privately printed in 1880 and produced (without success) in 1882. More sensationally, Stevenson had a nightmare, in 1885, about a man 'being pressed into a cabinet when he swallowed a drug and changed into another'. On the advice of his wife Fanny, Stevenson expressed the nightmare in allegorical form and *The Strange Case of Dr Jekyll and Mr Hyde* (1886) was unleashed upon the world. Stevenson, himself drawn to both the rewards of work and the delights of play, was fascinated by Brodie as an egregious example of the divided self.

Stevenson was not the only Scottish writer to utilise the Brodie story. Muriel Spark's *The Prime of Miss Jean Brodie* (1961) portrays an Edinburgh spinster psychologically disfigured by duality since she is narrowly self-righteous as well as expansively romantic. Jean tells two girls in the Brodie set: 'I am a descendent, do not forget, of Willie Brodie, a man of substance, a cabinet maker and designer of gibbets, a member of the Town Council of Edinburgh and a keeper of two mistresses who bore him five children between them. Blood tells.'

The personality who thus inspired Stevenson and Spark was born in the Old Town of Edinburgh where his father, Francis, was a wright (cabinet maker) who rose to the rank of Deacon (leader) of the Wrights. An adventurous youth, William was attracted to the Theatre Royal in the North Bridge and loved to watch performances of his favourite play, John Gay's *The Beggar's Opera*. Already his nightlife was given over to excitement. Apart from the histrionic delights of the Theatre Royal, there was the cockpit and the Cape Club – a fraternity of men fond of conversation and conviviality.

William eventually succeeded his father as Deacon of Wrights (from 1781 to 1783 and from 1786 to 1787. He also obtained a seat on the Town Council. Part of his work as Deacon was to fit new doors and locks to shops in the city and this put him a privileged position. With his grand home in Brodie's Close, the Deacon was a respectable man about town – during the day that is, for there were rumours that by night he kept the company of two mistresses and some rather disreputable men.

In August 1786 Edinburgh was alarmed by the news that the bank of Messrs Johnston and Smith had been robbed. In October, the goldsmith James Wemyss of Parliament Close, was relieved of a substantial amount of jewellery. Throughout 1787 the burglaries continued and the gang responsible seemed to have an almost supernatural ability to open locked doors. On Wednesday 8 March 1788, there was an audacious attempt to break into the General Excise office in Chessel's Court, by the Canongate. Although the burglars did not manage to take much, their willingness to mount a robbery on such a scale caused consternation. On the Friday evening John Brown, an Irishman, came to see the Sheriff-Clerk about the Secretary of State's offer of a free pardon to anyone giving information leading to the arrest of the notorious gang who were undermining the security of Edinburgh. Brown persuaded an official to come with him to the King's Park and showed him a collection of countfeit keys hidden under a stone at the Salisbury Crags.

Brown named some of the members of the gang and George Smith, a Cowgate grocer, and Andrew Ainslie, a High Street shoemaker, were arrested and confined in the Tolbooth. Brown also hinted that the leader of the gang was a well-known man in a privileged position.

When he heard that Brown was talking and Smith and Ainslie were in prison, Brodie got out of Edinburgh. Realising that the Deacon had abandoned him, Smith made a full confession that implicated Brodie as the mastermind behind the burglaries. Brodie, Smith explained, had made copies of keys he himself had fitted to shops. For the break-in at the General Excise Office he had sent Smith to make a putty impression of a key then made a duplicate. The Sheriff-Clerk's office reacted to this information by offering a reward of £150 for 'William Brodie, a considerable House-Carpenter and Burgess of the City of Edinburgh'.

The Deacon had escaped to Holland but before leaving he sent some letters to Edinburgh where they were examined by Harry Erskine, Dean of the Faculty of Advocates, then passed to the Sheriff. In a letter to his friend Michael Henderson, Brodie wrote 'Were I to write to you all that has happened to me and the hairbreadth escapes I made from a well-scented pack of bloodhounds, it would make a small volume'.

Brodie was arrested in Amsterdam and brought back to Edinburgh to stand trial, in August, before Lord Braxfield. At the trial Brodie was accused of 'breaking into a house used or kept as an Excise Office, or other public office, under cloud of night, and from thence abstracting and stealing money'. He was found guilty and sentenced to death. Braxfield told Brodie:

It's much to be lamented that those vices, which are called gentlemanly vices, are so favourably looked upon in the present age. They have been the source of your ruin; and, whatever may be thought of them, they are such as assuredly lead to ruin. I hope you will improve the short time which you have now to live by reflecting upon your past conduct, and endeavouring to procure, by a sincere repentance, forgiveness for your many crimes.

On 1 October 1788 Brodie went to the gallows at the Edinburgh Tolbooth. Apparently he tried to outwit death by wearing a steel collar under his neckerchief and bribing the hangman to make a short drop. However, the rope was adjusted and Brodie dropped to his death. His bizarre personality is perhaps best conveyed by the will he made before he died:

> And lastly my neck being now about to be embraced by a halter I recommend to all Rogues, Sharpers, Thieves and Gamblers, as well in high as in low stations to take care of theirs by leaving of all wicked practices and becoming good members of society.

Henry Mackenzie

A doctor's son, Henry Mackenzie (1745–1831) was born on 26 July 1745 in Libberton Wynd which ran north and south between the Lawnmarket and the Cowgate where George IV Bridge now stands. He was educated at the High School and Edinburgh University and died, on 14 January 1831, at his home in 6 Heriot Row, facing Queen Street Gardens. He is buried in Greyfriars Churchyard, on the north side of the terrace. Mackenzie's sentimental novel, *The Man of Feeling* (1771), was greatly admired by Burns (see below) and others. In 1779 Mackenzie edited the *Mirror* and from 1785–7 edited the *Lounger* which carried, in its issue of 7 December 1786, Mackenzie's enormously influential essay on Burns, the 'heaven-taught ploughman'.

Robert Fergusson

Robert Fergusson (1750–74) was born on 5 September 1750 in Cap and Feather Close (off the High Street, site built over on the east side of the North Bridge). He was educated privately at a school in Niddry's Wynd and at the High School before going, on a bursary, to the High School of Dundee (in 1762) and St Andrews University which he left in May 1786 without taking a degree. Returning to Edinburgh he took a job as a copyist in the office of the Commissary Clerk and, after his father's death in 1767, supported his mother and sister by clerking.

In 1771 Fergusson began to contribute verse to Walter Ruddiman's *Weekly Magazine* which was henceforth the main platform for his poetry. His first efforts were in English but in January 1772 Ruddiman published 'The Daft Days' in which Fergusson demonstrated a mastery of Scots and established himself as more than the equal of his predecessor Allan Ramsay. He followed this with a series of brilliantly observed and eloquently expressed Scots poems which made him the toast of literary Edinburgh.

On 10 October 1772 Fergusson was elected a member of the Cape Club whose members met regularly to eat, drink and debate in The Isle of Man's Arms, Craig's Close (265 High Street). Dubbed 'Sir Precentor' by the Cape Club, Fergusson also enjoyed drinking in Lucky Middlemist's tavern in the Cowgate; and in Johnnie Dowie's tavern, Libberton's Wynd (demolished when George IV Bridge was built).

In 1773 Ruddiman published *Poems by Robert Fergusson* but the same year the poet's poor health and deeply depressive temperament made it impossible for him to continue with clerking. In July 1774 he fell down a flight of stairs and in a state of mental distraction was taken to the Edinburgh Bedlam (demolished), the annexe to Darien House, the old Workhouse, Bristo. He died in the Edinburgh Bedlam on 17 October 1774. Significantly, the West House asylum (Royal Edinburgh Hospital) at Morningside was erected by public subscription following an appeal by Dr Andrew Duncan (1744–1828) who attended Fergusson and was appalled at the conditions the poet endured in the Edinburgh Bedlam. In 1789 Robert Burns, who was always glad to acknowledge Fergusson's influence on his own work, had a headstone set up in Canongate Churchyard, Canongate. Burns's inscription reads:

No sculptur'd Marble here nor pompous lay
No storied Urn nor animated Bust
This simple Stone directs pale Scotia's way
To pour her sorrows o'er her Poet's Dust.

Fergusson's poetry celebrates both the vice and vitality of his native place. In 'Auld Reekie' (a poem of 328 lines published as a pamphlet in 1773) he paints a memorable and profound verbal portrait of Edinburgh as a city of startling contrasts:

Now Morn, wi' bonny purple smiles,	
Kisses the air-cock o' Saunt Giles;	
Rakin their een, the servant lasses	
Early begin their lies an' clashes.	
Ilk tells her friend o' saddest distress	
That still she bruiks frae scoulin mistress;	*scolding*
An' wi her joe, in turnpike stair,	*sweetheart*
She'd rather snuff the stinkin' air,	
As be subjected to her tongue,	
When justly censur'd i' the wrong.	
On stair, wi' tub or pat in hand,	*pot*
The barefoot housemaids lo'e to stand,	
That antrin fouk may ken how snell	*different, sharp*
Auld Reekie will at mornin' smell;	
Then, wi' an inundation big as	

> The burn that 'neath the Nor' Loch brig is,
> They kindly shower Edina's roses,
> To quicken an' regale our noses

> *Robert Burns*

Robert Burns (1759–96), astonished by the success of the Kilmarnock edition of his *Poems, Chiefly in the Scottish Dialect* (31 July 1786), arrived in Edinburgh on 29 November 1786 to be met by his Mauchline friend John Richmond who took him to share his first-floor room in Baxter's Close, Lawnmarket, overlooking Lady Stair's House (where there is a museum, open to the public, celebrating Burns, Scott and Stevenson). Though the Baxter's Close house has gone there is a plaque over the Lawnmarket entrance to Lady Stair's Close. Burns was welcomed into Edinburgh as a social and cultural phenomenon. The Earl of Glencairn enthused over his poetry and persuaded the influential Caledonian Hunt to subscribe for 100 copies of a new edition (which was duly dedicated to them). Glencairn introduced Burns to the parsimonious publisher-bookseller William Creech who became his literary agent in Edinburgh.

Eleven days after Burns's arrival in the capital the *Lounger* appeared with a review by its editor, Henry Mackenzie, author of *The Man of Feeling* (1771), a book Burns prized 'next to the Bible'. Mackenzie's opinion was law among the literati. By acclaiming 'this heaven-taught ploughman' as a 'genius of no ordinary rank' Mackenzie not only made Burns the darling ingredient of any social gathering, but gave him a role which the poet relished. With his lightning wit and brilliant, if provocative, conversation Burns, a stocky man of five-foot-nine, dominated Edinburgh. He wore a dark coat, light waistcoat, ruffled shirt, boots, buckskin breeches, and arranged his unpowdered hair by spreading it over his forehead and tying it at the back.

He was welcomed by the Crochallan Fencibles, a club, founded by William Smellie (who printed the Edinburgh edition of Burns's poems) which met in Dawney Douglas's Tavern in Anchor Close (gone), conveniently near Smellie's printing works. He was made a member of the Canongate Kilwinning Masonic Lodge (whose members included the Earl of Glencairn, Henry Mackenzie, William Creech and the painter Alexander Nasmyth). For his own satisfaction Burns honoured his poetic debt to Robert Fergusson (see above) by arranging for a tombstone to be erected over his neglected grave.

On 17 April 1787 Burns accepted 100 guineas from Creech for the copyright of the Edinburgh edition of his poems. This contained, in addition to the dedication to the Caledonian Hunt, an 'Address to Edinburgh' beginning

Edina! Scotia's darling seat!
　All hail thy palaces and tow'rs,
Where once, beneath a Monarch's feet,
　Sat Legislation's sov'reign pow'rs:
　From marking wildly-scatt'red flow'rs,
As on the banks of Ayr I stray'd,
　And singing, lone, the ling'ring hours,
I shelter in thy honor'd shade.

The Edinburgh edition sold 3,000 copies, and made a handsome profit for Creech. On 4 May 1787 Burns sent off a song to James Johnson, the engraver, for his traditional song anthology, the *Scots Musical Museum*, and next morning set off on horseback with Bob Ainslie, a convivial law student, to tour the Borders. After another tour, of the Highlands with the boorish Latin master William Nicol, Burns returned to Edinburgh in the winter of 1787 and stayed in a house on the south-west corner of St James's Square in the New Town. On 4 December 1787 Burns met, at a tea party, Mrs Agnes McLehose, a grass widow anxious to keep the company of Edinburgh's latest literary lion. Agnes, or 'Nancy', had left her profligate husband and, thanks to her cousin William Craig, was staying in the Potterrow (house gone). If Burns's poems had excited her interest, this meeting in the flesh positively thrilled her and she asked the poet to take tea with her. Before he could accept he dislocated his knee in a fall from a coach. This enforced passivity led to the celebrated correspondence between Sylvander (Burns) and Clarinda (Nancy), Arcadian names suggested by Mrs McLehose.

After exchanging formalities Burns admitted to 'unnamed feelings' which Mrs McLehose agreed were delightful when 'under the check of reason and religion'. Burns was not to be put off and while ostensibly flattering her insipid verses as 'good poetry' slipped in a reference to the 'God of love'. This epistolary courtship inflamed the poet. After a month's correspondence with this attractive woman (of his own age) who had, after all, instigated the affair, Burns told a friend 'I am at this moment ready to hang myself for a young Edinburgh widow'.

Intent on physical conquest, Burns made his first call – in a sedan chair – early in the new year of 1788. Five more visits followed rapidly, yet Sylvander must have acted with propriety because Clarinda wrote happy in the knowledge that an exquisite evening 'did not lead beyond the limits of virtue', to which he declared that he would deny himself 'the dearest gratification on earth' in deference to her reputation and 'inward peace'. One evening he did go too far for Clarinda's comfort for in a written reprimand he was asked to observe 'the strictest delicacy'. As it happened the poet was on the point of leaving for Mossgiel and apologised for compromising her reputation before he left Edinburgh.

In September 1791 Burns moved into a house in Dumfries and there heard from Clarinda who told him that Jenny Clow, a servant girl, was destitute in Edinburgh with a two-year-old son by Burns. In reply he claimed he had always been willing to look after the boy and asked Clarinda to give Jenny some money. Learning that Clarinda intended to join her now prosperous husband in Jamaica Burns came up to Edinburgh to bid a last farewell, staying in the **White Hart Inn** on the north side of the Grassmarket. That it was a genuinely tender meeting is confirmed by the poem Burns sent to Clarinda on his return to Dumfries.

> Ae fond kiss, and then we sever!
> Ae farewell, and then forever!
> Deep in heart-wrung tears I'll pledge thee,
> Warring sighs and groans I'll wage thee.

A **Burns Monument** was erected on the south side of Regent Road in 1830; the statue (by Flaxman) it once contained is in the National Portrait Gallery; the relics are in Lady Stair's House. In 1985 a **Robert Burns Memorial Window**, designed by Leifur Breidfjörd, was installed in St Giles' Cathedral.

James Hogg

When James Hogg (1770–1835), the Ettrick Shepherd, came to Edinburgh in 1810 to establish his literary weekly, *The Spy*, he had high hopes that the capital would applaud his editorial energy and creative ingenuity. Among other features *The Spy* published a section of 'Love Adventures of Mr George Cochrane', an autobiographical novella in which the narrator, 'an old bachelor' (Hogg being an unmarried man of forty at the time of his arrival in Edinburgh) relates with relish his affairs with five different women: a pretty servant girl, an exalted lady, the Catholic Mary, the Cameronian Jessy, and a middle-aged Presbyterian 'paragon of sanctity and devotion'.

'Love Adventures of Mr George Cochrane' offended many subscribers to *The Spy* and contributed to its collapse after a run of only one year. Hogg was disgusted by the hypocritical response of his Edinburgh readers and took his revenge on them in the final issue (24 August 1811) of *The Spy*:

> Enemies, swelling with the most rancorous spite, grunted in every corner [and] pretended friends . . . took every method in their power to lessen the work in the esteem of others, by branding its author with designs the most subversive of all civility and decorum.

During the years 1810 to 1815 he spent in Edinburgh, Hogg lived in Anne Street (demolished when Waverley Bridge was built); the Harrow

Inn, Grassmarket (46–54 Candlemaker Row representing the remains of the Harrow Inn); and Deanhaugh Street, Stockbridge, where he completed *The Queen's Wake* (1812) and thus established his reputation as an accomplished poet. Part of Hogg's fictional masterpiece, *The Private Memoirs and Confessions of a Justified Sinner* (1824), unfolds in and around Edinburgh. For example, the sinner Wringhim is drawn towards Arthur's Seat where he sees 'a lady, robed in white', has conversations with his diabolic second self, and contemplates killing his brother by pushing him off 'the dizzy pinnacle'.

Sir Walter Scott

Sir Walter Scott (1771–1832) was born on 15th August 1771 in a house at the top of College Wynd, the university part of Edinburgh's new town: a plaque on 8 Chambers Street notes that Scott's birthplace was 'near this spot'. He was the ninth of twelve children born to Walter Scott – a Writer to the Signet and thus part of the Scottish legal elite – and his wife Anne, daughter of Edinburgh University's Professor of Medicine. Six of the Scotts' children had already died in infancy so there was great concern when, at eighteen months, Walter lost the power of his right leg as a result of polio. On the advice of his maternal grandfather, Dr John Rutherford, he was sent to the Borders to get the benefit of fresh country air.

At seven, Scott settled into his father's house at 25 George Square (plaque), Edinburgh, and this was his home until his marriage in 1797. As part of a family and no longer a 'single indulged brat' (as in the Borders) Scott was ill-at-ease in George Square. While he appreciated his mother's love of poetry, his father's strictly orthodox Calvinism was anathema. Sundays were a hell of a Calvinist boredom.

With only a few private lessons in Latin behind him Scott was sent to the High School to study (he recalled) under 'Mr Luke Fraser, a good Latin scholar and a very worthy man'. Scott did not excel as a scholar but 'glanced like a meteor from one end of the class to the other, and commonly disgusted my kind master as much by negligence and frivolity, as I occasionally pleased him by flashes of intellect and talent'. He was, however, able to hold his own in the rough and tumble of the playground and became popular among his schoolmates by his apparently effortless ability to tell entertaining stories.

In 1781 the eleven-year-old Scott entered the class of the brilliant and humane Rector of the High School, Dr Alexander Adam. Now equipped to understand Latin, Scott began to appreciate the resources of the language and delighted Dr Adam with his translations of Horace and Virgil. He finished the High School when he was twelve then spent another period in the Borders.

In 1783 Scott began his studies at Edinburgh University, attending

Professor John Hill's Latin class and Professor Andrew Dalzel's Greek class. The Latin class was too unruly to be informative and Scott, with no previous knowledge of the language, pretended such indifference to Greek that he earned, among his fellow-students, the nickname 'the Greek Blockhead' while the professor pronounced him an incurable dunce. It was time, his father decided, for his non-academic son to concentrate on legal studies.

In 1785 Scott was apprenticed to his father as Writer to the Signet. He was bored by the office routine and spent his allowance for copy-money on the theatre and in James Sibbald's circulating library in Parliament Square so that his office desk was crammed with romantic reading matter. When away from the office Scott would seek out the easily-accessible desolation of Arthur's Seat and Salisbury Crags and exchange tales of his own invention with friend and fellow-apprentice John Irving. In the second year of his apprenticeship Scott suffered an internal haemorrhage and was confined to bed. Apart from occasional games of chess, and glimpses of troops on the Meadows, Scott had only books to amuse him. After recovery, and a period of convalescence at Kelso, Scott came back to claim his place in Edinburgh. In the company of robust friends such as John Irving, Scott attended the literary societies and took his full share of frequent conviviality – 'the error of my youth' as he later called this adolescent over-indulgence. In the 1789–90 session of Edinburgh University, Scott had an opportunity to consider moral philosophy in the class of Professor Dugal Stewart 'whose striking and impressive eloquence riveted the attention even of the most volatile student'.

Scott decided to go a step further than his father, and told him that, instead of going into partnership with him, he intended to qualify as an advocate. Scott studied civil and municipal law and was called to the Scottish Bar on 11 July 1792. He was, as he put it in the concluding sentences of his autobiography, 'a gentleman, and so welcome anywhere, if so be I could behave myself, as Tony Lumpkin says "in a concatenation accordingly".'

After being discouraged by Williamina Belsches, the great love of his life (and Green Mantle in *Redgauntlet*), Scott devoted his energies to literary and physical pursuits. His first book – two Bürger ballads translated as *The Chase, and William and Helen* – appeared anonymously in 1796 (a year before Williamina married William Forbes, a banker's son). In February 1797 Scott helped form the Edinburgh Light Dragoons of which he was Quartermaster, Secretary and, for a time, Paymaster. He married a French girl, Charlotte Charpentier, in Carlisle on 24 December 1797 and set up home in 39 South Castle Street (where there is a plaque on the wall and a statuette of Scott above the door). This was Scott's town home until 1826, the year of his financial crash. To settle his debts of almost £117,000 (including private debts of around £20,000) Scott agreed to pay the money made from his writing into a trust. He was allowed to remain in Abbotsford but had to sell 39 North Castle Street. Henceforth he lived in Edinburgh in lodgings, retired from the Court in 1830, and spent most of the time left to him at Abbotsford where he died. The **Scott Monument**, in Princes Street, was completed in 1846 and stands 200ft high. It features figures from Scott's books as decorations; and contains John Steel's Carrara marble statue of Scott who is shown sitting, with his deerhound Maida at his side.

The **Grassmarket**, a rectangular area (230 yards long) under the cliff of Edinburgh Castle, was once the place of public executions and at the east end of the Grassmarket the site of the gallows is marked by a St Andrew's Cross in rose-coloured cobblestones with the inscription 'For the Protestant faith on this spot many Martyrs and Covenanters died.' Criminals as well as Covenanters died on the Grassmarket gallows and the criminal connotations of the area were increased by the activities of William Burke (1792–1829) and William Hare who lived in Log's lodging house in Tanner's Close (demolished) by the West Port (the gate at the western end of the Grassmarket):

> Up the close an' doon the stair,
> Roon' the toun wi' Burke an' Hare:
> Burke's the butcher, Hare's the thief,
> Knox the boy that buys the beef.

That jingle is still in oral circulation in Edinburgh where Burke and Hare, between them, murdered sixteen unfortunates whose bodies were destined to further the study of anatomy as practised by the brilliant Dr Robert Knox, the most popular teacher at the Medical School.

Burke's name has passed into the English language. It is preserved, in the *Oxford English Dictionary*, as a verb meaning 'To murder, in the same manner or for the same purpose as Burke did; to kill secretly by suffocation or strangulation, or for the purpose of selling the victim's body for dissection. . . . To smother, "hush up", suppress quietly.' Burke, Hare and Knox have featured as characters in a play, *The Anatomist* (1930), by James Bridie and in a filmscript, *The Doctor and the Devils*, by Dylan Thomas. Burke and Hare continue to haunt the imagination of Edinburgh.

After Burke and Hare were arrested, in Log's lodging house, on 1 November 1828, the *Edinburgh Courant* published Burke's confession in which the particular method of murder is described:

When they first began this murdering system they always took them to Knox's after dark; but being so successful, they went in the daytime and grew more bold. . . . They often said to one another that no person could find them out, no one being present at the murders but themselves two; and that they might as well [be] hanged for a sheep as a lamb. They made it their business to look out for persons to decoy into their houses to murder them. Burke declares, when they kept the mouth and nose shut a very few minutes, they could make no resistance, but would convulse and make a rumbling noise in their bellies for some time; after they ceased crying and making resistance, they left them to die of themselves: but that their bodies would often move afterwards, and for some time they would have long breathings before life went away.

As the crown had problems in making a convincing case against the murderers, Hare was promised his freedom if he turned king's evidence and testified against Burke. He did so and Burke was found guilty .

When Burke was hanged, before a crowd of some 25,000 spectators, Sir Walter Scott wrote in his journal for 28 January 1829:

Burke the murderer hanged this morning. The mob, which was immense, demanded Knox and Hare, but though greedy for more victims, received with shouts the solitary wretch who found his way to the gallows out of five or six who seem not less guilty than he. But the story begins to be stale, although I believe a doggerel ballad upon it would be popular, how brutal soever the wit.

On 7 March 1829 Scott, out of sorts, 'felt like one of the victims of the wretched Burke, struggling against a smothering weight on my bosom, till nature could endure it no longer'. Ironically, Scott was to endure the image of Burke until the end of his life. On 18 May 1831 he put in an appearance at Jedburgh on behalf of the Tory candidate for Roxburgh-shire. As Scott's carriage passed a group of radical Hawick weavers, it was stoned and his attempt to make a speech was drowned out in abuse. The Tory candidate was, predictably, elected and Scott left Jedburgh to a hail of stone and cries of 'Burke Sir Walter'. This hostility had a profoundly disturbing effect on Scott who, on his deathbed in 1832, several times reiterated the phrase 'Burke Sir Walter'.

Scott's novel *The Heart of Midlothian* (1818) is an historical fiction founded on facts of 1736 in and around the Grassmarket. Captain John Porteous, of the City Guard, conveys a smuggler called Wilson to the place of execution, to the fury of the mob who resent Porteous's callous displays of cruelty. For example, Porteous forces onto the large wrists of Wilson handcuffs that are evidently too small for him. Wilson complains of the excruciating pain and Porteous replies: 'It signifies little, your pain will be soon at an end.' There is considerable popular sympathy for Wilson and when he is hanged the mob becomes restless, throwing stones at Porteous and his guards. Infuriated by this, Porteous springs from the scaffold, takes a musket from one of the soldiers, and opens fire on the crowd.

Tried before the High Court, Porteous is found guilty of murder and condemned to death. When a royal reprieve is granted to Porteous, the Edinbugh mob decide to take the law into their own hands. They remove Porteous from the Tolbooth and take him to the Grassmarket so he can die 'on the common gibbet . . . where he spilled the blood of so many innocents'. Having determined the destiny of Porteous, the crowd take him to the Grassmarket. The Grassmarket thus features powerfully as a presence in *The Heart of Midlothian* and Scott's description of the area is both informative and evocative:

> In former times, England had her Tyburn, to which the devoted victims of justice were conducted in solemn procession up what is now called Oxford-road. In Edinburgh, a large open street, or rather oblong square, surrounded by high houses, called the Grassmarket, was used for the same melancholy purpose. It was not ill-chosen for such a scene, being of considerable extent, and therefore fit to accommodate a great number of spectators, such as are usually assembled by this melancholy spectacle. On the other hand, few of the houses which surround it were, even in early times, inhabited by persons of fashion; so that those likely to be offended or over deeply affected by such unpleasant exhibitions were not in the way of having their quiet disturbed by them. The houses in the Grassmarket are, generally speaking, of a mean description; yet the place is not without some features of grandeur, being overhung by the southern side of the huge rock on which the castle stands, and by the moss-grown battlements and turreted walls of that ancient fortress.
>
> It was the custom, until within these thirty years, or thereabouts, to use this esplanade for the scene of public executions. The fatal day was announced to the public, by the appearance of a huge black gallows-tree towards the eastern end of the Grassmarket. This ill-omened apparition was of great height, with a scaffold surrounding it, and a double ladder placed against it, for the ascent of the unhappy criminal and the executioner. As this apparatus was always arranged before dawn, it seemed as if the gallows had grown out of the earth in the course of one night, like the production of some foul demon. . . . On the night after the execution the gallows again disappeared, and was conveyed in silence and darkness to the place where it was usually deposited, which was one of the vaults under the Parliament-house or courts of justice.

The title of *The Heart of Midlothian* derives from the name given to the Old Tolbooth prison (1466–1817) in Parliament Square where the site is marked by brass plates in the roadway and a heart-shaped design of setts.

Lord Jeffrey

Francis Jeffrey, Lord Jeffrey (1773–1850) was born in a four-storeyed house at 7 Charles Street. In 1801 he started his married life (with Catherine Wilson who died four years later) on the third floor of 18 Buccleuch Place (plaque) where he discussed with Henry Brougham (1778–1869) and Sydney Smith (1771–1845) the launching of the *Edinburgh Review* which ran from 10 October 1802 until 1929. In 1802 Jeffrey moved to 62 Queen Street, facing the gardens, and in 1810 went to 92 George Street, Under Jeffrey's editorship, from 1803 to 1829, the *Edinburgh Review* became a powerful organ of literary opinion. Its anonymous review (probably by Brougham) of Byron's *Hours of Idleness* (1808) resulted in Byron's satirical reply in *English Bards and Scotch Reviewers* (1808). In 1829 Jeffrey (who was remarried, to Charlotte Wilkes, in 1813) was appointed Dean of the Faculty of Advocates and the following year became Lord Advocate. He was raised to the Bench as Lord Jeffrey in 1834. Jeffrey's last home was at 24 Moray Place where he died on 26 January 1850. His sarcophagus stands near the west wall of Dean Cemetery.

William Blackwood

The publisher William Blackwood (1776–1834) was born in Edinburgh on 20th November 1776 and set himself up as a bookseller and publisher at 64 South Bridge in 1804. In 1816 he decided to transfer his business from the Old to the New Town and at 17 Princes Street created both a business and a literary saloon which was memorably described in John Gibson Lockhart's *Peter's Letters to his Kinsfolk* (1819):

> you have an elegant oval saloon, lighted from the roof, where various groups of loungers and literary dilettanti are engaged in looking at, or criticising among themselves, the publications just arrived by that day's coach from town. In such critical colloquies, the voice of the bookseller himself may ever and anon be heard mingling the broad and unadulterated notes of its Auld Reekie music; for unless occupied in the recesses of the premises with some other business, it is here that he has his usual station.

On 1 April 1817 Blackwood began to publish the *Edinburgh Monthly Magazine* as a radical Tory alternative to the Whig *Edinburgh Review*. As edited by Lockhart and John Wilson the magazine, renamed *Blackwood's Magazine* for the October 1817 issue, was a spectacular success. *Black-*

wood's (known also as 'Maga' because of Blackwood's pronunciation of 'magazine') continued in existence until December 1980.

Thomas Campbell

Thomas Campbell (1777–1844) studied law at Edinburgh University in 1796 and the following winter taught Greek and Latin to private pupils. Campbell recalled:

> In this vocation I made a comfortable livelihood as long as I was industrious. But *The Pleasures of Hope* (1798) came over me. I took long walks about Arthur's Seat, conning over my own (as I thought them) magnificent lines; and as my 'Pleasure of Hope' got on, my pupils fell off.

The best known lines in the poem – "Tis distance lends enchantment to the view,/And robes the mountain in its azure hue' – are supposed to have come to Campbell while walking on Calton Hill. Campbell lodged in Alison Square (demolished) 'in the second floor of a stair on the north side of the central archway, with windows looking partly into the Potterrow and partly into Nicolson Street'.

Susan Ferrier

Susan (Edmonstoune) Ferrier (1782–1854) was born in Edinburgh on 7 September 1782; her father, a Writer to the Signet, was Walter Scott's colleague in the Court of Session and Susan Ferrier enjoyed a long friendship with Scott. She lived in London from 1800 to 1804 and on her return to Edinburgh stayed with her father in Canaan Lane, Morningside. The first of her three novels, *Marriage* (1818), comments on the contrasts built into Edinburgh: 'Beneath, the Old Town reared its dark brow, and the New one stretched its golden lines, white, all around, the varied charms of nature lay scattered in that profusion, which nature's hand alone can bestow.' Susan Ferrier's home at 25 George Street is now part of the George Hotel. She died on 5 November 1854 and is buried in St Cuthbert's churchyard, behind St John's Church, at the West End of Princes Street.

John Wilson

Having lost a fortune in the Lake District, John Wilson (1785–1854) came to Edinburgh in 1812 in which year he published *Isle of Palms and Other Poems* and *The Magic Mirror*. On the evidence of these poetic works Wilson was admitted to Edinburgh's literary circles and he naturally gravitated towards William Blackwood's saloon at 17 Princes Street where he met John Gibson Lockhart (1794–1854), a fellow student of law. Lockhart and Wilson edited, in October 1817, the first issue of *Blackwood's Magazine* which contained a sensational attack on the Whig *Edinburgh Review*.

Wilson also wrote, for *Blackwood's Magazine*, many of the 'Noctes Ambrosianae'. This series, published between 1822 and 1835, comprised imaginary conversations between such characters as 'The Ettrick Shepherd' (James Hogg) and 'Christopher North' (Wilson himself). The convivial conversations were set in Ambrose's Tavern in Gabriel's Road (gone, but possibly located in the alley between the Cafe Royal and Register House at the East End of Princes Street).

An imposing figure with an irascible manner, Wilson lived at 53 Queen Street, near Castle Street, in a three-storey house looking on to Queen Street Gardens. In 1819 he moved to 29 Anne Street, near the Water of Leith. He was (despite his lack of qualifications for the post) appointed Professor of Moral Philosophy at Edinburgh University in 1820 and in 1826 settled at 6 Gloucester Place – now the Christopher North Hotel, complete with plaque – where he died on 3 April 1854.

Thomas De Quincey

Encouraged by his friend John Wilson, Thomas De Quincey (1785–1859) came to Edinburgh in December 1820 with the intention of becoming a regular contributor to *Blackwood's Magazine*. Though he had little literary experience at the time, his conversational brilliance convinced Wilson, who had known De Quincey in the Lake District, that his friend could make an outstanding essayist. De Quincey worked on various essays, including an 'opium article', for *Blackwood's* but fell out with William Blackwood in January 1821 and left Edinburgh for Grasmere. But for this argument *Blackwood's* might have published De Quincey's masterpiece *Confessions of an English Opium Eater* (1821) which appeared instead in the *London Magazine*.

De Quincey settled in Edinburgh in 1830 but almost immediately found himself in financial trouble. Between 1831 and 1841 some thirty-five suits for debt were filed against De Quincey who frequently put himself beyond the reach of his creditors by staying in one of the houses of refuge at the Holyrood Sanctuary. There, within 100 yards of Holyrood Palace, debtors could live with impunity and on Sundays leave the sanctuary and visit their families without fear of arrest. Apart from his periods at the sanctuary, De Quincey lived in Great King Street, in Forres Street, at Duddingston and in the left-hand flat on the second floor of 42 Lothian Street (demolished). He is buried in St Cuthbert's churchyard.

Percy Bysshe Shelley

In 1811 Percy Bysshe Shelley (1792–1822), the most politically radical of the English Romantics, came to Edinburgh to marry the sixteen-year-old Harriet Westbrook; a certificate was issued on 28 August and they were married, either that day or the next, in the house of Reverend Joseph Robertson at 225 The Canongate. For five weeks Shelley and Harriet lived in a ground-room suite of floors at 60 George Street. In 1814 Shelley eloped with Mary Godwin who became his second wife in 1816 after Harriet drowned herself in the Serpentine, London.

Thomas Carlyle

On the eve of his fourteenth birthday in November 1809, Thomas Carlyle (1795–1881) walked (in three days) the hundred miles from Ecclefechan to Edinburgh to study at the University. In 1813 he left Edinburgh University, without taking a degree, and taught mathematics in his old school, Annan Academy. He returned to Edinburgh in 1817 to study theology but abandoned this religious calling for a literary career. Carlyle married Jane Baillie Welsh on 17 October 1826 and the couple spent the first eighteen months (October 1826 to May 1828) of their married life in a house rented by Jane's mother at 21 Comely Bank (where there is a plaque). In *Reminiscences* (edited by James Anthony Froude and published in 1881 within weeks of Carlyle's death) Carlyle writes of his life at Comely Bank:

> we did grow to 'know everybody of mark', or might have grown; but nobody except [Francis, Lord Jeffrey, editor of the *Edinburgh Review*] seemed to either of us a valuable acquisition. Jeffrey much admired [Jane], and was a pleasant phenomenon to both of us. . . . We had a little tea-party (never did I see a smaller or a frugaller, with the tenth part of the human grace and brightness in it) once a week – the 'brown coffee-pot,' the feeble talk of dilettante – pretty silly – etc.; ah me, how she knit up all that into a shining thing! . . . Oh she was noble, very noble, in that early as in all other periods; and made the ugliest and dullest into something beautiful! I look back on it as if through rainbows, the bit of sunshine hers, the tears my own.

While living at 21 Comely Bank, Carlyle worked on a didactic novel as well as writing the contents of the first volume of *Critical and Miscellaneous Essays* (1839), two of the essays ('Jean Paul Richter', 'State of German Literature') having first appeared in Jeffrey's *Edinburgh Review*. Goethe was an admirer of Carlyle and his second letter to his fellow writer arrived at Comely Bank, along with Goethe's marriage gifts. During the eighteen months at Comely Bank, Carlyle was an unsuccessful candidate for two professorships – one at London University; the other, the Chair of Moral Philosophy at St Andrews. In 1865 Carlyle was elected Lord Rector of Edinburgh University.

Dr John Brown

Born in Biggar, Lanarkshire, on 22 September 1810 Dr John Brown (1810–82) came to Edinburgh in 1822 and was educated at the High School and Edinburgh University where he studied medicine. From 1850 until his death he lived at 23 Rutland Street (where there is a memorial to him carved in the stonework of the wall to the left of the front window). His essays, in *Horae Subsecivae* (3 vols, 1858–82), established him as an entertaining and observant stylist. 'Marjorie Fleming' (in which he describes a close friendship between 'Pet Marjory' and Sir Walter Scott) and 'Our Dogs' are among his finest essays but he is best-remembered for 'Rab and His Friends' which introduces the heroic mastiff thus:

> There, under the large arch of the South Bridge, is a huge mastiff, sauntering down the middle of the causeway, as if with his hands in his pockets; he is old, grey, brindled; as big as a little Highland bull, and has the Shakespearian dewlaps shaking as he goes.

Robert Louis Stevenson

Robert Louis Stevenson (1850–94) was born on 13 November 1850 at 8 Howard Place, where there is a plaque. In 1853 the family moved to 1 Inverleith Terrace and in 1857 moved again to 17 Heriot Row; on the railings opposite the Heriot Row house there is an interpretation point on the Robert Louis Stevenson Heritage Trail. Stevenson's father Thomas was a lighthouse and harbour engineer; his mother Margaret Isabella Balfour was the daughter of a minister. They stood solidly for the respectability their son was later to reject.

Stevenson's nurse Alison 'Cummie' Cunningham, daughter of a Fife fisherman, filled the young boy's mind with biblical stories and fired his imagination with tales of the Covenanters. Stevenson's *A Child's Garden of Verses* (1885) is dedicated to Cummie and memorably describes 'The Lamplighter' he used to watch from his nursery window in 17 Heriot Row. The poem begins:

> My tea is nearly ready and the sun has left the sky;
> It's time to take the window to see Leerie going by;
> For every night at teatime and before you take your seat,
> With lantern and with ladder he comes posting up the street.

and ends:

For we are very lucky, with a lamp before the door,
And Leerie stops to light it as he lights so many more;
And O! before you hurry by with ladder and with light,
O Leerie, see a little child and nod to him to-night!

Stevenson attended Edinburgh Academy before travelling abroad for
the sake of his health. Back in Edinburgh he was educated privately then
went to Edinburgh University in 1867 to study engineering. By 1871 he
was enthusiastic enough about his literary ambitions to tell his father he
intended to abandon engineering. Thomas Stevenson persuaded his son
to secure his financial future by reading for the Scottish Bar; in 1872,
accordingly, Stevenson joined the office of Messrs Skene, Edwards and
Bilton, Writers to the Signet. In July 1875 he was admitted to the Scottish
Bar though he did not seriously attempt to pursue a legal career.

Before becoming an advocate, Stevenson and his father had the kind
of domestic clashes subsequently absorbed into the narrative tension of
Weir of Hermiston (1896). In 1873, for example, Stevenson was confronted
by his father when he came home one January evening to 17 Heriot Row
after spending some convivial hours with his best friend Charles Baxter.
Thomas Stevenson had discovered the written constitution of the L.J.R.
(Liberty, Justice and Reverence) Society founded by Stevenson, Baxter
and other like-minded young men. As the constitution commenced with
the words 'Disregard everything our parents have taught us', Thomas
Stevenson remonstrated with his son who admitted his agnosticism and
intellectual unrest. The scene was described in a letter Stevenson wrote
to Charles Baxter:

The thunderbolt has fallen with a vengeance now. . . . My father put
me one or two questions as to beliefs, which I candidly answered. . . .
I am, I think, as honest as they can be in what I hold. I have not
come hastily to my views. I reserve (as I have told them) many points
until I acquire fuller information. I do not think I am thus justly to
be called a 'horrible atheist'; and I confess I cannot exactly swallow
my father's purpose of praying down continuous afflictions on my
head.

For several years, in fact, Stevenson had been spending much of his time
exploring the duality of Edinburgh, symbolised by the contrast between his
father's home in Heriot Row and the social and sexual underground
of Edinburgh. 'Social inequality is nowhere more ostentatious than at
Edinburgh', he wrote in *Edinburgh: Picturesque Notes* (1879). Stevenson
enjoyed keeping the company (in Lothian Road and Leith Walk) of
prostitutes who knew him as 'velvet coat' on account of his sartorial
stylishness. He also liked drinking in Rutherford's bar in Drummond
Street. J.M. Barrie recalled a chance encounter with Stevenson in Princes

Street and how Stevenson took him by the arm 'away from the Humanities [class at Edinburgh University] to something that he assured me was more humane, a howff called Rutherford's'.

Though Stevenson's marriage to Fanny Osborne, in 1880, took him away from Edinburgh – to Bournemouth, America and eventually Samoa – the city of his birth remained a powerful presence in his work. In 1885, while living with Fanny at Bournemouth, he wrote *Dr Jekyll and Mr Hyde* (1888) and the impulse for the story came from the career of Edinburgh's Deacon Brodie about whom Stevenson and W.E. Henley had written a play in 1879. Though Stevenson's story is ostensibly set in London there is little doubt that it recreates Victorian Edinburgh. G.K. Chesterton, in his *Robert Louis Stevenson* (1927) observed:

It seems to me that the story of Jekyll and Hyde, which is presumably presented as happening in London, is all the time very unmistakably happening in Edinburgh . . . there is something decidedly Caledonian about Dr Jekyll; and especially something that calls up that quality in Edinburgh that led an unkind observer (probably from Glasgow) to describe it as 'an east-windy, west-endy place'.

In 1887, on the death of his father, Stevenson visited Edinburgh for the last time. **Lady Stair's House**, in the Lawnmarket, is open to the public as a museum containing relics of Stevenson, Sir Walter Scott and Robert Burns.

There are plans to erect a Stevenson monument in Edinburgh. Few writers have evoked the spirit of the city so brilliantly; for example Princes Street, now the busiest thoroughfare in Edinburgh, was once as Stevenson describes it in *Catriona* (1893), a novel that explores the capital in considerable detail:

I came forth, I vow I know not how, on the *Lang Dykes*. This is a rural road which runs on the north side over against the city. Thence I could see the whole black length of it tail down, from where the Castle stands upon its crags above the loch in a long line of spires and gable ends, and smoking chimneys . . .

Kenneth Grahame

Kenneth Grahame (1859–1932) was born on 8 March 1859 at 30 Castle Street (plaque) then was taken, as a child, to Inverary when his father became Sheriff-Substitute of Argyllshire. After his mother died, in 1864, Grahame was brought up by his grandmother in Cookham Dean, Berkshire. His novel *The Wind in the Willows* (1908) is a children's classic and was successfully dramatised as *Toad of Toad Hall* by A. A. Milne.

Sir Arthur Conan Doyle

Sir Arthur Conan Doyle (1859–1930) was born on 22 May 1959 at 11 Picardy Place, where there was a plaque until the building was demolished in 1969. A public house, the Conan Doyle, now stands near the site of his birthplace. Doyle studied medicine at Edinburgh University and two of his most celebrated fictional characters are modelled on Edinburgh men. As a medical student in Edinburgh in the 1870s Doyle had been hugely impressed by the deductive skills of Dr Joseph Bell (1837–1911) who was consultant surgeon at Edinburgh Infirmary, professor at Edinburgh University, and editor of the *Edinburgh Medical Journal*. In creating Sherlock Holmes, so he writes in his *Memories and Adventures* (1924), Doyle 'thought of my old teacher Joe Bell, of his eagle face, of his curious ways, of his eerie trick of spotting details'. Writing to Dr Bell on 4 May 1892 Doyle declared:

> It is most certainly to you that I owe Sherlock Holmes. . . . I do not think that his analytical work is in the least an exaggeration of some effects which I have seen you produce in the out-patient ward.

Doyle served as Bell's out-patient clerk and prepared notes before each patient was presented to Bell for diagnosis. When Doyle settled down, in March 1886, to write *A Study in Scarlet* (1887) he recalled Dr Bell and so Sherlock Holmes was born. Bell himself, however, told Doyle: 'You are yourself Sherlock Holmes, and well you know it.'

In *The Lost World* (1912), first and most famous of the Professor Challenger stories, Doyle created his notoriously irascible zoologist Professor George Edward Challenger. As he revealed, in *Memories and Adventures*, Doyle based Professor Challenger on Professor William Rutherford (1839–99) of Edinburgh University. Doyle vividly remembered Rutherford who 'would sometimes start his lecture before he reached the classroom so that we would hear a booming voice saying: "There are valves in the veins", or some other information, when the desk was still empty'. Doyle added that Rutherford was 'a rather ruthless vivisector'.

John Gray, Oscar Wilde

St Peter's Church, Falcon Avenue, Churchill – designed by Sir Robert Lorimer in 1906 and blessed the following year – is structured as a Italian-Byzantine church complete with campanile and forecourt. It was financed by André Raffolovich, the aesthete whose London salon was ridiculed when Oscar Wilde described it as more of a saloon than a salon. Raffolovich had St Peter's built for his friend John Gray (1866–1934), rumoured to be the original of Wilde's character Dorian Gray. Wilde's novel *The Picture of Dorian Gray* (1891) is a sumptuously told tale of a vain young man who exchanges his soul so he will retain his youth while his portrait ages. Gray is a collector of exquisite experiences and, for example,

> the Roman ritual had always a great attaction for him. . . . The fuming censers, that the grave boys, in their lace and scarlet, tossed into the air like great gilt flowers, had their subtle fascination for him. . . . He had a special passion, also, for ecclesiastical vestments, as indeed he had for everything connected with the service of the Church.

Although Dorian Gray never succumbs formally to the call of the Roman Catholic Church, John Gray – the friend Wilde referred to as 'Dorian' – eventually became Father John Gray of St Peter's Church.

Son of a Scottish journeyman carpenter, Gray met Wilde in 1889 at a session of the Rhymers' Club in London. Wilde felt that Gray had all the makings of the perfect disciple for he was good-looking and wrote suitably decadent poems. After Wilde met Lord Alfred Douglas in 1891 he lost interest in John Gray but felt guilty enough about this to pay for the cost of publication of Gray's first collection of poems, *Silverpoints* (1893). Gray decided to enter the priesthood after the arrest of Wilde in 1895 and instructed a barrister to attend Wilde's trial to take action should his name be mentioned. In a letter, written to Lord Alfred Douglas from Reading Gaol, Wilde said 'When I compare my friendship with you with such still younger men as John Gray and Pierre Louys, I feel ashamed. My real life, my higher life was with them and such as they.'

Sir Compton Mackenzie

Sir Compton Mackenzie (1883–1972) settled in 31 Drummond Place in 1953 and until the end of his life divided his time between Edinburgh and the south of France. He describes the house in the final volume of his autobiography *My Life and Times* (10 vols, 1963–71):

> Drummond Place was the first addition made to the New Town after Waterloo. The building of it began in October 1815 and in consequence all the floors in Drummond Place are of soft wood. . . . At this date it was touch and go whether Drummond Place would maintain the dignity it had enjoyed until the Second World War had 'popularised' it. The railings of the big central garden had been pulled down in that fatuous campaign for scrap iron, and the residents were just getting together to re-fence the garden and prevent it becoming the playground of destructive youngsters.

Mackenzie redecorated 31 Drummond Place and lined the house with bookshelves. He was a genial host and many literary visitors to 31 Drummond Place cherished the memory of Mackenzie's company. In the summer of 1955, for example, James Thurber visited Mackenzie and wrote to him, on 13 August 1955: 'We have been telling everyone since we left Edinburgh of our two enjoyable evenings at your house, and we shall go on remembering them fondly, and hope to see you again next year.' Shortly after Thurber's visit Mackenzie entertained Thornton Wilder but found him 'less exhilarating' than Thurber.

Helen Cruickshank

Helen Burness Cruickshank (1886–1975) was born on 15 May 1886 in Hillside, Angus, and was educated at Montrose Academy until 1903 when she joined the Civil Service, working first in London for ten years before settling in Edinburgh in 1912, spending another thirty years in her chosen profession. At her home, Dinnieduff at 4 Hillview Terrace, Corstorphine, she entertained many Scottish writers including Hugh MacDiarmid (Christopher Murray Grieve, 1892–1978) who, when Secretary of the Scottish Centre of PEN (formed in summer, 1927) stayed at Dinnieduff when he visited Edinburgh. He slept in the tiny front room which Helen Cruickshank named the Prophet's Chamber after the story of Elijah and the pious widow who placed her small 'chamber in the wall' at the prophet's disposal. When MacDiarmid went to London in 1929, Helen Cruickshank took over his position as Secretary of Scottish PEN and did this honorary work for seven years. Because of advancing years and ill health she moved, in 1973, to Queensberry Lodge, Canongate, where she died on 2 March 1975.

As a poet she published work in both English and a dialect Scots that drew on her Angus upbringing – her *Collected Poems* appeared in 1971 and her *Octobiography* in 1976. Her poem 'Corstorphine Woods' ends optimistically:

> And, as I roon the corner, best of a'
> The mavis, singing on my gavel wa' –
> Happy am I, altho' I bide my lane,
> To ha'e a singin' hert that's a' my ain.

Siegfried Sassoon, Wilfred Owen

The great English war poets Siegfried Sassoon (1886–1967) and Wilfred Owen (1893–1918) were both patients, during the First World War, at Craiglockhart War Hospital, Colinton Road: originally built, 1877–80, as Craiglockhart Hydropathic Institution, it is now Craiglockhart College of Education. On 27 July 1917, Sassoon published 'A Soldier's Declaration' in the *Bradford Pioneer* giving the text of a statement made to his commanding officer, explaining his grounds for refusing to serve further in the army. Thanks to the intervention of Robert Graves, Sassoon was sent to Craiglockhart War Hospital for neurasthenics in July 1917. Here Sassoon settled down to write the poems that would constitute his finest collection, *Counter-Attack* (1918). Some of the poems received their first publication in the hospital magazine, the *Hydra*, edited by another neurasthenic, Wilfred Owen, admitted to Craiglockhart in June 1917.

After experiencing war at the Somme in January 1917 Owen had broken down. Temperamentally his poetic inclinations tended towards Keatsian introspection but his sensitivity had been hardened in the trenches and in Sassoon's *The Old Huntsman* (1917) he had found a model for the satirical poems he felt he must now write. By coincidence he had, at Craiglockhart, an opportunity to meet his hero face to face and one evening at the beginning of August 1917 knocked on Sassoon's door and entered carrying under his arm several copies of *The Old Huntsman*. This meeting was a major source of inspiration to Owen.

Owen was discharged from Craiglockhart in November 1917 and was killed in action on 4 November 1918 while taking his company over the Sambre Canal. *The Collected Poems of Wilfred Owen* (edited by C. Day Lewis, 1964) contains a poem, 'Six o'clock in Princes Street' which begins:

> In twos and threes, they have not far to roam,
> Crowds that thread eastward, gay of eyes;
> Those seek no further than their quiet home,
> Wives, walking westward, slow and wise.

Edwin Muir

In 1942 Edwin Muir (1887–1959), then living in St Andrews, was offered work in Edinburgh with the British Council. His duties involved arranging lectures and concerts for international houses established for European refugees. Muir lived first in lodgings at 47 Manor Place then rented a flat at 8 Blantyre Terrace. Poetically it was a productive time, resulting in work included in *The Voyage and Other Poems* (1946). After the war, Muir went to Prague as the Director of the British Council Institute there until the Communist coup of 1948.

Hugh MacDiarmid

Christopher Murray Grieve (1892–1978) – the poet Hugh MacDiarmid – was a pupil at Broughton Junior Student Centre, Macdonald Road, from 1908 to 1911. During this time he was encouraged by his English teacher George Ogilvie (1871–1934) with whom he subsequently corresponded for many years; and he edited the *Broughton Magazine* (1909). Ogilvie was an elder of Lothian Road Church (now Film House), under the Rev. Dr R. J. Drummond, and Grieve attended the meetings of the Lothian Road

Church Literary and Debating Society. When Grieve was married to Margaret (Peggy) Skinner, on 13 June 1918, Dr Drummond performed the ceremony at 3 East Castle Road.

After settling at Biggar in 1951, Hugh MacDiarmid was a frequent visitor to Edinburgh and liked to drink with his friends in Milne's Bar, Hanover Street; The Abbotsford, Rose Street; and the Café Royal, West Register Street. **Milne's**, in particular, was MacDiarmid's 'favourite howff' and in 1985 the bar was redecorated in honour of MacDiarmid's memory with photographs of the poet inside and a painted sign outside. MacDiarmid's legendary association with Milne's is mentioned in Alasdair Gray's novel *1982 Janine* (1984). After climbing the Scott Monument, the narrator Jock McLeish lunches (in Milne's) on

> a pie and a pint in a basement in Hanover Street. The bar was crowded except where three men stood in a small open space created by the attention of the other customers. One had a sombre pouchy face and upstanding hair which seemed too like thistledown to be natural, one looked like a tall sarcastic lizard, one like a small shy bear. 'Our three best since Burns', a bystander informed me, 'barring Sorley of course',

The three bards thus portrayed are (respectively) MacDiarmid, Norman MacCaig (see below) and Sydney Goodsir Smith (see below). Sorley is Sorley MacLean (born 1911), the great Gaelic poet who taught at Boroughmuir School, Edinburgh, from 1943 to 1956.

Rebecca West

Cicily Isabel Fairfield (1892–1983) was born in London as the youngest of three daughters of Isabella McKenzie, a Scottish pianist, and Captain Charles Fairfield. After the death of her father the family moved to Edinburgh where she was educated at George Watson's Ladies College. She adopted her Ibsenesque pseudonym (from the heroine of *Rosmersholm*) in 1912, and published her second novel, *The Judge*, in 1922. The autobiographical heroine, Ellen Melville, is introduced as a 'wee typist' in Edinburgh, which is vividly described at twilight:

> She took her mind by the arm and marched it up and down among the sights of Edinburgh. . . . Now the Castle Esplanade, that all day had proudly supported the harsh, virile sounds and colours of the drilling regiments, would show to the slums its blank surface, bleached bone-white by the winds that raced above the city smoke. Now the Cowgate and the Canongate would be given over to the drama of the disorderly night; the slum-dwellers would foregather about the rotting doors of dead men's mansions and brawl among

the not less brawling ghosts of a past that here never speaks of peace, but only of blood and argument.

Albert Mackie

Albert Mackie (1904–85) was born on 18 December 1904 in Brunswick Road, near Easter Road, on the Edinburgh side of the boundary with Leith. He was brought up in Shaw's Square and Gayfield Street (both north of Calton Hill and Leith Walk) and in 34 North Castle Street (directly opposite Sir Walter Scott's house at No. 39) where he lived when he published his first book *Poems in Two Tongues* (1928). Educated at London Street Primary School, Broughton Secondary School and Edinburgh University, Mackie worked first as a schoolteacher then as a journalist, editing the *Edinburgh Evening Dispatch* from 1946 to 1954. Under the pseudonym 'Macnib' he contributed humorous poems to the *Edinburgh Evening News*.

J. K. Annand

J(ames) K(ing) Annand was born on 2 February 1908 at 11 Mackenzie Place; though Mackenzie Place no longer exists the house remains and is known as St Bernards' Cottage since it is the nearest building to St Bernard's Well on the banks of the Water of Leith (between Stockbridge and the Water of Leith village). In a letter of 28 May 1983 Annand writes:

> The house was virtually on the edge of a pocket of the countryside within the town. Many birds nested in our garden, and my father instilled in me an interest in nature with his visits to the western woods and shores of the town. Here too, began my interests in Scots language and traditions. Both my parents spoke Scots and my paternal granny who lived with us, told me old tales and rhymes. It was here that my first writings, as a schoolboy and student, were produced. I lived here until my marriage in 1936.

Annand was educated at Broughton Secondary School and Edinburgh University and subsequently supported himself by schoolteaching, mainly in Edinburgh. He lived at 1 Silverknowes Loan, Davidsons Mains, from 1936 to 1958; at 174 Craigleith Road from 1962 to 1980; and thereafter at 10 House O'Hill Row. Annand made his literary reputation as a distinguished writer of Scots verse for children in his collections *Sing it Aince for Pleasure* (1965), *Twice for Joy* (1974), and *Thrice to Show Ye* (1979).

116

Robert Garioch

In 1983 the Saltire Society put up a plaque at 4 Nelson Street, the home of Robert Garioch Sutherland (1909–81). Born in Edinburgh on 9 May 1909 Robert Garioch (he dropped the surname in his published work) spent most of his working life as a schoolteacher though, traumatically, he was a prisoner of war in Italy and Germany from 1942 to 1945 (an experience that informs his poem 'The Wire'). As an Edinburgh man, Garioch decided to take as his poetic model Robert Fergusson who had previously inspired the young Robert Burns. Like Fergusson, Garioch reflected the life of the city in his verse and he recorded his impressions and opinions in a series of Edinburgh sonnets that add up to a comic vision of Edinburgh. 'In Princes Street Gairdens' begins:

> Doun by the baundstaund, by the ice-cream barrie,
> there is a sait that says, Wilma is Fab.
> Sit doun aside me here and gieze your gab,
> just you and me, a dou, and a wee cock-sparrie.

Like his good friend Sydney Goodsir Smith (see below) Garioch enjoyed his evenings in the Rose Street pubs. He was also known, to various literary colleagues, as a superb brewer of his own ale.

George Bruce

In 1956 the poet George Bruce (born 1909), a BBC Producer from 1946 to 1970, moved from Aberdeen to Edinburgh where he settled in a Georgian house in 25 Warriston Crescent. His poem 'Houses' ends with a stanza about his Edinburgh home:

> Our house is different; it is very old,
> it creaks a bit in the wind,
> is water-tight now and then,
> comfortable for mice with good runways:
> it should do my time.

Norman MacCaig

Norman MacCaig was born on 14 November 1910 in London Street and, after an few months moved to Dundas Street where his father worked in, then owned, a chemist's shop. MacCaig was educated at the High School and at Edinburgh University where he read Classics (from 1928 to 1932). From 1934 to 1970 MacCaig earned his living as a teacher in Edinburgh and gradually built up a reputation as a subtle poet successfully using the metaphysical idiom to explore his own surroundings in Edinburgh and in Assynt (where he has a summer holiday home).

MacCaig's Edinburgh poems perceive the city from a singular point of view and the poet generally operates as an ironic observer. His most sustained meditation on Edinburgh, 'Inward Bound' from *The White Bird* (1973), is rich in reference to his upbringing in the city:

> Journeys. Mine were
> as wide as the world is
> from Puddocky to Stockbridge
> > minnows splinter in a jar
> > and a ten-inch yacht
> > in the roaring forties of Inverleith Pond
> > crumples like a handkerchief
> till the web enlarged
> > chocked once with a zeppelin
> > that dropped the beginning of the end of the world
> > on the Grassmarket.

MacCaig's home at 7 Leamington Terrace is a well-known literary address in Edinburgh for there he entertained his close friend Hugh MacDiarmid and there he has been host to many visiting writers.

Fred Urquhart

Novelist and storyteller Fred Urquhart was born on 12 July 1912 at 8 Palmerston Place where he spent the first three years of his life. The first born son of Frederick Burrows Urquhart, a chauffeur, and his wife Agnes Harrower, Urquhart came back to Edinburgh in 1919 to stay in 37 West Cottages, Granton: the cottages, situated between the middle and the west piers, were demolished before World War Two, but are featured in Urquhart's novel *Time Will Knit* (1938). Mirren, grandmother of Spike in the novel, tells herself 'You can't rear seven children in a three-roomed cottage on thirty shillings a week without finding out that life isn't a bed of roses.'

Urquhart lived in Granton from 1919–20 and returned to Edinburgh, after a period in Wigtonshire, to stay in two rooms on the top flat of 12 Queen Street for eighteen months from 1925. He remembers the General Strike taking place while living in Queen Street and attending Broughton Secondary School. After school and on Saturday mornings he had a job delivering parcels for a firm of tailors in George Street. In a letter of 19 June 1983 he writes:

> I got four shillings and sixpence a week for this [job], also a wide knowledge of Edinburgh. I travelled with parcels on tramcars as far afield as Portobello and Joppa, Morningside and Newington.
> Whenever possible, I used to walk long distances, to save the

tramfares so that I could use the few coppers to pay my way into the cheapest seats in picture houses like The Salon in Leith Walk, and The Savoy and The Grand in Stockbridge.

He later used the background of the tailors' shop in the story 'Sweet' collected in *I Fell for a Sailor* (1940).

Early in 1927 the Urquhart family moved into 1 Fraser Grove, Wardie, and in 1930 shifted to 10 Fraser Grove where his parents lived until his father died in 1958. In 1 Fraser Grove, Urquhart wrote two unpublished novels; in 10 Fraser Grove he wrote his first published short stories and his first published novel *Time Will Knit*.

Sydney Goodsir Smith

In his later years Sydney Goodsir Smith (1915–75) lived at 25 Drummond Place (where there is a plaque, with a relief of the poet's head) with his wife Hazel. Born in New Zealand in 1915, Smith arrived in Edinburgh (when his father became Professor of Forensic Medicine at the University) at the age of twelve. Henceforth he took the city to his heart and became, quite consciously, the boozy bard of Auld Reekie. His most characteristic theme was a dialogue between himself (usually with a glass in hand) and a personified Edinburgh. In 'Lament in the Second Winter of War' he wrote:

Auld Embro's bluid is thin, the bars 're toom	*empty*
An cauld is her fierce iren hert, her black banes	*bones*
Rigid wi cauld, the bluid's fell thin aneth the snaw.	

His affair with the personified city (note the image of Edinburgh, in *Under the Eildon Tree*, 'Flat on her back sevin nichts o' the week,/Earnan her breid wi her hurdies' sweit') was conducted with good humour and grace. Smith's masterpiece, the elegiac sequence *Under the Eildon Tree* (1948, revd 1954), involves the poet in various adventures as 'Smith the Slugabed' counterpoints his own misfortunes with those of legendary lovers.

Edinburgh is omnipresent in three conversational poems published by Smith. *The Vision of the Prodigal Son* (1960) finds the poet celebrating the 200th birthday of Burns in reflective mood before the poem dissolves into a pubscape, a territory well known to Smith. *Kynd Kittock's Land* (1965), a television poem, is Smith's guided tour of the city he so lovingly adopted.

> This rortie city
> Built on history
> Built on history
> Born of feud and enmity

The third conversational poem, *Gowdspink in Reekie* (1974), is an irreverent meditation on Goldsmith's 'Where Wealth Accumulates and Men Decay'. Inevitably, Smith finds himself in a pub:

> I cannae mind the howff, in Rose Street onyweys,
> The 'Abbotsford' maybe or 'Daddy Milne's' –
> But we were standing at the bar . . .

These poems give some of the quality of Smith's personality for he was a familiar figure in the Rose Street pubs and known as a man of great charm, immense fun and fascinating conversation. When he lived in 25 Drummond Place he frequented the bar of the Drummond Hotel on Sundays.

In Smith's high-spirited novel *Carotid Cornucopius* (1964) the heroine, Colickie Meg, gives birth to a daughter at **Portobello** in one of the most memorable scenes of the book. With his penchant for puns Smith first sets the scene on 'the gowden sands of Pottiebellie'. Colickie Meg and Jock O'Leerie, the father of the child, go out on the sea in a boat (or 'boatle') and she feels the pains beginning (or 'the puns begunning').

> At this megicull mamberment, at the fairy seacunt of tume that the
> bibbie Aphrobridgetie Dampobottomie slud like an aell or
> merrimaide frae ute Meg's swooming wambe, flickering lythlie as an
> angel-shrimp thorough the jawing yetts of Megma Mater to seek the
> wattery rowme of Faither Learie, then Plewviose and Sol were in their
> splenitude, ilkane in his grandier gied all . . .

Smith notes that 'there was a hjailuva din and seeliberotion all ovair Portibellio for the bairth of Bride'.

Muriel Spark

Muriel Spark was born Muriel Sarah Camberg in 1918 in Edinburgh which figures in her verse ('Litany of Time Past' refers to a chant remembered from childhood) as well as her fiction. She was brought up in Bruntsfield Place and, as an imaginative girl who composed poems from the age of nine, spent her free hours in Morningside Public Library. 'Edinburgh', she wrote, 'had an effect on my mind, my prose style and my ways of thought.' Her best-selling novel *The Prime of Miss Jean Brodie* (1961) follows the heroine as she takes her special set of chosen girls on a walk through the old parts of Edinburgh. While they are walking it occurs to Sandy Stranger – the girl who eventually betrays Miss Brodie to the headmistress of Marcia Blaine School (modelled on James Gillespie's School for Girls where Mrs Spark was educated in Edinburgh) – that 'the Brodie set was Miss Brodie's fascisti'. As Miss Brodie brings these respectable girls into the recesses of the Old Town they come to the Grassmarket whose appearance in the 1930s is vividly conveyed by Spark:

Now they were in a great square, the Grassmarket, with the Castle, which was in any case everywhere, rearing between a big gap in the houses where the aristocracy used to live. It was Sandy's first experience of a foreign country, which intimates itself by its new smells and shapes and its new poor. A man sat on the icy-cold pavement; he just sat. A crowd of children, some without shoes, were playing some fight game, and some boys shouted after Miss Brodie's violet-clad company, with words that the girls had not heard before, but rightly understood to be obscene. Children and women with shawls came in and out of the dark closes.

Joan Lingard

Joan Lingard was born in Edinburgh, left the city at the age of two to live in Belfast (which provides the background for her 1970 novel *The Lord on Our Side*) then resettled in Edinburgh at the age of eighteen. Her second novel, *The Prevailing Wind* (1964) is set in the Marchmont district of Edinburgh, drawing on Lingard's experience as a student living in Warrender Park Terrace in the 1950s. In the book the heroine, Janet Robertson, returns to Edinburgh with her daughter Sally and looks for a place to live:

> First she went to Marchmont, the Mecca of bed-sitters. A notice in the window of a ground floor flat said: *Accommodation.* . . . The room was gloomy. Thick net curtains clung to the windows and at their sides hung thick brown drapes, unpleasant to the touch. . . . The walls were dun coloured, the ceiling had no colour at all; the furniture was sparse but heavy and the divan beds sagged under scratchy grey blankets. The kitchenette was a cupboard; it contained two gas rings and a shelf with a hole which held a polythene basin. The walls were spattered with grease.

The Headmaster (1967), Lingard's fourth novel, is set in the Grange, on the south side of Edinburgh, and the year she completed it she found a house in Chalmers Crescent, on the edge of the Grange, so (said Lingard in a letter of 16 May 1983) 'it was a case of life following art'. Edinburgh is also present in *A Sort of Freedom* (1969); *The Gooseberry* (1978), a children's novel set in the Stockbridge area; and *The Second Flowering of Emily Mountjoy* (1979).

EDNAM, Roxburghshire   (Border)   2m N of Kelso on A699

James Thomson

Son of the parish minister, James Thomson (1700–48) was born in the former manse at Ednam on 11 September 1700 and is commemorated by a monument on Ferny Hill, just beyond the village. He attended school in Jedburgh and studied divinity at Edinburgh University. When his Professor condemned the imaginative tone of his sermons, he abandoned his religious calling and moved to London, in 1725, to work as a tutor and develop as a writer – in the company of Pope, Gay and other colleagues. Thomson's majestic sequence *The Seasons* (1730) established him as a major Augustan poet and a master of natural description. 'Winter' has an almost Wordsworthian wealth of detail:

> The loosened ice,
> Lets down the flood, and half dissolved by day,
> Rustles no more; but to the sedgy bank
> Fast grows, or gathers round the pointed stone,
> A crystal pavement, by the breath of heaven
> Cemented firm.

Thomson wrote the song 'Rule Britannia' for *The Masque of Alfred* (1740).

Francis Lyte

'Abide With Me' was, like 'Rule Britannia', the work of a native of Ednam. Francis Lyte (1793–1847). the hymnist who wrote 'Praise, My Soul, the King of Heaven' as well as 'Abide With Me', was born in a house (gone) by the Eden Water. He is commemorated by a plaque (of 1952) on Ednam Bridge where supporters of the Old Pretender gathered in 1715.

EILEAN AIGAS, River Beauly,   Inverness-shire   (Highland)

John Sobieski Stolberg Stuart, Charles Edward Stuart

In 1838 John Sobieski Stolberg Stuart (1795–1872) and Charles Edward Stuart (1799–1880) settled on Eilean Aigas, in a shooting lodge built for them by Lord Lovat. On this islet on the River Beauly, the two brothers completed their massive catalogue on tartans, *Vestiarium Scoticum* (1842) which is more impressive for its inventiveness than its authenticity. Nevertheless, many of the imaginary tartans they concocted are still worn as the genuine articles. As well as devising tartans for Scottish clans, the Stuart brothers claimed to be descended from Prince Charles Edward Stuart.

Sir Compton Mackenzie

Sir Compton Mackenzie leased the lodge from 1931 to 1933 and writes, in the seventh volume of his autobiography *My Life and Times* (10 vols, 1963–71):

> The carriage drive up to the house was on the other side of a bridge under which the Beauly came foaming and leaping from the gorge that separated Eilean Aigas on one side from the mainland. Once it had emerged from that gorge between sheer cliffs it flowed round the other side of the island as gently as sweet Afton itself. There the woodland with its undergrowth of rhododendrons and azaleas sloped down to a level green bank whitened with lilies-of-the-valley in their season. At the narrowing northerly end the river flowed in from the torrential gorge as placidly as a pool and it was shallow enough to wade in and search for the mussels in which one sometimes had the luck to find a sizable pearl.

Mackenzie put a billiards-table in what had been the Stuart brothers' library and worked – on, for example, *Water on the Brain* (1933) – in a den beyond. He later looked back to his time on Eilean Aigas as 'one of the golden ages I have enjoyed in my life'.

ELDERSLIE, Renfrewshire (Strathclyde) 2½m W of Paisley, off A373

Elderslie is traditionally the birthplace of Sir William Wallace (*c.* 1270–1305), the Scottish patriot whose exploits inspired writers from Blin Harry the Minstrel, author of *Wallace* (written around 1477); to Sydney Goodsir Smith, whose play *The Wallace* was successfully staged at the Edinburgh International Festivals of 1960 and 1985. A **Wallace Memorial** stands at the west entrance to the town.

John MacDougall Hay

John MacDougall Hay (1881–1919), author of *Gillespie* (1914), became minster at Elderslie in 1909, the year he married Catherine Campbell (daughter of a minister). *Gillespie* was probably first drafted around 1907 and completed at Elderslie.

George Campbell Hay

John MacDougall Hay's son George Campbell Hay (1915–84) was born in The Manse, Elderslie. Hay was educated at Oxford where he studied modern languages. During the Second World War he served in North Africa and had a mental breakdown attempting unsuccessfully to get out of the army. He wrote fluently in Gaelic, Scots and English and his lyrical gift is seen to advantage in 'The Old Fisherman' (which was memorably set to music by Francis George Scott):

> The old boat must seek the shingle,
> her wasting side hollow the gravel,
> the hand that shakes must leave the tiller;
> my dancing days for fishing are over.

Hay was, in his later years, sometimes incapacitated by his depressive illness. For a while he returned to Tarbert, where he spent his childhood, but eventually moved to Edinburgh (6 Maxwell Street) where he died on 25 March 1984.

ELGIN, Moray   (Grampian)   On A96

Elgin, the administrative and commercial capital of the District of Moray, has a celebrated Cathedral, founded in 1224 as the seat of the Diocese of Moray. It was burned by the Wolf of Badenoch, son of Robert II, in 1390. Rebuilt, it was in use until the Reformation then, in 1567, the lead was stripped from the roof by order of the Privy Council (and Regent Moray) and deterioration began. The great central tower fell in 1711 and by the end of the eighteenth century the Cathedral was being used as a quarry for building stone.

Dr Samuel Johnson, James Boswell

Dr Samuel Johnson and James Boswell visited Elgin, and its cathedral, on Thursday 26 August 1773, as both men noted in separate accounts. Johnson, in *A Journey to the Western Islands of Scotland* (1774), wrote:

> The ruins of the cathedral of Elgin afforded us another proof of the waste of reformation. There is enough yet remaining to shew, that it was once magnificent. Its whole plot is easily traced. On the north side of the choir, the chapter-house, which is roofed with an arch of stone, remains entire; and on the south side, another mass of building, which we could not enter, is preserved by the care of the family of Gordon; but the body of the church is a mass of fragments.

Boswell, in *The Journal of a Tour to the Hebrides* (1785), added:

We dined at Elgin, and saw the noble ruins of the cathedral. Though it rained much, Dr Johnson examined them with a most patient attention. He could not here feel any abhorrence at the Scottish reformers, for he had been told by Lord Hailes, that it was destroyed before the Reformation, by the Lord of Badenoch, who had a quarrel with the bishop. The bishop's house, and those of the other clergy, which are still pretty entire, do not seem to have been proportioned to the maginficence of the cathedral, which has been of great extent, and had very fine carved work.

The Cathedral is open to the public.

Andrew Young

The poet Andrew Young (1885–1971) was born in Elgin on 29 April 1885 and in 1981 his daughter, Mrs Alison Lowbury, unveiled a plaque at Elgin railway station marking the site of his birth. The plaque is situated on the exterior wall of the passenger station which stands on the site of the old stationmaster's house where Young was born when his father was stationmaster. Young was educated in Edinburgh where he studied theology; in 1939 he risked the wrath of his ninety-three-year old Presbyterian father by entering the Anglican Church as Vicar of Stonegate, Sussex. Young retired from his ministry in 1959 and, already a Canon of Chichester Cathedral, settled in the village of Yapton, near Chichester.

The *Poetical Works* of Andrew Young, edited by Alison (Young) Lowbury and her husband Edward Lowbury, show some local associations. 'Memorial Verses' (1918) commemorates the poet's friend: Cecil Barclay Simpson, minister of Elgin's Moss Street Church, who was killed in October 1917 on active service in France. 'Culbin Sands' has a regional relevance for at Culbin, on the coast between Nairn and Elgin, a sandstorm of 1694 buried fields and houses, leaving a desert where there had been a community.

Hilton Brown

Hilton Brown (1890–1961) was the son of the procurator fiscal at Elgin and lived at 23 Hay Street. He was educated at Elgin Academy and St Andrews University before entering the Indian Civil Service in 1913. He published *A Study of Kipling* in 1945. Later he settled in Kenya and died in Nairobi.

James Wood

The novelist James Wood (1919–84) was born in Elgin where his mother, Margaret, kept a gown shop on the corner of South Street and Gordon Street. He published more than two dozen novels (mainly between 1950 and 1970). After working as a revenue assistant with the Customs and Excise in Speyside, he retired and was living at 2 Gordon Street at the time of his death.

Jessie Kesson

Jessie Kesson (born 1916 in Inverness) grew up in Kelby's Close (demolished), off the High Street of Elgin: it was one of a group of closes beneath Ladyhill. Before going at the age of eight to Skene Orphanage, Aberdeenshire, her childhood world was shaped by the dimensions of Kelby's Close. In her novel *The White Bird Passes* (1958) she draws on her memories of Elgin and features Kelby's Close as Our Lady's Lane:

> [Our] Lady's Lane was a tributary of High Street, one of many such tributaries of long, narrow wynds that slunk backwards from the main street, gathering themselves into themselves, like a group of women assuring each other proudly, 'We keep ourselves to ourselves', and, at the same time, usually knowing more than most people of what is going on around.
> If you rushed down High Street in a hurry, you wouldn't notice Lady's Lane at all, so narrowly and darkly does it skulk itself away, but Lady's Lane would most certainly see you.

It is this enclosed world that Janie (the autobiographical heroine) tries to make sense of as she grows up in the somewhat red light of her mother Liza and in the shadow left by a father she had never seen. When Janie's mother attracts the attentions of the authorities the child (like Jessie Kesson herself) is sent to an orphanage.

In the mid-1940s Jessie Kesson settled, with her husband and daughter, at Linksfield Farm Cottage, Elgin. Subsequently she moved to London.

ELLISLAND, Dumfriesshire   (Dumfries and Galloway)   6m N of Dumfries on A76

Robert Burns

In the summer of 1787 Robert Burns (1759–96) went to Dumfriesshire to look over **Ellisland farm**, six miles north of Dumfries, which had been offered to him at a moderate rent by an admirer Patrick Miller. Though the farm's position on the River Nith was visually attractive Burns was experienced enough to suspect its agricultural viability. Visiting the farm the following year, with a friend, he was advised to accept the seventy-seven-year lease at an initial rent of £50 per year. Burns was now a married man, having set up house as man and wife with Jean Armour in Mauchline, in February 1788 when he was in the town to take three weeks' Excise instruction. Whether the Excise insisted he become a married man or whether Burns felt he needed a reliable woman to look after his newly leased farm, the fact is that Jean was to make him a devoted, if undemanding, wife. She represented the peasant reality he knew, whereas sophisticated Edinburgh ladies such as Agnes McLehose were unpredictable and often bewildering.

Ellisland, on the west bank of the Nith, was 'a poet's choice, not a farmer's'. Burns soon found the soil was too exhausted to support crops. He had seen Mount Oliphant and Lochlea farms help kill his father, while brother Gilbert was only able to keep Mossgiel going because Robert lent him about half the money he got for the Edinburgh edition of his poems. Now Burns was stuck with a farm 'in the last stage of worn-out poverty'. Little wonder that while his farmhouse was being built, Burns made frequent visits to Jean fifty miles away at Mossgiel and that

> Of a' the airts the wind can blaw   *directions*
>   I dearly like the west,
> For there the bonie lassie lives,
>   The lassie I lo'e best.
>
> There wild woods grow, and rivers row,
>   And monie a hill between,
> But day and night my fancy's flight
>   Is ever wi' my Jean.

From the vantage point of Ellisland farm, the summer sun sinks towards Mossgiel.

Burn's certificate of competence for the Excise was issued in July 1788 and in September of the following year he began his arduous duties. This meant that in addition to running Ellisland farm, Burns had to cover about 200 miles per week on horseback, often in pouring rain. He had to provide his own horse, do his own books at night and for this work he got £50 a year, half the goods seized, and £50 per arrested smuggler. Not surprisingly, considering the rewards, he was good at his job, going in for the big fish and overlooking the petty tax evasions of the poor.

He was also a 'kind and indulgent master' at Ellisland. One of his farmworkers recalled how he would help with the ploughing and sowing and how he would pour his men a dram of whisky as an additional reward for extra work. At home he 'usually wore a broad blue bonnet, a blue or drab long-tailed coat, corduroy breeches, dark-blue stockings, and *cootikens*, and in cold weather a black-and-white checked plaid wrapped round his shoulders'.

A mile north of Ellisland farm, at Friar's Carse, the home of Captain Robert Riddell of Glenriddell, there was always a warm welcome for Burns. An amateur of the arts, Captain Riddell gave Burns a key to the little Hermitage on the estate where he might meditate and compose poetry (a kind but largely impractical thought considering how Burns's time was taken up by Excise work). It was at Friar's Carse that Burns met the corpulent antiquarian Captain Francis Grose researching for a book on the *Antiquities of Scotland*. Burns got on well with this 'fine, fat, fodgel wight/O' stature short but genius bright' and asked him to include an illustration of Kirk Alloway (where his father was buried) in his book. Grose agreed, on condition that Burns provide a witch story to accompany the drawing. A letter to Grose beginning 'On a market day, in the town of Ayr, a farmer from Carrick . . .' (see p. 35) contains the narrative germ of 'Tam O' Shanter'. Burns is supposed to have composed the poem, in a fury of creativity, in one day's absence from the Excise, while pacing the path at Ellisland overlooking the Nith. Visitors to Ellisland farm can follow the poet's footsteps on **Shanter Walk** where Burns wrote his best-known narrative poem in the autumn of 1790. Before Burns was released from the Ellisland lease in September 1791 (whereupon he moved to Dumfries) he had contributed such lyrics as 'Auld Lang Syne' and 'A Red, Red Rose' to James Johnson's *Scots Musical Museum* (1787–1803). At Ellisland too, in 1788, he wrote 'On Seeing a Wounded Hare Limp by Me which a Fellow Had Just shot At' which ends by combining a lament and a curse:

> Oft as by winding Nith I musing, wait
> The sober eve, or hail the cheerful dawn,
> I'll miss thee sporting o'er the dewy lawn,
> And curse the ruffian's aim, and mourn thy hapless fate.

ERISKAY, Outer Hebrides   (Western Isles)

Sir Compton Mackenzie

With its 'low green land and white beaches', Eriskay features as Little Todday in Compton Mackenzie's novel *Whisky Galore* (1947). In fact, Eriskay lies to the north-east of Barra; in Mackenzie's fiction Little Todday lies west of the larger island. *Whisky Galore* opens in 1943 with the people of Little Todday lamenting the lack of whisky owing to wartime restrictions; there has not been a drop of whisky on the island for twelve days. Suddenly, like manna from heaven, whisky is delivered on (as it were) the islanders' doorstep when the *SS Cabinet Minister*, carrying a cargo of 50,000 cases of whisky, strikes a reef in the Minch. The islanders are quick to use all their native ingenuity to dispose of the drink in the most suitable way. Mackenzie based his novel on an actual event. In February 1941 the *SS Politician*, a ship considered fast enough to outrun the U-boats in the Atlantic, foundered on a reef in the Sound of Eriskay with her cargo of 264,750 bottles of whisky. Inevitably the men of Eriskay illegally salvaged the drink. Mackenzie (who built a bungalow on Barra in 1934) changed one local detail for comic effect. Eriskay is a Roman Catholic island whereas Little Todday is depicted as a Presbyterian stronghold. This causes problems as the islanders are obliged to observe the Sabbath – the day on which the *SS Cabinet Minister* is wrecked.

ERRAID, Argyllshire   (Strathclyde)

Robert Louis Stevenson

Erraid is a tidal island off the south-west tip of Mull. Robert Louis Stevenson (1850–94) spent three weeks on the isle in the summer of 1870 while his father supervised the construction of the lighthouse on Dhu Hearteach with local stone. In *Kidnapped* (1886) Stevenson has the kidnapped David Balfour shipwrecked on Erraid, an experience he finds alarming (as the author explains in the fourteenth chapter of the novel):

> Earraid . . . is nothing but a jumble of granite rocks with heather in among. . . . The time I spent upon the island is still so horrible a thought to me, that I must pass it lightly over. . . . All day it streamed rain; the island ran like a sop; there was no dry spot to be found; and when I lay down that night, between two boulders that made a kind of roof, my feet were in a bog.
>
> The second day I crossed the island to all sides. There was no one part of it better than another; it was all desolate and rocky; nothing living on it but game birds which I lacked the means to kill, and the gulls which haunted the outlying rocks in a prodigious number.

After four days it dawns on David (thanks to signals from fisherman in the Sound) that Erraid is a tidal island and that he can easily cross to Mull at the right moment.

There is presently a small community on Erraid.

ETTRICK, Selkirkshire   (Border)   16m SE of Selkirk, off B709

James Hogg

James Hogg (1770–1835), the Ettrick Shepherd, was born at Ettrickhill farm. His birthplace is gone but marked by a 20ft monument with a bronze portrait medallion. In a letter of 22 July 1802 to Sir Walter Scott – included in Hogg's *Highland Tours* (1981) – Hogg describes his native place:

I must tell you what sort of a place Etterick is. . . . The name Etterick is of great antiquity. The Gaelic term, from which I am told it is derived, hath some reference to darkness; and it is believed to have been descriptive of sylvan scenery, rather of a dismal nature – probably in the near neighbourhood of the parish church, as it is there only that sundry places are thus particularized as Old Etterick-hill, Etterick-house, Etterick-hall, Etterick-pen, although the whole country is termed Etterick Forest.

The hills are generally of a beautiful deep green, thick covered with sheep, though no-wise rugged or tremendous. The highest is Phauppenn, which rises 2,370 feet above the level of the sea. The view from the top of this mountain is very extensive to the south and east, but northwards is immediately intercepted by the interposition of Hertfell and the White Coom, betwixt which the palm has been disputed as the highest in Scotland south of the Forth – though it certainly belongs to the latter. Its elevation above the sea being 2,840 feet. . . .

The river Etterick taketh its rise five miles SSE of the village of Moffat and runs a course of 30 miles. About a mile anda half above Selkirk it is augmented one half by the tribute of its sister Yarrow; and as far below that ancient burgh, the Tweed is increased nearly one half by these united streams.

The two rivers, Etterick and Yarrow, form properly what is called Etterick Forest – which was the Sylva Caledonia of the ancients and is now the Arcadia of Britain, the whole scene, life and manners of the inhabitants being truly pastoral.

It was John Wilson who featured Hogg as 'The Ettrick Shepherd' in his 'Noctes Ambrosianae' in *Blackwood's Magazine* (from 1822 to 1835). Hogg's early years were passed in farm service and he became a shepherd, in Yarrow, at the age of twenty. He achieved success with his poetic sequence *The Queen's Wake* (1813). His novel *The Private Memoirs and Confessions of a Justified Sinner* (1824) is one of the masterpieces of Scottish fiction.

FAILFORD, Ayrshire   (Strathclyde)   2m E of Mauchline on A758

Robert Burns

Failford, where the Water of Fail flows into the River Ayr, plays a crucial part in the story of Robert Burns (1759–96) and his Highland Mary. A footbridge, in the centre of the village, leads to a grassy mound and monument supposed to mark the exact spot where Burns bid farewell to Mary Campbell (1763–86).

Like many of his contemporaries Robert Burns frequently thought of seeking his fortunes overseas from Scotland. In 1786 he had good reason to contemplate a new life: he got a girl, Jean Armour, pregnant and had been rejected as a possible son-in-law by a man who disliked his behaviour and deplored his lack of prospects. Accordingly Burns accepted a job as a plantation book-keeper in Jamaica and turned his bruised affections to another girl – Mary Campbell, a Coilsfield dairy-maid who had worked as a nursemaid in the Mauchline home of the poet's friend Gavin Hamilton. On the second Sunday of May 1786 Burns and Highland Mary met 'in a sequestered spot by the banks of Ayr'. Over the Fail Water they clasped hands and plighted their troth by exchanging bibles. (The bible Burns gave to Mary is preserved in the Burns Monument at Alloway.) Then, as Burns put it, they 'spent the day in taking farewell, before she should embark for the West Highlands to arrange matters among her friends for our projected change of life'. The scene is recreated in Burns's 'Will Ye Go to the Indies, My Mary' which ends:

> O plight me your faith, my Mary,
>   And plight me your lily-white hand;
> O plight me your faith, my Mary,
>   Before I leave Scotia's strand.
>
> We hae plighted our troth, my Mary,
>   In mutual affection to join;
> And curst be the cause that shall part us!
>   The hour, and the moment o' time!

It seems that Burns and Mary intended to marry and emigrate to Jamaica together: the publication of Burns's first book would alleviate his financial worries for he was well on the way to raising the necessary subscriptions. *Poems, Chiefly in the Scottish Dialect*, published on 31 July 1786, was an immediate success. Burns was scheduled to meet Mary at Greenock in September so they could both sail for Kingston: meanwhile he went to Mossgiel farm where he heard that Jean Armour had given birth to twins. Then, from Greenock, came the shattering news of Mary's death – Burns claimed she died from a 'malignant fever' but there is a possibility she died in childbirth. Suddenly the journey to Jamaica seemed pointless and Burns headed, instead, for Edinburgh where he was lionised as a cultural phenomenon. Burns lamented, in 'Highland Mary',

> O, pale, pale now, those rosy lips
> I aft hae kiss'd sae fondly;
> And clos'd for ay, the sparkling glance
> That dwalt on me sae kindly;
> And mouldering now in silent dust
> That heart that lo'ed me dearly!
> But still within my bosom's core
> Shall live my Highland Mary.

FALKIRK, Stirlingshire   (Central)   11m SSE of Stirling

Robert Burns

Robert Burns (1759–96) made two visits to Falkirk. On 25 August 1787 he and his friend William Nicol stayed at the Cross Keys Inn, High Street. A plaque was unveiled on 25 June 1889 commemorating his visit and is still set in the wall of the building, now 187 High Street. On his first visit Burns was refused admission to the Carron Ironworks (established in 1759) but was admitted on a subsequent visit in October 1787. The works, to the north of the town near Carron bridge, went into receivership in 1982.

Robert Buchanan

Robert Buchanan (1835–75), the local poet of Falkirk, was born in the Steeple area of Falkirk on 22 June 1835. He was apprenticed as a carrier to his uncle, John Gillespie, whose shop was at the foot of Bell's Wynd. Later he worked as an exciseman at Grangemouth; he died in Londonderry on 31 December 1875. Buchanan contributed prose and poetry to the *Falkirk Herald* and his work was collected as *Poems, Songs and Other Writings by Robert Buchanan, Falkirk* (1901). A monument was erected in Falkirk cemetery to Buchanan's memory in 1899

Francis George Scott

Francis George Scott (1880–1958), the composer who was an important influence on the modern Scottish Literary Renaissance, was a teacher of English at the Northern School, Falkirk, where he served a probationary period of two years from September 1901, gaining his certificate, after which he was promoted to the newly opened Carmuirs Public School, Camelon, Falkirk. Scott left Falkirk to teach at Langholm Academy where one of his pupils was Christopher Murray Grieve, better known in later years as the poet Hugh MacDiarmid.

James Wedgewood Drawbell

James Wedgewood Drawbell (1899–1979), the novelist, was born in Falkirk and died in Edinburgh. His autobiography *The Sun Within Us* (1963) contains descriptions of Falkirk at the beginning of the century.

FALKLAND, Fife (Fife) 11m N of Kirkcaldy on A912

The great glory of Falkland is Falkland Palace, an imposing example of sixteenth-century French Renaissance architecture. It was completed from 1530 to 1540 on the instructions of James V: the tennis court, built in 1539 and still in use, indicates the king's interest in the game. It was to Falkland Palace that James V came after the disastrous defeat of the Scots at Solway Moss (24 November 1542). His last days are described in Antonia Fraser's biography *Mary Queen of Scots* (1969):

> From [Linlithgow] he went to Falkland, the beloved palace which he had built for himself in admiration of the French Renaissance, and which like an animal now he chose as his lair in which to die. Incapable of digesting the disasters of his hopes, his personal humiliation and the humiliations of his country, the king now underwent a complete nervous collapse. . . . Into this sad sick-room came a messenger from Linlithgow who brought the news that the queen had been confined, and given birth to a daughter. The onlookers hoped that the king's sorrow might be somewhat alleviated by the fact that he now had an heir once more. But the king observed cynically: 'Adieu, fare well, it came with a lass, it will pass with a lass'. . . . Six days later, on 14 December King James was dead at the age of thirty.

Born on 8 December 1542, Mary was just one week old when she became Queen of a newly defeated Scotland and, as John Knox observed in his *History of the Reformation in Scotland* (1586), 'All men lamented that the realm was left without a male to succeed.'

David Herd

Falkland folklore insists that the walled garden of the palace is haunted by Jenny Nettles, the heroine of a song collected in *Ancient and Modern Scottish Songs* (1776) by David Herd (1732–1810):

I met ayont the cairnie
Jenny Nettles. Jenny Nettles
Singing til her bairnie
Robin Rattles bastard
To fleet the dool upon the stool   *remove, sorrow*
And ilka ane that mocks her
She round about seeks Robin out
To stap it in his oxter

It seems that this folksong was founded on fact and that a real Jenny Nettles took her own life rather than endure the social disgrace of illegitimacy. After being deserted by her lover she committed suicide near the foot of the Ochil Hills, a spot now marked by a cairn.

Using lines from the song of Jenny Nettles, Hugh MacDiarmid constructed the first quatrain of his lyric 'Empty Vessel' in *Penny Wheep* (1926):

I met ayong the cairney
A lass wi' tousie hair
Singin' til a bairnie
That was nae langer there.

William Dunbar

The most celebrated character associated with Falkland is Kynd Kittock, the heroine of the 'The Ballad of Kynd Kittock', a poem often attributed to William Dunbar (1460–1520). As the first stanza explains, Kynd Kittock was known for her astonishing thirst when she lived in Falkland which the poem places, for comic effect, in France:

My Guddame was a gay wife, but she was richt gend.   *simple*
  She dwelt furth far into France, upon Falkland Fell.
They callit her Kynd Kittock, whasae her weill kend.   *knew her well*
  She was, like a cauldron cruke, clear under kell.
                 she was as beautiful under hat as a pot-hook
They threepit that she deeit of thirst, and made a gude end.

After dying of thirst, Kynd Kittock heads for an alehouse near heaven:

  Sae she had hap to be horsit to her herbry   *lodging*
    At an ailhouse near hevin, it nichtit them there.
  She deeit of thirst in this warld, that gert her be so dry; *caused*
    She never ate, but drank owre meisure and mair.   over

Sneaking past Saint Peter, Kynd Kittock makes her way into heaven and lives a good life. However she finds the ale of heaven sour and returns to the alehouse to get a fresh drink. When she comes back to heaven's gate, Saint Peter hits her with a club:

> Then to the ailhouse again she ran, the pitchers to pour,
>> And for to brew and to bake.
>> Freindis, I pray you hertfully.
>> Gif ye be thirsty or dry,
>> Drink with my guddame, as ye gae by,
> Anys for my sake.   *once*

Mrs Brown of Falkland

The most celebrated of ballad singers was Mrs Brown of Falkland who learned ballads from the singing of three women: her mother, her nurse, and her aunt Anne Farquharson. She was born Anna Gordon (1747–1810) in Aberdeen where her father Thomas was Professor of Humanity at King's College. She later married the Rev. Andrew Brown, minister at Falkland. Francis James Child, editor of *The English and Scottish Popular Ballads* (1882–98), said 'No Scottish ballads are superior in kind to those recited in the last century by Mrs Brown, of Falkland'. She preserved thirty-three ballads, with variations, and all of them were canonised by Child, who made twenty of them A texts and four of them B texts.

FALLS OF BRUAR, Perthshire   (Tayside)   3m W of Blair Atholl on A9

Robert Burns

The Falls of Bruar, where Bruar Water flows into the Garry three miles west of Blair Atholl, was visited by Robert Burns on Sunday 2 September 1787. After spending two of the happiest days of his life at Blair Castle, the seat of the Duke of Atholl, Burns left on Monday 3 September and continued his Highland Tour with his friend William Nicol. Reaching Inverness on 5 September, Burns wrote to Josiah Walker (later Professor Walker of Glasgow University), tutor to the Duke of Atholl's family, and enclosed 'the effusion of a half-hour I spent at Bruar. I do not mean it was *extempore*, for I have endeavoured to brush it up as well as Mr Nicol's chat and the jogging of the chaise would allow.' The poem, 'The Humble Petition of Bruar Water to the Noble Duke of Athole', is a plea by the water for shade:

> Here, foaming down the skelvy rocks.   *shelvy*
>> In twisting strength I rin;
> There high my boiling torrent smokes,

Wild-roaring o'er a linn: *fall*
Enjoying large each spring and well,
  As Nature gave them me,
I am, altho' I say't myself,
  Worth gaun a mile to see.

Would, then, my noble master please
  To grant my highest wishes,
He'll shade my banks wi' tow'ring trees
  And bonie spreading bushes.
Delighted doubly then, my lord,
  You'll wander on my banks,
And listen monie a grateful bird
  Return you tuneful thanks.

In response to this plea, the Duke of Atholl had firs planted at the Falls of Bruar. Later plantings, replacing the Duke's firs, keep the area green.

FALLS OF LEDARD, Perthshire (Central) W of Loch Ard, off B829

Sir Walter Scott

In Sir Walter Scott's *Waverley* (1814), the Highland chieftain Fergus MacIvor describes Edward Waverley as 'a worshipper of the Celtic muse' when he introduces the Englishman to his sister, Flora MacIvor. Flora, a prominent translator of Gaelic poetry, agrees to recite to Waverley and arranges to meet him at her Highland Helicon so he can appreciate the atmospheric scenery appropriate to the Celtic muse. Thus Waverley is directed to 'a romantic waterfall':

It was not so remarkable either for great height or quantity of water, as for the beautiful accompaniments which made the spot interesting. After a broken cataract of about twenty feet, the stream was received in a large natural basin filled to the brim with water, which, where the bubbles of the fall subsided, was so exquisitely clear, that although it was of great depth, the eye could discern each pebble at the bottom. Eddying round this reservoir, the brook found its way as if over a broken part of the ledge, and formed a second fall, which seemed to seek the very abyss; then, wheeling out beneath from among the smooth dark rocks, which it had polished for ages, it wandered murmuring down the glen, forming the stream up which Waverley had just ascended.

In a note to the novel, Scott identified his romantic waterfall as the Falls of Ledard which he considered 'one of the most exquisite cascades it is possible to behold'. Flora performed her recitation for Waverley at a short distance from the waterfall so that its sound 'should rather accompany than interrupt that of her voice and [small Scottish harp]'.

FOREST MILL SCHOOL, Forest Mill   (Central)   6m W of Alloa on B913

Michael Bruce

In summer 1766 the poet Michael Bruce (1746–67) took a teaching job at Forest Mill School, near Alloa. While making this journey Bruce's pony stumbled in the Black Devon river and the consumptive poet was soaked. His health was not improved by the damp building used as a school. It was at Forest Mill that Bruce wrote his longest poem, 'Lochleven', which ends with a bitter description of his circumstances at the time: 'Thus sung the youth, amid unfertile wilds/And nameless deserts, unpoetic ground.' Bruce left Forest Mill in February 1767 and walked a distance of more than twenty miles to his native Kinnesswood. The present Forest Mill School is in the original two-room building which has been upgraded over the years. There is a plaque in honour of Michael Bruce on the adjacent schoolhouse front wall.

FORFAR, Angus   (Tayside)   12m N of Dundee on A94

A. S. Neill

A. S. Neill (1883–1975), the radical educationist who founded the International School, Hellerau, Dresden, in 1921, was born in 16 East High Street, Forfar on 17 October, 1883. When he subsequently set up his school at Summerhill at Leiston, Suffolk, he became internationally known as an eloquently anti-authoritarian voice in education. His books include *The Problem Child* (1926), *The Problem Parent* (1932), and *Summerhill* (1962). In *Neill! Neill! Orange Peel!* (1973) Neill writes: 'it gives me no thrill to imagine that one day in my native town of Forfar some town council may put up a brass plate on the house in which I was born'. When Neill was eight his father took the family to live in the schoolhouse at Kingsmuir, two miles from Forfar.

FORTH BRIDGES

Hugh MacDiarmid

Hugh MacDiarmid (Christopher Murray Grieve, 1892–1978) moved to Forfar in 1913 to work on the *Forfar Review*. In a letter of 20 August 1916 to George Ogilvie, Grieve wrote:

> Forfar is the booziest place in Earth [though] a sudden access of unaccountably good sense made me take a house, four miles in the country by Glamis Castle way, and invite my mother to keep house for me. The result was eminently satisfactory. I had an easy and well-paid job: my mother had claims upon my time which kept me out of 'company' in my spare time, and I had peace to write.

FORTH BRIDGES, Firth of Forth   Connecting Lothian and Fife

The Forth Rail Bridge, designed on the cantilever principle by John Fowler and Benjamin Baker, was constructed from 1883 to 1890. The Marchioness of Tweedale drove the first train across the bridge on 24 January 1890 and the Prince of Wales declared the bridge open on 4 March. The Forth Road Bridge, a suspension bridge, was started in 1958 and opened by the Queen in 1964.

Sydney Goodsir Smith, Edwin Morgan

In his collection *Fifteen Poems and a Play* (1969) Sydney Goodsir Smith (1915–75) includes his poem 'The Twa Brigs' (the two bridges). In this he pays tribute to the rail bridge:

> The wonder o' the day, that aye stands there
> A monument o' strenth and grace
> Til the dour age o' coal and steam
> that foundit Britain's grandeur in the warld . . .

and welcomes the road bridge:

> this braw new brig that streetches owre the Frith
> Wi a lichtsome streetch,
> Twa bonny airms o' lassies jynin owre the water,
> Wi their feet in the water tae –
> Didnae Venus rise frae the wave, for luve's sake?

The Second Life (1968) by Edwin Morgan (born 1920) contains a poem, 'The Opening of the Forth Road Bridge, 4.IX.64', which begins

> Like man in the universe –
> rising through mist, half seen,
> walking the gulfs.

Alasdair Gray

Alasdair Gray (born 1934), in his novel *1982 Janine* (1984), describes the 'railway bridge crawling across like a steel Loch Ness monster into the distinctly hedged and wooded fields and hills of Fife'.

FOVERAN, Aberdeenshire   (Grampian)   4½m SE of Ellon

David Toulmin

A 'fee'd loon' earning a meagre living from farm work for most of his life, David Toulmin (born John Reid in 1913) moved to Foveran parish in 1950. He lived first in a cottage at Rashierieve farm (the south cottage of the twin cottages) and here wrote most of his diaries as well as some articles that were published locally. Then, from 1958 to 1971, he lived at Aikenshill, Foveran, as he explains in a letter of 1 May 1983:

> We lived for thirteen wonderful years in the double cottage visible from the road in the end nearest the farm. I say 'wonderful' because it was on this farm that my writing abilities reached maturity and my first stories were broadcast. My first short stories were all written here and published in the local papers, particularly in the *Buchan Observer* of Peterhead where they came to the notice of the BBC in Glasgow.

At Aikenshill, Toulmin collected and revised the stories published as *Hard Shining Corn* in 1972; and wrote most of his second book *Straw Into Gold* (1973).

FRASERBURGH, Aberdeenshire   (Grampian)   15m NW of
Peterhead on A92

George Bruce

George Bruce, the poet, was born on 10 March 1909 in a white granite, north-facing house on 2 Victoria Street. 'My House', one of the poems in his first collection *Sea Talk* (1944), describes his childhood home in characteristically taut lines:

> My house
> Is granite
> It fronts
> North,

Where the Firth flows,
East the sea.
My room
Holds the first

Blow from the North,
The first from East,
Salt upon
The pane.

Bruce's father was head of A. Bruce and Company, the oldest herring-curing firm in the north-east of Scotland, and as a child Bruce visited the homes of many Buchan fisherman. Buchan, the region that contains Fraserburgh, extends for forty miles from the Ythan to the Deveron in north-east Aberdeenshire and Bruce's *Sea Talk* made his reputation as the poet of Buchan. He was educated in Fraserburgh (and at Aberdeen University) and returned imaginatively to the seaport long after he had physically left the place. When Bruce was living in Wormit, Fife, in the early years of the Second World War he wrote a poem about 'Kinnaird Head', the low promontory on the Moray Firth at Fraserburgh. It begins:

I go North to cold, to home, to Kinnaird,
Fit monument for our time.

This is the outermost edge of Buchan.
Inland the sea birds range,
The tree's leaf has salt upon it,
The tree turns to the low stone wall.
And here a promontory rises towards Norway.

GAIRNEY BRIDGE, Kinross (Tayside)   3m S of Kinross on B996

Ebenezer Erskine

On 6 December 1883 the Rev. John Cairns laid the Foundation Stone of the **Secession Memorial** at Gairney Bridge. Ebenezer Erskine (1680–1754), minister of Portmoak (1703–31) then Stirling, was a member of the Evangelical wing of the Church of Scotland. He defended the doctrine of the predestined salvation of the Elect as expressed in *The Marrow of Modern Divinity* (1646, republished by James Hogg of Carnock in 1718), a work condemned by the General Assembly in 1720. As a leading Marrowman, Erskine believed that congregations should have a say in the choice of ministers and was censured for a sermon on the subject in 1731. Erskine was suspended by the General Assembly, the same year. His response was to meet with three associates at Gairney Bridge and denounce the 'prevailing party in the Church' in contrast to 'the first, free, faithful and reforming General Assembly'. This meeting of 1731 is regarded as the origin of the Secession Church.

John Brown, Michael Bruce

In the hamlet of Gairney Bridge there was an old cottage which served as a school. John Brown (1722–87), the author of the *Self-Interpreting Bible* (1778), taught there in 1750 before taking up his ministry at Haddington. In 1765, after leaving Edinburgh University at the age of nineteen, the poet Michael Bruce (1746–67), taught in the same schoolhouse for a few months. On 17 June 1765 he completed a short poem, 'The Fall of the Table', which begins:

> Within this school a table once there stood –
> It was not iron – No! 'twas rotten wood.
> Four generations it on earth had seen –
> A ship's old planks composed the huge machine.

GARTMORE, Perthshire (Central) 4m S of Aberfoyle, off A81

Robert Graham

Robert Graham (1735–97) was born at Gartmore House, a seventeenth-century mansion half-a-mile north-east of the village and visible from the A81. In his teens Graham left Scotland for Jamaica where he settled as a plantation-owner and Receiver-General. He returned to Scotland in 1772 and in 1777 moved to Gartmore House which he inherited after the death of his father and elder brother. At Gartmore House he wrote lyrics such as the well known one beginning

> If doughty deeds my lady please,
>   Right soon I'll mount my steed;
> And strong his arm and fast his seat,
>   That bears frae me the meed.
> I'll wear thy colours in my cap,
>   Thy picture in my heart;
> And he that bends not to thine eye
>   Shall rue it to his smart!

A staunch Whig, Graham was MP for Stirlingshire and in 1785 became Rector of Glasgow University. On inheriting Finlaystone (on the Clyde, two-and-a-half miles east of Port Glasgow) he added Cunninghame to his

141

name. He is buried, with his wife and young son, in the walled burial ground. His celebrated grandson R. B. Cunninghame Graham (see below) wrote *Doughty Deeds: An Account of the Life of Robert Graham of Gartmore, Poet and Politician, 1735–1797, Drawn from his Letter-books and Correspondence* (1925).

Robert Bontine Cunninghame Graham

As a child Robert Bontine Cunninghame Graham (1852–1936) usually spent his summers at Gartmore and the rest of the year in London (where he was born on 24 May 1852). The Cunninghame Grahams had a claim to the title of Menteith, an earldom dormant since the seventeenth century, and R. B. Cunninghame Graham was, according to Andrew Lang (1844–1912), a direct and legitimate descendant of Robert II. He once told a woman in Scotland; 'I ought, madam, if I had my rights to be the king of this country.' Educated privately and at Harrow, he left Britain in 1870 and during the next seven years spent much of his time in Argentina and Paraguay. On 24 October 1878 he married, in London, Gabriella de la Belmondière, the Chilean poet with whom he collaborated on *Father Archangel of Scotland, and Other Essays* (1896).

His father, William Cunninghame Bontine, died on 6 September 1883 and Robert inherited the estates of Gartmore, Ardoch, and Gallangad along with the surname Cunninghame Graham. In 1886 the new Laird of Gartmore became Liberal MP for North-West Lanarkshire (a seat he held until 1892); after the formation of the Scottish Labour Party in 1888 he was its first president.

Because of the debts he had inherited, Graham lived frugally at Gartmore with Gabriella. During his occupation of the house he published *Notes on the District of Menteith* (1895), *Mogreb-el-Acksa: A Journey in Morocco* (1898), *The Ipané* (1899), and *Thirteen Stories* (1900). In 1900 he put his furniture and pictures up for auction and sold Gartmore House and estate to Sir Charles Cayser, a Glasgow shipping tycoon, for £126,000 – a sum that gave him financial security for the rest of his life. On 6 October 1900 Graham expressed his feelings on leaving Gartmore House in a letter to Edward Garnett: 'This has been a long & a heart-rending day. . . . It is bright moonlight now & the familiar trees look spiritual & perhaps reproachful. I wish it would rain, & look ugly.' Graham describes the last hours at Gartmore in his story 'A Braw Day' (*Charity*, 1912). He moved to London but, in 1904, returned to Scotland to live at Ardoch. Gartmore House was later acquired by the local authority and functioned as a Roman Catholic Church List D school. In December 1984 it was bought by the Way in Great Britain Ltd, an American-based biblical research, teaching and fellowship ministry as their European training centre.

GARTOCHARN, Dunbartonshire   (Strathclyde)   3m SW of Drymen

Maurice Lindsay

From 1949 to 1961 the poet Maurice Lindsay (born 1918) lived at Garto-charn which he describes, in his autobiography *Thank You for Having Me* (1983) as 'a tiny village at the middle of the base of the mountain-folded triangle of water which is Loch Lomond'. Lindsay lived first in a caravan then acquired Fir Tree Cottage for twelve hundred pounds in September 1950: 'It had a tiny living-room, a bedroom, a boxroom, a stone-floored kitchen and a rudimentary stone-floored bathroom'. Four years later 'we moved round the corner to the larger Rose Cottage, which we promptly re-christened "Corraith", after the Innellan holiday home of the thirties'. Lindsay was visited at 'Corraith' by the Scottish poet George Bruce, the English poet George Barker, and the Indian poet Dom Moraes.

GASK HOUSE, Perthshire   (Tayside)   6m NE of Gleneagles, off A9

Lady Nairne

Carolina Oliphant, Lady Nairne (1766–1845), was born on 17 August 1766 at Gask House, the home of her father Laurence Oliphant, an enthusiastic Jacobite. On 2 June 1806 she married her cousin Major William Murray Nairne who was restored to his forfeited estates and title in 1824. Under the pseudonym Mrs Bogan of Bogan she wrote lyrics for traditional tunes. 'Will ye no come back again?', a passionate lament for Bonnie Prince Charlie, begins:

> Bonnie Charlie's now awa,
>   Safely owre the friendly main;
> Mony a heart will break in twa,
>   Should he ne'er come back again.

Lady Nairne lived in Edinburgh until 1830 when her husband died. After the death of her only son she returned to Gask House where she died on 26 October 1845. She is buried in the chapel. Some mementoes of Lady Nairne can be seen in Ardblair Castle (one mile west of Blairgowrie on A923).

GATEHOUSE OF FLEET, Kirkcudbrightshire   (Dumfries and Galloway)   6m NW of Kircudbright on A75

Robert Burns

In this little village at the head of Fleet Bay, Robert Burns (1759–96) wrote 'Scots Wha Hae' in August 1793. A room in the Murray Arms Hotel is pointed out as the place where he sat and wrote his manuscript. Burns composed the words of 'Scots Wha Hae' to the tune of 'Hey tuttie tatie' while walking in Gatehouse of Fleet. As well as being inspired, by the tune, to 'a pitch of enthusiasm on the theme of Liberty and Independence' he was disturbed by the government's reactionary response to the radical events associated with the Friends of the People and Thomas Muir of Huntershill. In a letter to George Thomson, Burns said his final two stanzas were prompted by contemporary events:

> By Oppression's woes and pains,
> By your sons in servile chains,
> We will drain our dearest veins
> But they shall be free!

> Lay the proud usurpers low!
> Tyrants fall in every foe!
> Liberty's in every blow!
> Let us do, or die!

Burns hoped Thomson would include the song, as written, in his *Select Scottish Airs* but poet and publisher disagreed over text and tune and the song was not published during Burns's lifetime. Eventually, after the story of the quarrel was told in James Currie's biography of Burns, Thomson published 'Scots Wha Hae' as Burns conceived and executed it.

GIGHT CASTLE, Aberdeenshire   (Grampian)   5m NW of Haddo, off B9005

The tower-house of Gight was owned by the Gordon family from 1479 to 1787 when Catherine Gordon, the mother of Lord Byron (1788–1824), had to sell it to pay off the debts of her husband Captain John 'Mad Jack' Byron. The house of Gight was attacked by the Covenanters in 1644 and it decayed thereafter. Byron's mother, who died in 1811, was the thirteenth and last laird of Gight.

GLASGOW, Lanarkshire   (Strathclyde)

Glasgow grew from a quiet university (founded 1451) and cathedral town into Scotland's largest city and industrial centre. One aspect of its modern character is conveyed in *The Dear Green Place* (1966), a novel by Archie Hind (born in Glasgow in 1928):

> Gles Chu! Glasgow! The dear green place! Now a vehicular sclerosis, a congestion of activity!. . . . A Calvinist, Protestant city. The influx of Roman Catholic Irish and Continental Jews had done nothing to change it, even if they had given to its slum quarters an air of spurious romance. Even they in the end became Calvinist. A city whose talents were all outward and acquisitive. Its huge mad Victorian megalomaniacal art gallery full of acquired art, its literature dumb or in exile, its poetry a dull struggle in obscurity, its night life non-existent, its theatres unsupported, its Sundays sabbatarian, its secular life moderate and dull on the one hand and sordid, furtive and predatory on the other.

Glasgow has, however, a considerable cultural past and present, the names listed below giving only an impression of the verbal vitality of the city.

Thomas Campbell

Thomas Campbell (1777–1844) was born on 27 July 1777 at 215 High Street (where there is plaque). He studied at Glasgow University where he won a prize for his poem 'On Description' and two further prizes for translations from Aristophanes and Euripides. Campbell's poem *The Pleasures of Hope* (1799) made him a literary celebrity and in 1803 – a year after marrying his cousin Matilda Sinclair – he settled in London. He was elected Lord Rector of Glasgow University in 1827, even though Sir Walter Scott was a rival candidate; then re-elected the two following years. Campbell recalled his Glasgow origins in two contrasting poems. 'Lines on Revisiting a Scottish River' laments the industrialisation of the Clyde:

> And call they this Improvement? – to have changed,
> My native Clyde, thy once romantic shore,
> Where Nature's face is banished and estranged,
> And Heaven reflected in thy wave no more;
> Whose banks, that sweetened May-day's breath before,
> Lie sere and leafless now in summer's beam,
> With sooty exhalations covered o'er;
> And for the daisied green sward, down thy stream
> Unsightly brick-lanes smoke, and clanking engines gleam.

'Lines on Revisiting Cathcart' begins less indignantly:

Oh! scenes of my childhood, and dear to my heart
Ye green waving woods on the margin of Cart,
How blest in the morning of life I have strayed,
By the stream of the vale and the grass-covered glade!

William Motherwell

William Motherwell (1797–1835) was born at 117 High Street (plaque) at
the south corner of College Street. Son of an ironmonger, Motherwell
was educated at William Lennie's school where he met Jeanie Morrison,
the subject of the song of that name written when he was fourteen and
included in *Poems, Narrative and Lyrical* (1832):

My head rins round and round about,
  My heart flows like the sea,
As ane by ane the thochts rush back
  O' schule-time and o' thee.
Oh, mornin' life! oh, mornin' love!
  Oh, lichtsome days and lang,
When hinnied hopes around our hearts
  Like simmer blossoms sprang!

Motherwell went to Glasgow University and moved to Paisley, serving as
Sheriff-Clerk Depute of Renfrewshire from 1819–1829. He was a scrupulously scholarly editor of ballads and his *Minstrelsy, Ancient and Modern*
(1827) was a significant publication. Motherwell returned to Glasgow in
1830 as editor of the *Courier*. He died of apoplexy on 1 November 1835
and his grave in the Necropolis is marked by a monument.

Alexander Smith

Alexander Smith (1830–67) worked as a pattern designer in Glasgow, a
city he celebrated in verse and prose. 'Glasgow', from *City Poems* (1857),
uses urban imagery to convey the character of the city:

City! I am true son of thine:
Ne'er dwelt I where great mornings shine
  Around the bleating pens;
Ne'er by the rivulets I strayed,
And ne'er upon my childhood weighed
  The silence of the glens.
Instead of shores where ocean beats
I hear the ebb and flow of streets.

In *A Summer in Skye* (1865) Smith writes of Glasgow: 'It is not in itself
an ugly city and it has many historical associations. Few cities are

surrounded by prettier scenery'. Glasgow features as Hawkhead in Smith's novel *Alfred Hagart's Household* (1866).

John Buchan, Anna Buchan

In 1888 the Rev. John Buchan, father of the novelist John Buchan (1875–1940), was called to the John Knox Free Church in the Gorbals. The family lived at 34 Queen Mary Avenue, Crosshill, and Buchan attended Hutchesons' Grammar School (founded in 1650 by two Glasgow merchants, moved to Crossmyloof in 1959, building demolished) before going to Glasgow University from 1892 to 1895. Buchan began his literary career while an undergraduate in Glasgow, editing *Essays and Apothegms of Francis Lord Bacon* (1894) and contributing to *Macmillan's* and the *Gentleman's Magazine*. As a Sunday school teacher in his father's church, Buchan got to know a group of 'eight very bad small boys' as his sister Anna observes in her *Unforgettable, Unforgotten* (1945). They were the originals of the Gorbals Die-Hards who appear in *Huntingtower* (1922), the first three novels about the Glasgow grocer Dickson McCunn:

> Behind [Dickson McCunn's] premises in Mearns Street lay a tract of slums, full of mischievous boys with whom his staff waged truceless war. But lately there had started among them a kind of unauthorised and unofficial Boy Scouts, who, without uniform or badge of any kind of paraphernalia, followed the banner of Sir Robert Baden-Powell and subjected themselves to a rude discipline. They were far too poor to join an orthodox troop, but they faithfully copied what they believed to be the practices of more fortunate boys.

Anna Buchan (1877–1948), who wrote novels under the name O. Douglas, was educated at Queen's Park Academy and Hutchesons' Girls School. Her second novel, *The Setons* (1917) is a fictional account of her father's life in Glasgow.

Catherine Carswell

Catherine Roxburgh Macfarlane (1879–1946) was born in Glasgow on 27 March 1879, the daughter of a merchant. She became a socialist after reading Robert Blatchford at the age of seventeen, studied English at Glasgow University, experienced a disastrous first marriage (to Herbert Jackson, who tried to kill her), and made a reputation as dramatic and literary critic of the *Glasgow Herald* from 1907 to 1915 when she married Donald Carswell (born 1882 in Glasgow), then a sub-editor on the same paper. She lost her job with the *Glasgow Herald* after writing an enthusiastic review of D. H. Lawrence's banned novel *The Rainbow* (1915), and it was Lawrence who encouraged her to complete her autobiographical

Glasgow novel *Open the Door!* (1920) and to do justice to the passionate nature of Burns in her *The Life of Burns* (1930). In *Open the Door!* Catherine Carswell features as the heroine, Joanna Bannerman; Donald Carswell as Lawrence Urquhart. Other characters are modelled on real-life originals: Joanna's lover Louis is Maurice Greiffenhagen, appointed Professor of the Life Class at Glasgow School of Art in 1906. Victorian Glasgow is a powerful presence to the Bannerman family in 1896:

> [The Bannerman] girls could remember watching the distant ascent of their first fireworks – rockets soaring in honour of Glasgow's earliest Exhibition. From the same windows they had seen with rapture the first lighting of the city by electricity. And three times they had hung out great flags over the sills for Royal Processions. Once Georgie was quite certain that Queen Victoria, driving up Sauchiehall Street, had waved her hand in special acknowledgement to their high window.

Catherine and Donald Carswell settled in London where he died, in an accident during the black-out, in 1940. She died in Oxford at the age of eighty-six.

Edwin Muir

The Muir family, including Edwin Muir (1887–1959), arrived in Glasgow, from Orkney, in 1901. During his years in Glasgow, Muir worked in an office, a beer-bottling factory and – after spending two years (1912–14) in Greenock where he was employed in a bone factory – a shipbuilding office (having been turned down by the army on medical grounds). He was coverted to socialism in Glasgow and joined the Clarion Scots and the Independent Labour party. He also began to write for the *New Age*. In 1918, in a Glasgow flat, he met Willa Anderson (then a lecturer in a London training college for teachers) and married her on 7 June 1919. 'My marriage,' Muir said, 'was the most fortunate event in my life.' The couple settled in London and Muir, psychologically supported by Willa, went on to make a reputation as one of the most distinguished poets of his time.

He regarded his years in Glasgow as a fall into a nightmarish labyrinth for in that period he was traumatically shocked by a series of personal tragedies: his father died of a heart atttack, his brother Willie of consumption, his brother Johnnie from a brain tumour, and his mother from an internal disease. His novel *Poor Tom* (1932) is set in Glasgow and describes the life and death of Tom Manson who, like Muir's brother Johnnie, suffers from a brain tumour. In *An Autobiography* (1954) Muir depicts the Glasgow slums:

> the crumbling houses, the twisted faces, the obscene words casually

heard in passing, the ancient, haunting stench of pollution and decay, the arrogant women, the mean men, the terrible children, daunted me, and at last filled me with an immense, blind dejection.

James Bridie

James Bridie – the pseudonym of Osborne Henry Mavor (1888–1951) – was born in Glasgow on 3 January 1888. In his autobiographical *One Way of Living* (1939) he writes: 'I have not re-visited my birthplace, but I understand that it was a flat in a decent, stone-built building in a residential district of Glasgow called Pollockshields.' At the age of six he lived in 101 Armadale Street, Dennistoun, Glasgow: 'It was a groundfloor flat in a red sandstone tenement, and I remember nothing else about it except the patch of seedy grass in front and a ferocious policeman on the beat.'

Bridie was educated at Miss Carter's school, the High School, Glasgow Academy and Glasgow University where he studied medicine. He qualified as a doctor in 1913 and joined the staff of the Royal Infirmary. In 1919 he bought a practice in the Langside district of Glasgow and also joined the staff of the Victoria Infirmary as a junior assistant physician: 'My mother, my brother Eric and I took up housekeeping in a little semi-villa with a garden in Langside Avenue.' Bridie's theatrical career took off with Tyrone Guthrie's production (in March 1928) of *The Sunlight Sonata* at the Lyric Theatre, Glasgow. Though Bridie's best-known play *The Anatomist* (1930) deals with the Burke and Hare murders in Edinburgh, an equally powerful drama, *Dr Angelus* (1947) is set in Glasgow and explores the mind of notorious poisoner Dr E. W. Pritchard (executed in 1865). Bridie was one of the most enthusiastic advocates of an indigenous Scottish theatre and helped found the Citizens Theatre in 1932 and the Glasgow College of Drama in 1950. He died on 29 January 1951 in Edinburgh.

Hugh MacDiarmid

In February 1942 the poet Hugh MacDiarmid – Christopher Murray Grieve, 1892–1978 – left the Shetland island of Whalsay and came to Glasgow after being conscripted for National Service. While completing a six-month government training course and qualifying as a precision fitter, MacDiarmid stayed at 44 Munro Road with his friend, the composer Francis George Scott (1880–1958), to whom *A Drunk Man Looks at the Thistle* (1926) is dedicated. Writing to Helen Cruickshank (1886–1975) from 27 Arundel Drive, on 21 December 1943, MacDiarmid describes his feelings on working in the copper shell band department of Mechan's engineering company, Scotstoun:

I have indeed practically no time or energy for anything at all except my engineering, which involves over and above the 47 hour week, a great deal of overtime and Sunday work. Work and sleep is practically all I can do – my reading is principally thrillers: all I am fit for in the hour or two after I come home and before I go to bed, and it has to be a jolly good thriller if I do not fall asleep over it at that.

After suffering serious injuries when a stack of copper-cuttings fell on him and cut both his legs, the poet was transferred to the Merchant Service and became a deck hand, then first engineer, on a Norwegian vessel chartered by the British Admiralty. During the period 1946 to 1948 in Glasgow, MacDiarmid stayed mainly at 32 Victoria Crescent Road, Dowanhill, Glasgow G12, and liked to drink at the Curlers pub, Byres Road, round the corner: a mural by Walter Pritchard (who owned the three-storey house below which MacDiarmid had the basement) shows the poet and his Glasgow friends in Scottish costume. In 1949 he moved to Dungavel House, Strathaven.

'Glasgow', from *Collected Poems* (1962), suggests:

> The houses are Glasgow, not the people – these
> Are simply the food the houses live and grow on
> Endlessly, drawing from their vulgarity
> And pettiness and darkness of spirit. . . .
> To see or hear a clock in Glasgow's horrible,
> Like seeing a dead man's watch, still going though he's dead.
> Everything is dead except stupidity here.

Maurice Lindsay

Maurice Lindsay, poet and energetic man of letters, was born (the son of an insurance manager) on 21 July 1918 at Lynedoch Nursing Home, Lynedoch Place (now offices in the Park Conservation Area of Glasgow). From 1913 to 1932 he lived, with his family, at 11 Ashton Terrace, on the north side. Lindsay describes the Ashton Terrace home in his auto-biography *Thank You For Having Me* (1983):

> The drawing-room, into which I was rarely allowed, had a huge mid-Victorian chandelier, the gas jets of which were only lit on special occasions. Sometimes my mother would play on the upright piano that stood stiffly against the wall, while my great-aunt sat quietly rocking herself in her favourite chair.

In 1930 the Lindsay family moved to 32 Athole Gardens, 'an enclosed, hilly U-shaped crescent built in the high Victorian manner of the 1870s round a private fenced common central garden containing a grass tennis court'. Lindsay was educated at Glasgow Academy and in 1936 enrolled as a student at the Scottish National Academy of Music (now the Royal

Scottish Academy of Music and Drama) where he took lessons in piano while continuing to study violin with Camillo Ritter. During the Second World War he served with the Cameronians and in 1946 returned to Glasgow to work as a broadcaster and journalist (being music critic of the *Bulletin* for fourteen years).

From 1946 to 1947 Lindsay and his wife Joyce stayed in a small rented flat at 10 Jedburgh Gardens, by Kelvingbridge. In 1947, eighteen months after his marriage to Joyce, he rented a flat at 13 South Park Avenue, off Great Western Road. In 1949 Linday left Glasgow to stay in Gartocharn, Dunbartonshire, and in 1961 became the first Programme Controller of Border Television in Carlisle. He came back to Glasgow in 1967 as Director of the Scottish Civic Trust and lived from 1967 to 1976 at 11 Great Western Terrace. In his autobiography he explains 'it was my wife, following a lead of her own, who discovered the ground-floor flat of a converted mansion in the palace-like range of Great Western Terrace which was to be our home for nine years'. In 1976 Lindsay settled in Dumbarton.

Lindsay is an authority on Glasgow as is evident from his prose *Portrait of Glasgow* (1972). His poems offer various observations on Glasgow, 'Glasgow Orange Walk' (*Collected Poems* 1979) bitterly depicting the evidence of intolerance in a city divided by religion:

> Spread women, ugly men and little children
> dressed in the Sunday best of bigotry,
> suffered to come unto intolerance
> down orange miles of bannered frippery;
> the gadfly flutes, the goading fifes,
> the yattering side-drums of expended wars
> forcing sectarian division through
> our public streets choked back with fuming cars.

Edwin Morgan

Edwin (George) Morgan was born in Glasgow on 27 April 1920. His father was first a clerk, then a director of a firm of iron and steel scrap merchants. Morgan lived in Hyndland, then Pollockshields, then Rutherglen. He was educated at Rutherglen Academy, Glasgow High School and Glasgow University where he took his degree in English. In 1947, after serving with the Royal Army Medical Corps in the Middle East during the Second World War, he returned to teach English at Glasgow University. From the position of Assistant Lecturer he rose to become Titular Professor in 1975. In 1980 he retired.

Since 1962 Morgan has lived at 19 Whittingehame Court, in the West End of Glasgow, and in that house has composed most of his Glasgow poems, some of which are based on direct observation and some of which have been prompted by newspaper reports. He has said that 'Although I travel about quite a bit, I like to have Glasgow to return to, and naturally I will write about it many times'. His *Poems of Thirty Years* (1982) contains many poems exploring his native city. In 'King Billy' he watches the march of prejudice, in 'The Suspect' he brings in the police, in 'In the Snack-Bar' he watches a pitiful old man struggling to keep body and soul together and ends by exclaiming 'Dear Christ, to be born for this!' 'Glasgow Green' gives the city back a startling image of itself;

> Clammy midnight, moonless mist.
> A cigarette glows and fades on a cough,
> Meth-men mutter on benches,
> pawed by river fog. Monteith Row
> sweats coldly, crumbles, dies
> slowly. All shadows are alive.

Many of Morgan's poems show Glasgow as mean, brutal and distressingly complacent about its own squalor. His *Glasgow Sonnets* begin, for example, as 'A mean wind wanders through the backcourt trash'. However Morgan is capable of going beyond the squalor into the vitality of the city. His comic poem 'The Starlings in George Square' counterpoints officialdom against the birds who 'lighten the heart'. And in the title poem of *The Second Life* (1968) the poet celebrates his fortieth birthday by experiencing a mood of renewal in the city:

> All January, all February the skaters
> enjoyed Bingham's pond, the crisp cold evenings,
> they swung and flashed among car headlights,
> the drivers parked round the unlit pond
> to watch them, and give them light, what laughter
> and pleasure rose in the rare lulls
> of the yards-away stream of wheels along Great Western Road!

Clifford Hanley

Clifford Hanley was born on 28 October 1922 at 628 Gallowgate. He writes, in a letter of 17 May 1983:

> There is no habitation there today, as there was in 1922 at my birth. It is a landscaped Sea of Tranquillity. I ate that location for my reminiscent book *Dancing in the Streets* [1958]. Then there was 11 Fleet Street, Sandyhills, Shettleston, Glasgow (the name may have been predictive, but wasn't in the event) while I attended Eastbank Academy, Shettleston, Glasgow, won every subject prize and the Dux medal. The house and the school still stand. I winched a tall

beautiful lassie who lived at 165 Ardgay Street, in Shettleston, Glasgow. I still have her.

Hanley is well known as a witty broadcaster and popular journalist who regularly surveys the world from his vantage point at 36 Munro Road. His novel *The Taste of Too Much* (1960) deals with life in a Glasgow school and in his study of *The Scots* (1980) he comments on snobbery in Glasgow:

> Glasgow has its own graduations of geographical status. The Kelvinside district is nothing very special, but it is a legendary state of mind to lowlier residents, an area where people speak in genteel or 'pan-loaf' accents and demonstrate their impoverished gentility by having lace-curtains on the windows and no sheets on the beds.

Alasdair Gray

Alasdair Gray's hugely successful novel *Lanark* (1981) explores, among many other aspects of life, the mentality of artist Duncan Thaw whose ambition is 'to write a modern Divine Comedy with illustrations in the style of William Blake'. Thaw grows up in Glasgow, specifically in Riddrie:

> Thaw lived in the middle storey of a corporation tenement that was red sandstone in front and brick behind. The tenement backs enclosed a grassy area divided into greens by spiked railings, and each green had a midden. . . . Someone told Mrs Thaw that the former tenants of her flat had killed themselves by putting their heads in the oven and turning the gas on. She wrote at once to the corporation asking that her gas cooker be changed for an electric one, but as Mr Thaw would still need food when he returned from work she baked him a shepherd's pie, but with her lips more tightly pursed than usual.

Although Thaw is an inventive creation, the character is an autobiographical projection of Gray who was born in 11 Findhorn Street, Riddrie, on 28 September 1934, 'one stair up in a good corporation flat with a livingroom window in the gable wall facing the Cumbernauld Road' (letter of 10 February 1985 to the present author).

During the war he was evacuated with his mother and sister, first to a farm near Auchterarder, then to Stonehouse, a Lanarkshire mining town. Later the whole family lived in a hostel for munition workers in Wetherby, Yorkshire, where Gray's father was manager. After the war the family returned to 11 Findhorn Street where Gray lived until the age of twenty-five. He attended Riddrie Primary School (still standing), Whitehill Senior Secondary School (in a building now demolished) and Glasgow School of Art. After leaving Riddrie, Gray lived near the Glasgow School of Art in 158 then 160 Hill Street. In his letter of 10 February 1985 Gray explains,

My wife and I shared the first of these flats with friends – it was rented – later exchanging it for the second, which was larger and on the ground floor, and had rooms we could sublet to lodgers. This building was demolished when that side of the hill was cut away to let the approach road to the Kingston motorway bridge. The corporation kindly rehoused us in one of their older properties (large late 19th-century tenement again) in Hillhead, where I still live [in 39 Kersland Street].

Gray's novel *1982 Janine* (1984) is told by a narrator ensconced in the bedroom of a hotel in 'Peebles or Selkirk'. *The Fall of Kelvin Walker* (1985), Gray's third novel, is set in London.

Tom Leonard

The poet Tom Leonard was born on 22 August 1944 at 8 Annette Street, Govanhill, and was brought up (from 1948 until the early 1960s) at 200 Leithland Road, Pollok. The road is referred to in 'A Priest Came on at Merkland Street' (included in *Intimate Voices*, 1984):

> my name is Ozymandias
> king of Leithland Road
> Pollok
> Glasgow SW3

Again, in 'Pollock Poster No 1' Leithland Road is featured with the poet:

> sitting in the garden
> behind the toolshed
> reading Thomas Mann
> Beethoven on the transistor
> a blackbird in the potato patch
> the grass full of daisies

As a poet Leonard is renowned for his ability to use the Glasgow patois in an imaginative manner. For example, 'The Good Thief' is a dramatic monologue which puns cleverly on the Glaswegian pronounciation of 'in saying':

> heh jimmy
> ma right insane yirra pape
> ma right insane yirwanny us jimmy

Leonard was educated at Lourdes Secondary School and at Glasgow University; since his marriage in 1971 he has lived mainly at 56 Eldon Street.

GLENCOE, Argyllshire   (Highland)

Glencoe, a wild valley guarded on the south by the Three Sisters and on the north by the Chancellor, is the scene of one of the most notorious massacres in Scotland. When William of Orange came to the throne in 1689 his government demanded that all Highland chiefs had to take the oath of allegiance by 1 January 1692. From all the clans, only two chiefs failed to swear by that date – MacDonnell of Glengarry and MacIan MacDonald of Glencoe. The latter duly signed on 6 January. However, on the advice of his Secretary of State, William of Orange gave the powerful Glengarry another chance but vowed to teach MacIan and his 'sect of thieves' a lesson. The act was entrusted to Robert Campbell of Glenlyon who was a relative, by marriage, of old MacIan. Under the command of Campbell, 120 men from the Earl of Argyll's Regiment of Foot went to Glencoe to be billeted in the cottages there. They were received with the customary Highland hospitality and for fifteen days shared food and drink with the Glencoe MacDonalds. Then on 13 February 1692 the slaughter began early in the morning. MacIan was shot in his bed and his wife had her rings wrenched from her fingers by a soldier's teeth. Thirty-nine MacDonald clansmen were attacked in their sleep, bound hand and foot, and murdered in the snow. Cottages were put on fire as fresh snow fell and the surviving MacDonalds made for the caves. Many died in the snow.

Sir Walter Scott

Glencoe has remained a subject certain to arouse strong feelings in Scotland. Sir Walter Scott (1771–1832) published his poem 'On the Massacre of Glencoe' in 1814. It includes this stanza:

> The hand that mingled in the meal
> At midnight drew the felon steel,
> And gave the host's kind breast to feel
>   Meed for his hospitality!
> The friendly hearth which warm'd that hand,
> At midnight arm'd it with the brand,
> That bade destruction's flames expand
>   Their red and fearful blazonry.

Thomas Campbell, William Aytoun

Thomas Campbell (1777–1844) imagines a MacDonald forgiving a Campbell in his *Pilgrim of Glencoe* (1842) and William Aytoun (1813–65) comments on the massacre in his 'Widow of Glencoe'.

John Prebble, Alistair MacLean

Glencoe continues to haunt the imagination of writers. John Prebble's definitive account of the massacre, *Glencoe*, appeared in 1966. An aside in Alistair MacLean's thriller *When Eight Bells Toll* (1966) states:

> Many places have evil reputations. Few, at first seeing, live up to those reputations. But there are a few. In Scotland, the Pass of Glencoe, the scene of the infamous massacre, is one of them.

Bertrand Russell

In his *Autobiography* (1967–9) Bertrand Russell describes a drive 'through the gloomy valley of Glencoe, as dark and dreadful as if the massacre had just taken place'.

GORDON ARMS, Selkirkshire (Border)   Crossroads of A708 and B709

Sir Walter Scott, James Hogg

Sir Walter Scott (1771–1832) and James Hogg (1770–1835) are said to have met here, when the hotel was an inn. A plaque notes their last meeting here in autumn 1830. Scott's interest in Hogg continued and on 23 March 1832 (a matter of months before his death on 21 September 1832) Scott wrote from Naples, on the subject of Hogg's London success:

> I am glad Hogg has succeeded so well. I hope he will make hay while the sun shines; but he must be aware that the Lion of this season always becomes the Boar of the next. . . . He has another chance for comfort if he will use common sense with his very considerable genius.

GREENOCK, Renfrewshire (Strathclyde)   Clydeside port on A8

Jean Adam

Jean Adam (1710–65), the daughter of a shipmaster, was born at Carts-dyke (now part of Greenock) where she was orphaned at an early age. Encouraged by the local minister she developed her interest in poetry and her *Miscellany Poems* (1734) was published by subscription. She set up a school for girls in Greenock but when this failed became a hawker. She died in a Glasgow workhouse. 'There's nae luck aboot the house', which appeared in David Herd's *Scottish Songs* (1776), has been attributed to her though the case for William Julius Mickle as author is more convincing. Her poem 'A Dream, or the Type of the Rising Sun' shows a strong imagination at work:

> Forward I went, and saw society,
> The pleasure-garden of the deity;
> In which almighty Jove took such delight,
> He walked around her walls both day and night.
> At his own cost he built the threefold wall
> So high, that thieves could never miss to fall.

Robert Burns

On the evidence of his 'Highland Mary' poems it seems that Robert Burns (1759–96) intended to marry Mary Campbell (1763–86) in 1786 and emigrate to Jamaica with her. On 31 July 1786 the Kilmarnock edition of Burns's *Poems, Chiefly in the Scottish Dialect* appeared and was an immediate success, the 612 copies selling in a month. Burns was scheduled to meet Mary at Greenock in September so they could both sail for Kingston; meanwhile he went to Mossgiel farm where he heard that Jean Armour (later his wife) had given birth to twins. Then, from Greenock, came the shattering news of Mary Campbell's death – Burns claimed she died from a 'malignant fever' but there is a possibility that she died in childbirth. Suddenly the journey to Jamaica seemed pointless and Burns headed, instead, for Edinburgh where he was lionised as a cultural phenomenon. Burns, in 'Highland Mary', wrote: 'But still within my bosom's core/Shall live my Highland Mary.'

Mary and her brother (from whom she may have caught typhus, the 'malignant fever') were buried in the West Kirk churchyard and when the church was rebuilt in the nineteenth century the coffins were re-interred in the new cemetery in Nelson Street West where there is a monument.

John Galt

When John Galt (1779–1839) was ten his family moved to Greenock where he spent the next fifteen years of his life. As he noted in his *Autobiography* (1833) he enjoyed his life in Greenock as:

> a large oasis in the desert of my life, and much of my good nature towards mankind is assuredly owing to my associates there. I have met, no doubt, with many more accomplished, but never with better men.

Galt was educated at the local Grammar School, became a member of

Greenock Subscription Library (founded 1783) and worked as a junior clerk with James Miller and Company. He moved in local literary circles and in 1804 – the year he left Greenock for London after an altercation with a client at his work – invited James Hogg to Greenock for a dinner in his honour. The Ettrick Shepherd subsequently recalled:

[Galt's] stories of old-fashioned and odd people were so infinitely amusing, that his conversation proved one of the principal charms of that enchanting night. The conversation of that literary community of friends at Greenock as well as their songs and stories, was much above what I had ever been accustomed to hear.

Galt was a prolific writer who achieved major success with his novels, including *The Ayrshire Legatees* (1820), *Annals of the Parish* (1821), *The Provost* (1822), and *The Member* (1832). When Thomas Carlyle met him at a dinner party in London, in January 1832, he observed that 'Galt . . . has the air of a sedate Greenock Burgher'. Galt returned to Greenock in 1834 and lived at West Blackhall Street (at the junction with West Burn Street, the site is now indicated by a plaque). He died on 11 April 1839 and was buried in the old cemetery in Inverkip Street (there is a plaque over the locked gate). He is commemorated by a fountain on the esplanade.

John Davidson

John Davidson (1857–1909) was born in Barrhead, Renfrewshire, and brought up in Greenock where his father, a minister of the Evangelical Union, had charge of Nelson Street Church. He was educated at the Highlanders' Academy, Greenock, then left when he was thirteen to work in the chemical laboratory of Walker's sugar refinery. He was assistant to the Public Analyst of Greenock the following year but in 1872 went back to the Highlanders' Academy as a pupil-teacher. Leaving Greenock in 1876 he studied for a year at Edinburgh University; taught in Perth, Glasgow, Paisley and Crieff; and in 1889 returned to Greenock to teach in a small private school.

At the end of 1889 Davidson moved to London, supporting himself by journalism while he created some remarkable works including the dramatic monologue 'Thirty Bob a Week' which T. S. Eliot described as 'a great poem for ever'. In his series of Testaments – *The Testament of a Man Forbid* (1901), *The Testament of a Vivesector* (1901), *The Testament of an Empire-Builder* (1902), *The Testament of a Prime Minister* (1904), *The Testament of John Davidson* (1908) – he attempted to extend the intellectual scope of poetry by drawing on scientific terms with a philosophical indignation inspired by Nietzsche.

Financial and emotional security, however, eluded him and on 23 March

1909 he drowned himself by walking into the sea off Penzance, Cornwall. Hugh MacDiarmid wrote a poem, 'Of John Davidson', in his honour and observed, in an essay, 'Davidson stood out head and shoulders above all the Scottish poets of his own time. He alone had anything to say that is, or should be, of interest to any adult mind.'

Davidson's poem 'A Ballad in Blank Verse of the Making of a Poet' - from *Ballads and Songs* (1894) – contains a vivid description of Greenock:

> this grey town
> That pipes the morning up before the lark
> With shrieking steam, and from a hundred stalks
> Lacquers the sooty sky; where hammers clang
> On iron hulls, and cranes in harbours creak,
> Rattle and swing, whole cargoes on their necks;
> Where men sweat gold that others hoard or spend,
> And lurk like vermin in their narrow streets:
> This old grey town, this firth, the further strand
> Spangled with hamlets, and the wooded steeps,
> Whose rocky tops behind each other press,
> Fantastically carved like antique helms
> High-hung in heaven's cloudy armoury,
> Is world enough for me. Here daily dawn
> Burns through the smoky east; with fire-shod feet
> The sun treads heaven, and steps from hill to hill
> Downward before the night that still pursues
> His crimson wake; here winter plies his craft,
> Soldering the years with ice; here spring appears,
> Caught in a leafless brake, her garland torn,
> Breathless with wonder, and the tears half-dried
> Upon her rosy cheek; here summer comes
> And wastes his passion like a prodigal
> Right royally; and here her golden gains
> Free-handed as a harlot autumn spends;
> And here are men to know, women to love.

Edwin Muir

After working for seven years in a Glasgow beer-bottling factory, the poet Edwin Muir (1887–1959) got a job in a bone factory in Greenock – which he calls Fairport in his *Autobiography* (1954). The factory, where Muir was employed from 1912 to 1914, reduced bones to charcoal and grease in furnaces, producing (Muir noted) 'a gentle, clinging, sweet stench, suggesting dissolution and hospitals and slaughter-houses, the odour of drains, and the rancid stink of bad, roasting meat'. Shortly after the outbreak of war Muir, who was turned down by the Army on medical grounds, returned to Glasgow to work in a shipbuilding office.

W. S. Graham

W(illiam) S(ydney) Graham was born on 19 November 1918 in Greenock and trained as an engineer before concentrating on writing and settling in Cornwall. In his poem 'To My Mother', in *Collected Poems* (1980), he writes:

> The flowing strongheld Clyde
> Rests me my earliest word
> That has ever matchlessly
> Changed me towards the sea.
>
> That deep investment speaks
> Over ship-cradles and derricks
> And ebbs to a perfection's
> Deadly still anatomies.

Alan Sharp

Alan Sharp was born in Alyth, Perthshire, in 1934 and adopted by a Greenock couple; his father worked in the shipyards by day and served in the Salvation Army by night. Sharp left school at fourteen and spent the next four years working in the shipyards. After his National Service he did a variety of odd jobs including working as assistant to a Greenock private detective. He achieved a critical and commercial triumph with *A Green Tree in Gedde* (1965) which was announced as the first part of a trilogy; the middle part, *The Wind Shifts*, appeared in 1976 but then Sharp himself shifted from Scotland to Hollywood to enjoy the life of a highly paid screenwriter. *A Green Tree in Gedde* works by juxtaposition, the whole being the sum of three interdependent parts: Moseby's Book; Ruth's Book; Gibbon's and Cuffee's Book. John Moseby had been adopted into the middle class and is settling into a routine as a Glasgow University student. His best friend, Harry Gibbon is a carpenter ponderously seeking the meaning of life under the influence of his great-uncle Robert Gibbon who came to Greenock and developed into a peripatetic preacher who prophesied a new world and partly populated it with his illegitimate children.

A Green Tree in Gedde is dedicated 'to Greenock, to its buildings and chimneys and streets and the glimpses they have afforded me of the river and the hills'. The opening paragraph of the novel invokes the town:

Greenock lies along the Clyde littoral and is built up on to the hills behind. Thus it is a long lateral town and the streets rise steeply and provide open view of the river and the Argyllshire hills. . . . They are seen across an expanse of roofs and chimneys, the slates dull purple scales and the ridges presided by clumps of lums, cans churning and smoke pennons flying. The buildings are of sandstone block, greybuffs and occasional reds, and are erected in monolithic tenements, achieving their only rhythm in the flowing lines enforced by the land.

Bill Bryden

The dramatist and director Bill Bryden, who was born in Greenock in 1942, draws on the political past of the town in his play *Willie Rough*, first performed at the Royal Lyceum Theatre, Edinburgh, on 10 February 1972. Set in Greenock between February 1914 and June 1916, the play follows the political and psychological progress of Willie Rough who gets a job in a Greenock shipyard then, under the ideological influence of the Scottish Republican leader John MacLean, organises a strike which is brutally suppressed. Towards the end of the play Willie is sent to jail for writing a seditious article. It is a powerful drama that uses the vernacular speech-rhythms of Greenock effectively.

GREY MARE'S TAIL, Dumfriesshire   (Dumfries and Galloway)
8½m NE of Moffat, off A708

Sir Walter Scott

The waterfall is formed by the Tail Burn which drops more than 200ft from Loch Skene to join the Moffat Water. It, and the Giant's Grave (the hollow below), are described in the Introduction to Canto II of *Marmion* (1808):

> Yet him, whose heart is ill at ease,
> Such peaceful solitudes displease:
> He loves to drown his bosom's jar
> Amid the elemental war:
> And my black Palmer's choice had been
> Some ruder and more savage scene,
> Like that which frowns round dark Loch-Skene.
> There eagles scream from isle to shore;
> Down all the rocks and torrents roar;
> O'er the black waves incessant driven,
> Dark mists infect the summer heaven;

Through the rude barriers of the lake,
Away its hurrying waters break,
Faster and whiter dash and curl,
Till down yon dark abyss they hurl.
Rises the fog-smoke white as snow,
Thunders the viewless stream below,
Diving, as if condemn'd to lave
Some demon's subterranean cave
Who, prison'd by enchanter's spell,
Shakes the dark rock with groan and yell.
And well that Palmer's form and mien
Had suited with the stormy scene,
Just on the edge, straining his ken
To view the bottom of the den,
Where, deep deep down, and far within,
Toils with the rocks the roaring linn;
Then, issuing forth one foamy wave,
And wheeling round the Giant's Grave,
White as the snowy charger's tail,
Drives down the pass of Moffatdale.

In 1962 the National Trust for Scotland acquired 2,383 acres around the falls.

HADDINGTON, East Lothian (Lothian)   15m E of Edinburgh,
off A1

John Knox

Haddington (which has been a royal burgh since the twelfth century) is celebrated for its ecclesiastical associations. **St Mary's Parish Church** (built in the late fourteenth and early fifteenth centuries and now restored) is one of the largest churches of its period; John Knox (1513–72), the driving force behind the Scottish Reformation, was born in Giffordgate, Haddington, just across the river from St Mary's. In December 1545 Knox attached himself to the Protestant preacher George Wishart and was present, as a bodyguard, when Wishart preached before a small congregation in St Mary's early in 1546. Wishart was arrested the following day and (on 1 March 1546) burned for heresy in the presence of Cardinal Beaton in St Andrews Castle. The Protestant response to this was to assassinate Beaton on 29 March and Knox subsequently became chaplain to the Castilians (as the Protestant holders of St Andrews Castle were called). From then on his life was wholly dedicated to the cause of the

Scottish Reformation which became an established fact when the Scottish parliament approved, on 11 August 1560, the Protestant Confession of Faith prepared by Knox and his colleagues.

A man of enormous intellectual energy, Knox was a powerful polemicist and gifted writer. His manifesto *The First Blast of the Trumpet against the Monstrous Regiment of Women* (published anonymously in the summer of 1558) opens provocatively:

> To promote a Woman to beare rule, superioritie, dominion, or empire above any Realme, Nation, or Citie, is repugnant to Nature; contumelie to God, a thing most contrarious to his revealed will and approved ordinance, and finallie, it is the subversion of good Order, of all equitie and justice.

Knox had specific women such as 'Bloody Mary' Tudor and Mary of Guise in mind and was by no means a misogynist; in fact he married twice, and fathered five children.

On 15 January 1561 the First Book of Discipline was presented to the Scottish parliament as largely Knox's work. It allowed congregations to elect their own pastors, divided Scotland into parishes and – most significant of all – proposed educational reforms that created mass literacy in Scotland. Each parish was to provide a minimum of four years schooling for every child; there were to be secondary schools in the larger towns; and Scotland's three universities (St Andrews, Glasgow, and Aberdeen) were to be improved. Parliament did not actually pass the First Book of Discipline because the nobles were afraid they would personally have to finance the educational programme; nevertheless it was implemented and it became possible for a poor child in Scotland to earn a university education on account of his brains. Knox, a peasant's son, thus repaid the people for their faith in him. Knox's classic (if inevitably prejudiced) account of the *Historie of the Reformation of Religioun Within the Realm of Scotland* (completed 1586) is a vivid and vigorous narrative impressive for its eloquence and evocative atmosphere.

At the wish of Thomas Carlyle (who died on 5 February 1881) an oak tree was planted, on 29 March 1881, near the site of Knox's birthplace. The tree is fenced off and up a few steps from the street at Giffordgate (across the river from St Mary's). The commemorative stone beside the tree mistakenly gives the year of Knox's birth as 1505 whereas on the evidence of a letter, sent on 13 November 1579 from Sir Peter Young to Calvin's successor Beza, the actual year was 1513. Carlyle said (in 1840) that Knox was 'The one Scotchman to whom of all others, his country and the world owe a debt'. There is also a possible personal link between Carlyle and Knox for Carlyle liked to cite the story that his wife's father, John Welsh, was descended from John Knox, a Welsh having married Knox's daughter and become minister at Ayr. However as this Welsh was a second son and John Welsh was descended from the elder brother the story seems without substance.

Thomas Carlyle, Jane Welsh Carlyle

In his *Reminiscences* (1881), Thomas Carlyle (1795–1881) describes the house where his wife Jane Baillie Welsh (1801–66) spent the first twenty-five years of her life:

> At home was opulence (*without* waste), elegance, good sense, silent practical affection and manly wisdom; from threshold to roof-tree, no paltriness or unveracity admitted into it. I often told her how very beautiful her childhood was to me, – so authentic-looking withal, in her charmingly naive and humourous way of telling; – and that she must have been 'the prettiest little Jenny Spinner' (Scotch name for a long-winged, long-legged, extremely bright and airy insect) that was dancing on the summer rays in her time.

This house, in Lodge Street, is now the **Jane Welsh Carlyle Museum**, open to the public from April to September (Wed., Thurs., Fri., Sat. 2pm–5pm). In 1981, on the centenary of Carlyle's death, the Lamp of Lothian Trust (a charity based in Haddington) undertook the restoration of the drawing-room, the adjoining Doctor's dressing-room and the garden room in order to make the house and garden accessible to the public. It contains reproductions of portraits of the Carlyles, pictures of the places they stayed, and has been furnished in the Regency style.

The house, which dates from 1750, was the property of Jane's father Dr John Welsh, medical practitioner in Haddington from 1799 until his death from typhus at the age of forty-four in 1819. Jane, the only child of John and Grace Welsh, was born on 14 July 1801. From 1810 to 1812 she was tutored by Edward Irving (1792–1834) who had been appointed to take charge of the new Mathematical School in Haddington. Irving was an inspired teacher who took Jane on walks in and around Haddington. Before he left the town in 1812, to become a schoolmaster in Kirkcaldy, his athletic agility had ensured that his name would live on in Haddington: his jump over the Mill lade was remembered as Irving's leap.

In 1818 Irving saw Jane in Edinburgh and fell in love with her, a feeling she reciprocated. However, Irving had pledged himself to Isabella Martin whose father, the Kirkcaldy minister, refused to release him from his promise to marry. Irving and Jane were disappointed and depressed. His future included marriage to Isabella, fame in London as a millenialist preacher, and infamy when he was charged with heresy and deprived of his Church of Scotland ministry in 1833. (He died the following year and is buried in the crypt of Glasgow Cathedral.) Jane's future lay with Thomas Carlyle.

Carlyle admired Irving and met him in Edinburgh in 1815 and in Annan the following year. By 1816 both men were schoolteaching in Kirkcaldy where they became close friends. In *Reminiscences*,Carlyle acknowledges that it was from Irving that he first heard of Dr Welsh and his daughter:

it was from him (probably in 1818) that I first heard of her Father and her; some casual mention, the loving and reverential tone of which had struck me. Of the Father he spoke always as one of the wisest, truest, and most dignified of men; of her as a paragon of gifted young girls.

In May 1821 Irving came to Edinburgh to attend the General Assembly and persuaded Carlyle to come with him on an excursion to Haddington. Thus Carlyle was introduced, by Irving, to the nineteen-year-old Jane and her widowed mother. As Irving was unable to pursue his love of Jane, the way was clear for Carlyle to attend to 'the Flower of Haddington'. Accordingly he courted her by correspondence.

Jane realised that Carlyle was a brilliant man but she also felt he was somewhat more serious than herself and told him, in 1823, that she looked on their relationship as an affair of friendship: 'Your Friend I will be, your truest most devoted Friend, while I breathe the breath of life; but your Wife! Never, never!' Carlyle persevered and Jane eventually agreed to marry him. On 2 April 1826 – a few months before the marriage of 17 October 1826 – Carlyle told Jane his ideal of domestic harmony:

It may be stated in a word: *The Man should bear rule in the house and not the Woman*. This is an eternal axiom, the Law of Nature herself which no mortal departs from unpunished. I have meditated on this many long years, and every day it grows plainer to me; I must not and I cannot live in a house of which I am not head. I should be miserable myself, and make all about me miserable.

In the event he was both head of the house *and* often miserable, a situation that did nothing to lift Jane's moods of depression. She suffered from headaches and insomnia as she adjusted to life with Carlyle.

As her letters show, Jane was a naturally gifted writer and acute observer. Indeed, Charles Dickens hoped she would complete a novel since (so he told John Forster) 'None of the writing women come near her at all.' Instead of developing her own talents, she devoted herself to Carlyle, living with him in Edinburgh; enduring the isolation of Craigenputtock; and watching him grow into the 'Sage of Chelsea' in London. Only the letters remain as evidence of her artistry. The following passage, from a letter of 8 March 1824 to Eliza Stodart, is an assessment of Haddington:

Well! my beloved Cousin, here I am once more at the bottom of the pit of dullness, hemmed in all round, straining my eyeballs, and stretching my neck to no purpose. Was ever Starling in a more desperate plight? But I *will 'get out'* – by the wife of Job I *will*. Here is no sojourn for me! I must dwell in the open world, live amid life; but *here* is no life, no motion, no variety. It is the dimest, deadest spot (I verily believe) in the Creators universe: to look round in it, one might imagine that time had made a stand: the shopkeepers are to be seen standing at the doors of their shops, in the very same postures in which they have stood there ever since I was born; *'the thing that hath been is that also which shall be';* everything is *the same*, every thing is stupid; the very air one breathes is impregnated with stupidity. Alas my native place! that Goddess of dullness has strewed it with all her poppies!

But it is my native place still! and after all there is much in it that I love. I love the bleaching-green, where I used to caper, and roll, and tumble, and make gowan necklaces, and chains of dandelion stalks, in the days of my *'wee existence'*; and the schoolhouse where I carried away prizes, and signalised myself not more for the quickness of my parts, than for the valour of my arm, above all the boys of the community; and the mill-dam too where I performed feats of agility which it was easier to extol than to imitate, and which gained me at that time the reputation of a sticket callant (un garçon assasiné) which I believe I have maintained with credit up to the present hour; and above all I feel an affection for a field by the side of the river, where corn is growing now, and where a hayrick once stood – you remember it? For my part I shall never forget that summer's day; but cherish it *'within the secret cell of the heart'* as long as I live – the sky was so bright, the air so balmy, the whole universe so beautiful! I was very happy then! all my little world lay glittering in tinsel at my feet! but years have passed over it since; and storm after storm has stript it of much of its finery . . .

On 2 April Carlyle was in Edinburgh delivering his Rectorial Address at the University, Jane remaining in London as she was not well enough to travel. On Saturday 21 April, two days before Carlyle was due back in London, Jane went for a drive in her carriage. When she stopped in the park to give Tiny, a friend's dog, some exercise, another carriage knocked the dog over. Tiny recovered but Jane was shaken when she climbed back into her carriage. The coachman drove round the park twice before asking for further instructions. There was no answer – Jane had died of a heart attack.

Her body was brought back to Haddington and buried, beside her father, in the choir of St Mary's Parish Church. Over the grave is an epitaph composed by Carlyle who clearly meant every word of it:

In her bright existence she had more sorrows than are common; but also a soft invincibility, a clearness of discernment, and a noble loyalty of heart, which are rare. For forty years she was the true and everloving helpmate of her husband; and by act and word, unweariedly forwarded him, as none else could, in all of worthy that he did or attempted. She died in London, 21st April 1866; suddenly snatched away from him, and the light of his life as if gone out.

HART FELL, Dumfriesshire   (Dumfries and Galloway)   5m N of
Moffat

Nikolai Tolstoy

Standing at a height of 2,652ft above sea level, Hart Fell is the apex of the group of hills from which the rivers Annan,Clyde and Tweed rise. In Nikolai Tolstoy's *The Quest for Merlin* (1985), Hart Fell is identified as the Black Mountain, in the Caledonian Wood, to which Merlin retreated after the Battle of Arderydd in 573 AD. According to Tolstoy, Merlin was an historical figure of crucial importance. A pagan bard (or druid) who composed heathen poetry, Merlin flourished in the second half of the sixth century. His patron Gwenddolau was a pagan prince of the tribe known to the Romans as Selgovae.

As a champion of Celtic paganism, Gwenddolau came into conflict with Christianity and was killed fighting a Christian army at the battle of Arderydd, just north of Longtown near the English border. After the defeat and death of Gwenddolau, Merlin took refuge in the mountain of Hart Fell which, Tolstoy claims, was the centre of the tribal territory of the Selgovae. As its name implies, Hart Fell was celebrated for its harts, the last of which was reportedly killed in 1754. Merlin, says Tolstoy, was associated with a stag-cult and personified the horned deity who watched over men and beasts, and received the souls of the departed into his habitation in the sky:

He wore an antlered helm (possibly deerskins as well), and in some degree acted out the part of the stag itself. His station was by a sacred spring on the edge of a mountain [Hart Fell] in the centre of the Caledonian Forest, from whose summit he could look down upon the world spread out below. A sacred apple tree or orchard grew nearby, and the recluse was believed to be attended by animal familiars in the form of a pig and a wolf. The whole area of the mountain was regarded with awe and fear.

As well as placing Merlin on a Scottish mountain, Tolstoy also traced the prophet's sacred spring to Hartfell Spa, a chalybeate spring emerging from the hillside by the stream known as Spa Well Burn. From Tolstoy's account, Hart Fell was once regarded as the Sacred Centre of North Britain between the Roman Walls; and Hartfell Spa was Merlin's mountain spring, the oracular source of his prophecies.

HAWICK, Roxburghshire   (Border)   40m SE of Edinburgh on A7

Sir Walter Scott

In **Haggisha'**, in a row of cottages used as stables, a plaque marks the birthplace of Robert Paterson (1715–1801), the original of Scott's Old Mortality. By the framing format of Scott's 'Tales of My Landlord' series of novels, *Old Mortality* (1816) is narrated by Peter Pattieson who bases his text on anecdotes told him by the wandering inscription-carver Old Mortality. Pattieson's favourite walk, from the village schoolhouse of Gandercleugh, ends in a deserted burial ground where stand stones to the Covenanters. One summer evening, Pattieson sees old Mortality:

An old man was seated upon the monument of the slaughtered presbyterians, and busily employed in deepening, with his chisel, the letters of the inscription, which, announcing, in scriptural language, the promised blessings of futurity to be the lot of the slain, anathematised the murderers with corresponding violence. A blue bonnet of unusual dimensions covered the grey hairs of the pious workman . . . I had no difficulty in recognising a religious itinerant whom I had often heard talked of, and who was known in various parts of Scotland by the title of Old Mortality. . . . In the language of Scripture, he left his house, his home, and his kindred, and wandered about until the day of his death, a period of nearly thirty years. During this long pilgrimage, the pious enthusiast regulated his circuit so as annually to visit the graves of the unfortunate Covenanters, who suffered by the sword, or by the executioner, during the reigns of the two last monarchs of the Stewart line. . . . Their tombs are often apart from all human habitation, in the remote moors and wilds to which the wanderers had fled for concealment. But wherever they existed, Old Mortality was sure to visit them when his annual round brought them within his reach.

In his introduction to the 1830 'Magnum Opus' edition of the novel, Scott explains that he met the original Old Mortality, Robert Paterson, in Dunnottar churchyard around 1800. Paterson was born at Haggisha' (also known as Burnflat) in 1715 (though the memorial tablet at Haggisha' gives the year 1712). A reliable account of Paterson's origins was given to Scott by his friend Joseph Train, supervisor of excise at Dumfries:

Robert Paterson, *alias* Old Mortality, was the son of Walter Paterson and Margaret Scott, who occupied the farm of Haggisha', in the parish of Hawick, during nearly the first half of the eighteenth century. Here Robert was born, in the memorable year 1715.

At the age of thirteen Paterson was apprenticed to his brother Francis of Corncockle Quarry, Lochmaben, where he studied stonecraft. In 1743 he married Lizzie Gray and obtained a lease of Gatelawbridge Quarry in the parish of Morton. As an ardent member of the religious sect known as Hill-men or Cameronians (after their Covenanting founder Richard Cameron) Paterson took it upon himself to repair the Cameronian monuments in Galloway even though this responsibility led to the neglect of his wife and children. Gradually he extended his work throughout the Lowlands and beyond, hence Scott's meeting with him in Dunnottar Churchyard.

Francis George Scott, Hugh MacDiarmid

Francis George Scott (1880–1958), the composer, was born on 25 January (Burns's birthday) 1880 at his parents' home at 6 Oliver Crescent (plaque put up on the centenary of Scott's birth). He was educated at Hawick Academy and Brand's Teviot Grove Academy, a private school. He left Hawick in 1887 to enrol at Edinburgh University and as a pupil-teacher at Moray House College of Education, Edinburgh. From 1903 to 1912 Scott taught English at Langholm Academy where one of his pupils was Christopher Murray Grieve (1892–1978) – the poet Hugh MacDiarmid.

Scott was one of the most important figures to feature in MacDiarmid's career: the fact that *A Drunk Man Looks at the Thistle* (1926) is dedicated 'to my friend, Francis George Scott, the composer, who suggested it' is evidence of that. MacDiarmid wrote, in *The Company I've Kept* (1966):

I had got to the point [in shaping *A Drunk Man*] when I had ceased to be able to see the forest for the trees. I found the necessary imaginative sympathy in F. G. Scott and handed over the whole mass of my mansucript to him. He was not long in seizing on the essentials and urging the ruthless discarding of the unessentials. I had no hesitation in taking his advice and in this way the significant shape was educed from the welter of stuff and the rest pruned away.

Scott's sympathetic settings of MacDiarmid's lyrics are contained in *Scottish Lyrics set to Music* (5 vols, 1922–39). One of the MacDiarmid lyrics set by Scott, 'The Sauchs in the Reuch Heuch Hauch' describes – according to MacDiarmid's footnote in *Sangschaw* (1925) – 'A field near Hawick'. The field was in nearby Wilton, across the Teviot, but has been built over since MacDiarmid's youth.

HELENSBURGH, Dunbartonshire (Strathclyde) 8m NW of Dumbarton

W. W. Blackie

The residential coast town of Helensburgh is situated at the entrance to Gare Loch, on the north shore of the firth of Clyde. The **Hill House**, Upper Colquhoun Street – now in the care of the National Trust for Scotland – is one of the great architectural works of Charles Rennie Mackintosh (1868–1928). In 1902 the publisher W. W. Blackie moved from Dunblane to Helensburgh and commissioned Mackintosh to build him a family home on a site at the crown of the hill in Upper Helensburgh. When Blackie met Mackintosh he was astonished at his youth (he was thirty-four in 1902): 'I myself was not terribly old,' Blackie observed, 'but here was a truly great man who, by comparison with myself, I esteemed to be a "mere boy".' Blackie told Mackintosh he 'fancied grey roughcast for the walls and slate for the roof; and that any architectural effect sought should be secured by the massing of the parts rather than adventitious ornamentation.' Mackintosh's design, comprising two wings, combines Scottish Baronial with contemporary features; for example, the garden tower invokes the barmkin tower of the old Scottish keeps; by contrast the bay window in the drawing room, with its expanse of glass and flat roof, is conspicuously modern. Every aspect of the interior was supervised by Mackintosh, as Blackie noted approvingly: 'Every detail, inside as well as outside, received his careful, I may say loving attention; fireplaces, grates, fenders, fire irons; inside walls treated with a touch of stencilled ornament delightfully designed and properly placed.' The result is a unity displaying Mackintosh's interest in traditional Scottish architecture, his innovative contributions to modern architecture, and his decorative approach to interior design (as in the geometrically patterned chairs and carpet). The library – now an information centre but formerly the room in which Blackie considered manuscripts for publication – contains a desk originally designed by Mackintosh for the editor of the *Glasgow Herald*.

Neil Munro, James Bridie, George Blake

Three distinguished Scottish authors were drawn to Helensburgh at various times: the novelist Neil Munro (1864–1930) spent the last three years of his life at Craigendoran, less than a mile south-west of Helensburgh; the dramatist James Bridie (O. Mavor, 1888–1951) lived at Rockbank after retiring from his medical practice in Glasgow; George Blake (1893–1961) divided his time from 1932 onwards between Glasgow and Helensburgh which he used as the setting for his novel *Down to the Sea* (1937).

C. Day Lewis

In July 1928, C. Day Lewis (1904–72), the Irish-born poet who came to prominence as one of the English leftist poets of the 1930s, was offered a job at Larchfield Academy, Colquhoun Street, which had become a preparatory school in 1919. On 12 September 1928 he began teaching (games as well as English) at Larchfield whose former pupils included Sir James George Frazer (1854–1941), author of *The Golden Bough* (1890); and John Logie Baird (1888–1946), the pioneer of television. While in Helensburgh, which he called the 'Wimbledon of the North', Day Lewis worked on his *Transitional Poem* (1929). When Day Lewis married Mary King, his first wife, at Sherborne on 27 December 1928, his friend W.H. Auden sent him 'Epithalamium for C. Day-Lewis' with the lines 'The corridors are still/Within the empty school'. On 10 January 1929 Mr and Mrs Day Lewis moved into 128 West King Street, a council house on an estate overlooking the Clyde estuary to Greenock and on 27 February Auden came from Berlin for a visit. By June 1929 Day Lewis was weary of his Scottish sojourn for he wrote to L. A. G. Strong: 'I don't think we can stand more than another year in this hole . . . the parents and the directors at this place make life a positive misery.' Nevertheless, at Christmas 1929 Day Lewis and Larchfield's music master E. W. Hardy produced a Larchfield school song;

> School of the mountain and the lochside
> School of the white and blue,
> Make our hearts as bright and brave
> As the mountain and the wave
> So Scotland may be proud of you.

The song was dedicated to T. T. N. Perkins, the headmaster, but not used after he retired. Before leaving Helensburgh on 3 April 1930, Day Lewis recommended W. H. Auden as his successor at Larchfield, a proposal that was accepted by the school.

W. H. Auden

Auden began teaching at Larchfield in Easter 1930 and shortly after his arrival learned that Faber and Faber had accepted his *Poems* (1930) for publication. In 1931 the novelist Edward Upward stayed at Larchfield with Auden who lived in the staff living-quarters at the school. During the summer of 1931 Auden completed Book One of *The Orators* (1932) and completed the work by the late autumn of 1931. In October 1931 Auden was weary of Larchfield, as he explained in a letter to Gabriel Carrit: 'The school gathers mildew. Numbers down, the headmaster partially blind, his wife growing gradually mad in a canvas shelter in the garden. I spend most of my time adjusting the flow of water to the lavatories.' In 1932, his last year at Larchfield, Auden wrote a poem called 'The Watchers' which cites the town:

> Under the darkness nothing seems to stir;
> The lilac bush like a conspirator
> Shams dead upon the lawn, and there
> Above the flagstaff the Great Bear
> Hangs as a portent over Helensburgh.

Larchfield remained a private fee-paying boys' preparatory school until 1977 when it was amalgamated with St Bride's School to form Lomond School.

THE HERMITAGE, Perthshire   (Tayside)   2m W of Dunkeld, off A9

James Macpherson

A folly set above a fall on the River Bran, the Hermitage was built in 1758 for the third Duke of Atholl. This rectangular pavilion with slated roof and circular lookout platform, was originally surrounded by a wild garden but in 1783 was renamed 'Ossian's Hall' and furnished in honour of the legendary Gaelic bard, Ossian, whose name became a byword for romantic rhetoric on account of the fabricated Ossianic poems in James Macpherson's *Fingal* (1761) and *Temora* (1763). A little vaulted building up the river was named 'Ossian's Cave'. In 1943 the Hermitage was presented to the National Trust for Scotland in fulfilment of a wish by the Trust's first President, the eighth Duke of Atholl. It was restored in 1952 and the Trust opened a Nature Trail in 1966.

William Wordsworth

William Wordsworth (1770–1850) visited the Hermitage in 1814 and as a result wrote his 'Effusion in the Pleasure-Ground on the Banks of the Bran, near Dunkeld' after being shown shown a picture of Ossian. The poem begins:

> What He – who, mid the kindred throng
> Of Heroes that inspired his song,
> Doth yet frequent the hill of storms,
> The stars dim-twinkling through their forms!
> What! Ossian here – a painted Thrall,
> Mute fixture on a stuccoed wall;
> To serve – an unsuspected screen

For show that must not yet be seen;
And, when the moment comes, to part
And vanish by mysterious art;
Head, harp, and body, split asunder,
For ingress to a world of wonder:
A gay saloon, with waters dancing
Upon the sight wherever glancing;
One loud cascade in front, and lo!
A thousand like it, white as snow –
Streams on the walls and torrent-foam
As active round the hollow dome,
Illusive cataracts! of their terrors
Not stripped, nor voiceless in the mirrors,
That catch the pageant from the flood
Thundering adown a rocky wood.
What pains to dazzle and confound!
What strife of colour, shape and sound
In this quaint medley, that might seem
Devised out of a sick man's dream!
Strange scene, fantastic and uneasy
As ever made a maniac dizzy,
When disenchanted from the mood
That loves on sullen thoughts to brood.

After reflecting on the unsuitability of the Ossianic folly, Wordsworth appeals for an artist worthy of Ossian's reputation:

Then let him hew with patient stroke
An Ossian out of mural rock,
And leave the figurative Man –
Upon thy margin, roaring Bran! –
Fixed, like the Templar of the steep,
An everlasting watch to keep;
With local sanctities in trust,
More precious than a hermit's dust;
And virtues through the mass infused,
Which old idolatry abused.

Wordworth's effusion ends:

Thus (where the intrusive Pile, ill-graced
With baubles of theatric taste,
O'erlooks the torrent breathing showers
On motley bands of alien flowers
In stiff confusion set or sown,
Till Nature cannot find her own,

Or keep a remnant of the sod
Which Caledonian Heroes trod)
I mused; and, thrusting for redress,
Recoiled into the wilderness.

Robert Burns

The great Scottish fiddler Neil Gow (1727–1807) was born in the neighbouring village of **Inver** where he was visited by Robert Burns in 1787. Burns found Gow 'a short, stout-built, honest, Highland figure, with his greyish hair shed on his honest social brow'. Burns's poem 'To Mr Gow, Visiting Dumfries' begins;

Thrice welcome, king o' rant and reel!
Whaur is the bard to Scotia leal
Wha wadna sing o' sic a chiel   *such*
    And sic a glorious fiddle.

HESSILHEAD, Ayrshire   (Strathclyde)   2m ĖSE of Beith

Alexander Montgomerie

Alexander Montgomerie (*c.* 1545–98) was born in Hessilhead Castle (whose ruins remain). He was the acknowledged leader of the Castalian Band of poets formed by James VI in 1583. His metrical agility is apparent in, for example, the lyric beginning:

Hay! now the day dawis;
The holie cok crawis;
Now shroudis the shawis,   *groves*
    Throu Natur anone.
The thiseel-cok cryis   *missel-thrush*
On lovers wha lyis.
Now skaillis the skyis:
    The nicht is near gone.

The king acclaimed Montgomerie as 'maistre of our art' and involved him in an undercover mission to Catholic Spain in 1586. Montgomerie was imprisoned as a result of this and resented what he took to be James VI's indifference to his plight. Montgomerie subsequently became involved in a Catholic plot and was outlawed on 14 July 1597. His masterpiece, the long allegorical *The Cherrie and the Slae* (1597), contemplates the rival temptations of a cherry tree and a bush of sloe berries.

174

HUNTLY, Aberdeenshire   (Grampian)   33m NW of Aberdeen on
A96

George MacDonald

George MacDonald (1824–1905) was born in Bogie Street in a building
(now the Huntly Carpet Shop) marked by a plaque. A farmer's son
supposedly descended from MacDonalds who escaped the Glencoe
massacre, MacDonald was educated at Aberdeen Grammar School; King's
College, Aberdeen; and Highbury Technical College. He became a
Congregational minister in 1859 but resigned five years later (for reasons
of health) and turned to journalism. In 1859 he became a Professor at
Bedford College, London and in later years retired to Bordigheera, Italy,
where he died on 18 September 1905. The Huntly library houses the
George MacDonald collection of books and manuscripts.

MacDonald published *Poems* in 1857, then explored an imaginative
world of fantasy in *Phantastes* (1858) and *Lilith* (1859), romances that
influenced the work of J. R. R. Tolkien and C. S. Lewis. His novels *Alec
Forbes* (1865) and *Robert Falconer* (1868) draw on his Huntly origins.
There is an ecstatic quality in many of MacDonald's poems, such as
'Longing':

> White dove of David, flying overhead,
> Golden with sunlight on thy snowy wings,
> Outspeeding thee my longing thoughts are fled
> To find a home afar from men and things.

INCHINNAN, Renfrewshire   (Strathclyde)   10m W of Glasgow

Douglas Dunn

The poet Douglas Dunn was born on 23 October 1942 in Inchinnan where
he lived until November 1964 when he married and went to the USA for
a year. He was educated at the local primary school, then Renfrew High
School and Camphill Senior Secondary School. After leaving school he
worked in Renfrew County Library and in 1961 attended the Scottish
School of Librarianship. From 1966 he lived in Hull and after the death
of his wife, Lesley, in 1981 decided to return to Scotland, settling in
Taymouth. Several of his poems concern Inchinnan and Renfrewshire.
'Drowning', from *Barbarians* (1979), is an elegy for a boy who drowned
in the River Gryfe, near Inchinnan:

> Why give the place its name, when it has changed,
> Where, in the grasping waters of the Gryfe,

He, his name forgotten now, was drowned?
What is remembered is his little life.

Later, in the same poem, Dunn imagines the impact the death has had on those who were boys with him in Inchinnan:

Ask any man of forty-odd or so
Around that parish by the Clyde's run sweat,
He'll shake his head as if he has forgotten,
Then walk away, and wish he could forget.

INNERLEITHEN, Peeblesshire   (Border)   6m SE of Peebles on A72

Sir Walter Scott

St Ronan's Well (1823), by Sir Walter Scott (1771–1832), is set early in the nineteenth century with action involving the well near Aultoun (that is, Innerleithen). After the publication of the novel, the well (follow the road above the car park on the north side of the High Street) became much-frequented.

INVERARY, Argyllshire   (Strathclyde)

Dr Samuel Johnson, James Boswell

Inverary, on the west side of Loch Fyne, was planned in its present form in 1743 on the instructions of the third Duke of Argyll who wanted a new castle in an appropriate environment. Dr Samuel Johnson (1709–84) and James Boswell (1740–95) visited Inverary on their Scottish tour of 1773. Boswell's entry of Monday 25 October 1773, in his *Journal of a Tour to the Hebrides* (1785) tells of a visit to the castle and how 'Dr Johnson was much struck by the grandeur and elegance of this princely seat'. The castle was badly damaged by fire in 1877 and 1975 but both times restoration work preserved the character of the building.

Mathew 'Monk' Lewis, Sir Walter Scott

In 1798, Mathew 'Monk' Lewis (1775–1818) met Sir Walter Scott at Inverary Castle. Lewis dedicated *Romantic Tales* (1808) to his host's daughter, Lady Charlotte Campbell. Scott's *A Legend of Montrose* (1819) describes the Marquis of Montrose's victory at Inverary (1644).

INVERARY

Alexander Smith

In *A Summer in Skye* (1865) Alexander Smith (1829–67) relates how he crossed Loch Fyne in a 'small wash-tub of a steamer' to Inverary:

> Arriving, you find the capital of the West Highlands, a rather pretty place, with excellent inns, several churches, a fine bay, a ducal residence, a striking conical hill – Duniquoich the barbarous name of it – wooded to the chin and with an ancient watch-tower perched on its bald crown. The chief seat of the Argylls cannot boast much of architectural beauty, being a square building with pepper-box-looking towers stuck on the corners.

Neil Munro

Neil Munro (1864–1930) was born on 2 June 1864 at Inverary. As a child he had his fair share of domestic strain since he did not know his father though he knew who his father was. Munro was a fluent writer and journalist; he eventually edited the *Glasgow Evening News* and enjoyed great popularity with his tales of *The Vital Spark* (1906) and its eccentric crew comprising Para Handy, Dougie Mcphail, Tar, Sunny Jim and Hurricane Jack. Munro's finest writing is contained in three historical romances: *John Splendid* (1898), *Doom Castle* (1901), *The New Road* (1914). Set partly in Inverary, *John Splendid* is narrated by Elrigmore, an educated Gael who intones his quaintly archaic English like a pibroch. Archibald, Marquis of Argyll (or Argile as the novel spells it) is the Clan Campbell figure of authority. John Splendid is Argile's kinsman and silver-mine manager. The three respond in in their various ways to Montrose's war on Lorn. Munro's evocation of Inverary is a strong feature of the novel, as in the following description of market-day at 'Inneraora':

> The market-day came on the morning after the day John Splendid and I [i.e. Elrigmore the narrator] foregathered with my Lord Archibald . . . All day the town hummed with Gaelic and the round bellowing of cattle. It was clear warm weather, never a breath of wind to stir the gilding trees behind the burgh. At ebb-tide the sea-beach whitened and smoked in the sun, and the hot air quivered over the stones and the crisping wrack. In such a season the bustling town in the heart of the stern Highlands seemed a fever spot. . . . A constant stream of men passed in and out at the changehouse closes and about the Fisherland tenements, where seafarers and drovers together sang the maddest love-ditties in the voices of roaring bulls; beating the while with their feet on the floor in our foolish Gaelic fashion.

177

INVERNESS, Inverness-shire (Highland)   16m SW of Nairn

Adamnan's 'Life' records that St Columba visited the Pictish King Brude around 565 at a castle 'near the Ness' and the site of this is believed to be Craig Phadrig, a 550ft hill two miles west of Inverness across the Caledonian Canal.

Dr Samuel Johnson, James Boswell

Dr Samuel Johnson (1709–84) and James Boswel (1740–95) visited Inverness on their Scottish tour of 1773, Boswell noting in his *Journal of a Tour of the Hebrides* (1785, entry for Saturday 28 August 1773) 'We got safely to Inverness, and put up at Mackenzie's inn'. (The inn has disappeared but a shop stands in its place at 50 High Street.) The next day the two men visited 'Macbeth's castle [which] perfectly corresponds with Shakespeare's description': the site of Macbeth's castle (where Duncan was murdered) is at Auldcastle Hill where a Victorian villa, Dun Macbeth, now stands.

Edwin Muir

Edwin Muir (1887–1959) described Inverness, in his *Scottish Journey* (1935), as being 'inconveniently crowded with vehicles of all kinds, most of them stationary'.

Neil Gunn

The novelist Neil Gunn (1891–1973) married Jessie Dallas Frew (known as Daisy) in 1921 and two years later arrived in Inverness as excise officer attached to the Glen Mhor distillery. The Gunns lived, first, in Bruce Gardens (the house, Moyness, occupies the site) then moved in 1926, the year Neil's first novel *Grey Coast* was published, to their bungalow Larachan, at the north end of Dochfour Drive, off Bruce Gardens. This was Gunn's home until 1937 when, encouraged by the popular success of his novel *Highland River* (1937), he resigned from the Customs and Excise service, sold Larachan for £950 and (as the title of his next book explains) went *Off in a Boat* (1938) with Daisy, sailing from Skye to Inverness.

INVERSNAID, Stirlingshire (Central)   3m NE of Tarbet

William and Dorothy Wordsworth

The hamlet of Inversnaid, on the east side of Loch Lomond, was visited by William Wordsworth (1770–1850) and his sister Dorothy (1771–1855), in 1803. Wordsworth's fulsome tribute 'To a Highland Girl (from *Memorials of a Tour in Scotland*, 1803) was written, as the subtitle explains, 'At Inversneyde, Upon Loch Lomond'. After walking to Loch Katrine, seven miles east, the Wordsworths were given dinner at Invernsnaid by the ferryman's daughter. Wordsworth's poem to her begins;

> Sweet Highland Girl, a very shower
> Of beauty is thy earthly dower!
> Twice seven consenting years have shed
> Their utmost bounty on thy head:
> And these grey rocks; that household lawn;
> Those trees, a veil just half withdrawn;
> This fall of water that doth make
> A murmur near the silent lake;
> This little bay; a quiet road
> That holds in shelter thy Abode –
> In truth together do ye seem
> Like something fashioned in a dream;
> Such Forms as from their covert peep
> When earthly cares are laid asleep!

A lochside path leads one mile north to Rob Roy's Cave, sometime home of the outlaw featured in Sir Walter Scott's *Rob Roy* (1818).

Gerard Manley Hopkins

'Inversnaid', by Gerard Manley Hopkins (1844–89), is an ecstatic affirmation of the place:

> This darksome burn, horseback brown,
> His rollrock highroad roaring down,
> In coop and in comb the fleece of his foam
> Flutes and low to the lake falls home.
>
> A windpuff-bonnet of fáwn-fróth
> Turns and twindles over the broth
> Of a pool so pitchblack, féll-frówning,
> It rounds and rounds Despair to drowning.
>
> Degged with dew, dappled with dew
> Are the groins of the braes that the brook treads through,
> Wiry heathpacks, flitches of fern,
> And the beadbonny ash that sits over the burn.

What would the world be, once bereft
Of wet and of wildness? Let them be left,
O let them be left, wildness and wet;
Long live the weeds and the wilderness yet.

INVERURIE, Aberdeenshire   (Grampian)   16m NW of Aberdeen on
A96

Arthur Johnston

Arthur Johnston (1587–1641) was born at Caskieben, now Keith Hall, an estate near Inverurie. Educated at King's College, Aberdeen, he left Scotland in 1608 to study in Padua and subsequently at the Protestant University of Sedan. In 1637 he became Lord Rector of King's College. Johnston, the 'Scottish Ovid', completed the editing of the anthology *Delitiae Poetarum Scotorum* (1637), containing the Latin verse of thirty-seven Scottish poets. He wrote descriptive poems and produced Latin translations of the Psalms.

William Thom

From 1840 to 1844 William Thom (1798–1840) lived at 23 North Street (plaque removed to public library after rebuilding); his weaving shop was at the junction of Burns Lane and North Street. In December 1840 Thom composed one of his best-known poems, 'The Blind Boy's Pranks', which appeared in the *Aberdeen Herald* on 2 January 1841. When Jean Stephen – the mother of four of Thom's seven children – died the 'Inverurie poet' composed 'The Mitherless Bairn':

The mitherless bairn gangs till his lane bed,	*goes, lonely*
Nane covers his cauld back or haps his bare head;	*covers*
His wee hackit heelies are hard as the airn,	*chapped, iron*
An' litheless the lair o' the mitherless bairn! ·	*comfortless*

After the success of his *Rhymes and Recollections of a Handloom Weaver* (1844) Thom was lionised in London as the 'weaver poet' but his heavy drinking prevented him from enjoying his success and he died in poverty in Dundee.

IONA, Argyllshire   (Strathclyde)   1m W of Ross of Mull

James Boswell, Dr Samuel Johnson

In May 563 Columba landed (according to tradition) at Port na Churaich (Port of the Coracle) on the island of Iona. The present monastic buildings are supposed to occupy the site of the Church and hutments of Columba's foundation (of which no trace remains). St Oran's Chapel (built in 1080 and restored), the oldest building on the island, contains the tomb of Lord Ronald, the Lord of the Isles featured in Sir Walter Scott's poem (1815) of that name. In the entry for Tuesday, 19 October 1773 in his *Journal of a Tour to the Hebrides* (1785) James Boswell (1740–95) describes a visit he and Dr Samuel Johnson (1709–84) made to Iona (or Icolmkill as he calls it, using the Gaelic name):

> When we had landed upon the sacred place, which , as long as I can remember, I had thought of with veneration, Dr Johnson and I cordially embraced. We had long talked of visiting Icolmkill; and, from the lateness of the season, were at times very doubtful whether we should be able to effect our purpose. To have seen it, even alone, would have given me great satisfaction; but the venerable scene was rendered much more pleasing by the company of my great and pious friend, who was no less affected by it than I was; and who had described the impressions it should make on the mind, with such strength of thought, and energy of language, that I shall quote his words, as conveying my own sensations much more forcibly than I am capable of doing: 'We were now treading that illustrious Island, which was once the luminary of the Caledonian regions, whence savage clans and roving barbarians derived the benefits of knowledge, and the blessings of religion. . . . That man is little to be envied, whose patriotism would not gain force upon the plan of *Marathon*, or whose piety would not grow warmer among the ruins of *Iona!*'

Iain Crichton Smith

While living in Oban (from 1955 to 1982) the poet Iain Crichton Smith (born 1928) visited Iona and wrote one of his finest poems, 'For the Unknown Seamen of the 1939–45 War Buried in Iona Churchyard'. It begins:

> One would like to be able to write something for them
> not for the sake of writing but because
> a man should be named in dying as well as living,
> in drowning as well as on death-bed, and because
> the brain being brain must try to establish laws.

IRONGRAY, Kirkcudbrightshire   (Dumfries and Galloway)   1½m S
of B729, 4m NW of Dumfries

Sir Walter Scott

A flat tombstone (near the east porch of the church) commemorates Helen
Walker (1712–91), the original of Sir Walter Scott's Jeanie Deans, heroine
of *The Heart of Midlothian* (1818). The stone, donated by Scott in 1831,
bears an epitaph stating (in Scott's words): 'This humble individual practised in real life the virtues with which fiction has invested the imaginary
character of Jeanie Deans'.

The source of the sentimental story that is at the heart of *The Heart of
Midlothian* came to Scott in a letter from an admirer, Mrs Helen Goldie,
who told the tale of Helen Walker:

> She had been left an orphan, with the charge of a sister considerably
> younger than herself, and who was educated and maintained by her
> exertions. Attached to her by so many ties, therefore, it will not be
> easy to conceive her feelings, when she found that this only sister must
> be tried by the laws of her country for child-murder, and upon being
> called as principal witness against her.

Scottish law stipulated that, in the case of a child being dead or missing,
a woman who gave birth without seeking assistance should be charged
with infanticide and executed if found guilty. Helen Walker could have
spared her sister the death sentence if she had testified to her preparation
for the birth but she declared 'It is impossible for me to swear to a
falsehood; and, whatever may be the consequence, I will give my oath
according to my conscience.' When her sister was duly sentenced to death
Helen had a petition drawn up, then set out on foot to London to present
herself (as Mrs Goldie told Scott) 'in her tartan plaid and country attire,
to the late Duke of Argyle, who immediately procured the pardon she
petitioned for, and Helen returned with it, on foot, just in time to save
her sister.'

From this moral tale Scott fashioned the character of plain Jeanie Deans
who, by a similar strategy, saves her beautiful half-sister from execution
in Edinburgh in whose Tolbooth prison (known as the Heart of Midlothian) Effie is confined at the beginning of the book. Jeanie, daughter
of the staunchly Presbyterian Douce Davie Deans, rises to the moralistic
occasion by saying 'I will bear my load alone – the back is made for the
burden'.

IRVINE, Ayrshire (Strathclyde) 12m N of Ayr on A78

James Montgomery

James Montgomery (1771–1854) was born on 4 November 1771 in a house (demolished) subsequently called Montgomery House, in Montgomery Street. Son of a missionary of the Moravian Brethren, he was educated at the Moravian School at Fulneck, near Leeds. He settled in Sheffield in 1792 and by 1796 had become editor of the *Sheffield Iris;* as such he went twice to prison for political articles he had printed. He published *Prison Amusements* in 1797 and the heroic poem *Greenland* in 1819. 'For ever with the Lord' is the most endurable of his many hymns.

Robert Burns

Robert Burns (1759–96) – to whom there is a statue on Irvine Moor – spent seven months in Irvine from midsummer 1781. Certain he should 'set about doing something in life' the poet chose to learn flax-dressing in Irvine, lodging first at 4 Glasgow Vennel (where a plaque marks the site). Disastrously his partner turned out to be 'a scoundrel of the first water who made money by the mystery of thieving' and, celebrating the New Year of 1782, the flax-dressing shop was burned down 'by the drunken carelessness of my partner's wife'.

Other events at Irvine were to have a more productive influence on Burns's career. He fell under the influence of Richard Brown, an obstreperous sailor whose spectacular adventures included being captured and abandoned on the wild Connaught coast. Brown encouraged his acolyte to indulge his sexual appetite whenever possible and also suggested he should publish the few poems he had written. This proposal, reinforced by the discovery of Robert Fergusson's Scots poems, 'strung anew my wildly-sounding, rustic lyre with emulating vigour' but did not prevent an onslaught of despair and depression caused by his heart condition. Irvine Burns Club, one of the oldest in the country, has a museum open to the public on Saturdays.

John Galt

John Galt (1779–1834), son of a sea captain, was born on 2 May 1779 in the High Street (site marked by a plaque with a relief portrait of Galt). He was ten when his family moved to Greenock. Galt's *The Provost* (1822) is set in Irvine, called Gudetown in the novel:

> In ancient times, Gudetown had been fortified with ports and gates at the end of the streets; and in troublesome occasions, the country

people, as the traditions relate, were in the practice of driving in their families and cattle for shelter. This gave occasion to that great width in our streets, and those of other royal boroughs, which is so remarkable; the same being so built, to give room and stance for the cattle.

Edgar Allan Poe

In 1815 Edgar Allan Poe (1809–49), the master of the supernatural short story, came to Irvine to stay with relatives of Galt (in the house Galt was born in) and attend the Royal School.

JEDBURGH, Roxburghshire (Border) 10m NE of Hawick on A68

James Thomson

Jedburgh Abbey was founded by David I around 1138 as a priory for Augustinians from Beauvais; by 1152 it was raised to the status of Abbey of St Mary. It was ruined by warfare though the Abbey Kirk continued to be used for worship until 1875. Jedburgh Grammar School was housed in the Abbey and James Thomson (1700–84), author of *The Seasons* (1730) was educated there.

Robert Burns

Robert Burns (1759–96) visited Jedburgh in 1787 and recorded, in his journal, the 'charming, romantic situation of Jedburgh, with gardens, orchards, etc. intermingled among the houses – fine old ruins, a once magnificent Cathedral'. He was honoured with the freedom of the burgh and stayed at 27 Canongate (gone), enjoying the 'fine romantic little river [Jed]'.

William and Dorothy Wordsworth

During their Scottish tour of 1803, William Wordsworth (1770–1850) and his sister Dorothy (1771–1855) visited Jedburgh in September. As the inn was taken by the county judge and his court, they were given lodgings in 5 Abbey Close (plaque). where they were looked after by an old lady whose vitality delighted them. Wordsworth paid tribute to his hostess in 'The Matron of Jedborough and Her Husband' (published 1807):

> Age! twine thy brows with fresh spring flowers,
> And call a train of laughing Hours;

And bid them dance, and bid them sing;
And thou, too, mingle in the ring!
Take to thy heart a new delight;
If not, make merry in despite
That there is One who scorns thy power: –
But dance! for under Jedborough Tower
A Matron dwells who, though she bears
The weight of more than seventy years,
Lives in the light of youthful glee,
And she will dance and sing with thee.

Sir Walter Scott

The Wordsworths were visited by Sir Walter Scott (1771–1832), Sheriff of Selkirkshire, who read them part of his yet-unpublished *The Lay of the Last Minstrel*. Dorothy noted in her journal:

We had our dinner sent from the inn, and a bottle of wine, that we might not disgrace the Sheriff, who supped with us in the evening, – stayed late, and repeated some of his poem.

Jedburgh had both positive and negative connotations for Scott. It was in Jedburgh that he first appeared as an advocate in a criminal trial, thus beginning his legal career. In 1831, the year before his death, Scott had two unpleasant experiences at Jedburgh. Determined that the doctrine of parliamentary reform should not be aired without some comment from him, he went to Jedburgh on 21 March 1831 and was hissed while speaking against the Reform Bill. Scott told his hecklers: 'I regard your gabble no more than the geese of the green'. In view of this reception and because he had suffered a third stroke his family urged him to refrain from further public involvement in politics.

However, on 18 May 1831 Scott decided to put in an appearance in Jedburgh on behalf of the Tory candidate for Roxburghshire, Henry Scott of Harden, even though the result of the election was a foregone conclusion. As Scott's carriage passed a group of radical Hawick weavers it was stoned and his attempt to make a speech was drowned out in abuse. Henry Scott was, predictably, elected (forty to nineteen) and Scott left Jedburgh to a hail of stones and cries of 'Burke Sir Walter' (a reference to the suffocating method of murder associated with William Burke, hanged in 1829 on the evidence of his accomplice William Hare). Though Sheriff Scott had a better reception a few days later at Selkirk (where he personally apprehended a jostling radical) the hostility of the Jedburgh crowd had a profoundly disturbing effect on Scott who, on his deathbed, several times reiterated the phrase 'Burke Sir Walter'.

JEMIMAVILLE, Ross-shire   (Highland)   5m E of Cromarty on B9163

Jane Duncan

From 1959 the novelist Jane Duncan (1910–76) lived at Jemimaville in the old barn which she had converted into her home (retaining the name, the Old Barn, as her address). She regarded the Black Isle, in fact and in fiction, as her home as her father was born in The Colony, a croft on the Black Isle, but had gone south to join the Dunbartonshire police (first in Helensburgh, then in Glasgow where Jane Duncan was born on 10 March 1910). The Colony (now a farm by another name but still indicated on the Ordnance Survey map of the area) was the origin of Reachfar, the hilltop croft (on the Black Isle) linking nineteen related novels, collectively known as the *Friends* series. Reachfar, where the narrator Janet Sandison was raised, is also a symbol of the childhood idyll of innocence. As the first *Friends* novel – *My Friends the Miss Boyds* (1959) – has it, 'Reachfar was the one unchanging place in a world of constant change'.

Jane Duncan spent all her holidays at The Colony until the age of twenty-one when she went to live in England and in novel after novel The Colony is recreated as Reachfar, a little heaven in an increasingly ugly world. In *My Friends the Hungry Generation* (1968) Janet Sandison comes home to Scotland for a holiday in Aberdeenshire. She discovers that her brother's three children are sustained by stories of Reachfar:

> This myth of Reachfar that they were creating for themselves was something that they needed, something that had kinship with a deep need in all humanity. They felt the need for life to contain something that was wonderful, a sorta miracle that had clouds and clouds of glory and, above all, permanence. This myth that was rooted in the past, beyond the horizon of memory was a wispy tenuous thing that came and went in the mind like a rainbow in the April sky over Reachfar hill but it had, yet, the strength to be a bulwark which could defend the spirit and hold it unshaken amidst the erupting chaos of growing up and pressing on through day-to-day life.

When Jane Duncan's father retired from the police force, he worked on The Colony and settled in Jemimaville. At the time of his death in 1951 Jane Duncan was living with her husband in the West Indies. Her husband's death in 1958 made Jane Duncan decide to return to Scotland so she settled in her father's cottage in Jemimaville in 1959. She describes the village in *Letter from Reachfar* (1975). As she explains, there is a large 'rather beautiful' old house called Poyntzfield about a mile from the village post office. Poyntzfield got its name in a rather romantic manner for the house and estate were known as Ardoch in the eighteenth century when the house was inherited by 'a penniless lad wi' a lang pedigree who, like many more of his kind, went south to find himself a wealthy bride'. In Suffolk (or possibly Norfolk) he came across Jemima Poyntz, daughter of a Dutch father and an English mother. Taking his bride to his Highland home, the laird of Ardoch used her dowry to improve and enlarge the house, adding two wings to the rectangular block to make a three-sided courtyard and adding, at the back of the original block, a tower with an onion-shaped roof;

> The effect of these additions is curiously Dutch or perhaps merely foreign to Ross-shire. Then, in further compliment to his bride, [the laird of Ardoch] renamed both house and estate Poyntzfield but this was not all. He went on to build a row of cottages for his workers on the north seaward boundary of the estate and this has grown into the village of some twenty-five houses which bears the name of Jemimaville, where I now live. Miss Jemima Poyntz, if this story is true, and it is fairly well documented, is well commemorated.

Jane Duncan died in the Old Barn on 20 October 1976.

JURA, Argyllshire   (Strathclyde)

George Orwell

From May 1947 until the end of 1948 George Orwell – Eric Arthur Blair (1903–50) – looked on **Barnhill**, near the northern end of the Hebridean island of Jura, as his home during a crucial critical period of his life. He finished *Nineteen Eighty-Four* in 1948 – hence the title which simply reverses two digits to establish a different time. The first draft of the novel was ready by the end of October 1947, the revision completed in November 1948, and the typescript posted to his publisher on 4 December 1948. It was his last novel, his farewell performance, and he died (in England) of a lung haemorrhage on 21 January 1950. Between the first draft and the authorised version Orwell spent seven months (from Christmas Eve 1947) in Hairmyres Hospital, East Kilbride. Though he disliked Scots, Orwell had composed his masterpiece in Scotland, a place he described as 'almost an occupied country'.

For years Orwell had dreamed of getting away from it all to a Scottish island where presumably he would be able to avoid the natives. In his war-time diary of 20 June 1940 he admitted to 'Thinking always of my island in the Hebrides, which I suppose I shall never possess or see.' The island he came to inhabit was Jura which he first visited in 1944. His influential land-owning friend, David Astor, helped him find a remote farmhouse and so Orwell eventually moved into Barnhill, Jura, on 23 May 1947. He took with him his younger sister Avril, his adopted son Richard and a good amount of distress and desolation. He had lost his first wife Eileen in 1945, his sister Marjorie a few weeks before the move to Jura, and his personal sadness was deepened by a distrust of the Labour Government. Orwell's socialism was an emotional affair and he was disappointed that the Labour Government had not abolished public schools, the House of Lords and titles. Ironically, for a sick man, he despaired at Aneurin Bevan losing himself in 'all this administration about housing and hospitals'.

Orwell always liked to dwell on the worst aspects of any situation – whether it was his schooldays or his time ostensibly spent down and out in Paris and London – and it is tempting to read into the pages of *Nineteen Eighty-Four* some of the difficulties he endured in his abandoned farmhouse in Jura. There is, in the novel, a description of a property where 'plaster flaked constantly from ceilings and walls, the pipes burst in every hard frost, the roof leaked whenever there was snow, the heating system was usually running at half steam'. That could well be a reflection on life in the Orwell household at Barnhill farmhouse; if it is then Orwell would have enjoyed the misery of it. When the young David Holbrook visited Jura he noted a grimly masochistic streak in the great writer and wrote an unpublished novel in which Orwell serves a meal cooked by his sister. When Avril has transformed a goose into 'a deep brown carbonised relic [Orwell], with every line in his face turned down in contented displeasure, carved off meat baked as hard as bootlaces'. Life in Jura, with its discomforts, was very much to Orwell's liking and he intended to make Barnhill his permanent home.

The orthodox version of the making of *Nineteen Eighty-Four* is that Orwell's bleak vision was the work of a sick man who had isolated himself on a remote Scottish island in order to rid himself of the world he detested. Orwell's hatred, expressed in many articles and essays, was directed towards left-wing intellectuals whose arrogant ideology made them easy meat for brutal autocrats. So when Winston Smith, the hero of *Nineteen Eighty-Four*, dares to allow his mind to open on an optimistic opinion he pins his hopes on the proles:

If there was hope, it *must* lie in the proles, because only there, in those swarming disregarded masses, 85 per cent of the population of Oceania, could the force to destroy the Party ever be generated. The Party could not be overthrown from within.

Smith's faith is misplaced, it transpires, and he is finally at the mercy of the intellectually adroit O'Brien who tortures him into such submission that at the end of the novel Smith 'had won the victory over himself. He loved Big Brother'. Ingsoc, or English Socialism, has triumphed. The world is in a state of terror. As O'Brien tells Winston Smith: 'If you want a picture of the future, imagine a boot stamping on a human face – for ever.'

Orwell's biographers differ in their accounts of the Jura days. Bernard Crick, in *George Orwell* (1980), shows Orwell to be more of an imaginative than a documentary writer, claims that Orwell planned the novel as early as 1943 and concludes that '*Nineteen Eighty-Four* was no last testament: it was simply the last major book he wrote before he happened to die.' T. R. Fyvel's anecdotal memoir (1982) looks askance at the decision to live in Jura. 'Barnhill,' writes Fyvel, 'was in no way a good place for a man in Orwell's precarious state of health [but possibly] he wanted to put the maximum distance between himself and the atomic threat. It's a thought.' Apart from Crick's view of Jura as a suitable retreat for a writer and Fyvel's view of it as a desperate escapist measure there is the evidence of the novel itself which suggests that Orwell injected into his fiction the clinical facts of his own human condition.

After Winston Smith has been tortured by O'Brien he has an opportunity to examine himself and is suitably appalled:

> the truly frightening thing was the emaciation of his body. The barrel of the ribs was as narrow as that of a skeleton; the legs had shrunk so that the knees were thicker than the thighs. . . . The thin shoulders were hunched forward so as to make a cavity of the chest, the scraggy neck seemed to be bending double under the weight of the skull.

That is an exteme projection of what was happening to Orwell's own tubercular body as he indicated in a hospital notebook of 21 May 1948: 'Discomfort in gums. Chest more or less always constricted. Feeling in the morning of being almost unable to stand up. . . . Eyes always watering.'

It would be misleading to regard *Nineteen Eighty-Four* as merely a novel containing the details of how Orwell's dream of Jura turned into the nightmare of a dying man. However it is reasonable to assume that a writer of Orwell's disposition would use his immediate predicament in a dramatic way. *Nineteen Eighty-Four* is one of the most disturbing books in English literature, a brilliant satire on what can happen when citizens take political power for granted. Yet there is a strong autobiographical element. As Orwell worked in Jura typing the final text of his novel in a bedroom heated by a paraffin-stove he was well aware of his physical deterioration and must have pondered on his alternative title for *Nineteen Eighty-Four – The Last Man in Europe*. In the novel O'Brien tells Winston Smith:

> You are rotting away, you are falling to pieces. . . . Now turn round and look into that mirror again. Do you see that thing facing you? That is the last man. If you are human, that is humanity.

In the circumstances Orwell must have had moments when he felt exactly like that.

KELSO, Roxburghshire   (Border)   10m NNE of Jedburgh on A698

Sir Walter Scott

Kelso, on the banks of the Teviot and the Tweed, is a market town associated with Sir Walter Scott (1771–1832). Kelso Abbey, at Bridge Street, was the largest of the Border abbeys and a delight to Scott. It was founded in 1128 and razed by the Earl of Hertford in 1545. The tower is part of the original building.

When he was twelve Scott finished at the High School in Edinburgh but, because of growing pains, went for six months to his maiden aunt Janet's in Kelso instead of going straight to Edinburgh University. Her Garden Cottage (a little house in an elaborate garden) was later renamed **Waverley Lodge**. Scott attended the Grammar School in the nave of the abbey and became friendly with a classmate, James Ballantyne (1772–1833), a native of Kelso.

In these surroundings Scott felt (he recalled) the first 'awakening of that delightful feeling for the beauties of natural objects which has never since deserted me'. He thought Kelso 'the most beautiful, if not the most romantic village in Scotland', fell in love with the river Tweed, and was imaginatively excited by the ruined abbey. Moreover, 'the modern mansion of Fleurs, which is so situated as to combine the ideas of ancient baronial grandeur with those of modern taste' planted in his mind a seed that was to grow into Abbotsford. **Floors Castle** built by William Adam in 1721, is two miles north-west of Kelso and open to the public (July–Sept., daily except Fri. and Sat., grounds and gardens 12.30–5.30pm, house 1.30–5.30pm).

Having learned 'the love of natural beauty, more especially when combined with ancient ruins', Scott went back to Edinburgh to begin his studies at the University. In 1785 he was apprenticed to his father as Writer to the Signet and in the second year of his apprenticeship suffered an internal haemorrhage. Part of his convalescence was spent at Rosebank, the newly acquired home of his uncle Captain Robert Scott. At this villa on the Tweed, just below the town, Scott enjoyed magnificent views. He not only made a complete recovery but developed into a tall, physically fit youth so little troubled by his lameness that he undertook thirty-mile walks and spent much time horse riding. He also, at seventeen, took the time to fall in love with Jessie, a local tradesman's daughter, whom he honoured with a poem:

KILDERMORIE LODGE

Lassie can ye love me weel?
Ask your heart, and answer true,
Doth that gentle bosom feel
Love for one that loveth you?

In 1804 Scott inherited Rosebank, sold it for a profit and invested the money in the printing business of James Ballantyne. As a partner, Scott was badly hit by the collapse of the firm in 1826 and had to work off his debts by paying the money made from his writing into a trust.

KILDERMORIE LODGE, Ross-shire   (Highland)   10m NE of Alness

Hugh MacDiarmid

Kildermorie Lodge (ten miles up a road, passing Strathrusdale and Braentra, from Ardross filling station) was occupied from October 1920 to April 1921 by Christopher Murray Grieve (1892–1972) – before he adopted (in 1922) the pseudonym Hugh MacDiarmid. Grieve taught (under the Ross and Cromarty Education Authority) the two daughters of the head stalker in a side-school five minutes from the lodge. The property was owned by Dyson Perrins, the Worcester sauce millionaire who also owned Ardross castle. In a letter (of 13 November 1920) Grieve observed: 'my employer is C.W. Dyson-Perrins . . . one of the most delightful and original little good-hearted freaks in Christendom!'

Grieve's first impression of the place was favourable for he wrote to his old teacher, George Ogilvie, on 24 October 1920:

You must have wondered how I was enjoying this. It has been the most unqualifiedly successful experience I have yet made in a life of ups and downs. I intend to remain here as long as circumstances will permit.

In November 1920 he wrote to Ogilvie:

A lean week! Nothing of interest to report. My wife [Peggy] returned (after 5 weeks absence) on Thursday: and we are busy entrenching ourselves, in all the ways that one needs must at a distance of 17 miles from the nearest village, against the rigours to come – rigours already most unmistakably adumbrated in a terrific and soul-freezing frost. Praise be it is luxuriously comfortable indoors – and I have barely five minutes walk to school.

Grieve planned a sequence of fifty 'Sonnets of the Highland Hills' – eleven of which are included in *The Complete Poems of Hugh MacDiarmid* (1985) edited by W. R. Aitken and Michael Grieve – while staying at Kildermorie Lodge. One of the sonnets, 'The Wind-Bags', is subtitled 'Gildermorie, November 1920' and begins:

191

Rain-beaten stones; great tussocks of dead grass
And stagnant waters throwing leaden lights
To leaden skies: a rough-maned wind that bites
With aimless violence at the clouds that pass,
Roaring, black-jowled, and bull-like in the void,
And I, in wild and boundless consciousness,
A brooding chaos, feel within me press
The corpse of Time, aborted, cold, negroid.

During his stay at Kildermorie Lodge, Grieve also worked on his first book, *Annals of the Five Senses* (1923), and planned his periodical *Scottish Chapbook* (launched in 1922).

KILMARNOCK, Ayrshire   (Strathclyde)   12m NE of Ayr, off A77

Robert Burns

On the corner of Waterloo Street and King Street, in Starr Inn Close, stood **John Wilson's printing shop** (now gone, site marked by a granite slab) which produced *Poems, Chiefly in the Scottish Dialect* (1786) by Robert Burns (1759–96). At the foot of the title page is the imprint *'Kilmarnock/Printed by John Wilson/M,DCC,LXXXVI'* – hence the phrase 'Kilmarnock edition'.

Burns's first book was published by subscription. The poet sent Wilson proposals for the book in April 1786 and it appeared on 31 July 1786 when Burns was twenty-seven. It was stitched in blue paper, cost three shillings a copy and the edition of 612 was sold out in a month at a profit, to the poet, of £20. Wilson refused to print a second, enlarged edition of the book so Burns had that printed in Edinburgh by William Smellie.

The Kilmarnock edition is a remarkable first collection, containing the bulk of Burns's poetic achievement – though it omitted 'The Twa Herds', 'Death and Dr Hornbook', 'Address to the Unco Guid' and 'Holy Willie's Prayer'; and, of course, 'Tam O' Shanter' (1790) was still to come. In the last ten years of his life, with the glorious exception of 'Tam O' Shanter', Burns concentrated on songwriting rather than the composition of verse.

Poems, Chiefly in the Scottish Dialect was greeted by a storm of applause. In 1786 the *Edinburgh Magazine* commented: 'The author is indeed a striking example of native genius bursting through the obscurity of poverty and the obstructions of a laborious life.' Henry Mackenzie, author of *The Man of Feeling* (1771), felt even more strongly on the subject. In the *Lounger* (9 December 1786), as well as pinning the label of 'heaven-taught ploughman' to Burns, he made the point that the poet:

has been obliged to form the resolution of leaving his native land, to seek under a West Indian clime that shelter and support which Scotland has denied him. But I trust means may be found to prevent this resolution from taking place; and that I do my country no more than justice, when I suppose her ready to stretch out her hand and cherish and retain this native poet.

Burns, in other words, was too precious a Scottish commodity to export to the West Indies. He had to be kept in Scotland and the success of the Kilmarnock edition ensured just that for Burns abandoned his plans to sail to Jamaica and headed instead for Edinburgh where he was lionised.

The **Laigh Kirk** (Bank Street) provides the setting for 'The Ordination' which begins:

> Kilmarnock wabsters, fidge an' claw, *weavers, shrug, scratch*
>   An' pour your creeshie nations; *greasy*
> An' ye wha leather rax an' draw, *stretch*
>   Of a' denominations;
> Swith! to the Laigh Kirk, ane an' a',
>   An' there tak up your stations;
> Then aff to Begbie's in a raw,
>   An' pour divine libations
>   For joy this day.

Begbie's (the Angel Inn in Market Lane) has gone. 'Tam Samson's Elegy' commemorates a Kilmarnock seedsman who lived in London Road (house gone):

> Kilmarnock lang may grunt an' grane, *groan*
> An' sigh, an' sab, an' greet her lane, *weep alone*
> An' cleed her bairns – man, wife an' wean – *clothe, child*
>   In morning weed;
> To Death she's dearly pay'd the kain: *rent in kind*
>   Tam Samson's dead!

There is a Burns monument and museum – complete with Kilmarnock edition – in the **Kay Park**. Kilmarnock is the headquarters of the Burns Federation.

Alexander Smith

Alexander Smith (1829–67) was born on 31 December 1829 in Kilmarnock (site unknown). The son of a lace pattern designer, Smith followed his father's trade until the success of his first collection *A Life Drama* (1852). In Smith's autobiographical novel *Alfred Hagart's Household* (1866) Kilmarnock becomes Spiggleton.

William McIlvanney

The novelist William McIlvanney was born in Kilmarnock on 25 November 1936 and educated at Kilmarnock Academy and Glasgow University. His most acclaimed novel, *Docherty* (1975), is set in Graithnock, a fictional version of Kilmarnock. The book opens in 1904 with the birth of Tam Docherty's fourth and final child, Conn, just after Christmas when hope is high in the High Street of Graithnock. Conn is symbolic of a new life as Tam, a miner, says: 'He'll never be ready fur the pits. No' this wan. He'll howk wi' his heid. Fur ideas.' Tam Docherty is, however, gradually martyred by the economic burden he (as a representative of his class) has to carry. Conn has, after all, to go into the pits which represents a major defeat: Tam 'had fathered four children and all he had ever been able to give them was their personal set of shackles'. Tam eventually sacrifices himself so that a fellow-worker might survive a pit collapse; Tam is projected as the proletarian saint of Graithnock.

KINNAIRD, Perthshire   (Tayside)   1½m NE of Pitlochry on A924

Robert Louis Stevenson

A tablet on the garden wall of a roadside house indicates that Robert Louis Stevenson (1850–94) completed his supernatural Scots story 'Thrawn Janet' while staying here in 1880. 'In the fated year,' Stevenson wrote in the *Idler* of August 1894 (in an account of the making of *Treasure Island*):

> I came to live with my father and mother at Kinnaird, above
> Pitlochry. . . . I love my native air, but it does not love me; and at
> the end of this delightful period was a cold, a fly-blister, and a
> migration to the Castleton of Braemer [where *Treasure Island* was
> written].

Stevenson sent 'Thrawn Janet' to Leslie Stephen's *Cornhill Magazine* where it was published the following October.

KINNESSWOOD, Kinross-shire   (Tayside)   3½m E of Kinross

Michael Bruce

Michael Bruce (1746–67) was born on 27 March 1746 in Kinnesswood; the cottage in which the poet was born was restored in 1906 and is open to the public on request (key with curator). Bruce is associated with the landscape at the foot of the Lomond Hills by the northern shore of Loch

Leven; from the age of ten until he was sixteen he spent his summers herding sheep on the hills. Bruce's brief life was dominated by the faith of his father – a weaver who was an elder of the Secessionist church – and the fact of his own consumptive illness. He studied, at Edinburgh University, for the ministry and produced metrical paraphrases that still circulate in the Church of Scotland. His best-known poem is 'Ode to the Cuckoo' but some of his finest lines occur in his longest poem 'Lochleven' in which he describes Kinnesswood:

> Fair from his hand, behold the Village rise
> In rural pride, 'mong intermingled trees!
> Above whose aged tops the joyful swains
> At even-tide, descending from the hill,
> With eye enamoured, mark the many wreaths
> Of pillared smoke, high curling to the clouds.
> The street resounds with Labour's various voice,
> Who whistles at his work. Gay on the green,
> Young blooming boys, and girls with golden hair,
> Trip nimble-footed, wanton in their play,
> The village hope. All in a reverend row,
> Their grey-haired grandsires, sitting in the sun,
> Before the gate, and leaning on the staff,
> The well-remembered stories of their youth
> Recount, and shake their aged locks with joy.

After working as a teacher, Bruce returned to Kinnesswood in February 1767, enjoying his last days in the cottage on the 'Loaning of the Hill'. He died on 15 July 1767 and is buried in Portmoak Churchyard (on east side of Loch Leven) where there is a monument. The Michael Bruce Memorial Trust was established in 1903 and maintains the poet's cottage which contains books and information. Since 1935 annual memorial services have been held, on a Sunday in July, in Portmoak Church to honour the memory of Bruce.

KINROSS, Kinross-shire   (Tayside)   10m NNE of Dunfermline on
M90

Michael Bruce

Kinross stands on the west side of Loch Leven and in his poem 'Lochleven' the poet Michael Bruce (1746–67) mentions 'gay Kinross, whose stately tufted groves/Nod o'er the loch'. In autumn 1765 Bruce became a student of divinity at the theological hall of the Secession Church in Kinross. (The building still stands, in Swan's Acre, and is now the Loch Leven Inn). Within six months of Bruce's enrolment as a student the college closed.

KIRKCALDY, Fife (Fife) On A92

Adam Smith

A royal burgh since 1644, Kirkcaldy (known as the 'lang toun' because of the length of the High Street) proudly proclaims itself as the birthplace of Adam Smith (1723–90) whose *The Wealth of Nations* (1776) is regarded as one of the most influential economic texts ever written. It argued the case for free trade over mercantilist assumptions, brought the classical British school of political economy into being, and virtually established economics as an autonomous discipline. Baptised on 5 June 1723, Smith spent his youth at 220 High Street (demolished 1834) and it was here he wrote *The Wealth of Nations* as a plaque (near the Clydesdale Bank) explains:

> Here stood the birthplace of *Adam Smith, LL.D., F.R.S.* Born 1723. Died 1790. Professor of Moral Philosophy in Glasgow University 1751–1754. Lord Rector – Glasgow University 1787. Commissioner of Customs, Edinburgh 1778–1790. *The Wealth of Nations* was written here while the author was resident here, 1767–1776. Buried in Canongate churchyard, Edinburgh. Erected 1952.

However, C. R. Fay argues, in *Adam Smith and the Scotland of His Day* (1956):

> But it was not his birthplace, for he once took a friend who was staying with him there [220 High Street] to see 'the house in which he first drew breath' – and though the site of this is unmarked, there is good evidence that it was at the corner of High Street and Rose Street on land now covered by a furniture shop.

Smith was educated at the burgh school from 1730 to 1737 then went to Glasgow University. He later studied at Balliol College, Oxford; earned a living as a lecturer in Edinburgh and was Professor of Moral Philosophy at Glasgow University from 1751 to 1762. After leaving Glasgow, in December 1762, he lived in London and the Continent. He explained, in a letter of 1780 to the Commissioner of the Danish Board of Trade:

> Upon my return to Great Britain [in October 1766] I retired to a small town in Scotland, the place of my nativity, where I continued to live for six years in great tranquillity and almost in complete retirement. During this time I amused myself principally with writing my 'Enquiry

concerning the Wealth of Nations', in studying Botany (in which, however, I made no great progress), as well as some other sciences to which I had never given much attention before.

The Adam Smith Centre, opposite the War Memorial Gardens, was opened (by philanthropist Andrew Carnegie) as the Adam Smith Hall in 1899 and modernised as the Adam Smith Centre in 1871. In 1973, on the 250th anniversary of the economist's birth, an international Adam Smith Symposium was held in the Adam Smith Centre.

Pet Marjory

Marjorie Fleming ('Pet Marjory', 1803–11) was born on 15 January 1803 at 130 High Street, which was rebuilt in 1920 and is now A. K. Melville's, the outfitters. Before she died on 19 December 1811, Marjory had written a three-volume journal combining prose observations with compositions (often of an historical nature) in verse. In 1788 Marjory's parents – James Fleming, an accountant, and Isabella Rae, daughter of an Edinburgh surgeon – settled in Kirkcaldy, living at the 'Lion House' before moving to 130 High Street. Marjory liked to play at the policies of Raith, the family seat of the Fergusons and now Raith Park. She also learned to love books, an interest encouraged by her father who often read to her.

In 1808 Marjory was visited by her cousin, Isabella Keith, who became her greatest friend. When Marjory went to Edinburgh, with Isabella, she stayed at Mrs Keith's house at 1 North Charlotte Street and there she began her journals. Often the journals assume a highly moralistic tone, as in this passage from the First Journal:

> I am sure I get acquainted with boys and girls almost every day wickedness and vice makes one miserable & unhappy as well as a concousness of guilt on our mind Dr Swifts works are very funny & amusing & I get some by hart Vanity is a great folly & sometimes leads to a great sin disumulation I think is worse this was a bad day but now is a good one Self-denial is a good thing and a virtue. St Paul was remarkable for his religion and piety he was in a great many periels & dangers.

Her verse, however, was more forceful as in the lines 'Dedicated to Mrs H. Crawfurd by the Author – MF':

> Three turkeys fair their last have breathed
> And now this world for ever leaved
> Their Father & their Mother too
> Will sigh and weep as well as you
> Mourning for their osprings fair
> Whom they did nurse with tender care

Indeed the rats their bones have cranched
To eternity are they launched
There graceful form and pretty eyes
Their fellow fows did not despise
A direful death indeed they had
That would put any parent mad
But she was more than usual calm
She did not give a single dam
She is as gentel as a lamb
Here ends this melancholy lay
Farewell Poor Turkeys I must say

Her most ambitious poetic work, 'The Life of Mary Queen of Scots', was also written in octosyllabic couplets.

The final page of Marjory's third and last journal is dated 'Kirkaldy, July 19', the month she returned to her home in Fife after three years in Edinburgh. By November she was ill, a victim of an epidemic of measles. After her death, on 19 December 1811, she was buried in Abbotshall Churchyard (found by following Abbotshall Road from the Adam Smith Centre). The simple gravestone of 1811 was incorporated in the monument of 1930 which features an impressive stone sculpture of Marjory by C. d'O. Pilkington Jackson (who also created the equestrian bronze of Robert the Bruce at Bannockburn). H. B. Farnie, a London journalist, edited Marjory's journals in 1858 and in 1863 Dr John Brown, in his essay 'Marjorie Fleming', publicised the legend that Marjory was a friend of Sir Walter Scott's:

> Sir Walter was in that house [Mrs Keith's home at 1 North Charlotte Street] almost every day, and had a key, so in he and the hound went, shaking themselves in the lobby. 'Marjory! Marjory!' shouted her friend, 'where are ye, my bonnie wee croodlin' doo?' In a moment a bright, eager child of seven was in his arms, and he was kissing her all over. . . . Scott used to say that he was amazed at her power over him, saying to Mrs Keith, 'she's the most extraordinary creature I ever met with, and her repeating of Shakespeare overpowers me as nothing else does.'

Though neither Scott nor Marjory mention each other in their journals it is possible they met in Edinburgh.

Mark Twain was one of Marjory's great admirers. In an article on 'Marjorie Fleming: the Wonder Child', in *Harper's Bazaar* in 1909, he wrote:

> She was made out of thunder-storms and sunshine, and not even her little perfunctory pieties and shop-made holinesses could squelch her spirits or put out her fires for long. . . . I have adored Marjorie for

six-and-thirty years; I have adored her in detail, I have adored the
whole of her; but above all other details . . . I have adored her because
she detested that odious and confusing and unvanquishable and
unlearnable and shameless invention, the multiplication table.

Thomas Carlyle

The old Burgh School of Kirkcaldy stood at the junction of Hill Street
and Kirk Wynd and there Thomas Carlyle (1795–1881) taught from 1816
to 1818. During his time in Kirkcaldy he had two important relationships.
His friendship with Edward Irving (1792–1834) developed as both men
were teaching in the same town. Like Carlyle, Irving was a former pupil
of Annan Academy and former student of Edinburgh University. Like
Carlyle, too, Irving had a prophetic outlook. Whereas Carlyle gradually
built a reputation as one of the greatest of all Victorians, Irving watched
his own career collapse. He became a millenialist preacher in London,
obsessed by the Second Coming and the phenomenon of 'speaking in
tongues'. In 1833 he was deprived of his Church of Scotland ministry
because of his supposed heresy, and died the following year. Carlyle
however, remained faithful to the memory of his friend and discussed his
life in *Reminiscences* (1881). It was Irving, after all, who introduced
Carlyle to Jane Baillie Welsh in Haddington in 1821 – a grand gesture
since Irving himself wanted to marry the woman who became Carlyle's
wife. However, Irving had pledged himself to Isabella Martin of Kirkcaldy
and did not feel free to pursue Jane.

Carlyle's other close friend in Kirkcaldy was Margaret Gordon, his first
love. Unfortunately for Carlyle he was considered a poor match for her.
Carlyle disliked teaching and soon 'tired of the trade', especially as Irving
had decided to leave Kirkcaldy in 1818 (becoming assistant to the Rev.
Thomas Chalmers in Glasgow in 1819). After leaving Kirkcaldy, Carlyle
did some tutoring in Edinburgh where, on 8 January 1819, he wrote to
James Johnstone:

It is superfluous to say that I have bid farewell to Fife. My resolution
was taken without advice, because none was to be had; but not
without long & serious meditation. I could not leave Kirkcaldy but
with regret. There are in it many persons of a respectable – several
of an exemplary character; and had the tie which united us been of a
less irritating nature, my time might have been spent very happily
among them. . . . P.S. I forgot to say (what was indeed of no
consequence) that I spent, along with Irving, the Christmas holidays
in Fife. They were the happiest, for many reasons which I cannot at
this time explain, that for a long space have marked the tenor of my
life.

Possibly, Carlyle saw Margaret Gordon in the Christmas holidays, hence the happiness. The old Burgh School and Carlyle's lodgings at 22 Kirk Wynd were both demolished but his association with Kirkcaldy is marked by a plaque on the Trustee Savings Bank.

John and Anna Buchan

Pathhead, now part of Kirkcaldy, was formerly a separate little town between Kirkcaldy and Dysart on the Firth of Forth. In 1876 the Rev. John Buchan, father of the novelist John Buchan (1875–1940), was called to Pathhead Free Church where he remained until 1888 when he moved to the John Knox Free Church in the Gorbals, Glasgow. Pathhead Free Church manse was a grey stone building beside a railway, a linoleum factory, a coal-pit, a bleaching-works and a ropewalk; in this manse, 'Inglewood' in Smeaton Road, John Buchan's sister Anna was born (the novelist 'O. Douglas', 1877–1948) was born. The church was demolished in 1963, the manse more recently, but Ravenscraig Castle, along the shore, stands as John and Anna Buchan saw it. The castle dates back to 1460 when James II had it constructed as part of Scotland's defence of the Forth against pirates and the English. During the Reformation the castle witnessed various skirmishes and in 1651 it was occupied by Cromwell's troops who left it in disrepair. Buchan knew of the sad tale of Rosabelle, from Scott's *Lay of the Last Minstrel* (1805, VI, xxiii):

> 'Moor, moor the barge, ye gallant crew!
> And gentle lady, deign to stay!
> Rest thee in Castle Ravensheuch.
> Nor tempt the stormy firth to-day.
>
> The blackening wave is edg'd with white:
> To inch and rock the sea-mews fly;
> The fishers have heard the Water-Sprite,
> Whose screams forebode that wreck is nigh.
>
> Last night the gifted seer did view
> A wet shroud swathed round lady gay;
> Then stay thee, Fair, in Ravensheuch;
> Why cross the gloomy firth to-day!'

Rosabelle, who drowns in Scott's poem, is remembered in the name of Kirkcaldy's Rosabelle Street.

Buchan was educated at Pathhead Board School, then at the Burgh School of Kirkcaldy (formerly at the junction of Hill Street and Kirk Wynd), then at the High School. He described Pathhead sands in the first chapter of *Prester John* (1910) when David Crawfurd recalls the town of Kirkcaple (Kirkcaldy) and the parish of Portincross (Pathhead):

> The town of Kirkcaple, of which and its adjacent parish of Portincross my father was the minister, lies on a hillside above the little bay of Caple, and looks squarely out on the North Sea. Round the horns of land which enclose the bay the coast shows on either side a battlement of stark red cliffs through which a burn or two makes a pass to the water's edge. The bay itself is ringed with fine clean sands, where we lads of the burgh school loved to bathe in the warm weather. But on long holidays the sport was to go farther afield among the cliffs; for there there were many deep caves and pools, where podleys might be caught with the line, and hid treasures sought for at the expense of the skin of the knees and the buttons of the trousers. Many a long Saturday I have passed in a crinkle of the cliffs, having lit a fire of driftwood, and made believe that I was a smuggler or a Jacobite new landed from France.

In *The Free Fishers* (1934) – set on the Fife coast where the Free Fishers of Forth, at the time of the Napoleonic Wars, have their brotherhood – Buchan evokes the weavers of Gallatown and the nailmakers of Pathhead:

> The looms were clacking in every cot-house as he [Anthony Lammas] rode through the weaving village of Gallatown; hammers were busy among the nailmakers of Pathhead; the smell of a tan-pit came to his nostrils with a pleasing pungency; when he descended the long slope of the Path the sight of scaly fisherfolk and tarry sailormen gave him an inconsequent delight.

Long before Buchan was famous, however, he was writing in (if not of) Fife. His first published work was a New Year's Hymn, composed in 1887 'By a Scholar' for the Pathhead Free Church Sabbath School:

> To Thee, our God and Friend,
> We raise our hymn today,
> O, guard and guide us from above
> Along life's troubled way.

KIRKCOLM, Wigtonshire (Dumfries and Galloway) 5m NNW of Stranraer on A718

Fred Urquhart

Kirkcolm, a village on the west side of Loch Ryan, is featured as Cairncolm in one of the funniest stories by Fred Urquhart (born 1912). Maggie, inspired by the benefits of the National Health Service, makes up her mind that 'she must get her money's worth'. She plagues her doctor with requests for treatment until 'the cupboard in Maggie's back bedroom was filled to overflowing with full, near-full and half-empty bottles of coloured water, as well as with boxes of pills of all shape and colours. This does not suffice so she has her teeth out, cuts her hair off, and works out a way to get a free artificial leg – with fatal results. 'Maggie Logie and the National Health' was written more than thirty years after Urquhart had left Kirkcolm where he stayed from 1921 to 1925 when his father was chauffeur to Carrick Buchanan of Corswall House. Urquhart went to Kirkcolm village school and for a year to Stranraer High School.

KIRKCONNELL, Dumfriesshire (Dumfries and Galloway) 3½m NW of Sanquhar

Alexander Anderson

Alexander Anderson (1845–1909) was born on 30 April 1845 at Kirkconnell and is buried in the churchyard, at the top of the village, where there is a monument. A platelayer who wrote under the pseudonym 'Surfaceman', he published *A Song of Labour and Other Poems* (1873) and in 1881, encouraged by Thomas Carlyle (1795–1881), became assistant librarian at Edinburgh University.

KIRKCUDBRIGHT, Kirkcudbrightshire (Dumfries and Galloway) 25m SW of Dumfries on A711

The town, on the estuary of the Dee, has a ruined castle (built 1582 by Sir Thomas Maclellan, former provost of Kirkcudbright) and a harbour, once envisaged as a landing place by the Spanish Armada. John Paul Jones (1747–92) – who received a privateer's commission from Congress on the outbreak of the American War of Independence – was born at Kirkbean, near Kirkcudbright. For a while he was imprisoned in the **Old Tolbooth**.

Robert Burns

Robert Burns (1759–96) was a visitor to Kirkcudbright and local folklore insists that he wrote the Selkirk Grace at the **Selkirk Arms Hotel**:

> Some hae meat and canna eat,
> And some wad eat than want it.
> But we hae meat, and we can eat
> And sae the Lord be thankit.

KIRKFIELDBANK, Lanarkshire   (Strathclyde)   1m W of Lanark

Robert McLellan

The dramatist Robert McLellan (1907–85) was born at his grandparents' farm, Linmill, Kirkfieldbank, on 28 January 1907. In a letter of 14 June 1983 (to the present writer) he recalled:

> Linmill had the main influence on my work, not only because my Linmill stories [*Linmill and Other Stories*, 1977] are about my childhood there, but because there I learned my first language in an atmosphere of great love and trust, and it has been my favourite ever since.
>
> My parents didn't live at Linmill. They were in let houses or lodgings until I was of school age, and my mother went home to Linmill to have her children, and sent them there in all their holidays. When I went to school it was in Milngavie . . . Milngavie and district had very little apparent effect on my work, not because one couldn't have written about it in Scots, but because I was wary of putting people who were alive around me into my work. The Linmill people were so far away (I thought) that I could mention them with impunity. I was to learn later that most of them were just as alive as I was, some, although not favourably mentioned in my stories, delighted to be remembered in them nevertheless, others, mainly my cousins, threatening, not too seriously, to sue me.

McLellan lived (from 1938) on Arran where he died on 30 January 1985.

KIRKOSWALD, Ayrshire   (Strathclyde)   10m SW of Ayr on A77

Robert Burns

The misery of Robert Burns's last two years of working on his father's farm at Mount Oliphant was relieved in the summer of 1775 when he went to school on the 'smuggling coast' of Kirkoswald to study 'Mensuration, Surveying, Dialling, etc., in which I made a pretty good progress'. The **Shanter Hotel**, on the site of the school, has a pewter tankard supposedly used by Burns. The poet was taught by the village schoolmaster Hugh Rodger whose house, opposite the churchyard, is marked by a plaque. In the churchyard are the graves of Burns's maternal relatives (Broun) and of locals subsequently immortalised by the poet.

While Burns was at Kirkoswald he slept at Ballochniel Farm (one mile south) where his uncle worked. As well as making good progress as a scholar, he made great progress in 'the knowledge of mankind' in Kirkoswald. Among scenes of 'swaggering riot and roaring dissipation' the sixteen-year old learned to 'mix without fear in a drunken squabble' while a teenage crush on the 'charming Filette' Peggy Thomson distracted him from his studies and caused him many sleepless nights. Peggy lived next door to the school and is said to have inspired Burns's poem 'Peggy's Charms':

> Blest be the wild, sequester'd shade,
>   And blest the day and hour,
> Where Peggy's charms I first survey'd,
>   When first I felt their power!

'Tam O' Shanter' – composed at Ellisland farm in the autumn of 1790 – features characters from Kirkoswald. Douglas Graham (1738–1811) who rented the farm of Shanter (*seann tor* means 'old mound'), had a boat called the 'Tam O' Shanter' for the purposes of smuggling. Graham is the original of Tam O' Shanter. The village inn, adjacent to the church, was called the Kirkton; as the landlady Jean Kennedy affected airs, her hostelry was known as 'the Leddies' House'. In Burns's poem, we learn that the hero 'at the Lord's house, even on Sunday . . . drank wi' Kirkton Jean till Monday'. As well as farming and smuggling, Graham was a dealer in malt so every market day he would go to Ayr accompanied by his 'ancient, trusty, drouthy cronie' Souter Johnnie, modelled on the shoemaker John Davidson (1728–1806). These visits were anathema to Graham's wife Helen (*née* M'Taggart) who thus became a 'sulky sullen dame' (like Tam's wife Kate) in his absence. Burns's description of the boozy companionship between Tam and Souter Johnnie – that is, between Douglas Graham and John Davidson – is a highlight of his work:

> But to our tale: – Ae market-night,
> Tam had got planted unco right,
> Fast by an ingle, bleezing finely,
> Wi' reaming swats, that drank divinely;   *foaming, new ale*
> And at his elbow, Souter Johnie,
> His ancient, trusty, drouthy cronie:
> Tam lo'ed him like a very brither;
> They had been fou for weeks thegither.
> The night drave on wi' sangs and clatter;
> And ay the ale was growing better:
> The landlady and Tam grew gracious
> Wi' secret favours, sweet and precious:
> The Souter tauld his queerest stories;

The landlord's laugh was ready chorus:
The storm without might rair and rustle,
Tam did na mind the storm a whistle.

Shanter Farm is now gone, but **Souter Johnnie's House** is open to the public (April–Sept. 2.30–8pm) and maintained by the National Trust for Scotland. Davidson moved into this thatched house in 1785, five years before Burns composed his great narrative poem. The cobbler's house contains period furniture and Burns relics including the poet's Masonic Badge. On the sward which stands on Souter Johnnie's kailyard are stone figures, sculptured by James Thom, showing Tam, Souter Johnnie, the innkeeper and his wife.

KIRKPATRICK, Dumfriesshire (Dumfries and Galloway) 6m NW of Gretna, off A74

On a caravan camp, signposted for **Bruce's Cave**, a derelict mansion marks the site of Dunskelly Castle, ancestral home of Sir William Irving, Robert the Bruce's standard-bearer at the battle of Bannockburn (24 June 1314). Down from this, reached by a wooden platform on the cliffside, is Bruce's Cave which local folklore identifies as the cave where Bruce was inspired by the tenacity of a spider, hence the Scottish saw still in oral circulation: 'If at first you don't succeed, try, try, try again.' Bruce probably hid in this cave during 1313 gathering his resolve for the final push against the English, culminating in the victory over Edward II at Bannockburn. Above the cave a monk has carved:

Within this cave King Robert Bruce
From foes pursuant sought a truce,
Like my forebears who for him fell,
I, Irvingguard do guard it well.

James Currie

James Currie (1756–1805), the first editor and biographer of Robert Burns (1759–96), was born at Kirkpatrick Fleming on 31 May 1756. The son of a minister, Currie emigrated to Virginia in 1771 and fought in the Colonial Army during the American War of Independence. He returned to Scotland in 1777 to study medicine at Edinburgh University and settled in Dumfriesshire in 1792 when he met Robert Burns in Dumfries. Currie's *The Works of Robert Burns, With an Account of his Life and a Criticism on his Writings* (1800), the first collected edition, took a moralistic approach to the bard's behaviour and presented him as a wayward genius with the emphasis on wine (or whisky) and women rather than song. Currie died at Sidmouth on 31 August 1805.

KIRK YETHOLM, Roxburghshire (Border) 7m SE of Kelso, off B6352

Sir Walter Scott, John Keats

Since the sixteenth century Kirk Yetholm has been associated with the Scottish gypsies whose last 'Queen' died in 1883. The **Gypsy Palace**, a cottage, still stands. Meg Merrilies, in *Guy Mannering* (1815), by Sir Walter Scott (1771–1832), is described as 'A kind o' queen amang the gypsies'. Scott, who was fascinated by gypsy life, based the character of Meg on his grandfather's account of Jean Gordon of Kirk Yetholm. She was born around 1670, married Patrick Faa in her teens, and had many children. It is said that all her sons, except one, died at the hands of the hangman for such crimes as sheepstealing and that her husband was exiled to America for the crime of fire raising. Jean herself was ducked to death, at Carlisle in 1745, for loudly procliming her Jacobite sympathies. John Keats (1795–1821) wrote 'Meg Merrilies' in tribute to Scott's creation:

> Old Meg she was a gipsy.
> And lived upon the moors;
> Her bed it was the brown heath turf.
> And her house was out of doors.
> Her apples were swart blackberries,
> Her currants, pods o' broom;
> Her wine was dew of the wild white rose.
> Her book a church-yard tomb.

KIRRIEMUIR, Angus (Tayside) 12m N of Dundee on A926

J. M. Barrie

James Matthew Barrie (1860–1937) was born in Kirriemuir – the Thrums of his books – on 9 May 1860. **Barrie's birthplace**, in an upstairs room at 9 Brechin Road, in a row of cottages known as the Tenements, is now a National Trust for Scotland property open to the public (April–Oct. 10am–6pm, Sun. 2–6pm). The two-storeyed four-roomed, slate-roofed house, along with the communal wash-house in the yard (where young Barrie staged his first drama) was bought by Duncan Elliot Alves of Bryn Bras Castle, Caernarvon, in 1937 after Barrie's death and presented to the National Trust for Scotland. Restoration, begun in 1961, conformed to the arrangement made by Barrie's mother Margaret Ogilvy.

Barrie's birthplace contains the hair-bottomed chairs Margaret Ogilvy installed on the day Barrie was born, described in the opening sentences of *Margaret Ogilvy* (1896):

On the day I was born we bought six hair-bottomed chairs, and in our little house it was an event, the first great victory in a woman's long campaign; how they had been laboured for, the pound-note and the thirty threepenny-bits they cost, what anxiety there was about the purchase, the show they made in possession of the west room, my father's unnatural coolness when he brought them in (but his face was white) – I so often heard the tale afterwards, and shared as boy and man in so many similar triumphs, that the coming of the chairs seems to be something I remember, as if I had jumped out of bed on that first day, and run ben to see how they looked.

The house also contains the desk, couch and settle from Barrie's Adelphi Terrace flat; original manuscripts and first editions; his warrant of baronetcy (awarded in 1913) and coat of arms with seals; a portrait by Sir John Lavery; *Peter Pan* jerkins worn by Pauline Chase and Jean Forbes Robertson; letters, proof copies, photographs and press cuttings.

Barrie's father was a weaver whose workshop was located in a downstairs room in 9 Brechin Road. Like every other handloom weaver he kept a bunch of loose threads – or thrums – hanging beside the loom to repair broken threads in the fabric. Kirriemuir thus became Thrums in Barrie's books. Thrums was, for Barrie, a world in itself. In *A Window in Thrums* (1889) the Dominie who narrates the book says: 'To those who dwell in great cities Thrums is only a small place, but what a clatter of life it has for me when I come to it from my school-house in the glen.'

Barrie lived at a time of change for Kirriemuir, as he describes in *Margaret Ogilvy*:

Before I reached my tenth year a giant entered my native place in the night, and we woke to find him in possession. He transformed it into a new town at a rate with which we boys only could keep up, for as fast as he built dams we made rafts to sail in them; he knocked down houses, and there we were crying 'Pilly!' among the ruins; he dug trenches, and we jumped them; we had to be dragged by the legs from beneath his engines, he sunk wells, and in we went. . . . Where had been formerly but the click of the shuttle was soon the roar of 'power', handlooms were pushed into a corner as a room is cleared for a dance; every morning at half-past five the town was wakened with a yell, and from a chimney-stack that rose high into our caller air the conquerer waved for evermore his flag of smoke. Another era had dawned, new customs, new fashions sprang into life, all as lusty as if they had been born at twenty-one; as quickly as two people may exchange seats, the daughter, till now but a knitter of stockings, became the breadwinner, he who had been the breadwinner sat down to the knitting of stockings; what had been yesterday a nest of weavers was to-day a town of girls.

Barrie's father was a resourceful man who attempted to cope with the transformation of a community of handloom weavers to a factory town. At the age of fifty-six he became a book-keeper and, after two years of desk work in Forfar, became chief confidential clerk (in 1872) in **Gairie Linen Works** beside the **Gairie Burn** (at the foot of Bellies Brae).

Barrie's mother was the abiding influence in his life, as *Margaret Ogilvy* demonstrates. She was a 'great reader' and introduced her talented son to such books as *Robinson Crusoe*. She was brought up under the influence of the Auld Lichts – the seceders of 1773 who upheld the Solemn League and Covenant – and Barrie's *Auld Licht Idylls* (1888) retold her tales of Kirriemuir as stories of Thrums. On an emotional level Barrie's greatest ambition was to please his mother since when he was seven his older brother David was killed in a skating accident and Barrie attempted to take the place of Margaret Ogilvy's favourite son.

Barrie's education was supervised by his brother Alexander who obtained teaching posts at Glasgow Academy and Dumfries Academy, enrolling Barrie at both these schools. Barrie subsequently attended the university in Edinburgh where he wrote reviews for the *Edinburgh Courant* and *The Scotsman*. *Auld Licht Idylls* and *The Little Minister* (1891) brought him both fame and fortune and in 1894 he married the actress Mary Answell. According to Janet Dunbar's *J.M.Barrie: The Man Behind the Image* (1970) 'Barrie was impotent' and the marriage was never consummated. If the marriage, which ended in 1909 (when Mary left him for Gilbert Canaan) was a failure, his artistic career was astonishingly successful. He was one of the most popular of the kailyard novelists and as a dramatist – with *The Little Minister* (1897), *Quality Street* (1901), *The Admirable Crichton* (1902), *Peter Pan* (1904), *What Every Woman Knows* (1908), to name but five – he became one of the most acclaimed authors of his time. Though his great theatrical triumphs are associated with his life in London (from 1885 onwards) Barrie's artistic origins are embedded in Kirriemuir where he is buried. His **grave** is signposted: turn right along Brechin Road, pass the Bowling Club, turn left up Cemetery Road.

The **Auld Licht Kirk** (demolished in 1893, now the Evangelical Free Church), Bank Street, was the church Margaret Ogilvy attended and features in *Auld Licht Idylls*. Near this was the **Hanky School**, run by the Misses Adam, Barrie's first school. On her marriage, Margaret Ogilvy left the Auld Licht Kirk and attended the Free Church in Southmuir (on the site of the present **St Andrew's Church**, on the left of Glamis Road, near Strathview). *Auld Licht Idylls* is narrated by the Dominie (the school-master) from Glen Quharity, modelled on **Glen Clova** (on B955); the west road, on the approach to Glen Clova, passes the old **Wester Esk School-house** (on the right), the original of the Dominie's schoolhouse. 'The Courting of T'nowhead's Bell' (the eighth chapter of *Auld Licht Idylls*) describes how the farmer of **T'nowhead Farm** – which was on the opposite corner of the Forfar road from Strathview – goes with his wife and nine children to the Auld Licht Kirk. leaving their maid Bell with the baby. During the sermon Bell's two suitors leave the Auld Licht Kirk and go to propose to her, one going by **Bellies Brae**, the other across the **Commonty** (on the left of the hill going up to Strathview).

When a Man's Single (1888) opens in the **Kirkwynd** with the noise of the looms and closes with a marriage made in Thrums, complete with a proposal in Glen Quharity.

Like *Auld Licht Idylls*, *A Window in Thrums* (1889) is narrated by the Dominie, on holiday from the glen and lodging at the **House on the Brae**, described at the beginning of the book:

> On the bump of green round which the brae twists, at the top of the brae, and within cry of T'nowhead Farm, still stands a one-storey house, whose whitewashed walls, streaked with the discoloration that rain leaves, look yellow when the snow comes. In the old days the stiff ascent left Thrums behind, and where is now the making of a suburb was only a poor row of dwellings and a manse, with Hendry's cot to watch the brae. The house stood bare, without a shrub, in a garden whose paling did not go all the way round, the potato pit being only kept out of the road, that here sets off southward, by a broken dyke of stones and earth. On each side of the slate-coloured door was a window of knotted glass. Ropes were flung over the thatch to keep the roof on in the wind . . . [the kitchen] has a flooring of stone now, where there used to be only hard earth, and a broken pane in the window is indifferently stuffed with rags. But it is the other window I turn to, with a pain at my heart, and pride and fondness too, the square foot of glass where Jess sat in her chair and looked down the brae. . . . This is Jess's window. For more than twenty years she had not been able to go so far as the door, and only once while I knew her was she ben in the room. . . . The little window commands the incline to the point where the brae suddenly jerks out of sight in its climb down into the town. The steep path up the commonty makes for this elbow of the brae, and thus, whichever way the traveller takes, it is here that he comes first into sight of the window. Here, too, those who go to the town from the south get their first glimpse of Thrums. . . . Jess's window was a beacon by night to travellers in the dark, and it will be so in the future when there are none to remember Jess. . . . At this window she sat for twenty years or more looking at the world as through a telescope.

The House on the Brae (privately owned), on the Glamis road, stands opposite **Strathview** (also privately owned) which was the Barrie family home from 1872. Jess, in *A Window in Thrums*, has affinities with Margaret Ogilvy: both women have lost a favourite son and worry about another son. Just as Jess watches for Jamie (a brother in London) from the House on the Brae, so Margaret Ogilvy used to sit at a window in Strathview and wait for Barrie to return home.

The Little Minister, also narrated by the Dominie, describes the impact of twenty-one-year old Gavin Dishart on Thrums to which he has been invited as minister by the Auld Lichts. With his widowed mother Margaret he arrives at the 'white Manse among the trees', in the Tenements, the part of Kirriemuir where Barrie was born:

> The manse stands high, with a sharp eye on all the town. Every back
> window in the Tenements has a glint of it, and so the back of the
> tenements is always better behaved than the front. . . . The manse
> looks down on the town from the north-east, and is reached from
> the road that leaves Thrums behind it in another moment by a wide,
> straight path, so rough that to carry a draught of water to the manse
> without spilling was to be superlatively good at one thing.

The **Auld Licht Manse**, opposite the Tenements, was built around 1827. In 1893 the Auld Licht congregation, now absorbed into the United Free Church, built a new kirk on the site with shops below to provide an income. This is now used by the Evangelical Free Church.

Gavin Dishart is soon made aware that his every action is scrutinised by his congregation. When, for example,his tall hat blows off in the **Schoolwynd** this is a cause for comment: 'He should hae run after it mair reverently.' Inevitably, then, Gavin's involvement with Babbie, the gypsy girl he meets in **Windyghoul**, brings him problems from the beginning:

> In Windyghoul there is either no wind or so much that it rushes down
> the sieve like an army, entering with a shriek of terror, and escaping
> with a derisive howl. The moon was crossing the avenue. But Gavin
> saw only the singer.
>
> She was still fifty yards away, sometimes singing gleefully, and again
> letting her body sway lightly as she came dancing up Windyghoul. Soon
> she was within a few feet of the little minister, to whom singing, except
> when out of tune, was a suspicious thing, and dancing a device of the
> devil. His arm went out wrathfully, and his intention was to pronounce
> sentence on this woman.

To see Windyghoul and **Caddam Wood** go along Angle Road (turning left at the crossroads) and across the Cortachy Road.

Gavin is no match for the enchanting Babbie. She warns the weavers that soldiers are waiting by T'nowhead Farm to escort police who plan to arrest the weavers who resisted the manufacturers' reduction of the price of their cloth (as happened in 1839 when Margaret Ogilvy was nineteen). Babbie tricks the postman, Wearyworld, into blowing the warning horn from the top of the **Roods**. To reach the Roods and **Kirriemuir Hill**, turn right along Lochmill Road and right again into Glengate and the Town centre; go left by the Angus Milling Company – where there is a statue of Peter Pan – into St Malcolm's Wynd; take the next turning to the left.

Babbie next incites the crowd in the **Square** (turn left into **Schoolwynd** then right into Bank Street) to follow her down **Bellies Brae** and tricks Gavin into throwing a divot at an officer:

> [Gavin] had been watching the handsome young captain, Halliwell, riding with his men; admiring him, too, for his coolness. This coolness exasperated the gypsy, who twice flung at Halliwell and missed him. He rode on smiling contemptuously.
> 'Oh, if only I could fling straight!' the Egyptian moaned.
> Then she saw the minister by her side, and in the tick of a clock something happened that can never be explained . . . suddenly the Egyptian's beautiful face was close to [Gavin's] and she pressed a divot into his hand, at the same time pointing at the officer, and whispering 'Hit him.'
> Gavin flung the clod of earth, and hit Halliwell on the head. . . .
> Then shrank in horror.

After Babbie escapes from imprisonment in the **Town House** she persuades soldiers, by the Tenements, that she is 'Mrs Dishart' returning with the little minister to the manse. She and Gavin later meet at Nanny Webster's little mud-house by Caddam Wood. Babbie later tries to extricate herself from her relationship with Gavin after an encounter with a boy who has climbed the **Standing Stone** on the hill (to reach the Standing Stone, follow the track parallel to the wall of the cemetery, leaving the Cricket Pavilion on the left). The boy wishes the gypsy in hell since, because of her, his father has lost faith in the little minister and started drinking heavily again. Later Gavin learns that Babbie has been adopted by Lord Rintoul, of Glen Quharity, who intends to marry her. After a gypsy marriage, a great flood, and various incidents, Babbie and the little minister are reunited.

Barrie wrote much of *The Little Minister* at Strathview in the autumn of 1889 and 1890.

In *Sentimental Tommy* (1836), Thomas Sandys and his little sister Elspeth have been brought up, in a poor part of London, sustained on stories of Thrums told by their widowed mother. Before her death she asks Aaron Latta (whom she once jilted, a week before their wedding) to look after the children and he brings them to his cottage above the **Den** (signposted 'To the Den'). Nearby, in a house – modelled on **Lochmill House** by the **Coffin Brig** – lives the Painted Lady whose illegitimate daughter Grizel endures a difficult relationship with Tommy. Like Barrie, Tommy is sent to the **Hanky School**, the hankies being used to protect the carpet when kneeling in prayer.

An imaginative boy, Tommy listens to tales about the Thrums Jacobites and, inspired by Scott's *Waverley*, invents Jacobite adventures for himself. Every Saturday he and Elspeth meet Grizel, Corp, Gavin Dishart (the minister's son) and Gavinia in the Den to act out his fantasies. Their lair is by a waterfall, the **Reekie Broth Pot**, and one of their meeting places is the **Cuttle Well**. At the end of the book, in disgrace for failing to win a university bursary, Tommy is sent to be a farm labourer in **Glen Prosen** (turn off the B955 at Dykehead).

The sequel, *Tommy and Grizel* (1900) takes place after an interval of six years. Tommy escapes to London where he becomes a literary celebrity after publishing 'Letters to a Young Man About to be Married'. Returning to Thrums, he takes up with Grizel and eventually marries her, settling in the Painted Lady's house. After a visit to Lady Rintoul's house in Glen Quharity, Tommy dies.

On Kirriemuir Hill, the visitor can see the **Cricket Pavilion** and **Camera Obscura** Barrie presented to 'Thrums' on 7 June 1930. At **St Mary's Episcopal Church** on 24 June 1937, Barrie's funeral service was held. The church has a memorial window to Barrie's brother Alexander, who died in 1914.

'The Ball of Kirriemuir'

Kirriemuir, which advertises its connection with J. M. Barrie, is perhaps less proud of its association with the bawdy song 'The Ball of Kirriemuir' beginning

> Did ye hear about the ball, my lads?
> The Ball of Kirriemuir?
> Some came for the dancing
> But they mostly came to whore.

According to the Scottish novelist James Barke (1905–58) – in *Robert Burns: The Merry Muses of Caledonia* (1965) edited by Barke and Sydney Goodsir Smith – the song celebrates an actual barn-dance held near Kirriemuir in the 1880s. Gershon Legman, however, the authority on erotic folklore, dismisses this as fanciful. In *The Horn Book* (1964) Legman points out that the stanza-pattern of 'The Ball of Kirriemuir' was determined by the third quatrain of the song 'Blyth Will an' Bessie's Wedding' in the *c.* 1800 edition of *The Merry Muses*:

> Tammie Tamson too was there,
> Maggie Birnie was his dearie,
> He pat it in amang the hair,
> An' puddled there till he was weary,

A text of the song was included in *Forbidden Fruit* (*c.* 1875) so we can be sure that 'The Ball of Kirriemuir' was current in the mid-Victorian period when Barrie was a teenager.

LAKE OF MENTEITH, Perthshire   (Central)   6m SSW of Callander

Robert Bontine Cunninghame Graham

Notes on the District of Menteith (1885) was the first book published by Robert Bontine Cunninghame Graham (1852–1936) who was greatly appreciative of 'The lake, with its three islands, its giant chestnuts [and] mouldering priory'. The Cunninghame Grahams had a claim to the title of Menteith, an earldom dormant since the seventeenth century, and Robert knew the district intimately since he spent summers as a child at nearby Gartmore House (which he inherited in 1883 and sold seven years later). With his wife, the Chilean poet Gabriella de la Belmondière, he collaborated on *Father Archangel and Other Essays* (1896); Graham himself established a reputation as an outstanding storyteller with *Thirteen Stories* (1900) and *Success* (1902, containing his classic story 'Beattock for Moffat'). When Gabriella died (on 8 September 1906 at the Hotel de France, Hendaye) Graham had her body brought back to Scotland and buried in the ruined Augustinian priory on **Inchmahome**, the largest island on the Lake of Menteith. After Gabriella's death, Graham became increasingly involved in Scottish nationalism and in 1928 helped found the National Party of Scotland. He died, in Buenos Aires, on 20 March 1936 and, when his body was returned to Scotland, was buried beside his wife and ancestors in Inchmahome priory. Graham's tombstone, in the quire, has a carving of his cattle-brand (instead of the cross) and the simple inscription 'Robert Bontine Cunninghame Graham of Gartmore 1852–1936'.

LANGHOLM, Dumfriesshire   (Dumfries and Galloway)   31m E of
Dumfries on A7

Only eight miles from England, Langholm is a mill and market town where the rivers Esk and Ewes converge with Wauchope Waters. Its annual Common Riding festival features as emblems a spade, a thistle, a floral crown and a barley bannock (loaf) on which a salted herring is nailed.

William Julius Mickle

A tablet on the Town Hall, Town Square, records that William Julius Mickle (1735–88) was born in Langholm on 29 September 1734 (actually 28 September 1735). Son of a minister, Mickle was a clerk, then partner, in an Edinburgh brewery but when this ran into financial difficulties he went to London, in 1764, to work as a proofreader with the Clarendon press. His translation of Camoes's *Lusiad*, published 1771–5 by subscription, was a considerable success. He went to Portugal in 1781 as a naval secretary then later settled at Forresthill farm, near Oxford, where he died. He is credited with the composition of the song 'There's nae luck aboot the house' ('The mariner's Wife') whose chorus runs:

> For there's nae luck about the house,
>   There's nae luck at a',
> There's nae luck about the house,
>   When our gudeman's awa.

His 'Cumnor Hall' suggested the subject of *Kenilworth* to Scott.

William and Dorothy Wordsworth

William and Dorothy Wordsworth visited Langholm in 1803. In her *Recollections of a Tour Made in Scotland AD 1803* (1894) Dorothy (1771–1855) writes (entry for Friday, 23 September 1803):

> Arrived at Langholm at about five o'clock. The town, as we approached from a hill, looked very pretty, the houses being roofed with blue slates, and standing close to the River Esk, here a large river, that scattered its waters wide over a stoney channel. The inn neat and comfortable – exceedingly clean: I could hardly believe we were still in Scotland.

Thomas Scott Cairncross

Thomas Scott Cairncross (1872–1961) was minister of Langholm South United Free Church from 1901 to 1907. In 1905 he published *The Return of the Master* which contained an evocative tribute to 'Langholm':

> It lies by the heather slopes
> Where God spilt the wine of the moorland
> Brimming the beaker of hills. Lone it lies,
> A rude outpost; challenging stars and dawn,
> And down from remoteness
> And the Balladland of the Forest
> The Pictish Esk trails glory,
> Rippling the quiet eaves
> With the gold of the sun.

While living in Langholm, the Rev. Cairncross reviewed books for the *Irish Times* and worked on the essays collected in *The Steps of the Pulpit* (1910). One of these, 'Blawearie', is an imaginative portrait of Langholm: 'Blawearie is a little paradise'. *Blawearie* was also the title of a novel

214

Cairncross published in 1911, a fictional account of Langholm. In *The Scot at Hame* (1922), a volume published years after he left Langholm, Cairncross included a poem 'Tarras', about the Tarras Water, Langholm, which rises in a boggy wasteland known as Tarras Moss:

> Oh it's fine to be in Tarras
> When the leaves are comin' oot,
> Where the saughs and elders trimmle,   *willows*
> And there's money a peat-brown troot.

When C. M. Grieve (see below) edited his first *Northern Numbers* anthology in 1920 it featured, as one of the eleven contributors, T. S. Cairncross. In December 1920 the first of Grieve's three articles on 'Certain Newer Scottish Poets' appeared in the *National Outlook*: it was a eulogy on Cairncross. Later Grieve (writing as Hugh MacDiarmid) criticised Cairncross, in *Lucky Poet* (1943), as a man 'of fastidious upper-class temper' who resented the radical tone of the new Scottish poetry. Cairncross was hurt by this criticism from one he had encouraged when a member of his church.

Hugh MacDiarmid

Dedicating his collection *Stony Limits and Other Poems* (1934) to his wife Valda and son Michael, Hugh MacDiarmid wrote:

> *I had the fortune to live as a boy*
> *In a world a' columbe and colour-de-roy*
> *As gin I'd had Mars for the land o' my birth*   if
> *Instead o' the earth.*

MacDiarmid was born Christopher Murray Grieve on 11 August 1892 in Arkinholm Terrace, Langholm, Arkinholm being the name of a battle fought in 1445 and resulting in a victory for James I over James, ninth Earl of Douglas. Grieve's birthplace thus bore the name of Langholm's most famous battle and for the rest of his long life he was a combative character who fought many cultural and political battles. In his autobiography *Lucky Poet* (1943) he writes:

> my first bit of bad luck coincided with my first introduction to my
> native land, for my mother wrapped me well in a Shetland shawl and
> took me to the door to see – but, alas! my infant eyesight could not
> carry so far, nor, if I could have seen, would my infant brain have
> understood – the most unusual sight of the Esk frozen over so hard
> that carts and horses could go upon it for twenty miles as upon a
> road, and the whole population were out skating upon it all day and,
> by the light of great bonfires, at night.

Grieve's family moved to a house in Henry Street in 1896 and at the age of seven, the year Grieve enrolled in the primary department of Langholm Academy, he went with his family to a house in Library Buildings, Parliament Square, behind the post office (now tourist information centre, with plaque honouring MacDiarmid).

Grieve's father was employed as a postman and his mother worked as a caretaker in the town library upstairs. A passage in *Lucky Poet* explains:

It was that library, however, that was the great determining factor. My father was a rural postman, his beat running up the Ewes Road to Fiddleton Toll, and we lived in the post office buildings. The library, the nucleus of which had been left by Thomas Telford, the famous engineer, was upstairs. I had constant access to it, and used to fill a big washing-basket with books and bring it downstairs as often as I wanted to. . . . There were upwards of twelve thousand books in the library (though it was strangely deficient in Scottish books), and a fair number of new books, chiefly novels, was constantly bought. Before I left home (when I was fourteen) I could go up into that library in the dark and find any book I wanted. . . . I certainly read almost every one of them.

In Langholm, Grieve came under two important influences. As the son of a church elder, Grieve attended Langholm South United Free Church (now Border Fine Arts) whose minister from 1901 to 1907 was the Rev. Thomas Scott Cairncross (see above). As a boy, Grieve thought Cairncross's verse was 'great stuff' and he often visited the minister and borrowed books from him. At Langholm Academy, Grieve was taught English by Francis George Scott (1880–1958) who lived in Langholm from 1903 to 1912. Scott later distinguished himself as a composer who set many MacDiarmid lyrics to music. It was to Scott that MacDiarmid dedicated his Scots masterpiece *A Drunk Man Looks at the Thistle* (1926).

Grieve left Langholm in 1908 to attend Broughton Junior Student Centre in Edinburgh. After the death of his father, in 1911, he went to South Wales as a journalist then returned to Langholm in 1912 before resuming his journalistic career the following year in Clydebank. While living in Montrose, in 1922, Grieve created his pseudonymous alter ego Hugh MacDiarmid whose experimental Scots verse remade his nation's poetry in a modernist image. The work of MacDiarmid has many associations with Langholm. Every last Friday in July, Langholm's Common Riding festival (dating from 1759) is celebrated in style as MacDiarmid explains in *A Drunk Man*:

Drums in the Walligate, pipes in the air,
Come and hear the cryin' o' the Fair.

A' as it used to be, when I was a loon   *boy*
On Common-ridin' Day in the Muckle Toon.

The bearer twirls the Bannock-and-Saut Herrin',
The Croon o' roses through the lift is fairin',   *sky*

The aucht-fit thistle wallops on hie;   *eight-foot*
In heather besoms a' the hills gang by.

The Muckle Toon (big town) is the colloquial name of Langholm.

In the 1930s MacDiarmid projected a huge autobiographical poem, *Clann Albann*, with a first volume entitled *The Muckle Toon* recalling his years in Langholm. As it survives the *Muckle Toon* sequence consists of *First Hymn to Lenin and Other Poems* (1931), *Second Hymn to Lenin* (1932), *Scots Unbound and Other Poems* (1932) and isolated poems in *Scottish Scene* (1934), *Stony Limits and Other Poems* (1934), and *A Lap of Honour* (1967). For example: 'The Church of My Fathers' cites the kirk the poet attended in Langholm; 'The Seamless Garment' mentions a cousin in a Langholm mill; 'Water Music' mentions the three rivers (Wauchope, Esk, Ewes) that converge in Langholm; 'Tarras' refers to Tarras Water; 'The Monument' concerns the 100ft high 'muckle monument' of white sandstone on the top of Whita Hill, commemorating one of the Four Knights of Eskdale, Sir John Malcolm, Governor of Bombay and author of a history of Persia.

In his prose, too, MacDiarmid praises Langholm, as in *Lucky Poet*:

My boyhood was an incredibly happy one. Langholm was, indeed – and presumably still is – a wonderful place to be a boy in. . . . It certainly [flowed with milk and honey] in my boyhood – with a bountifulness so inexhaustible that it has supplied all my subsequent poetry with a tremendous wealth of sensuous satisfaction, a teeming gratitude of reminiscence, and that I have still an immense reservoir to draw upon. My earliest impressions are of an almost tropical luxuriance of nature – of great forests, of honey-scented hills, and moorlands infinitely rich in little-appreciated beauties of flowering, of animal and insect life, of strange and subtle relationships of water and light:
    The recurrent vividness of light and water
    Through every earthly change of mood and scene,
and of a multitude of rivers, each with its distinct music and each catering in the most exciting way for hosts of the most stimulating and wholesome pleasures a fellow can know in the heyday of his youth – ducking, guddling, girning, angling, spearing eels, and building islands in midstream and playing at Robinson Crusoe. . . . These were, indeed, the champagne days – these long, enchanted days on the Esk, the Wauchope, and the Ewes:

Vivid and impulsive in crystalline splendour,
Cold and seething champagne,
and the thought of them today remains as intoxicating as they must
have been in actual fact all those years ago. I have been 'mad about
Scotland' ever since.

In later years, the polemical impact of *Lucky Poet* (which contains
bawdy anecdotes about the poet's early years in Langholm) and MacDiarmid's reputation as a militant nationalist and fiery communist made him
a controversial figure in his home town. When there were reports (in
1963) that he might receive the Freedom of the Burgh of Langholm,
MacDiarmid wrote to the Town Clerk (28 March 1963): 'Please inform
your [Town] Council that if at any future time they should offer me the
Freedom I will refuse it, and will also refuse any other public recognition
offered to me by Langholm.' Still, when time permitted MacDiarmid
continued to come to Langholm for the Common Riding festival and he
was buried in Langholm Cemetery on 13 September 1978. His gravestone
quotes the following quatrain from *A Drunk Man*:

> I'll ha'e nae hauf-way hoose, but aye be whaur
> Extremes meet – it's the only way I ken
> To dodge the curst conceit o' bein' richt
> That damns the vast majority o' men.

After a public competition and much local controversy a MacDiarmid
Memorial Sculpture, by Jake Harvey, was installed at Whita Yett on 11
August 1985.

LAURENCEKIRK, Kincardineshire (Grampian) 14m SW of Stonehaven on A94

Thomas Ruddiman, Dr Samuel Johnson, James Boswell

Thomas Ruddiman (1674–1757), the grammarian whose *Rudiments of the
Latin Tongue* (1714) had a long life as a standard textbook, became a
schoolmaster in Laurencekirk in 1695, four years before moving to Edinburgh. When Boswell and Johnson visited Laurencekirk in 1773 they were
well aware of the town's association with Ruddiman. Boswell wrote, in
his *Journal of a Tour to the Hebrides* (1785):

> We stopped at Lawrence Kirk, where our great Grammarian,
> Ruddiman, was once a schoolmaster. We respectfully remembered
> that excellent man and eminent scholar, by whose labours a knowledge
> of the Latin tongue will be preserved in Scotland, if it shall be
> preserved at all.

218

Boswell further observed that:

Lord Gardenston is the proprietor of Laurence Kirk, and has
encouraged the building of a manufacturing village, of which he is
exceedingly fond, and has written a pamphlet upon it, as if he had
founded Thebes; in which, however, there are many useful precepts
strongly expressed. The village seemed to be irregularly built, some
of the houses being of clay, some of brick, and some of brick and
stone. Dr Johnson observed, they thatched well here.

James Beattie

James Beattie (1735–1803) was born near Laurencekirk, where his father
kept a shop, and was educated at the village school before studying at
Aberdeen University whose Professor of Moral Philosophy he became in
1760. As a philosopher Beattie criticised David Hume in *An Essay on the
Nature and Immutability of Truth* (1770). His long poem *The Minstrel; or,
The Progress of Genius* (1771, 1774) describes the development of a poet:

> And oft he traced the uplands, to survey,
> When o'er the sky advanced the kindling dawn,
> The crimson cloud, blue main and mountain grey,
> And lake, dim-gleaming on the smoky lawn;
> Far to the west the long long vale withdrawn,
> Where twilight loves to linger for a while;
> And now he faintly kens the bounding fawn,
> And villager abroad at early toil. –
> But, lo! the sun appears! and heaven, earth, ocean smile.

Beattie is also remembered for his *Scotticisms, Arranged in Alphabetical
Order, Designed to Correct Improprieties of Speech and Writing* (1779).
This itemised list, of Scottish expressions to avoid, is a revealing product
of a period when Scottish academics affected impeccably English manners
and attempted to suppress their distinctively Scottish origins.

Lewis Grassic Gibbon

As the principal town in the Howe of the Mearns, Laurencekirk is part
of the landscape of Lewis Grassic Gibbon's trilogy *A Scots Quair* (1932–4).
In *Sunset Song* (1932), the first volume, the heroine Chris and her husband
Ewan approach Laurencekirk which 'looked brave in the afternoon stir,
with its cattle mart and its printing office'. Gibbon adds: 'It had aye a
hate for Stonehaven, Laurencekirk, and some said that it should be the
county capital, but others said God help the capital that was entrusted to
it'.

Fred Urquhart

Novelist and storyteller Fred Urquhart (born 1912) worked at Bent farm as a farm labourer and farm secretary from January 1940 to 1944. It was here that Urquhart conceived and wrote some of his stories about the Howe of the Mearns. 'The Dying Stallion', from *Selected Stories* (1946), uses the horse as a symbol of vitality to point up the onset of impotence in an old man who has been something of a sexual stallion in his youth.

LAURIESTON, Kircudbrightshire (Dumfries and Galloway) 8m N
of Kircudbright on A762

Samuel Rutherford Crockett

Samuel Rutherford Crockett (1859–1914), who was born at Little Duchrae farmhouse (one mile south of Mossdale on A762), is buried at Balmaghie churchyard (turn left by bridge three miles east of Laurieston, on B795) where there is a memorial (at the foot of a tombstone to Isabella Young, twenty yards from the gate). Crockett was educated at the village school in Laurieston before moving, in 1867, to Castle Douglas with his parents. A cairn at the north of Laurieston commemorates Crockett and quotes Robert Louis Stevenson's poem 'To S. R. Crockett', written after receiving the dedication of Crockett's second book, *The Stickit Minister* (1893):

> Blows the wind today, and the sun and the rain are flying
>   Blows the wind on the moors today and now,
> Where about the graves of the martyrs whaups are crying,
>   My heart remembers how!
>
> Grey recumbent tombs of the dead in desert places,
>   Standing-stones on the vacant wine-red moor,
> Hills of sheep, and the howes of the silent vanished races,
>   And winds, austere and pure.
>
> Be it granted me to behold you again in dying,
>   Hills of home! and to hear again the call;
> Hear about the graves of the martyrs the peewees crying
>   And hear no more at all.

Author of more than forty novels, Crockett studied for the Free Church Ministry in Edinburgh from 1883 to 1886. The great success of *The Lilac Sunbonnet* (1894), one of the key works of the Kailyard school of fiction, encouraged him to leave the ministry and concentrate on writing. The book contains an idyllic vision of Galloway:

Overhead there was nothing nearer than the blue lift, and even that
had withdrawn itself infinitely far away, as though the angels
themselves did not wish to spy on a later Eden. It was that midsummer
glory of love-time, when grey Galloway covers up its flecked granite
and becomes a true Purple land.

LEADHILLS, Lanarkshire   (Strathclyde)   14m NW of Moffat on B797

Allan Ramsay

Allan Ramsay (1684–1758) was born at Leadhills, the second highest
village in Scotland, on 15 October 1684. His father – John Ramsay, factor
to the Earl of Hopeton who owned the local lead and gold mines – died
shortly after his birth and Ramsay was brought up by his stepfather, a
farmer. Ramsay was educated locally at Crawford School up to the age
of fifteen; after his mother's death he was apprenticed, in 1701, to a
periwig maker in Edinburgh. He was subsequently associated with Edinburgh, where he made an immense contribution to Scottish culture as a
poet and literary man of action, but he remembered his origins in Leadhills
in his poem 'To the Whin-Bush Club, The Bill of Allan Ramsay':

> Of *Crawfurd-Moor*, born in *Leadhill*,
> Where Min'ral Springs *Glengoner* fill,
>   Which joins sweet flowing *Clyde*,
> Between auld *Crawfurd-Lindsay's* Towers,
> And where *Deneetne* rapid pours
>   His Stream thro' Glotta's Tide;
> Native of *Clydesdale's* upper Ward,
>   Bred Fifteen Summers there,
> Tho, to my Loss I'm no a Laird
>   By Birth, my Title's fair
>   To bend wi' ye and spend wi' ye
>   An Evening, and gaffaw,
>   If Merit and Spirit
>   Be found without a Flaw.

LEUCHARS, Fife   (Fife)   5m NW of St Andrews

Edwin Muir

Edwin Muir's poem 'The Wayside Station' – from *The Narrow Place*
(1943) – was prompted by his experience of Leuchars Junction, the railway

station at Leuchars. The poem was written during the winter of 1940–41 when Muir was living at St Andrews and working at the Food Office in Dundee. Every morning he had to change trains at Leuchars, on his way to work, and (he said in a broadcast of 1952) 'in the winter mornings particularly there was generally a long wait in the cold and bleak station . . . and over everything hung the thought of war'. The poem begins:

> Here at the wayside station, as many a morning,
> I watch the smoke torn from the fumy engine
> Crawling across the field in serpent sorrow.
> Flat in the east, held down by stolid clouds,
> The struggling day is born and shines already
> On its warm hearth far off. Yet something here
> Glimmers along the ground to show the seagulls
> White on the furrows' black unturning waves.

LEWIS, Outer Hebrides   (Western Isles)

Derick Thomson

Gaelic poet and scholar Derick Thomson – Ruaraidh MacThómais – was born in Stornoway on 5 August 1921 and brought up the schoolhouse (where his father taught) between the villages of Bayble and Garrabost on the Eye Peninsula. In an autobiographical essay 'A Man Reared in Lewis' (in Maurice Lindsay's anthology *As I Remember*, 1979) Thomson writes:

> It was a kind of no-man's-land, near the boundary of the Garrabost
> Common Grazings, where Bayble cattle might easily stray over the
> line, and where there might be small misunderstandings over peat-
> cutting rights. . . . The schoolhouse [in which I lived] was a
> thoroughly bilingual environment. My father and mother habitually
> spoke in Gaelic to each other, but frequently enough spoke English
> to each other also, without any sense of strain.

Later Thomson was educated at the Nicolson Institute, Stornoway, then (between 1939 and 1950 during which time he served with the Royal Air Force in World War Two) at the universities of Aberdeen, Cambridge and Bangor.

Thomson co-founded the Gaelic magazine *Gairm* in 1951 and acted as its editor; became Professor of Celtic at Glasgow University in 1963; and helped found the Gaelic Books Council in 1968. He published a useful *Introduction to Gaelic Poetry* in 1974 and collected his poems under the title *Creachadh na Clàrsaich* in 1982.

LEWIS

Iain Crichton Smith

Born in Glasgow on 1 January 1928, poet and novelist Iain Crichton Smith was six months' old when his mother brought him to Lewis. From then, until the age of seventeen, Smith lived in Edgemoor Cottage, Upper Bayble, on the Eye Peninsula. In an autobiographical essay 'Between Sea and Moor' (in Maurice Lindsay's anthology *As I Remember*, 1979) Smith writes:

> My house lay between the sea and the moor; the moor which was often red with heather, on which one would find larks' nests, where one would gather blaeberries: the moor scarred with peatbanks, spongy underfoot: blown across by the wind (for there is no land barer than Lewis).

Smith was educated in the village school and at the Nicolson Institute in Stornoway, walking the eight miles to school every morning. He recalled:

> I moved between the two worlds – the world of the [Nicolson Institute] and the world of the village – travelling home every night by bus. At home I spoke Gaelic and in the school I spoke English. But in those days I didn't find this an extraordinary situation. I simply accepted it. I would never have dreamed to speaking English to anyone in the village, and of course most of the Stornoway people spoke only English.

In 1945 Smith went to Aberdeen University and, after graduating in 1949, moved to 5 Carrick Terrace, Dumbarton. He was at Jordanhill College of Education, Glasgow, from 1949 to 1950 and did his National Service, from 1950 to 1952 with the Royal Scots in Dreghorn Barracks, Colinton, Edinburgh. From 1952 to 1955 he taught at Clydebank High School (travelling from Dumbarton) and from 1955–1977 taught at the High School in Oban where he lived at 42 Combie Street. Smith retired from teaching in 1977, the year he married Donalda, and in 1982 settled in Tigh na Fuaran ('house of the spring') in Taynuilt, Argyll. His work, however, is rooted in Lewis and in his compassion for the plight of his widowed mother who once worked as a fishergirl to support her two sons; who adhered to the Free Church religion; and who developed a morbid fear of illness after her husband died of tuberculosis.

In Smith's published works there are several poems about old women and each of them draws from Smith his deepest emotions and/or his profoundest sympathy. The poem 'For my mother' is, naturally, full of admiration for a woman who has weathered the storms of seventy years:

> as if her voyage were
> to truthful Lewis rising
> most loved though most bare
> at the end of a rich season.

'Old Woman with Flowers' and 'If You Are About to Die Now' delicately invoke the poet's thoughts on the final moments of his mother whose death is recorded, and life celebrated, in the first part of the collection *Love Poems and Elegies* (1972).

Smith's attitude to Lewis is ambivalent since he recalls with affection the spirit of the place yet recoils from the institutional aspects of the religion he learned on the island. He said (in a letter of 16 May 1979) 'I was brought up in the Free Church and I have felt since that as a religion it is too constricting, dictatorial and lacking in joy.' In 'Sunday Morning Walk' Smith depicts the island of Lewis in the cold grip of a Free Church Sabbath, a bizarre situation in which the islanders have to affect indifference to the glorious summer that surrounds them:

> Sunday of wrangling bells – and salt in the air –
> I passed the tall black men and their women walking
> over the tight-locked streets which were all on fire
> with summer ascendant. The seas were talking and talking.

A prolific poet and novelist, Smith is a bilingual writer who despairs over the possibility of Gaelic dying as he indicates in 'Deer on the High Hills' (*Selected Poems*, 1985) in a passage on modern Lewis:

> Tinkers subdued to council houses learn
> to live as others do, earn as they earn
> and English growing as the Gaelic dies
> describes these vast and towering inland skies.
> God is surrendering to other gods
> as the stony moor to multiplying roads.
> Folk songs and country westerns in the bars
> displace the native music sweet and harsh
> which dilettantes soon will learn to prize
> when the last real brutal singer dies,
> too zealous and too tearful.

LIATHACH, Wester Ross   (Highland)

Hugh MacDiarmid

Pronounced 'Leeagach' and meaning 'the Grey One', Liathach is a five-mile, east-west ridge of mountains with seven tops (reaching 3,456 feet) in Torridon, a 16,100 acre estate run by the National Trust for Scotland. (Torridon itself is 8m WSW of Kinlochewe, off A896.) Capped partly by quartzite, Liathach's forms are founded on red-brown Torridonian sandstone 750 million years old. In his poem 'The North Face of Liathach'

– collected in *Complete Poems* (1978) – Hugh MacDiarmid begins by saluting the spectacle:

> The north face of Liathach
> Lives in the mind like a vision.
> From the deeps of Coire na Caime
> Sheer cliffs go up
> To spurs and pinnacles and jagged teeth.
> Its grandeur draws back the heart.
> Scotland is full of such places.
> Few (few Scots even) know them.

Later in the poem he meditates on the meaning of the mountain:

> I have seen a head blood-drained to this hue.
> But this cliff is not dead.
> It has an immense life of its own
> And will loom, as if it could come rushing
> To beat, to maim, to kill
> (Damned anti-climax of a notion!)
> Just as it looms to-day
> After every human being now alive
> Has returned, not to rock but to dust.

LOCHINVAR LOCH, Kircudbrightshire (Dumfries and Galloway)
5m N of Bal of Balmaclellan

Sir Walter Scott

In Sir Walter Scott's *Marmion* (1808) – subtitled 'A Tale of Flodden Field' and set in 1513, the year of the battle of Flodden in which Marmion is killed – Young Lochinvar appears ostentatiously to carry off his bride in one of Scott's best-known songs (V, xii):

> O, young Lochinvar is come out of the west,
> Through all the wide Border his steed was the best;
> And save his good broadsword he weapons had none,
> He rode all unarm'd, and he rode all alone.
> So faithful in love, and so dauntless in war,
> There never was knight like the young Lochinvar.
>
> He staid not for brake, and he stopp'd not for stone,
> He swam the Eske river where ford there was none;
> But ere he alighted at Netherby gate,
> The bride had consented, the gallant came late:

For a laggard in love, and a dastard in war,
Was to wed the fair Ellen of brave Lochinvar.

Young Lochinvar, of course, claims Ellen and rides off with the 'fair lady'. The ruins of Young Lochinvar's castle lie on the island in the middle of Lochinvar Loch.

LOCHLEA, Ayrshire   (Strathclyde)   2½m NW of Mauchline,
off B7444

Robert Burns

Robert Burns (1759–96) lived in **Lochlea farm** from 1777 to 1784. The house in which he composed some of the poems in *Poems, Chiefly in the Scottish Dialect* (1786) is now an outhouse, a newer farmhouse replacing it.

In 1777 the poet's father William Burnes left Mount Oliphant farm and made an oral agreement with David McLure to rent the 130 swampy acres of Lochlea farm in the parish of Tarbolton. Burns was well pleased with the move as it gave him access to Tarbolton and the Bachelors' Club. In 1781 Burns went to Irvine, to learn flax-dressing and when he returned to Lochlea the following year he found his father in difficulties: suddenly finding himself short of cash, McLure had demanded arrears of rent from William Burnes. Even amid these tribulations Burns began his *Commonplace Book 1783–85* of 'Observations, Hints, Songs, Scraps of Poetry, &c., by Robt. Burness; a man who had little art in making money, and still less in keeping it.' Significantly he noted his desire to be the poet of Ayrshire, to sing the praises of 'the fertile banks of Irvine, the romantic woodlands and sequestered scenes on Aire, and the healthy mountainous source, and winding sweep of Doon' (an ambition his muse, Coila, grants him in 'The Vision').

That William Burnes was in serious difficulty, with the impact of consumption and the worry of prolonged litigation, was common knowledge and, as a precaution against the worst Robert and his brother Gilbert Burns rented Mossgiel farm, near Mauchline, from Gavin Hamilton, a fellow freemason. In January 1784 the Edinburgh Court of Session upheld William Burnes's case but the legal costs took what little money he had: as Burns put it 'his all went among the rapacious hell-hounds that growl in the kennel of justice'. On 13 February, less than a month after the court decision, William Burnes died at the age of sixty-three and, in accordance with his wishes, was buried in the churchyard of Kirk Alloway, a few hundred yards from his 'auld clay biggin'.

LOCH KATRINE, Perthshire/Stirlingshire (Central) 8½m W of Callander

Dorothy and William Wordsworth

Eight miles long (by one mile broad at its widest), 364ft above sea-level and 495ft deep, Loch Katrine is surrounded by mountains including Ben Vane on the north; and Ben Lomond and Ben Venue on the south. It lies in the Trossachs (so called from the Gaelic word for 'bristly' which describes the texture of the countryside). During her Scottish tour of 1803, Dorothy Wordsworth (1771–1855) recorded a visit to Loch Katrine. When the boatman took her and her brother William (1770–1850) to 'the termination of the lake' she noted (entry for Saturday 27 August 1803):

> It was an entire solitude; and all that we beheld was the perfection of loveliness and beauty; we had been through many solitary places since we came into Scotland, but this place differed as much from any we had seen before, as if there had been nothing in common between them; no thought of dreariness or desolation found entrance here; yet nothing was to be seen but water, wood, rocks, and heather, and bare mountains above.

Sir Walter Scott

In *The Lady of the Lake* (1810) Sir Walter Scott (1771–1832) drew the attention of an adoring public to the loch. His heroine, Ellen Douglas (in whose honour one of the islands in Loch Katrine is called Ellen's Isle) is presented as a romantic model of feminine modesty (I, xix):

> And seldom o'er a breast so fair,
> Mantled a plaid with modest care,
> And never brooch the folds combin'd
> Above a heart more good and kind.
> Her kindness and her worth to spy.
> You need but gaze on Ellen's eye;
> Not Katrine, in her mirror blue.
> Gives back the shaggy banks more true.
> Than every free-born glance confess'd
> The guileless movements of her breast;
> Whether joy danced in her dark eye,
> Or woe or pity claim'd a sigh,
> Or filial love was glowing there,
> Or meek devotion to a prayer,
> Or tale of injury call'd forth
> The indignant spirit of the North.

One only passion unreveal'd,
With maiden pride the maid conceal'd,
Yet not less purely felt the flame; –
O need I tell that passion's name?

The public fell in love with Ellen and flocked to the Trossachs to see Loch Katrine for themselves.

William McGonagall

In 1859 Loch Katrine became a source of water supply for Glasgow, a fact featured in 'Loch Katrine' by William McGonagall (*c.* 1805–1902):

And as I gaze upon it, let me pause and think,
How many people in Glasgow of its water drink,
That's conveyed to them in pipes from its placid lake,
And are glad to get its water their thirst to slake.
Then away to Loch Katrine in the summer time.
And feast on its scenery most lovely and sublime;
There's no other scene can surpass in fair Scotland,
It's surrounded by mountains and trees most grand.

The steamer 'Sir Walter Scott' (built in 1900 at Dumbarton, then dismantled and reassembled on the loch) runs cruises during the summer.

LOCH LEVEN, Kinross-shire (Central)

Andrew of Wyntoun, Michael Bruce

From 1395 to 1413 Andrew of Wyntoun (*c.* 1355–1422) was Prior of St Serf's Inch, at the south-east of Loch Leven. In the monastery, whose ruins remain, he wrote most of his *Orygynale Cronykil of Scotland*, a metrical history of Scotland from antiquity to the reign of Robert the Bruce. It was published in two volumes in London in 1795 and the definitive text was published, in six volumes, by the Scottish Text Society from 1903 to 1914. In his long poem 'Lochleven', Michael Bruce (1746–67) describes St Serf's Inch as follows:

Fronting where Gairney pours his silent urn
Into the Loch, an island lifts its head.
Grassy and wild, with ancient ruin heap'd
Of cells; where from the noisy world retir'd
Of old, as same reports, Religion dwelt
Safe from the insults of the darken'd crowd
That bow'd the knee to Odin; and in times

Of ignorance, when Caledonia's sons
(Before the triple-crowned giant fell)
Exchang'd their simple faith for Rome's deceits.

Mary Queen of Scots was imprisoned in Lochleven Castle, a fifteenth-century structure, on the Castle Island, on 17 June 1567. On 24 July she was forced to abdicate in favour of James VI, the Earl of Moray assuming power as Regent. On 2 May 1568 she escaped from Lochleven Castle (open to the public from May to October, access by ferry from lochside). Mary's captivity, abdication and escape from the castle are described in Sir Walter Scott's novel *The Abbot* (1820), a sequel to *The Monastery* (1820). In 'Lochleven', Michael Bruce features:

high Lochleven Castle, famous once,
Th' abode of heroes of the Bruce's line;
Gothic the pile, and high the solid walls,
With warlike ramparts, and the strong defence
Of jutting battlements, and age's toil!
No more its arches echo to the noise
Of joy and festive mirth. No more the glance
Of blazing taper through its windows beams,
And quivers on the undulating wave:
But naked stand the melancholy walls
Lash'd by the wintry tempests, cold and bleak,
That whistle mournful thro' the empty halls,
And piece-meal crumble down the tow'rs to dust.

LOCHNAGAR, Aberdeenshire   (Grampian)   6m SE of Braemar

Lord Byron

Writing to Charles David Gordon in August 1805, George Gordon, Lord Byron (1788–1824) recalled:

passing near Abergeldie on an excursion through the Highlands; it was at that time a most lovely place. I suppose you will soon have a view of the eternal snows that summit the top of Lachin-y-Gair, which towers so magnificently above the rest of our *Northern Alps*. I still remember with pleasure the admiration which filled my mind when I first beheld it, and, further on, the dark, frowning mountains which rise near Invercauld, together with the romantic rocks that overshadow Mar Lodge.

Byron visited Lochnagar (3,786ft) when he was nine or ten and in the *Records of Invercauld* the Rev. J. G. Michie reported that a ghillie had escorted Byron during a visit to the area in the autumn of 1803. The mountain Lochnagar was celebrated in 'Lachin Y Gair', included in Byron's *Hours of Idleness* (1807). The poem ends:

Years have roll'd on, Loch na Garr, since I left you,
    Years must elapse ere I tread you again:
Nature of verdure and flow'rs has bereft you,
    Yet still are you dearer than Albion's plain.
England! thy beauties are tame and domestic
    To one who has roved o'er the mountains afar:
Oh for the crags that are wild and majestic!
    The steep frowning glories of dark Loch na Garr.

LOGIEALMOND, Perthshire   (Tayside)   10m NW of Perth

Ian Maclaren

Logiealmond lies on the north bank of the River Almond. Its Free Church minister, from 1873 to 1877, was John Watson (1850–1907) whose first charge was this parish. Under the pseudonym Ian Maclaren he published, in 1894, a miscellany of 'Idylls', *Beside the Bonnie Brier Bush*, that became a bestseller (quickly selling a quarter of a million copies in Britain and half a million copies in the USA). One of the best-known examples of the sentimental kailyard ('cabbage-patch') school of Scottish writing, *Beside the Bonnie Brier Bush* is set in Drumtochty, a parish based on Logiealmond: 'Drumtochty made up its mind slowly upon any new-comer, and for some time looked into the far distance when his name was mentioned' ('As a Little Child'). Maclaren's novel *Kate Carnegie and Those Ministers* (1896) is also set in Drumtochty. Watson, who wrote several theological works, died on 6 May 1907 during a lecture tour of America.

LONGNIDDRY, East Lothian   (Lothian)   10m E of Edinburgh on
A198

Hugh MacDiarmid

When the poet Hugh MacDiarmid (1892–1978) returned to Scotland, towards the end of 1932, he was given editorial employment on the *Free Man*, a Social Credit weekly published by Robin Black of Portobello, Edinburgh. Under his real name of C. M. Grieve, MacDiarmid contributed a weekly causerie, called 'At the Sign of the Thistle', to the *Free Man*. Earning £2 per week for this work, he rented – for ten shillings a week – a small cottage beside the old lime kilns near the railway at Longniddry. He and his wife Valda Grieve lived in the cottage for several months from 1932 to 1933. In May 1933 MacDiarmid and Valda moved to Whalsay, Shetland. Locals in Longniddry recall that MacDiarmid used to return on the late bus from Edinburgh, usually sitting at the back of the bus and smoking his pipe. Known as Fruit Farm Cottage, the little house still stands and was used, in 1984, as a dollmaker's workshop.

LOWER LARGO, Fife   (Fife)   On A915

Daniel Defoe, William Cowper

In this coastal village, on Largo Bay, Alexander Selkirk (1676–1721), the original of Daniel Defoe's Robinson Crusoe, was born; a statue of Selkirk stands in a niche on the site of his birthplace. Defoe's masterpiece describes – to cite the full title of the first part of the novel published on 25 April 1719 – *The Life and Strange Surprising Adventures of Robinson Crusoe of York, Mariner*. Defoe narrates the book in the first person and comes alive as the resourceful young sailor cast away in an island in the Caribbean Sea where he survives thanks to his ingenuity and the devotion of 'My man Friday'.

The extraordinary narrative was based on the life of Selkirk. As sailing master of the *Cinque Ports* galley, Selkirk sailed from the Downs to Brazil in 1703. When the captain of the *Cinque Ports* died in Brazil he was replaced by Thomas Stradling whose authority was undermined by Selkirk's hostility. After many quarrels Selkirk was, at his own request, put ashore in September 1704 on the island of Juan Fernandez where he lived, alone, for more than four years. Captain Woodes Rogers anchored the *Duke* off the island on 2 February 1709 and took Selkirk aboard as a mate before returning to England.

Later Rogers published his journal, *A Cruizing Voyage round the World* (1712), and described Selkirk's life on the island:

After he had conquered his melancholy, he diverted himself sometimes with cutting his name on the trees, and the time of his being left, and his continuance there . . . he came, at last, to conquer all the inconvenience of his solitude, and to be very easy.

From this principal source Defoe built up his adventure which is full of inventive touches and so Selkirk the celebrity became Crusoe, the hero of a classic fiction.

William Cowper (1731–1800) was also inspired by the story of Selkirk and wrote 'Verses Supposed to be Written by Alexander Selkirk' beginning:

I am monarch of all I survey,
My right there is none to dispute.

MANOR VALLEY, Peeblesshire   (Border)   3m SW of Peebles

Sir Walter Scott

Manor Valley, drained by the Manor Water, was the home of David Ritchie, the original of Sir Walter Scott's *The Black Dwarf* (1816). Ritchie built himself a cottage which was replaced, in 1802, by the present **Black Dwarf's Cottage** on the same site. The laird, Sir James Nasmyth of Posso, had the cottage constructed for Ritchie and retained the Black Dwarf's original 3ft 10in doorway and the tiny window in the wall through which he scrutinised passersby. Standing 3ft 6in, Ritchie is portrayed as Elshender the Black Dwarf in Scott's novel:

> His head was of uncommon size, covered with a fell of shaggy hair, partly grizzled with age; his eyebrows, shaggy and prominent, overhung a pair of small, dark, piercing eyes, set far back in their sockets. . . . The rest of his features were of the coarse, rough-hewn stamp, with which a painter would equip a giant in romance; to which was added the wild, irregular, and peculiar expression, so often seen in the countenances of those whose persons are deformed. His body, thick and square, like that of a man of middle size, was mounted upon two large feet; but nature seemed to have forgotten the legs and the thighs, or they were so very short as to be hidden by the dress which he wore. His arms were long and brawny, furnished with two muscular hands, and, where uncovered in the eagerness of his labour, were shagged with coarse black hair. It seemed as if nature had originally intended the separate parts of his body to be the members of a giant, but had afterwards had capriciously assigned them to the person of a dwarf, so ill did the length of his arms and the iron strength of his frame correspond with the shortness of his stature.

Ritchie's cottage is a mile beyond **Manor Churchyard** where Ritchie was buried after his death on 6 December 1811. In 1845 W. and R. Chambers, the publishing brothers, erected a tombstone in memory of David Ritchie. A statue of Ritchie can be seen (by special request) in the grounds of Hailyards House, Manor, where Scott stayed in the summer of 1797. Adam Fergusson, his friend, took Scott up the Manor Valley to meet David Ritchie, then around fifty-seven. Apparently Ritchie asked Scott: 'Man, hae ye ony poo'er?' (that is, magical power). Scott denied that he had and Ritchie signalled to a black cat which perched on a shelf. Ritchie then observed of Scott: 'He has poo'er. Ay, *he* has poo'er.'

MAUCHLINE, Ayrshire   (Strathclyde)   9m SE of Kilmarnock on A76

Robert Burns

In the period when Robert Burns (1759–96) lived at Lochlea, his father's farm, and himself farmed Mossgiel with his brother Gilbert – that is, from 1777 to 1786 – the poet was a frequent visitor to Mauchline which consequently features in many of his poems. **Mauchline Cross**, for instance, is cited in the first stanza of Burns's epistle 'To John Kennedy':

> Now, Kennedy, if foot or horse
> E'er bring you in by Mauchlin Corss   *Cross*
> (Lord, man, there's lasses there wad force
>   A hermit's fancy;
> And down the gate in faith! they're worse
>   An' mair unchancy) . . .   *dangerous*

'The Belles of Mauchline' runs, to the tune of 'Bonie Dundee':

> In Mauchline there dwells six proper young belles,
> The pride of the place and its neighbourhood a',
> Their carriage and dress, a stranger would guess,
> In Lon'on or Paris they'd gotten it a'.
>
> Miss Miller is fine, Miss Markland's divine,
> Miss Smith she has wit, and Miss Betty is braw,
> There's beauty and fortune to get wi' Miss Morton;
> But Armour's the jewel for me o' them a'.

Jean Armour lived with her father – a master mason – at the foot of the Cowgate, at its junction with Howard Place.

Gavin Hamilton, from whom Burns rented Mossgiel farm, lived in the house next to **Mauchline Castle**, a fifteenth-century ecclesiastical tower near the **parish church** and Burns married Jean Armour in a room in this house in 1788. Burns and Jean set up house in Castle Street, now open to the public (Mon–Sat. 10am–7pm; Sun. 2–7pm) as **Burns House** which contains the Armour family bible. The parish church is built on the site of the building in which Burns was publicly rebuked by the minister, Daddy Auld.

Of the inns Burns enjoyed, three are still in evidence. **Poosie Nansie's**, once a lodging house and still an inn, is the setting for the cantata 'Love and Liberty (The Jolly Beggars)' which Burns omitted from collections published in his lifetime (it was first published in Glasgow in 1799):

> When lyart leaves bestrow the yird,   *withered, earth*
> Or, wavering like the bauckie-bird   *bat*

Bedim cault Boreas' blast;
When hailstanes drive wi' bitter skyte,   *lash*
And infant frosts begin to bite
In hoary cranreuch drest;   *rime*
Ae night at e'en a merry core   *One, gang*
O' randie, gangrel bodies   *vagrant*
In Poosie-Nansie's held the splore,   *carousal*
To drink their orra duddies: *spare rags*
Wi' quaffing and laughing
They ranted an' they sang,
Wi' jumping an' thumping
The vera girdle rang

Near Poosie Nansie's is the site of the **Whitford Arms** (marked by a plaque). **Nanse Tinnock's**, near Mauchline Cross, was the change-house in 'The Holy Fair':

Now butt an' ben the change-house fills,   *tavern*
Wi' yill-caup commentators;   *ale-cup*
Here's crying out for bakes an' gills,   *biscuits*
An' there the pint-stowp clatters;
While thick an' thrang, an' loud an' lang,
Wi' logic an' wi' Scripture,
They raise a din, that in the end
Is like to breed a rupture
O' wrath that day.

In the **churchyard**, the scene of 'The Holy Fair', are the graves of the parish minister (Daddy Auld), William Fisher (Holy Willie), Nanse Tinnock, the Gibson family (who ran Poosie Nansie's) and – in the Armour family burial plot – the poet's in-laws and some of his children.

The Mauchline Burns knew was dominated by kirk politics and divided into two antagonistic groups. The strictly Calvinist Auld Licht (old light) party, who believed in preordained damnation or salvation, worshipped a God who punished sinners in a blazing hellfire: 'A vast, unbottom'd, boundless pit,/Fill'd fou o' lowin' brunstane'. The liberal New Licht faction held that a merciful God would reward good deeds. Burns was temperamentally drawn to the New Lichts, partly in reaction to his father's fundamentalism. He particularly resented the power of the Kirk Session – a council of parish elders presided over by the minister – who publicly condemned him for fathering (by one of his father's servant girls) 'dear-bought Bess', the first of his illegitimate children. (He later admitted to eleven illegitimate children, though the two pairs of twins by Jean were not strictly so.)

To express his feelings towards the kirk Burns wrote his three great ecclesiastical satires: 'Holy Willie's Prayer', 'The Holy Fair' and 'Address to the De'il'. The first, and greatest, of these immortalised the preposterous William Fisher, 'a rather oldish bachelor elder in the parish of Mauchline, and much and justly famed for that polemical chattering which ends in tippling orthodoxy, and for that spiritualised bawdry which refines to liquorish devotion'. Fisher instigated charges of irregular church attendance against Burns's lawyer friend, brother-mason and landlord, Gavin Hamilton. When these were dismissed, by the Presbytery of Ayr, Burns imagined the unctuous, unbearably self-righteous Willie praying to the Calvinist God who 'Sends ane to heaven and ten to hell'. Implicit in the poem is the presentation of Calvinism as an unChristian concept bent on vengeance rather than forgiveness. Willie asks for the 'Strong right hand' of God to come down on the non-elect, particularly Gavin Hamilton:

> Lord, mind Gau'n Hamilton's deserts:
> He drinks, an' swears, an' plays at cartes,   *cards*
> Yet has sae monie takin arts
>   Wi' great and sma',
> Frae God's ain priest the people's hearts
>   He steals awa.
>
> And when we chasten'd him therefore,
> Thou kens how he bred sic a splore,   *row*
> And set the warld in a roar
>   O'laughin at us:
> Curse thou his basket and his store,
>   Kail an' potatoes!

Of the reaction to this poem, circulated round Mauchline, Burns said it

> alarmed the kirk-Session so much that they held three several meetings
> to look over their holy artillery, if any of it was pointed against
> profane Rhymers. Unluckily for me, my idle wanderings led me, on
> another side, point-blank within the reach of their heaviest metal.

This was his affair with Jean Armour, a Mauchline girl eight years his junior. With her comely figure and fine dark hair she was, Burns felt, the best of the Mauchline beauties. Burns met Jean in 1785 at a Mauchline dance. Tradition has it that the poet's rakish reputation made it difficult for him to persuade any of the girls to dance with him. Before leaving he sarcastically wished aloud for a girl to follow him as faithfully as the collie dog he had brought with him. It was this remark that Jean teased him with when they met on the village green. The hint was well taken by Burns; they became intimate and by the end of 1785 Jean was pregnant. Delighted at the prospect of becoming a father, he gave her a paper declaring them man and wife (a perfectly legal procedure in Scotland where marriage by declaration remained valid up to 1939).

In March 1786, just before Burns sent John Wilson, the Kilmarnock printer, proposals for the publication of his *Poems, Chiefly in the Scottish Dialect* (31 July 1786), Jean's father James literally fainted on hearing of his daughter's condition. Like many another Mauchline father he disapproved of Burns's unorthodox ways and his obvious lack of prospects, so had the marriage declaration mutilated. Burns was horrified – as his poem 'The Lament' testifies – and, not for the first time, thought of making a fresh start. He accepted a job as a plantation book-keeper in Jamaica and turned his bruised affections to another girl, 'Highland' Mary Campbell. Poetic success and the death of Mary Campbell changed his plans and he married Jean in Mauchline in 1788.

On the outskirts of Mauchline, where the Tarbolton and Kilmarnock roads meet, there is a **National Burns Memorial**, planned by the Glasgow Mauchline Society in 1895 as a suitable tribute to the poet. In addition to the Burns Museum – in a baronial tower containing papers, photographs and relics including the poet's pocket-knife, his coffee cup, and the chair on which Jean Armour nursed his children – there are twenty cottages (mainly for the elderly). Initially the Glasgow Mauchline Society planned six cottages for deserving families but the project expanded into a community complete with hall and bowling green.

MAXWELTON HOUSE, Dumfriesshire   (Dumfries and Galloway)
13m NW of Dumfries on B729

William Douglas

Annie Laurie was born in Maxwelton House (to the east of Moniaive) in 1682 and subsequently became the subject of the popular love song ('Annie Laurie') by William Douglas (1672–1748) of Fingland:

> And for bonnie Annie Laurie
> I'll lay me doun and dee.

A seventeenth-century house, with part of a fifteenth-century castle, Maxwelton House is open to the public (May–Sept. 2.30–5, Wed. and Thurs.).

MAYBOLE, Ayrshire   (Strathclyde)   9m SW of Ayr on A77

William Dunbar, Walter Kennedy

Maybole was the capital of Carrick when Ayrshire was divided into three parts (the others being Kyle and Cunninghame). Walter Kennedy (*c.* 1460–*c.* 1508), the poet, was Provost of Maybole around 1594 when Carrick was a mainly Gaelic-speaking area. In the vituperative 'The Flyting of Dunbar and Kennedy', William Dunbar (*c.* 1460–*c.* 1520) and Kennedy exchange insults. Dunbar makes much of Kennedy's Carrick heritage and contrasts his own command of 'Inglis' (that is, the Lowland Scots vernacular) with Kennedy's supposed linguistic limitations:

> I tak on me ane pair of Lowthiane hippis   *buttocks*
>   Sall fairar Inglis mak, and mair parfyte,   *Scots*
> Than thow can blabbar with thy Carrik lippis.   *mutter, lips*

Rising to his theme, Dunbar tells Kennedy:

> Thow bringis the Carrik clay to Edinburgh cors
> Upoun thy botingis hobland, hard as horne . . .   *boots, hobbling*

On the evidence of this poem Kennedy was, at least technically, Dunbar's equal and he makes a vigorous defence of 'Irische' (that is, Gaelic):

> Thou lufis nane Irische, elf, I understand,
>   Bot it suld be all trew Scottish mennis lede;   *language*
> It was the gud language of this land,
>   And Scota it causit to multiply and sprede . . .

Kennedy was the third son of Lord Kennedy of Dunure. The Kennedys were the Earls of Cassilis and their castle (restored) was the home of the Countess of Cassilis who, in the ballad 'The Gypsy Laddie', is enchanted by Jockie Faa and his gypsies:

> The gypsies they came to my lord Cassilis' yett   *gate*
>   And O but they sang bonnie!
> They sang sae sweet and sae complete
>   That down came our fair ladie.
>
> She came tripping down the stairs,
>   And all her maids before her;
> As soon as they saw her weel-far'd face,   *well-favoured*
>   They coost their glamourie ower her.   *cast, spell*

When the Earl of Cassilis finds out that his lady has gone he rides after her with catastrophic consequences for the gypsies:

They were fifteen valiant men,
Black, but very bonny,
And they lost all their lives for one,
The Earl of Cassilis' ladie.

MELROSE, Roxburghshire   (Border)   3½m SE of Galashiels

Sir Walter Scott

In 1803 Sir Walter Scott (1771–1832) took William Wordsworth
(1770–1850) and his siter Dorothy (1771–1855) to see Melrose Abbey.
Founded in 1136 for Cistercian monks from Rievaulx, Melrose Abbey was
ruined by war and reduced by local builders in search of suitable stone.
Dorothy was impressed by the traceried stonework but also noted acidly:

> surely this is a national barbarism; within these beautiful walls is the
> ugliest church that was ever beheld – if it had been cut out of the
> side of a hill, it could not have been more dismal.

The minister of Melrose (ordained 1788) was the Rev. George Thomson
whose son, George Thomson – installed 'dominie' (teacher) at Abbotsford
around 1812 – was the original of Dominie Abel Sampson, the 'stickit
minister' of Scott's *Guy Mannering* (1815).

Melrose Abbey (open to the public) is memorably evoked in Scott's
The Lay of the Last Minstrel (II,i) which appeared in 1805:

If thou woulds't view fair Melrose aright,
Go visit it by the pale moonlight;
For the gay beams of lightsome day
Gild, but to flout the ruins grey.
When the broken arches are black in night,
And each shafted oriel glimmers white;
When the cold light's uncertain shower
Streams on the ruin'd central tower;
When buttress and buttress, alternately,
Seem fram'd of ebon and ivory;
When silver edges the imagery,
And the scrolls that teach thee to live and die;
When distant Tweed is heard to rave,
And the owlet to hoot o'er the dead man's grave,
Then go – but go alone the while –
Then view St David's ruin'd pile;
And, home returning, soothly swear,
Was never scene so sad and fair!

Scott enthusiastically approved of the restoration work carried out for the Duke of Buccleuch in 1822.

MINTO, Roxburghshire   (Border)   6m NE of Hawick, off A698

Jean Elliot

Jean Elliot (1727–1805) – the daughter of Sir Gilbert Elliot of Minto, Lord Justice Clerk for Scotland – was born at Minto House (not open to the public). According to tradition she composed 'The Flowers of the Forest' after her brother Gilbert challenged her to write a song about the battle of Flodden (1513). Using the lines 'I've heard them lilting at the ewes milking' and 'The flowers of the forest are a' wede away' from an old ballad, 'The Battle of Flodden', Jean Elliot produced her version which was admired by both Burns and Scott. It was included in David Herd's *Scottish Songs* (1776) and reprinted in Scott's *Minstrelsy of the Scottish Border* (1802–3). The first of the six stanzas runs:

> I've heard them lilting at our yowe-milking –   *ewe-milking*
>   Lasses a-lilting before dawn of day;
> But now they are moaning on ilka green loaning – *every*
>   The Flowers of the Forest are a' wede away.   *withered*

MOFFAT, Dumfriesshire   (Dumfries and Galloway)   23m NE of
Dumfries on A701

John Home, James Macpherson

During the eighteenth century Moffat, with its mineral springs, became a fashionable spa. In 1759 John Home (1722–1808), author of the popular verse drama *Douglas* (1757), was taking the waters at Moffat when he was introduced to James Macpherson (1736–96), then a young tutor with literary ambitions. When Home asked Macpherson, a crofter's son from Ruthven, about Gaelic poetry Macpherson replied that he had some examples to hand. Cannily, however, Macpherson asked Home if he knew any Gaelic. 'Not one word,' said Home. 'Then how can I show you them?' asked Macpherson. 'Very easily,' Home observed: 'translate one of the poems which you think a good one, and I imagine that I shall be able to form some opinion of the genius and character of Gaelic poetry.' Macpherson obliged and Home was impressed enough to encourage his friend to persevere with his poetic translations. This led to Macpherson's career as the creator of Ossianic poetry. In 1760 he published *Fragments of*

Ancient Poetry (1760) and the following year created a sensation with *Fingal* which purported to be a translation of Ossian, Fingal's son and a third-century Gaelic bard. On the basis of a few authentic fragments of Gaelic poetry, Macpherson had fabricated *Fingal* – and *Temora*, which followed in 1763. Dr Johnson exposed the element of fakelore though Macpherson refused to reveal his sources and continued to insist his translations were the result of scholarly research.

MONTROSE, Angus   (Tayside)   38m S of Aberdeen on A92

Willa Anderson, Edwin Muir

Willa Anderson (1890–1970), who married the poet Edwin Muir in 1919, was brought up rather reluctantly in Montrose as she explains in her book *Belonging* (1968):

> I did not feel that I belonged whole-heartedly to Montrose. Well before I was three, I explained [to Edwin], I had discovered that I did not really belong to the Montrose way of life. My people spoke Shetland at home, so my first words were in the Norse dialect of Shetland, which was not valid outside our front door. I remember standing in Bridge Street, where we lived, fingering my pinafore, dumb with embarrassment, while four or five older girls squealed in delighted mockery of what I had been saying and urged me to say it again.

Willa survived, she told Edwin, by learning to speak 'broad Montrose'.

In July 1924 – after a four-year period abroad in Prague, Dresden and Hellerau – Willa and Edwin Muir headed back to Scotland. Arriving in Montrose they stayed with Willa's mother who had a shop in the High Street. Edwin was disappointed with Montrose though, Willa recalled:

> The great round of sky, the wide links with their stretches of thyme and eyebright, the wild North Sea beating on sand dunes held together by tough pink liquorice and marram grass, were still as I remembered them; was it not a setting where the wind of the spirit had freedom to blow?

Both Muirs did some literary work, Edwin preparing critical essays for his collection *Transition* (1926); and Willa took the opportunity to teach Edwin to play golf. 'In Montrose, of all places,' said Willa, 'we first encountered Christopher Grieve, perhaps better known by his pen-name, Hugh MacDiarmid, who had been appointed editor of a local weekly, the *Montrose Review*'. Muir and MacDiarmid got on well at first but were to fall out after the publication of Muir's *Scott and Scotland* twelve years later.

In January 1925 the Muirs moved to England, to stay in a cottage at Penn, then returned to Montrose in November 1925 as Edwin wanted to finish *Transition*. Willa, pregnant, looked forward to her mother's 'dry, warm house in Montrose'. However, she had a miscarriage in Montrose and in February 1926 left the town when the couple were ready to leave Scotland again for their 'second European adventure'.

Hugh MacDiarmid

Apart from some months at Kildermorie Lodge, Alness, Hugh Mac-Diarmid (C. M. Grieve, 1892–1978) spent the decade 1919–29 at Montrose. These were arguably the most creative years of his life, the period in which he adopted (1922) the pseudonym Hugh MacDiarmid and wrote *Sangschaw* (1925), *Penny Wheep* (1926) and *A Drunk Man Looks at the Thistle* (1926). It was thus at Montrose that Scottish literature was remade in a MacDiarmidian image of combative self-confidence; at Montrose that MacDiarmid's immortal Drunk Man came to consciousness.

Christopher Murray Grieve first came to Montrose in 1919 as a recently-married (13 June 1918) man who had spent most of World War One as a soldier in Salonika. He obtained a job on the editorial staff of the *Montrose Review*, then situated in a close off the High Street (plaque at head of close commemorating MacDiarmid's association with the *Montrose Review*). After his spell at Kildermorie Lodge (October 1920-March 1921) Grieve returned to Montrose (and his job on the *Montrose Review*) with his wife Peggy in April 1921. They lodged at 19 Kincardine Street and 12 White's Place before moving into a new council house at 16 Links Avenue on 17 March 1922. This was his home and headquarters until he left Montrose in August 1929 to take up an editorial job with the radio critical journal *Vox* in London. Describing the Montrose years in *The Company I've Kept* (1966) the poet recalled:

> I became editor-reporter of the *Montrose Review*, and held that position until 1929. I threw myself whole-heartedly into the life of that community and became a Town Councillor, Parish Councillor, member of the School Management Committee and Justice of the Peace for the county.

He also produced a daughter, Christine (born 1924), and a son, Walter (born 1929). It was this apparent pillar of the community who was ready, willing and able to support a radically new Scotland. In the Montrose years Grieve founded the Scottish Centre of PEN in 1927 and helped found the National Party of Scotland in 1928.

The house at 16 Links Avenue provided the Scottish Literary

Renaissance, as sustained by the poet, with an address. It was there, in 1922 that Grieve began to put Montrose on the cultural map of the literary world. As a journalist he had access to print and set up as his own publisher and bookseller. On 26 August 1922 he produced the first number of a new literary monthly, the *Scottish Chapbook*, containing a conversational piece in English entitled 'Nisbet, An Interlude in Post-War Glasgow' and attributed to one 'Hugh M'Diarmid'. In October the third issue of the *Scottish Chapbook* featured, on its first page, 'The Watergaw' by Hugh M'Diarmid. In a 'Causerie' editor Grieve, conscious that Joyce's *Ulysses* had appeared in February of that year, enthused over the experimental implications of Synthetic Scots as 'a deliberate attempt to thrust the Doric on to a plane corresponding to the plane of the most advanced school of modern English'. In the same month that Hugh MacDiarmid made his poetic debut with 'The Watergaw', T. S. Eliot's *The Waste Land* appeared. Grieve wanted to save Scotland from its post-Union mood of defeatism and so cast his alter-ego MacDiarmid in the role of Scotland's cultural saviour: a man whose artistry would combine with qualities of leadership to make 'A greater Christ, a greater Burns'.

That calculated bit of blasphemy appeared at the opening of *A Drunk Man Looks at the Thistle* which was conceived in Montrose and composed at 16 Links Avenue. The poem describes the drunken odyssey of a Scot as he staggers homewards to his wife Jean, collapses on a hillside, then confronts an enormous thistle which alternately alarms and inspires him. The Drunk Man is presented as a Montrose man:

> And in the toon that I belang tae
> – What tho'ts Montrose or Nazareth? –
> Helplessly the folk continue
> To lead their livin' death!

So the Drunk Man addresses the Thistle. By the end of the poem the spirit-sodden Scot has attained a genuine spirituality. MacDiarmid's vision is of a Scotland transformed by the efforts of inviolable individuals. Inside every Drunk Man, MacDiarmid implies, there is Scotsman of intellect and integrity struggling to get out.

MacDiarmid left Montrose because his wife did not care for the small town atmosphere and he himself thought the offer of a job on *Vox* promised financial security as well as a journalistic challenge. Eventually MacDiarmid felt that cultural conditions in Montrose were no longer in his creative interests; that, at any rate, is the way he portrays the situation in *To Circumjack Cencrastus* (1930), a long poem that was planned as a worthy successor to *A Drunk Man*. Yet whereas *A Drunk Man* is triumphant, *Cencrastus* is defeatist. In *A Drunk Man* MacDiarmid portrays the thistle-crucified Scot rising to resurrection. In *Cencrastus* the saviour-poet has too many local difficulties as he acknowledges:

Thrang o' ideas that like fairy gowd
'll leave me the 'Review' reporter still
Waukenin' to my clung-kite faimly on a hill
O' useless croftin' whaur naething's growed
But Daith, sin Christ for an idea died
On a gey similar but less heich hillside.   *high*
Ech, weel for Christ: for he was never wed
And had nae weans clamourin' to be fed!

In later years MacDiarmid recalled his Montrose period with affection.
An article on 'The Angus Burghs' (published in *The Thistle Rises*, 1984)
observes:

> In a very real sense in the 'Twenties Angus (and particularly Montrose)
> was the cultural centre of Scotland. There was something in the
> atmosphere and lay-out of Montrose very conducive to creative work,
> and most of the discussions on which [various] forward-looking
> movements were based . . . took place there. . . . These were indeed
> great times in Montrose and will live in Scottish literary history.

In 1961 MacDiarmid contributed a poem to the 150th anniversary number
of the *Montrose Review*. It ends:

Model of the preference of quality to quantity
Montrose set here between the hills and the sea
On its tongue of land is a perfect example
Of multum in parvo – Earth's best in epitome.

Fionn Mac Colla

In his autobiography *Too Long in this Condition* (1975), the novelist Fionn
Mac Colla dwells on the Gaelic connotations of the name Montrose.

> I recollect being struck particularly by the enormous predominance of
> Gaelic names, plain or disguised. . . . Montrose is Gaelic – *monadh*
> meaning a moor and *ros* meaning a peninsula, which as Henry James
> might have said it so very much is. Even in my boyhood the oldest
> citizens still spoke of it as Monròs. During the period of French
> influence the *mon* was pronounced and spelt in the French fashion
> – *mont* – as in Mont Blanc, etc., the 't' of course being silent. When
> the French influence waned and English influence succeeded, the 't'
> began to be pronounced, hence the pronunciation in my time of
> Montrose , or as is now coming in, enforced by the BBC –
> Montrowse, or even Montráaooze. We were taught in school [by
> teachers who should have known better] that Montrose came from
> Latin, *mons rosarum*, a Mount or Mountain of Roses!!! Hence the

name Mount Road, and round the corner Rosemount Cemetery – one can only hope the denizens of that area of the town did not feel too much let down on taking up residence!

Mac Colla (1906–75) was born Tom MacDonald on 4 March 1906 at 9 White's Place, Montrose. Here, at the age of four, he had a mystical experience as he explains in *Too Long in this Condition*:

I was standing in the gairden at the back of the hoose. I had a companion, one of the retired sea captains of the days of sail [who] lived up oor stair. It may be that my sensibility was heightened because of the consciousness of so great a mass of amiability in my immediate vicinity – that is how we affect each other – but I was suddenly aware of some flowers, of the way the *existence* of some tall flowers was *blazing* in them. I was stooping forward 'breathless with adoration', I even, greatly daring, put forward my hand to turn, as it were gently to turn the blossom of the efflorescence towards me so that I might be exposed to the beam of its full light. I knew at that moment I was doing what I – what we were all – in the world for. A sort of *pietas* I had towards the whole world of life and its wonder.

On 12 April 1909 Mac Colla's grandfather died and the MacDonald family moved to a part of the novelist's grandmother's house at 104 Murray Street. Mac Colla was brought up as a Plymouth brother, but was never happy with the Protestant faith. Indeed in later years, in novels and his discursive volume *At the Sign of the Clenched Fist* (1967), he blamed the cultural ruin of Scotland on the consequences of John Knox's Reformation. An implacable enemy of what he saw as Knoxian negativity, Mac Colla was indignant from an early age: an angry young child in Montrose. In this condition he had, inside the room on the right on the first floor at 104 Murray Street, one of the most momentous experiences of his life:

My father [who grew up in Inverness] spoke a few words [of Gaelic] to himself. I was . . . rooted to the spot by a life-shaking experience [aware] that the sky was sun-filled and it was gloriously warm, that my father smelt faintly of leather, and had just caused the whole of my personal predicament and that of my contemporaries to become devastatingly clear, and that *it was so inevitable that it seemed I had always known it*. Although I knew perfectly well what had happened, I said, 'What was that?' My father, caught somewhat off balance, said off-handedly, 'Oh that's a language they speak in some parts of Scotland.' Then seeing my intense interest he relented. 'I said, *Nach i tha blath an diugh;* that means, Isn't it warm today.'

Mac Colla felt that English was foreign to his sensibility, that Scots was a language he enjoyed, but that Gaelic – the almost lost language of

Scotland – contained the spiritual essence of the Scottish nation. Hence-forth he was to explore, intellectually and imaginatively, the visionary quality of Gaelic culture and the historical attacks on Gaelic by Scottish Reformers and English invaders.

Mac Colla trained as a teacher (in Aberdeen) and after working in Wester Ross, taught in the Scots College in Safed, Palestine. When the National Party of Scotland was formed in 1928 he joined and when he returned to Scotland in 1929 he was determined never again to leave his native land. He made first for Montrose where his family now lived at 12 Links Avenue, near the council house of Hugh MacDiarmid (C. M. Grieve) at 16 Links Avenue. It was immensely stimulating living next door to the great poet and polemicist. Or almost next door, as Mac Colla explains in *Too Long in this Condition*:

> It wasn't difficult [renewing a relationship with MacDiarmid]; he lived next door. Or at least, lest I should be picked upon for making inaccurate statements there was a house between us; but as it was occupied by my Aunt Annie, widow of my still-regretted Uncle Charlie . . . then it amounted to living next door. To be precise we were in No. 12 Links Avenue, Aunt Annie in 14, and C. M. Grieve in 16. I used to step across the fence, walk across Aunt Annie's lawn, and step across another fence into C.M.G.'s. When I made the return journey there was seldom anyone around to observe what course I took, MacDiarmid and I having been setting the world to rights till morning. I want to emphasise however that while paying due respect to age and experience, I was in no sense a pupil. Although only 23 years I was precociously mature.

When MacDiarmid and his wife, Peggy Grieve, went to London in September 1929, Mac Colla went with them. Mac Colla started to write his novel *The Albannach* (1932) while living with the Grieves, then came back to Montrose to work on it at his parents' home, now at Grianan, 15 Blackfriars Street. (The novel was completed in St Andrews.) In 1939 Mac Colla and his wife Mary, whom he married in 1936, lived at 112 Murray Street, Montrose.

MORVEN, Aberdeenshire   (Grampian)   5m N of Ballater

Lord Byron

George Gordon, Lord Byron (1788–1824) spent eight years (1790–8) in Aberdeen and the north with his mother, Catherine Gordon (died 1811), the last laird of Gight (in the parish of Fyvie). He grew to love the Scottish mountains and in 'When I Roved a Young Highlander', from *Hours of Idleness* (1807), celebrates Morven (2,862ft) in the first stanza:

When I roved a young Highlander o'er the dark heath,
    And climb'd thy steep summit, oh Morven of snow!
To gaze on the torrent that thunder'd beneath,
    Or the mist of the tempest that gather'd below,
Untutor'd by science, a stranger to fear,
    And rude as the rocks where my infancy grew,
No feeling, save one, to my bosom was dear;
    Need I say, my sweet Mary, 'twas centred in you?

MOSSGIEL, Ayrshire   (Strathclyde)   1m N of Mauchline, on
                Tarbolton road

Robert Burns

When his father died – at Lochlea farm on 13 February 1784 at the age of sixty-three – Robert Burns (1759–96) became head of the family. Even before his father's death Robert and his brother Gilbert had taken the precaution of renting, from Gavin Hamilton, **Mossgiel farm** – a 118 acre property a mile outside the village of Mauchline. With its new head, the Burns family moved into Mossgiel in 1784, using the single-storey but and ben (replaced by the present farmhouse).

Burns 'entered on this farm with a full resolution'. He read manuals on farming, calculated crops, attended markets, but still bought in bad seed which, when confounded by a late harvest, deprived him of half his crops. Farming had once again failed Robert and, finally free from his father's restraining influence, he determined to assert himself in the parish or, as he put it, 'I now began to be known in the neighbourhood as a maker of rhymes'.

In the stable loft he used as a bedroom, Burns wrote some of his finest poems. For example, in November 1785 his ploughshare turned up the nest of a field-mouse and when the animal attempted to escape John Blane, one of the farm-servants, made after it with the pattle (plough-spade) before Burns stopped him. The result of this incident was 'To a Mouse' which ends with a philosophical flourish:

That wee bit heap o' leaves an' stibble,	*stubble*
Has cost thee monie a weary nibble!	
Now thou's turned out, for a' thy trouble,	
But house or hald,	*Without, holding*
To thole the winter's sleety dribble	*endure*
An' cranreuch cauld!	*hoar-frost*

But Mousie, thou art no thy lane,   *alone*
In proving foresight may be vain:
The best-laid schemes o' mice an' men
    Gang aft agley,   *askew*
An' lea'e us nought but grief an' pain,
    For promis'd joy!

Still thou art blest, compared wi' me!
The present only toucheth thee:
But och! I backward cast my e'e.
    On prospects drear!
An' forward, tho' I canna see,
    I guess an' fear

'The Vision', written at Mossgiel in 1785, indicates in the first two stanzas the creative exhaustion Burns experienced after a day's farming:

The sun had clos'd the winter day,
The curlers quat their roaring play,   *ceased*
And hunger'd maukin taen her way,   *hare*
    To kail-yards green,
While faithless snaws ilk step betray
    Whare she has been.

The thresher's weary flinging-tree,   *flail*
The lee-lang day had tired me;
And when the day had clos'd his e'e,
    Far i' the west,
Ben i' the spence, right pensivelie,   *back, parlour*
    I gaed to rest.   *went*

The majority of the poems in *Poems, Chiefly in the Scottish Dialect* (1786) were written as Mossgiel.

After meeting 'Highland' Mary Campbell, Burns planned to leave Mossgiel and explore the world outside Ayrshire. In 1786 he and Mary planned to emigrate to Jamaica together and Burns hoped the publication of his *Poems, Chiefly in the Scottish Dialect* would alleviate his financial problems and enable him to realise his immediate ambitions. Meanwhile, Jean Armour had acknowledged to the Kirk Session at Mauchline that she was pregnant by 'Robert Burns in Mossgiel' and Jean's father was after a substantial financial settlement. To safeguard his position Burns transferred his share in Mossgiel to Gilbert and announced that the profits were to be used to support an illegitimate daughter. Then, in hiding from Jean's father, he awaited the publication of his book. As a result of its success, and the tragic death of Mary Campbell, Burns abandoned his plans to go to Jamaica and went instead to Edinburgh – and immortality.

MULL, Argyllshire (Strathclyde)

Mull, meaning 'mass of hill', is so called after Ben More, the 3,169ft mountain of the island. Duart Castle (off A849, on east point of Mull) dominates the Sound of Mull; the keep was built in the thirteenth century, the castle extended in 1633. It was ruined by the Duke of Argyll in 1691 and recently restored by Sir Fitzroy Maclean. The Macleans of Duart supported the Stuarts and during the 1745 Jacobite rising Sir Hector Maclean was imprisoned in the Tower of London.

James Boswell, Dr Samuel Johnson

Dr Johnson and James Boswell (1740–95) visited Mull in 1773. In the entry for Thursday 14 October 1773 in his *Journal of a Tour to the Hebrides* (1785) Boswell described Tobermory:

> Tobermorie is an excellent harbour. An island lies before it, and it is surrounded by a hilly theatre. The island is too low, otherwise this would be quite a secure port; but, the island not being a sufficient protection, some storms blow very hard here . . . I went to the top of a hill fronting the harbour, from whence I had a good view of it. We had here a tolerable inn.

Johnson and Boswell rode to visit Sir Allan Maclean on Inch Kenneth which greatly impressed Johnson who wrote some Latin verses, 'Insular Sancti Kenneth'.

In the entry for Thursday, 21 October, in his *Journal*, Boswell describes a journey to Loch Buie 'where we were to pass the night'; the house where he and Johnson stayed, east of Carsaig Bay at the head of Loch Buie, is now a stables approached from Ardura. Johnson and Boswell went on to visit 'Moy, the seat of the Laird of Lochbuy' and visited Moy Castle (now a ruin) as Boswell explains:

> After breakfast, we surveyed the old castle, in the pit or dungeon of which Lochbuy had some years before taken upon him to imprison several persons; and though he had been fined in a considerable sum by the Court of Justiciary, he was so little affected by it, that while we were examining the dungeon, he said to me, with a smile, 'Your father knows something of this'; (alluding to my father's having sat as one of the judges on his trial).

James Hogg

Writing to Sir Walter Scott from 'the Johnson, Tobermory, Wednesday 30th May [1804]', James Hogg (1770–1835) described his visit to Mull:

As we dreaded again to encounter the tides in the sound of Mull, we came to an anchor in Loch Don [south of Duart Castle], and . . . went and spent the evening at the house of Achnacraig in Mull, which is a good inn, and kept by civil people. Here we tarried until a late hour, and then returned on board our vessel.

There is some green grass surrounding this bay but most of it is upon land which hath been tilled, and is thereby converted from a moss soil into a rich black loam. The mountains are high, the coast, except in the bay, bold and rocky . . . the ruins of Castle-Duart stood on the point beyond us, and upon the whole, the scene was rather interesting, though more so on account of its novelty to us than anything else.

William Wordsworth

William Wordsworth (1770–1850) wrote, during his 1831 tour of Scotland, a sonnet 'In the Sound of Mull', beginning:

> Tradition, be thou mute! Oblivion, throw
> Thy veil in mercy o'er the records, hung
> Round strath and mountain, stamped by the ancient tongue
> On rock and ruin darkening as we go.

Thomas Campbell

Thomas Campbell (1777–1844), son of the youngest son of a Highland laird, briefly studied law in the Glasgow office of a relative in 1793. In 1795, when the failure of a Chancery suit further reduced his father's income, Campbell obatined a tutorship in the family of a Mrs Campbell of Sunipol, eight miles west of Tobermory. Campbell was stimulated by his summer in Mull (he returned to Glasgow in the autumn) and liked to sit on a rock subsequently known as the Poet's Seat. It was while on Mull that his friend Hamilton Paul suggested to him the subject of his poem *The Pleasures of Hope* (1799) which includes the following well-known passage:

> 'Tis distance lends enchantment to the view,
> And robes the mountain in its azure hue.
> Thus, with delight we linger to survey
> The promised joys of life's unmeasured way;
> Thus, from afar, each dim-discovered scene
> More pleasing seems than all the past hath been;
> And every form, that Fancy can repair
> From dark oblivion, glows divinely there.

In Campbell's ballad 'Lord Ullin's Daughter', the heroine flees from her 'angry father' and seeks the safety of Ulva island (off mid-west Mull) with her lover, 'the chief of Ulva's isle'. To reach Ulva, the lovers have to be ferried across Loch-na-Keal (which Campbell calls Lochgyle). A tempest gathers over their boat:

> And still they rowed amidst the roar
>> Of waters fast prevailing:
> Lord Ullin reached that fatal shore,
>> His wrath was changed to wailing.

> For sore dismayed, through storm and shade,
>> His child he did discover:
> One lovely hand she stretched for aid,
>> And one was round her lover.

John Keats

John Keats (1795–1821) crossed Mull in 1818 with his friend John Reynolds whose spectacles aroused local interest.

Dugald MacPhail

Dugald MacPhail (1818–87), the Gaelic poet, was born in Strathcoil, at the head of Loch Spelve (south-east of the island). A memorial cites his 'An t'Eilean Mulach', the exile's song he wrote in Newcastle.

Robert Louis Stevenson

In *Kidnapped* (1886), by Robert Louis Stevenson (1850–94), David Balfour is shipwrecked on Erraid, off the south-west tip of Mull. Eventually discovering he is on a tidal island he crosses to the Ross of Mull:

> The Ross of Mull . . . was rugged and trackless, like the isle I had just left; being all bog, and briar, and big stone. There may be roads for them that know that country well; but for my part I had no better guide than my own nose, and no other landmark than Ben More.

NEIDPATH CASTLE, Peeblesshire (Border) 1m W of Peebles on A72

William Wordsworth

Standing on the north bank of the River Tweed, Neidpath was originally an old peel tower which passed from the Frasers, around 1310, to Sir

William Hay of Tweedale. In the fifteenth century Sir Gilbert Hay expanded the building to its present proportions. Hay's descendant became Earl of Tweedale and Neidpath Castle was sold in 1686 to the first Duke of Queensberry. In 1795 the fourth Duke of Queensberry sold the fine timber on the estate, an act that outraged William Wordsworth (1770–1850) on his first tour of Scotland. On 16 October 1803 Wordsworth sent Sir Walter Scott (1771–1832) a sonnet on the subject beginning (in the manuscript version):

> Now, as I live, I pity that great Lord
> Whom mere despite of heart could so far please,
> And love of havoc, (for with such disease
> Fame taxes him,) that he could send forth word
> To level with the dust a noble horde,
> A brotherhood of venerable Trees,
> Leaving an ancient dome, and towers like these,
> Beggared and outraged!

The printed text of 1807 altered the first line to read 'Degenerate Douglas! oh, the unworthy Lord!'.

Sir Walter Scott

Both Scott and Thomas Campbell (1777–1844) wrote ballads about 'The Maid of Neidpath' who was so disfigured by disease that her lover passed by and thus broke her heart. Scott's version (of 1806) begins:

> O lovers' eyes are sharp to see,
>   And lovers' ears in hearing;
> And love, in life's extremity,
>   Can lend an hour of cheering.
> Disease had been in Mary's bower,
>   And slow decay from mourning,
> Though now she sits on Neidpath's tower,
>   To watch her love's returning.

The poems ends:

> The castle arch, whose hollow tone
>   Returns each whisper spoken,
> Could scarcely catch the feeble moan
>   Which told her heart was broken.

Neidpath Castle is open to the public (Easter–Oct., 10am–6pm; Sun. 1–6pm).

251

NEW ABBEY, Kircudbrightshire   (Dumfries and Galloway)   7m S of
Dumfries on A710

The village of New Abbey takes its name from the ruined red stone abbey
that stands in its centre. It was founded (as was Balliol College, Oxford,
in 1282) by Dervorgilla on 10 April 1273 on the death of her husband,
John Balliol of Barnard Castle (north of England). Dervorgilla had
Balliol's heart embalmed and placed in an ivory casket bound with enam-
elled silver. She kept her relic of her 'sweet, silent companion' in her
presence until her death in 1289 when it accompanied her body to a
sepulchre in the sanctuary of the kirk of the monastery. In the south
transept chapel the reconstructed tomb of Dervorgilla lies beside the
decorated coffin lid of John, first Abbot of Sweetheart, who swore fealty
to King Edward I of England.

Andrew of Wyntoun, J. S. Richardson

As a tribute to the devotion of Dervorgilla to her husband, the Cistercian
monks called their abbey Dulce Cor – or Sweetheart Abbey. Andrew of
Wyntoun (c. 1355–1422) paid due tribute to Dervorgilla in the following
passage from his *Orygynale Cronykil of Scotland*, in the version cited by
J. S. Richardson in his *Sweetheart Abbey* (1951):

> She founded in Galloway
> An abbey of the Cistercian order:
> *Dulce Cor* she made them call [it],
> That is Sweet Heart, that abbey.
> And now the men of Galloway
> Call that place the New Abbey.
> She founded two houses of friars:
> They were Wigtown and Dundee.
> In increase also of God's service
> She founded two chaplainries in Glasgow;
> And in the University
> Of Oxford she caused
> A college to be founded. That lady
> Did all these deeds devoutly;
> A better lady than she were none
> In all the isle of Great Britain,
> She was right pleasing in beauty;
> Here were great tokens of bounty.

Fred Urquhart

The spirit of Devorgilla is invoked in the story 'The Lady of Sweetheart Abbey', included in *Proud Lady in a Cage* (1980) and *Seven Ghosts in Search* (1984) by Fred Urquhart (born 1912). The heroine, Maggie Campion, seems at a safe distance from Scotland as she lives with her husband in Oklahoma. However, it soon becomes apparent that she is tied to the past since her mother raised her by reciting 'every Scottish ballad she could remember and she got Maggie to learn them off by heart, too'. Maggie grows up with an awareness of Scotland and, increasingly, an empathy with the Covenanters who were dragged to their deaths at the stakes sunk in Solway Sands. Before she returns to her homeland in person Maggie has seen it in nightmares. The reality is both majestic and macabre as Devorgilla, the Lady of Sweetheart Abbey, imposes her spectral presence on Maggie and her no-nonsense American husband:

> Cass's hands tightened on the wheel, but he could not control the vehicle. Maggie's heart sickened at the sight of a signpost *Sweetheart Abbey 4 Miles*. . . . Yet when they reached the beautiful thirteenth-century Cistercian ruin, she could not help admiring it despite her fearsome feeling of dread. They sat for a moment, looking at the ruin, then Devorgilla opened the car door for Maggie. 'Welcome to Sweetheart, my children', she said. . . . She led them into the ruins. As they stood at the spot where she is buried, Devorgilla said to Maggie, ''Tis a pity, daughter, that we have to meet beside graves, but it is in the Balliol tradition. My son, John, who was king for such a short time, lost his kingdom in a graveyard at Strahcathro, far away from here, in Kincardineshire. . . . My poor John, he died in exile.'
>
> The late afternoon sun glinted on the silver casket as they walked beneath the arches of the nave. Devorgilla laid the casket on top of a broken pillar and said softly, 'Rest there a while, sweetheart, until I return for you.'

NEWARK CASTLE, Selkirkshire (Border)   4m W of Selkirk, off A708

Sir Walter Scott

Newark (or New Wark as distinct from Auldwark Castle which stood nearby) was first mentioned in 1423. A five-storeyed oblong tower house, standing within a barmkin, it was a royal hunting seat for Ettrick Forest: the Royal Arms of James I are on the west gable. It passed to the Scotts of Buccleuch and still belongs to the Duke of Buccleuch (entry on application to Buccleuch Estates). In *The Lay of the Last Minstrel* (1805),

Sir Walter Scott (1771–1832) sets the scene for his tale by bringing his old minstrel before the Duchess of Buccleuch some time after the execution of her husband, the Duke of Monmouth, in 1685:

> He pass'd where Newark's stately tower
> Looks out from Yarrow's birchen bower:
> The Minstrel gazed with wishful eye –
> No humbler resting-place was nigh;
> With hesitating step at last
> The embattled portal arch he pass'd,
> Whose ponderous grate and massy bar
> Had oft roll'd back the tide of war,
> But never closed the iron door
> Against the desolate and poor.

OBAN, Argyllshire   (Strathclyde)   9m W of Taynuilt on A85

James Boswell, Dr Samuel Johnson

Oban, on the Firth of Lorne opposite Mull, is a popular tourist centre with ferries running to Mull, Coll, Tiree, Barra, Colonsay and South Uist. In his entry for Friday, 22 October 1773 (*Journey of a Tour to the Hebrides*, 1785) James Boswell (1740–95) tells how he and Dr Samuel Johnson crossed by ferry-boat from Mull: 'We had a good day and a fine passage, and in the evening landed at Oban, where we found a tolerable inn.'

William Wordsworth

'Eagles', a sonnet by William Wordsworth (1770–1850), was composed at Dunollie Castle in the bay of Oban, in 1831. It begins:

> Dishonoured Rock and Ruin! that, by law
> Tyrannic, keep the Bird of Jove embarred
> Like a lone criminal whose life is spared.

Dunollie Castle, a mile north of Oban, was a thirteenth-century stronghold (now a keep and fragments) of the MacDougalls.

Alexander Smith

A Summer in Skye (1865) by Alexander Smith (1829–67) contains a memorable description of Oban:

Oban, which, during winter, is a town of deserted hotels, begins to get busy by the end of June. Yachts skim about in the little bay;

254

steamers, deep-sea and coasting, are continually arriving and departing; vehicles rattle about in the one broad and the many narrow streets; and in the inns, boots, chamber-maid, and waiter are distracted with the clangour of innumerable bells. Out of doors, Oban is not a bad representation of Vanity Fair. Every variety of pleasure-seeker is to be found there and every variety of costume . . . A more hurried, nervous, frenzied place than Oban, during the summer and autumn months, it is difficult to conceive. People seldom stay there above a night. The old familiar faces are the resident population. The tourist no more thinks of spending a week in Oban than he thinks of spending a week in a railway station. When he arrives his first question is after a bedroom; his second, as to the hour at which the steamer from the south is expected.

Robert Buchanan

Robert Buchanan (1841–1901) lived from 1866 to 1874 at The White House on the Hill (now Soroba Lodge, one mile south of Oban), during which period he published 'The Fleshly School of Poetry' in the *Contemporary review* (1871), an attack on the Pre-Raphaelite poets; and produced *The North Coast and Other Poems* (1868).

Virginia Woolf

Virginia Woolf (1882–1941) visited Oban in 1938 and wrote (in a letter of 28 June 1938 to Vanessa Bell):

We are now in Oban, which is, as far as I have seen it, the Ramsgate of the Highlands. Only the Scotch having melancholy in their bones . . . being entirely without frivolity build even bathing sheds of granite let alone hotels. The result is grim; and on every lamp post is a notice, Please do not spit on the pavement.

Iain Crichton Smith

From 1955–77 the poet, novelist and storyteller Iain Crichton Smith (born 1928) taught at the High School in Oban where he lived at 42 Combie Street.

OCHILTREE, Ayrshire   (Strathclyde)   10m E of Ayr on A70

George Douglas Brown

Ochiltree, a hillside village, is the birthplace of George Douglas Brown (1869–1902) and the Barbie of *The House with the Green Shutters* (1901), arguably the most influential of all modern Scottish novels. Born on 26 January 1869, the illegitimate son of a farmer and an illiterate dairy worker, Sarah Gemmell, Brown was named after his father who was known around Ochiltree as 'Smudden' (after his farm Drumsmudden). As a child young George had to endure unbearably malicious gossip, as James Veitch notes in *George Douglas Brown* (1952):

> He heard rough-tongued men refer to him as 'Smudden's bastard', and there was no doubt what the hateful term implied. Because his mother was unmarried, he was not the same as other children. And when he saw Smudden driving through Coylton [where Brown went to school], his face clouded. In his deep, secretive manner, he hated the small, dark man, hated him for being his father and yet for not being his father.

Brown's birthplace (marked by a plaque), is in one of a row of white-washed cottages on the brae that runs down to join the modern Ayr to Cumnock road (A70).

Brown left Coylton parish school to work as a pithead boy at Tarbolton. However, his old teacher from Coylton, impressed by the brilliance of the boy, got him a place at Ayr Academy where he was taken under the wing of the rector, William Maybin, an enthusiastic classicist. At Glasgow University, Brown took a First in Classics, won the Eglinton Fellowship of £100 per year, then won in 1891 the Snell Exhibition Scholarship which – at £130 for three years – took him to Balliol College, Oxford. At Oxford he fretted about the health of his mother (who died in 1895 from heart failure) and his loss of interest in academic studies was reflected in the Third he received at Oxford. In London he struggled to make a living from literary hackwork; eventually he went to a cottage in Haslemere, Surrey, to write the novel that had obsessed him since he first conceived of it as a long short story.

The House with the Green Shutters, written as a creative refutation of the sentimental kailyard school of fiction (represented by Barrie, Crockett and Maclaren), tells the story of a destructive man, John Gourlay, who is himself destroyed by the oppressive environment of Barbie (that is, Ochiltree), the town he desires to dominate. Gourlay is top man in Barbie, the biggest fish in a little pond, for Barbie is only 'a dull little country town'. He revels in his position of power as the only carrier in Barbie and, to emphasise his monopolistic power-base, builds the grandest house in the town. All Gourlay's pride is contained in the house and just as the house looks down on the 'dull little country town' so Gourlay looks down on the townspeople:

> At the beginning of a new day to look down on the petty burgh in which he was the greatest man, filled all his being with a consciousness of importance. His sense of prosperity was soothing and pervasive; he felt it all round him like the pleasant air, as real as that and as subtle; bathing him, caressing. It was the most secret and intimate joy of his life to go out and smoke on summer mornings by his big gate, musing over Barbie ere he possessed it with his merchandise.

Gourlay's pride, however, led to his downfall. Brown had personally suffered from malicious gossip and had formed a bitter impression of Scottish small-town life. Scots, according to Brown's experience, were motivated by malice and resented any man who surpassed the situation he inherited. Such a man would, thanks to the workings of a Calvinist God, get his just desserts. To the locals of Barbie, John Gourlay was, in all his arrogance, tempting fate. The Greeks had a word for it – hubris – and it was to the Greek model that Brown went for his bleak study of a Scottish tragedy. Gourlay's *hubris* invites disaster but he is also destroyed by the bodies, the malicious gossips who comment on his character, proleptically gloat over his downfall, and contribute to the inevitable catastrophe.

In elevating a group of Scottish gossips to the status of a Greek chorus, Brown made use of his classical training and his depiction of the chattering bodies has classic status:

> In every little Scotch community there is a distinct type known as 'the bodie'. 'What does he do, that man?' you may ask, and the answer will be, 'Really, I could hardly tell ye what he does – he's juist a bodie!' The 'bodie' may be a gentleman of independent means . . . or he may be a jobbing gardener; but he is equally a 'bodie'. The chief occupation of his idle hours (and his hours are chiefly idle) is the discussion of his neighbour's affairs. He is generally an 'auld residenter'; great, therefore, at the redding up of pedigrees. He can tell you exactly, for instance, how it is that young Pin-oe's taking geyly to the dram: for his grandfather, it seems, was a terrible man for the drink – ou, just terrible – why, he went to bed with a full jar of whiskey once, and when he left it, he was dead, and it was empty. So ye see, that's the reason o't.
>
> The genus 'bodie' is divided into two species: the 'harmless bodies' and the 'nesty bodies'. The bodies of Barbie mostly belonged to the second variety. . . . The Bend o' the Brae was the favourite stance of

the bodies; here they foregathered every day to pass judgement on the town's affairs.

They are there to gloat as the House of Gourlay is overwhelmed by tragedy. Gourlay is murdered by his son who is thereafter haunted by the fearsome image of the old domestic tyrant. Gourlay's daughter Janet is dying from a lung complaint and Gourlay's wife is, as a result of a blow inflicted on her by him, dying of an abscess of the breast. Having nothing to live for, the three of them take their own lives; first Gourlay's son, then his wife, then his daughter, take poison. The book ends as the postman spreads the news of the tragedy and we are left to imagine that the bodies of Barbie will dwell on the events for the remainder of their lives. Together, the personality of Brown and the character of Ochiltree (as Brown knew it) combined in one of the masterpieces of Scottish fiction. Brown died – of pneumonia on 28 August 1902 – after returning to London from a visit to Ayrshire. He left behind only one book, but that a great achievement. 'He had,' said J. B. Priestley, 'shot his bolt, but what a bolt.'

The House with the Green Shutters in Ochiltree, from which the novel takes its name, is now a Royal British Legion Club situated on the Cumnock to Ayr road (A70). It can be easily recognised as it still retains green shutters on the windows and bears a commemorative plaque.

ORKNEY, Orkney

'Orkneyinga Saga' (A. B. Taylor)

Orkney comprises a group of sixty-seven islands separated from Caithness by the Pentland Firth. *The Orkneyinga Saga* (translated by A. B. Taylor, 1938) is a thirteenth-century work composed and compiled in Iceland. Originally designed for recitation in Icelandic halls it tells the story of the Earls of Orkney from 874 to 1214 with an admirable regard for accuracy. Predominantly a prose composition, it includes eighty-three skaldic poems by eighteen skalds including Earl Rognvald Kolson.

Sir Walter Scott

The **Dwarfie Stone**, on the lower slopes of Hoy's Ward Hill (Orkney's highest hill) – approached by B9047 and side road, then by foot – features in Sir Walter Scott's novel *The Pirate* (1822). Scott (1771–1832) visited Hoy in 1814 during his six-week voyage round Scotland on the Lighthouse Yacht in the company of Robert Stevenson, grandfather of Robert Louis Stevenson. In his journal entry for Tuesday 16 August 1814 Scott describes a trip to see the Dwarfie Stone. In *The Pirate*, Norna of the Fitful Head

(Ulla Troil, who turns out to be the mother of the pirate Cleveland) tells Minna and Brenda Troil how the dwarf Trolld gave her power 'O'er tempest and wave':

> But, for my misfortune, I was chiefly fond to linger about the Dwarfie Stone, as it is called, a relic of antiquity, which strangers look on with curiosity, and the natives with awe. It is a huge fragment of a rock, which lies in a broken and rude valley, full of stones and precipices, in the recesses of the Ward Hill of Hoy. The inside of the rock has two couches, hewn by no earthly hand, and having a small passage between them. The doorway is now open to the weather; but beside it lies a large stone, which, adapted to grooves still visible in the entrance, once had served to open and to close this extraordinary dwelling, which Trolld, a dwarf famous in the northern Sagas, is said to have framed for his own favourite residence. . . . My vain and youthful bosom burned to investigate [many] mysteries, which the Sagas that I perused, or learned from Erland, rather indicated than explained; and in my daring mood, I called on the Lord of the Dwarfie Stone to aid me in attaining knowledge inaccessible to mere mortals.

In fact, as opposed to Scott's fiction, the Dwarfie Stane is the only rock-cut chambered tomb in Britain. Measuring 28ft long and 8ft high, it is a sandstone block in which a passage and two cells have been cut. The Dwarfie Stone is in the guardianship of the Department of the Environment.

Edwin Muir

Edwin Muir was born in the Folly (now gone), his father's rented farm in Deerness parish, Orkney, on 15 May 1887, the youngest of six children. When Muir was two his father rented the Bu, the largest (95 acres) farm on the tiny Orkney island of Wyre. The Bu lies below a mound on which there are remains of a twelfth-century castle. The farm was rented from General (later Sir) Frederick Burroughs, the owner of the island, and gave Muir his first experience of the Eden he repossessed in his mature poetry. He wrote in *An Autobiography* (1954):

> The farmers did not know ambition and the petty torments of ambition . . . they helped one another with their work when help was required, following the old usage; they had a culture made up of legend, folksong and the poetry and prose of the Bible; they had customs which sanctioned their instinctive feelings for the earth; their life was an order, and a good order.

Muir was seven when his father moved to the neighbouring farm of

Helzigartha and eight when General Burroughs's demands for a high rent drove his father, James Muir, to leave Wyre for the farm of Garth, three miles from Kirkwall on mainland Orkney.

Muir wrote a poem 'The Little General' – from *The Narrow Place* (1943) – about General Burroughs as he recalled him coming to Wyre every spring to shoot birds. The first two stanzas run:

> Early in spring the little General came
>   Across the sound, bringing the island death,
> And suddenly a place without a name,
>   And like the pious ritual of a faith,
>
> Hunter and quarry in the boundless trap,
>   The white smoke curling from the silver gun,
> The feather curling in the hunter's cap,
>   And clouds of feathers floating in the sun.

Garth farm was a failure which weakened James Muir's health and will. During his time at Garth, Edwin Muir attended Kirkwall Grammar School and when he was thirteen lived in a small house in Kirkwall following his father's decision to give up Garth. In 1901 the Muir family moved to Glasgow. Muir had to work in an office, a beer-bottling factory, a bone factory and a shipbuilding office and was psychologically shattered by a series of personal tragedies: his father died of a heart attack, his brother Willie of consumption, his brother Johnnie from a brain tumour, and his mother from an internal disease.

Muir looked back on his life, as a creative artist, and saw it as a fable. There was his idyllic childhood on Wyre, then the expulsion from the Orkney Eden and the trauma of life in a big industrial city, then the salvation of his marriage (in 1918 to Willa Anderson) and subsequent serenity. In his poetry and prose these stages represent Eden, the Fall into the labyrinth, and Paradise Regained. He increasingly strove to return to Eden via the imagination and to live there with an informed innocence as a result of experience. He saw his insular Orkney childhood as a time when he experienced 'the original vision of the world' and felt 'our first childhood is the only time in our lives when we exist within immortality'. In a late poem, 'The Horses' – from *One Foot in Eden* (1956), he sees the world recovering from destruction by endorsing the values Muir himself absorbed on Wyre, for the horses waited:

> Stubborn and shy, as if they had been sent
> By an old command to find our whereabouts
> And that long-lost archaic companionship.

ORKNEY

Eric Linklater

Merkister, at the north-eastern corner of the Loch of Harry, was the home
of Eric Linklater (1899–1974) from 1934 to 1947. The house was built in
1910 by Linklater's father and called Ingleneuk by the author's mother.
Though Linklater was born in Wales he thought of himself as an
Orkneyman (like his father): moreover, he was 'conceived in Orkney' he
claimed in *Fanfare for a Tin Hat* (1970). As a youth Linklater spent
summer holidays at the house and fell in love with the loch which he
explored in a little boat given to him by his father. He recalled the
experience in *The Man on My Back* (1944): 'Day after day I spent, solitary
as a dog at sea, or fishing with a mind intent only on the dropping flies
and the bubble of a rising trout. My chief talent was idleness, and to lie
in a drifting boat was a pleasure that did not grow stale.' When Linklater
returned to Orkney in the summer of 1934 he moved into Ingleneuk,
completed *Ripeness is All* (1935), renamed the house Merkister and set
about improving his property (which is now a hotel). On 11 November
1974 Linklater was buried in Harray churchyard. On a stone, some six
feet high, are the words '*Eric Linklater/1899–1974/Praise be to God*'.

George Mackay Brown

George Mackay Brown was born on 17 October 1921 in Victoria Street,
Stromness. When he was six his family moved to a house in Melvin Place.
Six years later the family moved to a council house in Well Park. Brown
attended Stromness Academy from 1926 to 1940 and a year after leaving
school was admitted to the sanatorium at Kirkwall suffering from tuberculosis. In 1951 he went to Newbattle Abbey College for a year then back
in Orkney spent another fifteen months in the Kirkwall sanatorium. In
1954 Brown's first collection of poems, *The Storm*, was published with an
introduction by Edwin Muir who was Warden of Newbattle Abbey College
when Brown studied there. Though Muir left Newbattle in 1955, Brown
returned for a second spell at Newbattle in summer 1956 to prepare
himself for entry to an English course at Edinburgh University the same
year.

In 1960 Brown graduated from Edinburgh University and almost
immediately another mild attack of tuberculosis took him to Tor-Na-Dee
Sanatorium at Aberdeen for a period of recuperation. He extended his
poetic reputation with *The Year of the Whale* (1965) and in 1967, the year
his mother died, published *A Calendar of Love*, a book of short stories.
Brown settled at 3 Mayburn Court, Stromness, and continued to publish
poems, stories and three novels: *Greenvoe* (1972), *Magnus* (1977) and
Time in a Red Coat (1984).

Brown has spent most of his life in Stromness and his work is rooted in the Orkney experience. *Fishermen with Ploughs* (1971), for example, is a poetic sequence set in the valley of Rackwick, on the Orkney island of Hoy. In *An Orkney Tapestry* (1969) Brown devotes a chapter to Rackwick and describes the desolation of the place:

> There is a fringe of tilth and pasture in the north of Hoy, along the shore: the road goes this far. Another road branches westward between the hills, into utter desolation, a place of kestrels and peatbogs. One thinks of the psalmist and his vale of death. After five miles the road ends abruptly at a glint of sea and the farm of Glen. The dark hills are still all round, but they hold in their scarred hands a green valley. This is Rackwick. The bowl is tilted seawards – its lip is a curving bay, half huge round sea-sculptured boulders, half sand. Out in the bay, like guardians, stand two huge cliffs, The Sneuk and The Too.

Stromness itself, with its single serpentine street of flagstones, its tiny closes, its 'pipe-spitting pierhead' (as Brown calls it in his poem 'Hamnavoe') is central to Brown's literary work. In his poems and stories, Brown prefers the Norse name Hamnavoe (meaning haven-bay) for his birthplace.

Some five miles from Stromness there is the chambered cairn of **Maes Howe**, the finest megalithic tomb in Britain. Apart from its immense archeological importance it has fired Brown's imagination in a striking way. Each midwinter, as Brown personally confirmed in 1972, the light of the setting sun penetrates the approach passage of Maes Howe to shine on the furthest wall of the tomb. Clearly this has sexual connotations; it is as if the sun had sown its seed in the womb-like shape of Maes Howe. The image is used in *An Orkney Tapestry*, is suggested in the title-story of *Hawkfall* (1974), and occurs at a crucial stage of 'A Winter's Tale' in *The Sun's Net* (1976). It is a ceremonial part of Brown's fascination with birth and resurrection. Maes Howe lies within the Stenness Brodgar complex along with the Ring of Brodgar, the Stenness Stones, the Ring of Bookan and Unstan Cairn. The twenty-seven extant stones standing in the great circle of Brodgar have provoked endless speculation as to their purpose; Brown has incorporated the phenomenon as the Temple of the Sun in *Hawkfall* while the area is used as the landscape of 'Brig-o-Dread' in *The Sun's Net*.

On the island of Egilsay, in 1116 AD, Earl Magnus Erlendson was martyred. Subsequently he became Orkney's saint and as such he is revered by Brown (a Roman Catholic since 1961). In Brown's first book of poems, *The Storm*, Magnus appears twice – in 'The Road Home' and 'Saint Magnus on Egilsay'; and in his first collection of stories, *A Calendar of Love*, the significance of Magnus is mentioned in two stories, 'The Three Islands' and 'Stone Poems'. A key chapter in *An Orkney Tapestry* deals with the martyrdom of Magnus and there are frequent references in Brown's books to the magnificent **St Magnus Cathedral** in Kirkwall which was founded by Earl Rognvald in 1137 as a monument to his saintly uncle.

Some twenty years after Magnus's brutal death on Egilsay, his life was recorded, in Latin, by an Orcadian priest Master Robert; the events of Magnus's life are also contained in the *Orkneyinga Saga* (a thirteenth-century work composed and compiled in Iceland). These accounts, and the scholarly biography of *St Magnus – Earl of Orkney* (1935) by the Kirkwall businessman John Mooney, are the sources of Brown's novel *Magnus*. It opens with Mans, the peasant representative of common humanity, ploughing Revay hill facing the tidal island, the Brough of Birsay, where a wedding is taking place between Erland and Thora, the parents of Magnus. Brown later set the martyrdom sacrifice of Magnus in the context of a German concentration camp, making it clear that the sacrifice is perpetually re-enacted.

Whether describing the prehistoric past, the recent history, or the possible future of Orkney, Brown explores the islands in an immensely imaginative manner and has based an impressive body of work entirely on the Orkney experience.

PAISLEY, Renfrewshire (Strathclyde) 8m W of Glasgow

Alexander Wilson

Paisley – synonymous with the weaving of fine patterned shawls in the nineteenth century and now the largest thread-producing town in the world – has notable literary associations. Poet and ornithologist Alexander Wilson (1763–1813), a weaver's son, is commemorated by a statue at Paisley Abbey (founded 1163, destroyed by the English 1307, rebuilt after 1450, restored after 1897). Wilson's satirical poem 'The Shark' attacked William Sharp (great-grandfather of 'Fiona Macleod', see below) for his conduct of his textile business. As a result of Sharp's libel action of 1792 Wilson emigrated to America where he published a collection of nature poems, *The Foresters* (1805) and worked on *American Ornithology* (1808–14).

Robert Tannahill

Robert Tannahill, another native of Paisley who knew Wilson at Lochwinnoch (9 miles south-west of Paisley) where they were both weavers, wrote a poem 'On Alexander Wilson's Emigration to America'. It ends:

> Since now he's gane, and Burns is dead,
> Ah! wha will tune the Scottish reed?

Her thistle, dowie, hangs its head;   *mournful*
   Her harp's unstrung;
While mountain, river, loch and mead,
   Remain unsung.

Farewell, thou much neglected bard!
These lines will speak my warm regard,
While strangers on a foreign sward
   Thy worth hold dear;
Still some kind heart thy name shall guard,
   Unsullied here.

Tannahill (1774–1810) was born on 3 June 1774 at 32 Castle Street where a memorial stone was placed in the front of his cottage on 3 June 1872. After leaving school, Tannahill was apprenticed as a handloom weaver and composed many of his poems at the loom to which he attached a plank board for writing. Douglas Dunn describes Tannahill's method of composition in his poem 'Tannahill' from *St Kilda's Parliament* (1981):

Composing verses at your bench,
Lines woven inch by linen inch
To follow each iambic hunch
   Into its art,
You sang, like a beginning finch,
   Your common heart.

Apart from his period at Lochwinnoch (with Alexander Wilson) and two years in Bolton, Tannahill spent his life in Paisley where he had a thatched cottage at 11 Queen Street,

Poems and Songs Chiefly in the Scots Dialect appeared in 1807 and Tannahill was encouraged by its reception and popularity. However when the publisher Constable refused to bring out a second, revised edition he drowned himself, on 17 May 1810, in the Maxwelton Burn at a spot now known as Tannahill's Pool. In 1858 the Tannahill Club was founded in Paisley and money was raised from open-air concerts on Gleniffer Braes to erect the Tannahill statue, near Paisley Abbey, in 1883. Gleniffer Braes was one of the poet's favourite haunts and features in 'The Braes of Gleniffer':

Keen blaws the wind o'er the braes o' Gleniffer,
   The auld castle's turrets are covered wi' snaw;
How changed frae the time when I met wi' my lover
   Amang the broom bushes by Stanley green shaw;
The wild flowers o' summer were spread a' sae bonnie,
   The mavis sung sweet frae the green birken tree;

But far to the camp they ha'e marched my dear Johnnie,
And now it is winter wi' nature and me.

The cottage in Queen Street can be visited by contacting Paisley Burns Club, which Tannahill helped found in 1803.

John Wilson

John Wilson (1785–1854) was born on 8 May 1785 at 63 High Street (plaque). His literary celebrity is associated with Edinburgh on account of the 'Noctes Ambrosianae' he contributed to *Blackwood's Magazine* between 1822 and 1835. In these James Hogg (who visited the Sun Tavern in Paisley at the invitation of Tannahill and his literary friends) is 'The Ettrick Shepherd' and Wilson himself 'Christopher North'.

William Motherwell

William Motherwell (1797–1835) spent some of his childhood in Paisley to which he returned as Sheriff Clerk Depute of Renfrewshire (1819–29) and editor of the *Paisley Advertiser* (1828–30). He was associated with the Whistle-Binkie poets, who allowed the Burnsian tradition to degenerate into a sentimental routine. However, his anthology *Minstrelsy Ancient and Modern* (1827) displayed a scrupulously scholarly approach to ballad texts and influenced the great American ballad scholar Francis James Child.

Fiona Macleod

William Sharp (1855–95) was born on 12 September 1855 at 4 Garthland Place (gone, but near Garthland Lane off the Glasgow Road) and spent the first thirteen years of his life in Paisley before his family moved to India Street in Glasgow. He never returned to his native town but travelled extensively in Australia, America and Europe; he died, at the age of fifty, on 12 December 1905 at Castello di Maniace, Sicily, and is buried under a Celtic cross carved in lava.

Sharp is best known through the works he published as Fiona Macleod, a name that became synonymous with the Celtic Twilight. The pseudonym Sharp adopted in 1894, on the publication of *Pharais: a Romance of the Isles*, was regarded by him as a genuine transformation rather than a literary strategy. Throughout his life Sharp refused to acknowledge his part in the creation of the Fiona Macleod canon which he felt was the work of his feminine soul as made in a particular image. *Pharais* was dedicated to E.W.R. and in her foreword to the 1910 edition, Sharp's widow Elizabeth states that the 'ultimate characteristic expression of his "dream self" was due to the inspiration and incentive of the friend to whom he dedicated *Pharais'*. Sharp himself said, in a letter to his wife, 'without her there would never have been any "Fiona Macleod" '. She was Mrs Edith Wingate Rinder with whom the Sharps sojourned in Rome in 1890–1. Some of the poems in Sharp's *Sospiri di Roma* (1891) suggest that he and Mrs Rinder had a passionate affair during the Roman period; Mrs Sharp said, in her *Memoir* of her husband: 'To me he came for sympathy in his work and difficulties and to others he went for gaiety and diversion.' (Mrs Rinder published *The Shadow of Arvor* (1896), a translation of Breton folktales and her husband, Frank, wrote an enthusiastic appreciation of Sharp when he died.) In her *William Sharp – 'Fiona Macleod'* (1970), Flavia Alaya writes: 'Mrs Rinder was of the same stuff as Sharp, for it was her flame that seems to have ignited him, spiritually if not otherwise.'

Sharp remains an enigmatic and romantic figure, an atypical Scot who rejected the stern Presbyterian ideas of his Paisley boyhood and sought spiritual release through the femininity of his alter ego Fiona Macleod. Alan, the hero of the third Fiona Macleod novel *Green Fire* (1896), looks for 'a woman saviour, who would come near to all of us, because in her heart would be the blind tears of the child, and the bitter tears of the man, and the patient tears of the woman'.

PEEBLES, Peeblesshire   (Border)   20m S of Edinburgh on A703

William and Robert Chambers

A county town at the confluence of the Tweed and Eddleston Water, Peebles was the birthplace of the brothers William and Robert Chambers: William (1800–83) was born on 16 April 1800, Robert (1802–71) on 10 July 1802, both of them at a small house (plaque) in Biggiesknowe (over the bridge, to the right). In 1814 the family moved to Edinburgh where the firm of W. and R. Chambers was established, publishing *Chambers' Journal* from 1832 to 1956 and developing into a prestigious imprint on reference books and dictionaries. Robert wrote books as varied as *Traditions of Edinburgh* (1824) and *The Vestiges of the Natural History of Creation* (1844); William became Lord Provost of Edinburgh (1865–8) and a philanthropist who presented the Chambers Institute (now the Peebles Museum, High Street) to his native town.

Mungo Park

Mungo Park (1771–1806), the explorer and travel writer, was a doctor in Peebles from October 1801 to October 1804: the site of his surgery is marked by a plaque at the east end of the High Street. In 1805 Park returned to Africa on an expedition to trace the source of the River Niger. Early the following year he was killed when his party was ambushed at rapids near Busa. Park's *Journal of a Mission to the Interior of Africa in the Year 1805* was published in 1815.

Anna Buchan

Anna Buchan (1877–1948), who wrote under the pseudonym O. Douglas, lived at Bank House, High Street (near the bridge), moving into the house after the death of her uncle William in 1906. Though overshadowed by her brother John, she was an extremely popular novelist who portrayed Peebles as Priorsford in her fiction. *The House That Is Our Own* (1940) depicts Peebles as the author knew it:

> Priorsford [was] the very ideal of a country town. . . . Inns and houses that held some of the graciousness of age were neighboured by shops and a cinema built in a new and fantastic mode, but the prevailing atmosphere was of the past, for, on the right-hand side of the street, going towards the Mercat Cross, stood a fine old building with turrets and narrow windows and steep-pitched roof.

PENICUIK, Midlothian (Lothian) 8m S of Edinburgh on A701

Allan Ramsay

In Cauldshoulders Park, in the grounds of Penicuik House (gutted by fire in 1899 and rebuilt) there is an obelisk erected in 1759 as **Allan Ramsay's Monument** to commemorate the poet (1684–1758).

Samuel Rutherford Crockett

From 1886 to 1895 Samuel Rutherford Crockett (1860–1914) was Free Church minister at Penicuik. One of the leading exponents of the sentimental Kailyard ('cabbage patch') school of Scottish writing he achieved success with his short stories, *The Stickit Minister* (1893), a volume dedicated to Robert Louis Stevenson (1850–94). After the appearance of *The Raiders* (1894) and *The Lilac Sunbonnet* (1894) Crockett resigned from his ministry in 1895. He lived at Bank House, in Penicuik Estate, until 1906 (when he moved to Torwood Villa, near Peebles) and there entertained literary friends such as Stevenson.

Dr John Brown

A memorial in the nave of the old church features a relief of a dog's head to draw attention to the literary significance of James and Ailie Noble who are buried in the churchyard. James and Ailie lived, with their dog Rab, at Howgate (one-and-a-half miles south-east of Penicuik) and are the central figures in Dr John Brown's celebrated essay 'Rab and his Friends'. When Ailie dies, Brown (1810–82) paints a verbal picture of grief:

> Rab all this time had been full awake and motionless: he came forward beside us: Ailie's hand, which James had held, was hanging down; it was soaked with his tears; Rab licked it all over carefully, looked at her, and returned to his place under the table.

PERTH, Perthshire   (Tayside)   21m SE of Dundee

The Kingis Quair

Scotland's chief town during the Middle Ages, Perth is rich in royal and literary associations: James I (1394–1437) held many parliaments and general councils in Perth and was assassinated on 21 February 1437 at Blackfriars Monastery at the North Inch of Perth. James I was a greatly gifted poet as well as a monarch. In 1405 he, the eleven-year-old son of Robert III, was captured by English pirates en route to France. For the next eighteen years he was a prisoner of the English though on the death of Robert III in 1406 he was recognised as James I by the Scottish parliament. In 1423, his final year of captivity, he fell in love with Lady Joan Beaufort – an experience poetically recorded in *The Kingis Quair* – and married her the following year when released on a ransom of 60,000 marks. He gradually restored respect for the monarchy but conspirators – who hoped to win the throne for Walter, Earl of Atholl, the younger son of Robert II's second marriage to Euphemia of Ross – murdered James I in the Dominican monastery. He was buried in the church of the Charter House (founded by him in 1425) – a site south of the hospital in King Street – as was his widow.

Gavin Douglas

After being Provost of the Collegiate Church of St Giles, Edinburgh, Gavin Douglas (*c.* 1474–1522) became Bishop of Dunkeld (from 1516–20), fifteen miles north of Perth. A plaque at the corner of St John Street and South Street draws attention to the site, through the archway pend, of Douglas's house in Perth. Douglas's masterpiece is his *Eneados*, a trans-

lation of Virgil into Middle Scots. The American poet Ezra Pound, in his
ABC of Reading (1956), said of Douglas's translation: 'I get considerably
more pleasure from the Bishop of Dunkeld than from the original highly
cultured but non sea-faring author'.

John Knox

Perth was formerly called St John's Toun (a name retained by the local
football team, St Johnstone) and it was in St John's church, St John's
Square, that John Knox delivered a celebrated sermon against idolatry on
11 May 1559. Knox's account of the impact of the sermon, in his *Historie
of the Reformatioun in Scotland* (completed 1586), is a vivid recreation of
the period when the Reformation was sweeping Scotland.

It chanceit, that the nixt Day, whiche wes the 11th of Maiii, efter,
that the Preichours wer exylled, that efter the Sermone, whiche was
vehement against Idolatrie, that a Preist, in Contempt, wald go to the
Mess; and to declair his malapairte Presumption, he wald oppin up
ane glorious Tabernacle, whiche stud upoun the hie Alter; thair stud
besyid certain godlie Men, and amongis utheris a young Boy, who
cryed with a loud Voice, 'This is intollerable, that quhen God by his
Worde hath planelie damned idolatrie, we sall stand and sie it used in
Despyte.' The Preist heirat offendit, gave the Child a grit Blowe; who
in Anger tuk up a Stone, and casting at the Preist, did hit the
Tabernacle, and brake down ane Image; and immediatly the haill
Multitude that war about cast Stanes, and put Hands to the said
Tabernacle, and to all uther Monuments of Idolatrie, whiche they
dispatched befoir the tenth Man in the Toun were adverteisit [=
informed], for the maist Parte war gane to Denner. Which noyssed
abrode, the hail Multitude conveinit [= collected], not the
Gentilmen, nouther of thame that war ernest Professours, bot of the
rascall Multitude, who finding nothing to do in that Churche, did rin
without Deliberation to the Gray and Black Freireis; and
notwithstanding that they had within thame verray stark [= strong]
Gairdis keipt for thair Defence, yit war thair Gaittis incontinent brust
up. The first Invasioun was upoun the Idolatrie; and thare efter the
comoun Pepill began to seik sum Spoyll.

After the 'rascal multitude' had indulged in an orgy of iconoclasm, Knox
marched to St Andrews to fulfil his prophecy, made in the galleys, that
he would return there in triumph. The uproar in Perth, on 11 May 1559,
marks the beginning of the last stage of the Scottish Reformation. Knox
felt he had might as well as right on his side, and his sermons generally
had the effect of rousing the 'rascal multitude'. St John's Church was
restored by Sir Robert Lorimer.

Sir Walter Scott

Sir Walter Scott's novel *The Fair Maid of Perth* (1828) opens with a tribute to Perthshire ('the fairest portion of the northern kingdom') and Perth ('so eminent for the beauty of its situation'). Having set the scene with romantic relish, Scott then introduces his heroine, Catharine Glover, the fair city's fairest inhabitant:

> To be called the Fair Maid of Perth would, at any period, have been a high distinction, and have inferred no mean superiority in beauty, where there were many to claim that much-envied attribute. . . . Such views might have dazzled a girl of higher birth than Catharine or Katie Glover, who was universally acknowledged to be the most beautiful young woman of the city or its vicinity, and whose renown, as the Fair Maid of Perth, had drawn on her much notice from the young gallants of the Royal Court, when it chanced to be residing in or near Perth; insomuch that more than one nobleman of the highest rank, and most distinguished for deeds of chivalry, were more attentive to exhibit feats of horsemanship as they passed the door of old Simon Glover, in what was called Couvrefew, or Curfew Street, than to distinguish themselves in the tournaments, where the noblest dames of Scotland were spectators of their address.

The Fair Maid's House, on the corner of Blackfriar's Wynd, was restored during the Victorian period and is now a shop and art gallery, conveniently close to the North Inch of Perth, now a popular park. (There is a local joke that Perth is the smallest town in Scotland because it is between two inches: in the South Inch a statue of Scott stands at the north-west entrance.)

It was in the North Inch that Blackfriars Monastery was founded (by Alexander II) in 1231. Situated at the southern end of the North Inch, the Dominican monastery stretched westwards to the area now marked by Barbossa Place and Murray Street. Scott notes the proximity of the Fair Maid's House to the monastery in his novel:

> So the Fair Maid of Perth laid aside the splendid hawking-glove which she was embroidering for the Lady Drummond, and putting on her holiday kirtle, prepared to attend her father to the Blackfriars Monastery, which was adjacent to Couvrefew Street, in which they lived.

It was in the North Inch, too, that the infamous Battle of the Clans took place on Palm Sunday, 30 March 1396. To settle a feud between the Clans Chattan and Kay (called Quhele in Scott's novel), thirty men from each clan fought a battle before Robert III and his queen and assorted

spectators who looked on it as a contest in the nature of a tournament.
Scott introduces the North Inch as:

> a beautiful and level plain, closely adjacent to the city, and
> appropriated to the martial exercises of the inhabitants.
> The plain is washed on one side by the deep and swelling Tay.
> There was erected within it a strong palisade, enclosing on three
> sides a space of one hundred and fifty yards in length, and seventy-
> four yards in width. The fourth side of the lists was considered as
> sufficiently fenced by the river. An amphitheatre for the
> accommodation of spectators surrounded the palisade, leaving a large
> space free to be occupied by armed men on foot and horseback, and
> for the more ordinary class of spectators. At the extremity of the
> lists, which was nearest to the city, there was a range of elevated
> galleries for the King and his courtiers, so highly decorated with
> rustic treillage, intermingled with gilded ornaments, that the spot
> retains to this day the name of the Golden, or Gilded Arbour.

This Gilded Arbour (or Gilten Herbar) was a green lea between the
monastery and the Inch and may have been land of Perth Castle which
was swept away by the flood of 1210.

Since one member of the Clan Chattan took fright and swam away
across the River Tay his place was taken by the armourer, Hal (or Harry)
of the Wynd who performed so ferociously that he helped secure victory
for the Clan Chattan. Scott writes:

> Thus ended this celebrated conflict of the North Inch of Perth. Of
> sixty-four brave men (the minstrels and standard-bearers included)
> who strode manfully to the fatal field, seven alone survived, who were
> conveyed from thence in litters, in a case little different from the
> dead and dying around them, and mingled with them in the sad
> procession which conveyed them from the scene of their strife. . . .
> It was some time ere Simon [Glover] ventured to tell his daughter of
> Henry's late exploits, and his severe wounds . . . Catharine sighed
> deeply, and shook her head at the history of bloody Palm Sunday on
> the North Inch.

However, she acknowledges the courage of Hal of the Wynd who marries
the Fair Maid of Perth 'within four months after the battle of the North
Inch'.

William Soutar (see below) has a poem 'Hal o' the Wynd' which explores
the humorous connotations of the combative Scot. The first quatrain
explains:

> Hal o' the Wynd he taen the field
> Alang be the skinklin Tay: *glittering*

And he hackit doun the men o' Chattan;
Or was it the men o' Kay?

John Ruskin

John Ruskin (1819–1900), arbiter of the aesthetic taste of Victorian England and champion of the Pre-Raphaelite painters, spent many boyhood holidays in Perth, staying either at Main Street, Bridgend (house demolished) or 10 Rose Terrace (see the plaque at the house) overlooking the North Inch. Ruskin's grandfather lived at Bowerswell (now a home for old people), north of the Tay, and took his own life in the house. In 1848 Ruskin married Euphemia (Effie) Chalmers Gray whose parents then lived at Bowerswell. Because of her tragic memories of Bowerswell, Ruskin's mother was unable to attend the wedding there. Six years after marrying Ruskin, Effie obtained a decree of nullity and subsequently married the painter Millais.

Sir Patrick Geddes

Born in Ballater, West Aberdeenshire, on 2 October 1854, Sir Patrick Geddes (1854–1932) came, with his parents, to Perth in 1857. On Kinnoul Hill they settled in a house which Geddes's father called Mount Tabor Cottage after the sacred mountain of Northern Palestine. Geddes lived at Mount Tabor Cottage (as a plaque notes) for the next seventeen years and he acknowledged that the house and garden played a crucial part in shaping his affirmative attitude towards the environment. In an essay (on 'Cyprus, actual and possible' in the *Contemporary Review* of June 1897) he referred to his memories:

> of trotting after Father with my little barrow and tools, or helping Mother with her flowers; and of watching things grow, of climbing the trees, of feeding the robins and pigeons out of my hand, and of many roamings. . . . I had my small barrow as my father the big one. His 'The Tally-Ho', mine 'The Express' – and what races when they were empty, what loads when they were full!

Geddes was educated at Perth Academy (then in Rose Terrace) though he valued his experiences at Mount Tabor Cottage above 'book-cram'. Geddes's innovative ideas on town planning extend the ecological balance he enjoyed at Mount Tabor Cottage when 'Life and its growth, beauty and use, were thus all realised together.'

Sir Walter Scott, Sydney Goodsir Smith

Kinnoul Hill, Geddes's beloved early environment, has greatly attracted writers. Scott, in *The Fair Maid of Perth*, refers to Kinnoul Hill 'rising into picturesque rocks, partly clothed with woods'. In his poem on Kinnoul Hill', Sydney Goodsir Smith (1915–75) writes of the hill in winter:

> O black's the ice on Kinnoul Brae,
> Dark scaurs like wa's o doom –
> But nane saw mirk 's this dumb wae
> That maks aa Perth a tomb.

John Buchan

Having been called to the Knox Church, Perth, in 1874 the Rev. John Buchan married Helen Masterton in December that same year. On 26 August 1875 their first child, John Buchan (1875–1940), the novelist, was born in the manse at 20 York Place. In 1876 the Rev. John Buchan was called to the Free Church, Pathhead, Fife, where he lived for twelve years. Buchan's birthplace was subsequently converted to offices and the only memento of the building's connection with the author is the bronze plaque on the right-hand side of the entrance door at 20 York Place.

William Soutar

William Soutar (1893–1943), the Scottish poet, was born at 5.30 am on Thursday 28 April 1898 at No. 2 South Inch Terrace, Perth. His father John was a master-joiner with, from 1907, his own business. John Soutar was also a devout member of the Auld Lichts (United Original Secession) sect of the Scottish kirk so William Soutar had an early training in somewhat grim Presbyterian ways. William was, however, an open and expansive personality as a child. Between the ages of five and fourteen he attended the Southern District school and distinguished himself at games, being captain of the football eleven in the Schoolboys' League. From 1912 to 1916 he attended Perth Academy where he was taught by George Mackinlay who died in action in 1917 and whose *Poems* were posthumously published in 1919. Soutar continued his interest in sport at Perth Academy, playing in the school soccer team and coming first in the high jump at the school sports of 1916.

In 1916 Soutar enlisted in the navy and was an enthusiastic able-seaman when he became ill from food poisoning. Unfortunately the illness was wrongly diagnosed as rheumatism, a mistake that was to have calamitous consequences for Soutar. From 1919 to 1923 he was at Edinburgh University and shortly before graduating (on 12 July 1923) published – anonymously – his first collection of poems, *Gleanings By an Undergraduate* (1923). He contemplated a career as a schoolteacher (or journalist) but his health was rapidly deteriorating.

On 23 May 1924 Soutar's parents moved into 'Inglelowe' (as Soutar called it), a semi-detached house, 27 Wilson Street, in the Perth suburb of Craigie. As Soutar was now an invalid he was unable to do anything but a few chores in the house and the garden and he began to have time to brood on the cause of his trouble – the damage done to his spine by the germ from food poisoning. After an unsuccessful operation of 1930 Soutar was permanently confined to his bed from 3 November of that year. From his bedroom on the ground floor of 'Inglelowe' – where a plaque marks Soutar's productive presence – he could look at the garden and, beyond it, Craigie Hill. In 1933 the poet's father enlarged his bedroom by pulling down the window-wall and extending it into the garden. Soutar now looked onto the garden through a big plate-glass window opposite the foot of his bed.

Describing Soutar's condition in *Still Life* (1958), Alexander Scott writes:

> From his bed, with the aid of the wall-mirrors and a small looking-glass in his hand, Soutar could locate any book he wanted, and those he required were arranged on small tables at his bedside. His work-table could be wheeled across the bed; it carried a desk, boxes for books and papers, and the indispensable ash-tray. Switches on the wall behind his head enabled him to control the lighting and to ring for attention.
>
> Soutar lay on his back, his head propped up by pillows; and since this position, and his inability to turn his head, made it uncomfortable for him to look at his visitors if they were by his bedside, the chairs were arranged at the far end of the room, in front of the window. They were high chairs, so that visitors sat on perches, as it were, lifted up into the recumbent man's line of vision.

Never given to public displays of self-pity, Soutar courageously coped with his predicament and set out to create poetry in both English and (influenced by his friend Hugh MacDiarmid) Scots. His poem 'Autobiography', written in 1937, poignantly sums up his situation:

> Out of the darkness of the womb
> Into a bed, into a room:
> Out of a garden into a town,
> And to a country, and up and down
> The earth; the touch of women and men
> And back into a garden again:
> Into a garden; into a room;
> Into a bed and into a tomb;
> And the darkness of the world's womb.

In November 1942 Soutar became ill from pneumonia and after learning that his lungs were affected he began, on 5 July 1943, 'The Diary of a Dying Man', extracts from which appear in Alexander Scott's edition of *Diaries of a Dying Man* (1954). Aware of the imminence of his own death, Soutar was still concerned to rise imaginatively above the physical limitations of his life. Writing his diary for Tuesday 10 August 1943 he reflects:

> How difficult, when invalidism is known to be progressive and finally fatal, to avoid an increasing consideration of the self. . . . Already I begin to meet the temptations of self-pity, by which one looks at himself against the background of the invalid state and not the normal day; with the implication that normality must be adapted to keep the abnormal in comparative comfort. So one might easily slide into complete egocentricity, relating all happenings not to general existence but to the particular corner of existence in which a life dwindled. This condition of a growing self-absorption is at this hour of time less excusable than in peace, when throughout half the world millions are in destitution, hunger and slavery, and millions are being mutilated or slaughtered. How easily a small inconvenience can cover the sun and make us forget the misery of a universe; and the tragic element in self-pity is this, that at last the power of maintaining proportion between the world and the self is lost, and is not known to have been lost, since what is now a world is within the deathly confines of a wholly involved self.

Souter died between 2am and 4am on Friday 15 October 1943 at 'Inglelowe'. He is remembered as a man of astonishing courage, as a powerful poet in English, and as a Scots poet whose vernacular verse for children is in a class of its own.

James Kennaway

Perth Repertory theatre, established in 1900 by David Steuart and Marjorie Dence, features in James Kennaway's first novel *Tunes of Glory* (1956). Jock Sinclair, the aggressive protagonist of the book, often seeks out the sympathetic company of Mary Titterington, a Belfast-born actress who works in repertory. Kennaway was concerned that he had modelled his repertory theatre so closely on Perth Rep. and asked his publishers, Putnam, to check the reference for libel. In the novel, Perth Rep. is described as a building somewhat the worse for wear, as Jock observes when he climbs the narrow staircase to the second floor where Mary has her dressing-room:

> The walls were badly in need of redecoration; the dressing-table, which had been bought at some sale years before, was as untidy as ever, and the big mirror still had a postcard slipped into the corner and one or two official notes pinned on to the frame. All around the room budding actors and actresses had scrawled their names on the walls, but none of the names meant anything now.

PETTYCUR, Fife   (Fife)   1m W of Kinghorn, off A92

Andrew of Wyntoun

A monument overlooking Pettycur harbour commemorates Alexander III who died in 1286. Under this Scottish king, the country enjoyed a golden age of prosperity; towns grew rich on foreign trade; wool, fur and fish were exported; churches and castles proliferated. Alexander dealt with the Norse threat and regained the Western Isles by defeating old king Hakon of Norway at the battle of Largs in 1263. However in 1275 the glitter began to fade when Alexander's queen, Margaret, and soon after their three children, died, leaving the king's grand-daughter, Margaret, Maid of Norway, as heir apparent. In the hope of producing a suitable male heir Alexander took a second wife, Yolande de Dreux, on 1 November 1285. Five months later the king chose a tempestuous night to ride to Kinghorn to be with his new wife. His horse stumbled and Alexander III was thrown over the cliff to his death. A song lamenting Alexander, quoted in Andrew of Wyntoun's *Orygynale Cronykil of Scotland* (written at the end of the fourteenth century), is regarded as the earliest extant example of Scottish poetry:

Sen Alexander our king wes deid
   That Scotland left in luve and lee,   *peacetime*
Away was sonse of aill and breid,   *abundance*
   Of wine and wax, of gamin and glee.   *entertainment*
The gold was changit all in leid.
   The frute failyeit on everik tree.
Christ succour Scotland and remeid   *remedy*
   That stad is in perplexitie.   *in a condition of*

Margaret, Maid of Norway, died (in Orkney from seasickness) on her voyage from Norway in 1290, thus bringing to an end the House of Canmore. Edward I put John Balliol on the Scottish throne and an English invasion of Scotland led to the Wars of Independence.

PITCALZEAN HOUSE, Nigg, Ross-shire   (Highland)   7m S of Tain, off B9175

Eric Linklater

From 1947 to 1971 Pitcalzean (pronounced Pitcalyan) House was the home of the novelist Eric Linklater (1899–1974). The oldest part of the house dates from the late eighteenth century and Linklater's predecessor had been a son of George Romanes, the biologist and friend of Charles

276

Darwin. In *A Year of Space: A Chapter in Autobiography* (1953) Linklater describes Pitcalzean house:

> I had bought, in 1946, a larger house than I needed. . . . We looked across the water to the coroneted height of Fyrish, dark against the snow on Ben Wyvis, and a pair of cruisers anchored in the bright firth off Invergordon; to the south, through a little wood carefully cleared, we saw the lights of Cromarty, the native place of the fantastical Sir Thomas Urquhart. . . . We began to regard the house, as well as the view, with some complacency; and on my fiftieth birthday I planted twelve hundred young beeches to make a frontal hedge.

The large walled garden allowed Linklater to develop his interests in market-gardening (which the Inland Revenue eventually accepted as a loss to set against his earnings from writing). Linklater left the house because the industrialisation of Nigg Bay altered his outlook. When a giant aluminium smelter was erected at Invergordon Linklater said he had previously enjoyed 'one of the best views in Scotland. The smelter has not improved it.' Of the construction of giant oil rigs on the beach at the bottom of his garden, he commented 'Everyone around here wanted it except me. . . . Unemployment is very serious in these parts. If I had stood out against it I should have been the most unpopular man in Ross-shire!' (*The Times*, 25 November 1971).

The house – where Linklater wrote such books as *Mr Byculla* (1950) – was bought by Highland Fabricators in 1971 when the Company was establishing a fabrication yard for the manufacture of steel North Sea production jackets in Nigg Bay. Containing the remains of Linklater's library it is used as a private guest house where Highlands Fabricators entertain representatives of the oil industry.

PORT GLASGOW, Renfrewshire   (Strathclyde)   3m E of Greenock
on A8

James Thomson

James Thomson (1834–82) – who used the initials B.V. in a pseudonym intended as a tribute to Shelley and Novalis – was born on 23 November 1834 in Port Glasgow. The son of a merchant seaman, Thomson is celebrated for his long poem *The City of Dreadful Night*, first published in instalments in the *National Reformer* in 1874 (then collected in 1880). It is a bleak poem haunted by the figure of motiveless modern man existentially alone in a Godless universe. Though it has been taken as, on one level, an expression of the personal anguish Thomson felt as a man dependent on alcohol and given to hallucination, it has a connection with the poet's birthplace

In an article in the *Port Glasgow Express* of 7 December 1906, Charles Brodie (a Port Glasgow poet and Thomson enthusiast) wrote:

> James Thomson (B.V.) of great and growing and enduring fame, was born at the head of Church Street in the house removed to make room for the heightening of the roof of Mr John Gibb's shop. The babe was almost immediately removed to a house in Black Bull Close, and was there for nearly a year.

Hugh McIntyre, a local historian, established Thomson's birthplace (house demolished) to have been on the corner of Princes Street and Church Street.

According to the Glasgow poet Tom Leonard (in an article in *The Scotsman* of 4 May 1985) Thomson was decisively influenced by his mother, Sarah Kennedy, as a child in Port Glasgow. Sarah was a follower of the millenialist preacher Edward Irving and felt it her duty to impart Irving's message to her son. Born two weeks before Irving's death, Thomson grew up with Irving's portrait on the wall and absorbed the apocalyptic tone of the preacher's prophetic insistence on a second coming. Leonard argues that *The City of Dreadful Night* can be read:

> as a bitter reply to the City of God as prophesied in the Book of Revelations – a central text for the followers of Irving. In Revelations, there is a city where there is no darkness, where God is ever present, and where there is a River of the Water of Life. In Thomson's poem, the city is always in darkness, God does not exist, and the river is called the River of Suicides.
>
> Yet the bitterness of Thomson's reply is the clearer illuminated by setting it beside the eagerness with which the Irvingites awaited the fulfilment of prophecy.

Although he moved to London in 1842 and subsequently taught in Ireland – he met Matilda Weller, whose death in 1853 drove him deeply into depression and drink, in Ballincollig, near Cork – Thomson composed his great poem to some extent by rejecting the spiritual lessons his mother had taught him. Thomson's masterpiece thus has its dark roots in Port Glasgow. He writes, in Canto III:

> No time abates the first despair and awe,
>   But wonder ceases soon; the weirdest thing
> Is felt least strange beneath the lawless law
>   Where Death-in-Life is the eternal king;
> Crushed impotent beneath this reign of terror,
> Dazed with such mysteries of woe and error
> The soul is too outworn for wondering.

As a result of internal haemorrhaging due to drinking, Thomson died in University Hospital, London, on 8 June 1882. He is buried at Highgate Cemetery.

QUARTER, Lanarkshire   (Strathclyde)   2m S of Hamilton

Walter Perrie

The poet Walter Perrie was born on 5 June 1949 in Quarter, a mining village which has (with the exception of the kirk, school, institute and pub) been entirely rebuilt since the mid-1960s when the miners' rows were demolished. Perrie was brought up in his parents' house at 49 Lime-kilnburn Road, in two facing miners' rows. Each row was built in sections, each section contained seven dwellings, and each dwelling consisted of a room, box-room and kitchen. The section of Limekilnburn Road where Perrie lived was known as 'up Dublin'.

Perrie was educated at Hamilton Academy and Edinburgh University (where he studied mental philosophy). His verse continues to reach back to Quarter which is evoked through the catalogue of pits at the beginning of his extended poem *A Lamentation for the Children* (1977):

> Thinacre, Knowetap,
> Plotock, Avonbraes,
> black roses once
> have closed to scabs
> on ancient sores.

> Monkey Row, Furnace Row,
> Dublin – all eaten away
>   by bungalows.
> Tidy gardens have consumed
>   the pigeon lofts.

RATHEN, Aberdeenshire   (Grampian)   4m S of Fraserburgh on A92

David Toulmin

Novelist and storyteller David Toulmin was born John Reid on 1 July 1913 at Strathellie Cottages, Rathen: the cottage (now all in one) is some three miles east of the A92 branching off a slip road at the Peterhead junction near Cortes Lake. Toulmin's birthplace features in the story

'Folks in Black' (from *Hard Shining Corn*, 1972) and his novel *Blown Seed* (1976). 'Folks in Black' is narrated by a girl frustrated by the dull routine of her life:

> So there was little else I could do but run barefoot around the doors of our thatched hovels, which were the cottar houses at Gowanlea, where my father and the foreman lived and worked on the farm. The orra pail stood at our doorstep, where it served as a sink for slop or dishwater, and meantime there was just enough water in it to cover the bottom.

Toulmin's first school was at Lonmay, in the next parish, and here (he writes in *Travels Without a Donkey*, 1980):

> I found the golden key which later in life was to open my mind to most of the treasures in the English language, though at the same time I was just beginning to master the native doric of my fathers.

Toulmin's formal education finished on his fourteenth birthday and he subsequently worked on the land as a 'fee'd loon' for £6.50 per half-year. He began to write, seriously, in 1946 and his first book, *Hard Shining Corn*, established him as an important writer when it appeared in 1972.

REAY, Caithness   (Highland)   9m WSW of Thurso on A836

Henry Henderson

Reay, a parish and village near Sandside Bay, is the subject of several poems by Henry Henderson (1873–1957). 'The Sands o' Reay' begins:

> There is a placie dear to me
> Nestlin' cosily by the sea,
> I'd like to sing an' gar it shine
> Mang ither placies, sae ye Nine –
> Gie inspiration that I may
> Sing o' the bonnie sands o' Reay

Henderson was born in a croft in Western Borrowston on 25 July 1873. After winning a local poetry competition for the 'Laureateship of Caithness' in 1895 he began to style himself 'Bard o' Reay'. He married Margaret Henderson on 12 September 1906 and four years later was appointed sub-postmaster at Dounreay in the post office at the Red Bungalow (which is now just outside the boundary of Dounreay Experimental Reactor Establishment). Henderson lived in the Red Bungalow until 1933 when the post office was transferred to Bulldoo, three miles north-east of Reay. In his capacity as Reay parish councillor, Henderson was involved in various local projects such as the new road from Dounreay to Shebster and the erection of the Reay War Memorial. He also campaigned for the preservation of St Mary's Chapel, Crosskirk (five miles west of Thurso). Henderson was president of the Reay Country Burns Association and Bard of the Reay Literary Society. He died on 3 October 1957.

RENTON, Dunbartonshire   (Strathclyde)   2m N of Dumbarton

Tobias Smollett

The **Smollett Monument** (behind railings on the site of the school playground, main road) in Renton – an industrial village established by Smollett's sister for workers in the bleach fields - consists of a Tuscan column on a square plinth complete with a Latin inscription. It was originally erected, in 1774, by James Smollett, the novelist's cousin. In his *Journal of a Tour to the Hebrides* (1785) James Boswell records a visit he and Dr Johnson made to Cameron House, at the south end of Loch Lomond, to see James Smollett. The entry for Thursday 28 October 1773 explains:

By the side of the high road to Glasgow, at some distance from his house, he had erected a pillar to the memory of his ingenious kinsman, Dr Smollett; and he consulted Dr Johnson as to an inscription for it. Lord Kames, who, though he had a great store of knowledge, with much ingenuity, and uncommon activity of mind, was no profound scholar, had it seems recommended an English inscription. Dr Johnson treated this with great contempt, saying, 'An English inscription would be a disgrace to Dr Smollett;' and, in answer to what Lord Kames had urged, as to the advantage of its being in English, because it would be generally understood, I observed, that all to whom Dr Smollett's merit could be an object of respect and imitation, would understand it as well in Latin; and that surely it was not meant for the Highland drovers, or other such people, who pass and repass that way.

We were then shewn a Latin inscription, proposed for this monument. Dr Johnson sat down with an ardent and liberal earnestness to revise it, and greatly improved it by several additions and variations.

Smollett – who was born at nearby Dalquhurn in 1721 and died at Leghorn in 1771 – would perhaps have disagreed with Boswell and Johnson on this linguistic point. In the event, Johnson's contribution was somewhat altered and the inscription reads as follows in English translation:

Stay, Traveller! If elegance of taste and wit, if fertility of genius, and an unrivalled talent in delineating the characters of mankind, have ever attracted your admiration, pause a while on the memory of Tobias Smollett, MD, one more than commonly endowed with those virtues which, in a man or a citizen, you would praise, or imitate.

Who, having secured the applause of posterity by a variety of literary abilities and a peculiar felicity of composition was, by a rapid and cruel distemper snatched from this world in the fifty-first year of his age.

Far, alas, from his country, he lies interred near Leghorn in Italy. In testimony of his many and great virtues this empty monument, the only pledge, alas, of his affection, is erected on the banks of the Leven, the scene of his birth and of his latest poetry, by James Smollett of Bonhill, his cousin, who would rather have expected this last tribute from him.

Try and remember this honour was not given alone to the memory of the deceased, but for the encouragement of others. Deserve like him and be alike rewarded.

In her *Journal of a Tour of Scotland* (1803) Dorothy Wordsworth gives her impression of the monument:

In a small enclosure by the wayside is a pillar erected to the memory of Dr Smollett, who was born in a village at a little distance, which we could see at the same time, and where I believe some of the family still reside. There is a long Latin inscription, which Coleridge translated for my benefit. The Latin is miserably bad – as Coleridge said, such as poor Dr Smollett, who was an excellent scholar, would have been ashamed of.

Just to the south-east of the Smollett Monument, on the banks of the Leven, Smollett was born – in Dalquhurn House, then a farm in the Vale of Leven on the Bonhill estates of his grandfather Sir James Smollett. A modern Dalquhurn House (used for Dalquhurn textile works' managers in the late nineteenth century) stands approximately on the site of Smollett's birthplace. Smollett's 'Ode to Leven Water' indicates his appreciation of the scenes of his youth:

> On Leven's banks, while free to rove
> And tune the rural pipe to love,
> I envied not the happiest swain
> That ever trod the Arcadian plain.
>   Pure stream, in whose transparent wave
> My youthful limbs I wont to lave,
> No torrents stain thy limpid source,
> No rocks impede thy dimpling course,
> That warbles sweetly o'er its bed,

With white, round, polished pebbles spread,
While, lightly poised, the scaly brood
In myriads cleave thy crystal flood -
The springing trout in speckled pride,
The salmon, monarch of the tide,
The ruthless pike intent on war,
The silver eel, and mottled par.
Devolving from thy parent lake,
A charming maze thy waters make,
By bowers of birch and groves of pine,
And edges flowered with eglantine.

   Still on thy banks, so gaily green,
May numerous herds and flocks be seen,
And lasses, chanting o'er the pail,
And shepherds, piping in the dale,
And ancient faith, that knows no guile,
And Industry, embrowned with toil,
And hearts resolved and hands prepared
The blessings they enjoy to guard.

RUTHWELL, Dumfriesshire   (Dumfries and Galloway)   10m SE of
Dumfries on B725

'The Dream of the Rood'

A signpost points to the village church where, in a special chamber (open
to the public, key available), stands the 18ft high **Ruthwell Cross** which
dates from 750. On this runic cross are passages from 'The Dream of the
Rood', one of the finest Old English religious poems and dated pre–750
by scholars on account of the evidence of the Ruthwell Cross. A brass
plaque on the chamber wall explains:

> The Ruthwell Cross dates from Anglo-Saxon times. Destroyed during
> the conflicts which followed the Reformation. Lay in the earthen
> floor of the church from 1642 to 1790. Erected in the Manse Garden
> in 1823. Sheltered here and declared a monument under the Ancient
> Monuments Act in 1887.

ST ANDREWS, Fife   (Fife)   13½ SE of Dundee

St Andrews is internationally known as the home of golf on account of the Royal and Ancient Golf Club (founded 1754), the ruling authority on the game.In 'The City of Golf', Robert F. Murray (1863–94) wrote:

> Would you like to see a city given over,
> Soul and body, to a tyrannising game?
> If you would, there's little need to be a rover,
> For St Andrews is the abject city's name.

In fact St Andrews is one of the most prominent places in Scotland for various historical, cultural, intellectual and academic reasons. St Andrews Castle (founded 1200, rebuilt late fourteenth century, now a ruin) played a crucial part in the Reformation for Cardinal Beaton was murdered here in 1546 and John Knox became the chaplain to the Protestants who occupied the castle. St Andrews Cathedral (built in the twelfth and thirteenth centuries), where Andrew of Wyntoun (*c.* 1355–1422), author of the *Orygynale Cronykil of Scotland*, was a canon regular, was once the largest church in Scotland.

Andrew Lang

St Andrews University (founded 1412) is the oldest university in Scotland and among those who studied here were William Dunbar (*c.* 1460–*c.* 1520); Sir David Lyndsay (*c.* 1490–1555); Gavin Douglas (*c.* 1474–1522), who was imprisoned in St Andrews Castle in 1515 during the regency of the Duke of Albany; Sir Robert Aytoun (1570–1638); John Arbuthnott (1667–1735); Robert Fergusson (1750–74) and Andrew Lang (1844–1912). Lang was a student from 1861–3 and always recalled St Andrews with great affection. His poem 'Almae Matres' (1887) is one of the best-known poetic tributes to the town:

> *St Andrews by the northern sea,*
>   *A haunted town it is to me!*
> A little city, worn and gray,
>   The gray North Ocean girds it round;
> And o'er the rocks, and up the bay,
>   The long sea-rollers surge and sound;
> And still the thin and biting spray
>   Drives down the melancholy street,
> And still endure, and still decay,
>   Towers that the salt winds vainly beat.
> Ghost-like and shadowy they stand
> Dim-mirrored in the wet sea-sand.

In later years Lang spent winters at 8 Gibson Place. He died at Banchory on 20 July 1912 and was buried in the East Cemetery of St Andrews. His grave is marked by a Celtic cross.

William Laughton Lorimer

Among those who taught at St Andrews were John Major (Mair) (1469–1550), author of *Historia Majoris Britanniae* (1521) and Provost of St Salvator's College from 1533; William Tennant (1784–1848), author of *Anster Fair* (1812) and Professor of Oriental Languages at St Andrews from 1834–48; and William Laughton Lorimer (1885–1967), translator of *The New Testament in Scots* (posthumously published in 1983). Born at Strathmartine, near Dundee, Lorimer was (in 1910) appointed Professor Burnet's Assistant in Greek at St Andrews University. After World War One (in which he served in the Intelligence Directorate of the War Office) he returned to St Andrews and in 1921 moved into 19 Murray Park, now Lorimer House. In 1953 Lorimer was appointed Professor of Greek at St Andrews. The last ten years of his life were devoted to translating the New Testament into Scots. It took him approximately eight years to complete his translation in draft and as long as that for his translation, expertly edited by his son Robin, to materialise in print. Lorimer's translation is a monumental achievement that could initiate a new era of Scots prose. Its quality is indicated by the following passage from John, 6:

> Whan it gloamed, his disciples cam doun aff the brae tae the lochside an, gaein abuird a boat, begoud crossin tae Capernaüm.
>
> Jesus hed ey no come tae them, gin it grew mirk; an nou the loch wis jawin and jawpin wi an unco storm o wind. Than, efter they hed rowed a five-an-twintie or threttie furlongs, they saw him gangin on the scriff o the watter an comin near the boat, an they war gliffed. But he cried tae them, 'It is een mysel; binna nane feared.'
>
> They war ettlin tae tak him abuird, but aa o a sudden an a clap the boat wis there at the shore they war airtin til.

James Boswell, Dr Samuel Johnson

Boswell and Johnson visited St Andrews in 1773. In his *Journey to the Western Islands of Scotland* (1774) Johnson wrote:

> In the morning we rose to perambulate a city, which only history shews to have once flourished, and surveyed the ruins of ancient magnificence, of which even the ruins cannot long be visible, unless some care be taken to preserve them; and where is the pleasure of preserving such mournful memorials? They have been till very lately so much neglected, that every man carried away the stones who fancied that he wanted them.

After further lamenting the decline of St Andrews, Johnson noted:

> St Andrews seems to be a place eminently adapted to study and
> education being situated in a populous, yet a cheap country, and
> exposing the minds and manners of young men neither to the levity
> and dissoluteness of a capital city, nor to the gross luxury of a town
> of commerce, places naturally unpropitious to learning.

James H. Whyte

From 1930 to 1939 James H. Whyte, a wealthy American, established a
cultural base in St Andrews. Whyte's father was Jewish but he adopted
the surname of his Scottish mother and enthusiastically supported the
ideals of the modern Scottish Literary Renaissance. At 3 South Street, a
building known as 'The Roundel', he installed his Abbey Bookshop in the
vaulted ground floor and converted the upper floors into the house he
lived in from 1931 to 1938 (when the bookshop closed and St Andrews
University bought the porperty). Whyte founded, and edited from 1930
to 1936, the *Modern Scot*, a progressive magazine of the arts. Whyte was
enthusiastic about the work of both Edwin Muir (1887–1959) and Hugh
MacDiarmid (1892–1978) who frequently contributed poetry and prose
to the magazine. MacDiarmid's translation of Alasdair MacMhaighstir
Alasdair's 'The Birlinn of Clanranald', for example, first appeared in the
Modern Scot of January 1935 and was then issued as a limited edition by
Whyte's Abbey Bookshop. In April 1936 the *Modern Scot* was incorporated into *Outlook* with Whyte as literary editor. In *Outlook*, June 1936,
there was a substantial extract from Muir's forthcoming book *Scott and
Scotland* (1936) containing the contention that Scots was an anachronism
and only 'a language for simple poetry'. MacDiarmid was horrified, since
Muir's argument apparently dismissed his achievements in *Sangschaw*
(1925), *Penny Wheep* (1926) and *A Drunk Man Looks at the Thistle*
(1926). He replied in a letter to *Outlook* but its belligerent tone offended
Whyte who rejected it. MacDiarmid therefore circulated (from Whalsay
on 1 July 1936) an open letter to Whyte denouncing *Outlook* as 'the
Scottish literary and fascist-nationalist quarterly' and Whyte as 'the
wealthy literary editor of *Outlook*'. It was the beginning of the long literary
war waged on Muir by MacDiarmid.

While in St Andrews, Whyte also acquired (in 1931) numbers 5 to 11
North Street – the old coast-guard building – and had it converted into
two houses with an art gallery on the upper level in between. According
to Maurice Lindsay's *Francis George Scott and the Scottish Renaissance*
(1980) the new edifice was known locally as 'the Moorish monstrosity'.
Whyte's friend John Tonge ('A. T. Cunningham'), journalist and author
of *The Arts of Scotland* (1938), lived in number 11.

Edwin Muir

After living for several years in Hampstead, London, Edwin Muir (1887–1959) decided to return to Scotland. In late August 1935 Muir moved, with his wife Willa (1890–1970) and son Gavin, to St Andrews where they rented Castlelea, The Scores, a house overlooking St Andrews Castle. As Willa had studied classics at St Andrews University and the town had both architectural and natural beauty, as well as an intellectual ambience, the Muirs had high hopes of their new life. However, Muir was unable to accept the class divisions he discerned in St Andrews, as he wrote in his diary for May 1938:

> The rich live on the poor; why should they sneer at them as well?. . . .
> In a small town where people know one another, the blatancy of the
> rich becomes more obvious; they sit more visibly on their money-bags.

In May 1938 the Muirs left Castlelea and settled into a house at 11 Queen's Gardens. Here they entertained guests such as the composer Francis George Scott (1880–1958) who spent summer holidays in St Andrews; and the poet Tom Scott (born 1918) who then lived and worked in the town. While staying at 11 Queen's Gardens, Muir wrote his autobiography *The Story and the Fable* (1940), later enlarged as *An Autobiography* (1954). Muir enjoyed walking by the sea and recorded, in August 1938, an early morning jaunt with Gavin to see the sunrise:

> We went along the East Sands, the light growing stronger and stronger;
> the land no longer rich and dark, but picked out in primitive colours:
> I was struck by the red roofs of the farms, as if red were newly created.
> Then I became conscious of light in itself, not as a mere medium for
> revealing objects: the whole world seemed to be over-flooded with
> light, flowing in a level river from the eastern fount.

During the War, Muir worked first in the Food Office at Dundee to which he travelled daily from St Andrews via Leuchars Junction. In 1942 he was offered work by the British Council in Edinburgh where he lived until 1945.

George Bruce

From 1943 to 1950 the poet George Bruce (born 1909) spent his summer holidays in St Andrews, lodging first with Mr and Mrs Ardagh at 66 South Street. Learning from the librarian Ardagh that four previous lodgers were airmen, each killed on separate missions over Germany, Bruce wrote his poem '66 South Street, St Andrews' (*Collected Poems*, 1970) which ends:

Now the deliberate four walls
Hold but memories. Four men
To be four air-men. All
Sweetness of life
In four known walls.

Another poem from this period, 'St Andrews, June, 1946' begins with a
tribute to the town:

Old tales, old customs and old men's dreams
Obscure this town. Memories abound.
In the mild misted air, and in the sharp air
Toga and gown walk the pier.
The past sleeps in the stones.

Tom Scott

Tom Scott (born in Partick, Glasgow, on 6 June 1918) moved to St
Andrews in 1931. His father, a foreman boilermaker, had to leave Glasgow
because of the slump on the Clyde and learn the building trade at the age
of forty-four. In a letter of 21 May 1983 Tom Scott writes:

My grandfather had lived and worked many years previously in St
Andrews when my mother was a girl, living in the famous (still) Ivy
Cottage in Louden's Close, South Street, and in the nearby village of
Denhead some four miles from St Andrews. . . . We lived at 42 South
Street (D'Arcy Thompson lived next door in 44, but ours was a block
of tenement but-and-bens while his was a family house) recently
restored as South Court, winning a Saltire Award for the restoration.
The Byre Theatre is at the back of the house, but didn't exist in my
day. I went to Madras College till June 1933, then worked as message
boy with Wm Niven, Butcher (no longer there), Church Street – the
original of Broun the Butcher [in *Brand the Builder*].

Scott's poem *Brand the Builder* (1975) is set in St Andrews. The sequence
describes characters Scott knew in St Andrews and explores the atmosphere of the town itself:

The sea crines aye awa alang the sands
And tint youth crines wi it, crines awa.
Yonder the rocks' lang fingers harp the tide
As ay they've duin, as aye they ever will,
Heron-sprayed amang their slimy weeds,
And in their pools the shrimp-life is strandit,
Partans, poodlies, and whitna ither life
Simple as water, savage whiles as war,

288

Gey like the life that's lived in the toun itself,
Sant-Andraes itsel a pool amang the rocks,
A tidal pool left high by the ebban sea,
We sic craters in't as wad dumfouner ye.

David Black

The poet David Black – born 8 November 1941 in Cape Town, South
Africa – came to Scotland, from Tanzania, in 1950 and throughout the
1950s lived, with his family, at 8 Dempster Terrace, St Andrews. A
sequence, 'St Andrews Poem', appears in his collection *The Happy Crow*
(1974).

ST MARY'S LOCH, Selkirkshire (Border) 13m SW of Selkirk, by A708

Sir Walter Scott

The six Cantos of *Marmion* (1808), by Sir Walter Scott (1771–1832), are
prefaced by verse epistles to the author's friends. The introduction to
Canto II, addressed to the Rev. John Marriot, approaches the subject of
solitude with reference to St Mary's Loch:

> Oft in my mind such thoughts awake,
> By lone Saint Mary's silent lake;
> Thou know'st it well, – nor fen, nor sedge,
> Pollute the pure lake's crystal edge;
> Abrupt and sheer, the mountains sink
> At once upon the level brink;
> And just a trace of silver sand
> Marks where the water meets the land.
> Far in the mirror, bright and blue,
> Each hill's huge outline you may view;
> Shaggy with heath, but lonely bare,
> Nor tree, not bush, nor brake, is there,
> Save where, of land, yon slender line
> Bears thwart the lake the scatter'd pine

William Wordsworth

William Wordsworth (1770–1850) was fascinated by the poetic fame of
the Yarrow, which rises above St Mary's Loch and flows into the Tweed.

Even before Wordsworth had seen the Yarrow he anticipated its beauty in 'Yarrow Unvisited':

> Let beeves and home-bred kine partake
> The sweets of Burn-mill meadow;
> The swan on still St Mary's Lake
> Float double, swan and shadow!

James Hogg

James Hogg (1770–1835) enjoyed convivial evenings at the **Tibbie Shiels Inn**, at the south end of St Mary's Loch. Tibbie was in service with Hogg's mother and is supposed to have described the Ettrick Shepherd as 'a gay, sensible man, for a' the nonsense he wrat'. She died in her 96th year, in 1878, and is buried in Ettrick churchyard. Just south-west of Tibbie Shiels Inn is **James Hogg's Statue**.

ST MONANS, Fife   (Fife)   2m E of Elie on A917

Christopher Rush

Poet and storyteller Christopher Rush was born in St Monans in 1944; though he has taught in Edinburgh since 1972 his work invariably explores the territory he knew as a child in the East Neuk of Fife among the fishermen. He lived first in 7 Station Road, on a hill going down to St Monans harbour and less than fifty yards from the water. In his introduction to the stories collected in *Peace Comes Dropping Slow* (1983) Rush writes: 'St Monans bore me. A salt-splashed cradle with a golden fringe.' In *A Twelvemonth and a Day* (1985) he laments, in lyrical prose, the death of the way of life he experienced as a child in St Monans. As a boy Rush felt he lived in a village of great communal vitality as colourful local characters went to sea and came back to swap stories of the great days of the herring industry. Life seemed to ebb and flow with the water, the people responded to the seasons, and there was an exhilarating sense of belonging to a cohesive group.

According to Rush, the glorious past is dead and buried, a perception that gives a melancholy tone to his account of his upbringing in the East Neuk. Like George Mackay Brown, whose work he so obviously admires, Rush is sickened by the consequences of technological advance and is an enemy of what passes for progress. Towards the end of *A Twelvemonth and a Day* he writes:

> St Monans I return to now with more than a tinge of reasonable regret.
> It has been quaintly taken over, like many such, by functionless

foreigners. The old shops of the butcher, the barber, the chemist, the cobbler – once the essential people in a community – have gone and their seaside homes have been prettified by the National Trust, shot right up outside the price-range of any local buyer. . . . I go back, I smell tar and tangle, I try to catch these old ghosts of the fishing that flutter in the meshes of the new nylon nets and linger in the smartly coloured lobster creels, where rubber and plastic piping take the place of the boughs my grandfather cut so carefully.

SCHIEHALLION, Perthshire   (Tayside)   14m E of Pitlochry

Hugh MacDiarmid

Schiehallion, known as the 'fairies' hill', is a mountain standing 3,547 feet. It is seen to advantage from the eastern end of Loch Rannoch. In 1920 Hugh MacDiarmid – C. M. Grieve (1892–1978) – planned a volume of fifty 'Sonnets of the Highland Hills'. Twenty-nine of these were sent to the poet's old teacher George Ogilvie and eleven survive in *The Complete Poems of Hugh MacDiarmid* (eds W. R. Aitken and Michael Grieve, 1985). 'Rivals', dedicated to the poet's first wife Margaret (Peggy) Grieve, ends:

> I know too well with what bright mysteries
> Your eyes on Braeriach turn: and how you run
> To where Schiehallion standing like a god
> Turns me to dust and ashes in the sun!

'Valedictory' ends

> Schiehallion and Calvary are one.
> All men at last hang broken on the Cross,
> Calling to One who gives a blackening sun.
> There is one hill up which each soul is thrust
> Ere all is levelled in eternal loss,
> The peaks and plains are one. The end is dust.

SHETLAND, Shetland

Shetland comprises one hundred islands, a minority of them inhabited. Mainland, the largest island, measures fifty-four miles north to south with a maximum breadth of some twenty-one miles.

Sir Walter Scott

Jarlshof, on Sumburgh Head, the most southerly tip of Shetland, is so called after the fictional house in Sir Walter Scott's novel *The Pirate* (1822). Scott visited Sumburgh Head in 1814 during his six-week voyage round Scotland on the Lighthouse Yacht in the company of Robert Stevenson, grandfather of Robert Louis Stevenson. In his journal entry for Tuesday 9 August 1814 Scott writes:

> The sea beneath rages incessantly among a thousand of the fragments which have fallen from the peaks and which assume an hundred strange shapes. It would have been a fine situation to compose an ode to the Genius of Sumburgh-head, or an Elegy upon a Cormorant – or to have written and spoken madness of any kind in prose or poetry. But I gave vent to my excited feelings in a more simple way; and sitting gently down on the steep green slope which led to the beach, I e'en slid down a few hundred feet, and found the exercise quite an adequate vent to my enthusiasm. I recommend this exercise (time and place suiting) to all my brother scribblers and I have no doubt it will save much effusion of Christian ink.

The journal dismisses 'the old house at Sumburgh' as 'a most dreary mansion'. In *The Pirate*, however, the house has a powerful presence from the beginning of the book:

> for a Norwegian chief of other times, or as other accounts said, and as the name of Jarlshof seemed to imply, an ancient Earl of the Orkneys had selected this neck of land as the place for establishing a mansion-house. It has been long entirely deserted, and the vestiges only can be discerned with difficulty; for the loose sand, borne on the tempestuous gales of those stormy regions, has overblown, and almost buried, the ruins of the buildings; but in the end of the seventeenth century, a part of the Earl's mansion was still entire and habitable. It was a rude building of rough stone, with nothing about it to gratify the eye, or to excite the imagination; a large old-fashioned narrow house, with a very steep roof, covered with flags composed of grey sandstone, would perhaps convey the best idea of the place to a modern reader.

The house cited by Scott dates from the sixteenth century and is but the last of eight distinct occupation phases of Jarlshof. On the site (open to the public) archaeological evidence reveals a hut from 2,000 BC; six late-Bronze Age dwellings; early-Iron Age circular stone huts; late-Iron Age broch and houses; wheelhouses from the second and third centuries; early ninth-century Norse farmsteads and hall; medieval farmstead; the Laird's 'new hall', dating from the sixteenth century. Jarlshof, the most complex excavated site in Shetland, is signposted.

Hugh MacDiarmid

Hugh MacDiarmid – Christopher Murray Grieve (1892–1978) – lived on the Shetland island of Whalsay from 1933 to 1942. Off the east coast of mainland Shetland, Whalsay ('whale island') is reached by driving north from Lerwick and taking the ferry from Laxo. The 'Hendra' sails through Dury Voe and passes the island of West Linga – where MacDiarmid set his poem 'On a Raised Beach' – on its way to Symbister harbour. An undulating island of hills and valleys textured by sedge and heather, Whalsay is rich in archeological relics: the Iron Age fort at the Loch of Huxter, the Standing Stones of Yoxie, the neolithic Bunzie House, the heel-shaped cairn of Pettigarths Field.

During the years MacDiarmid lived on Whalsay, with his second wife Valda Trevlyn and his son Michael, he rented – for 27 shillings a year – a four-roomed cottage standing on a hillside at Sodom (prounounced Sudam) overlooking Linga Sound. From this cottage (now derelict) the poet could see all of one raised beach on Linga and – partly obscured by the Calf of Linga – some of a longer raised beach near Croo Wick where the sheep are brought for shearing. When MacDiarmid was taken across to Linga in 1933, shortly after settling on Whalsay, he was a man desperately in need of spiritual sustenance. Shattered by the breakdown of his first marriage, to Peggy Skinner (who left him to live with a wealthy coal-merchant) he was (he acknowledged) 'in exceedingly bad state, psychologically and physically'. With characteristic courage he scrutinised the stones and empathised with them in his masterly 'On a Raised Beach' from *Stony Limits and Other Poems* (1934):

I must get into this stone world now.
Ratchel, striae, relationships of tesserae,
   Innumerable shades of grey,
   Innumerable shapes,
And beneath them all a stupendous unity,
Infinite movement visibly defending itself
Against all the assaults of weather and water,
Simultaneously mobilised at full strength
At every point of the universal front,
   Always at the pitch of its powers,
   The foundation and end of all life . . .

This is no heap of broken images.
Let men find the faith that builds mountains

> Before they seek the faith that moves them. Men cannot hope
> To survive the fall of the mountains
> Which they will no more see than they saw their rise
> Unless they are more concentrated and determined,
> Truer to themselves and with more to be true to,
> Than these stones, and as inerrable as they are.

Up the road from the Sodom cottage, MacDiarmid obtained, at a nominal rent, a two-roomed cottage at Hillhead near the laird's house (now a school). A young graduate, Henry Grant Taylor, came up to Whalsay to type for MacDiarmid and recalled that the poet spent most of his energy on his projected *Cornish Heroic Song for Valda Trevlyn*, an unfinished epic who linguistic and stylistic range is indicated by the extant parts: *In Memoriam James Joyce* (1955), *The Kind of Poetry I Want* (1961), *Dìreadh* (1974) and the various sections of *Impavidi Progrediamur* scattered through *The Complete Poems of Hugh MacDiarmid* (1985), edited by W. R. Aitken and Michael Grieve. It was planned as the longest poetic sequence in modern literature and celebrated a Celtic ideal of culture.

In *Lucky Poet* (1943), his intellectual autobiography, MacDiarmid describes the cottage at Hillhead:

> In addition to my home on Whalsay here I have (at a fair distance from the other) a separate cottage which I use as an office – an indescribable chaos stuffed with hundred of thousands of newspaper cuttings . . . and decorated in addition to mural paintings [by Barbara Niven] of my 'Curly Snake', the Green Spot-bellied Cencrastus, and a Cavorting Cow (developed from a doodle of my little boy's), with portraits of friends as diverse as Ezra Pound, Philip O'Connor, Mary Rhys (authoress of a book on the Scilly islands), Ruth Pitter, T. S. Eliot, James Joyce and Nazim Khikmet, the poet of Turkish liberation. . . . It is, no doubt, a very strange and utterly unexpectable cottage – incredibly unlike any of its neighbours (internally – outwards it is identical with these) – to find on a little Shetland island . . .

Unfortunately the murals have gone and the cottage is now used as an office. *Lucky Poet* was written on Whalsay which MacDiarmid left in February 1942 to go to Glasgow where he worked, initially, on the Clydeside 'doing hard manual labour'.

Vagaland

Thomas Alexander Robertson (1909–73) – who signed all his poems with the pseudonym Vagaland – was born at Westerwick, Skeld, on 6 March 1909. Before Vagaland was one year old, his father, a merchant seaman, was drowned and the poet's mother took her two sons to Stove, Walls (Waas). Vagaland was educated at Happyhansel School; the Anderson Educational Institute, Lerwick; and Edinburgh University where he graduated in 1932. After several temporary teaching jobs in Shetland, Vagaland was appointed Assistant Teacher of English and History at Lerwick Central School, a position he held until he retired in 1970. He died on 29 December 1973.

The Collected Poems of Vagaland (1975), edited by the poet's widow Martha, shows a profound attachment to the scenes of his childhood and an inventive use of the Shetland dialect. Vagaland was devoted to the culture of Shetland; he collaborated (with John J. Graham) on *Grammar and Usage of the Shetland Dialect* (1952) and was secretary of the Shetland Folk Society from 1945 to the time of his death. Introducing the collected edition of Vagaland, Ernest M. Marwick writes 'His clear accents set the tone for Shetland writing'. 'Stoorbra Hill', which describes one of Vagaland's favourite places, shows how lyrically Vagaland could use the Shetland dialect. The penultimate stanza runs:

> An mony a Hairst will bring da coarn *harvest*
> lang eftir we're awa,
> An generations still oon-boarn
> will skyug da Winter snaa. *take shelter from, snow*
> Dey'll watch da hedder turning green *heather*
> da dancing simmermil, *shimmer over the sea*
> An see da sun geng doon at nicht
> anunder Stoorbra Hill.

William J. Tait

William J. Tait was born, on 15 November 1918, in a cottage belonging to his maternal grandfather in Reafirth, Mid Yell. The poet's father had married a Mid Yell girl, Minnie Williamson, when he was headmaster in Burravoe, Yell. Subsequently Tait lived at Sandwick Schoolhouse, on Mainland, where his father was headmaster from 1918. After studying at the Anderson Educational Institute (now Anderson High School) and Edinburgh University, Tait supported himself mainly by schoolteaching. From 1942 to 1949 he was Principal Teacher of English and History at the Anderson Educational Institute and in 1984 he returned to Shetland, settling in Mid Yell where he was born. Tait writes in English and the Shetland dialect. His poem 'A Day Atween Waddirs', from *Collected Poems* (1980), was written in Sandwick and begins:

> Twa days fae syne I cam dis sam gait,
> Cut aff o da Cumlick rod an strack up da brae,
> Stansed dare at da tap o da rise an fan my fag
> Draain daid i my mooth wi my haest up da hill.

SKYE, Inner Hebrides   (Highland)

James Boswell, Dr Samuel Johnson

Skye, the largest of the Hebridean islands, measures some forty-nine miles from Rudha Hunish to the Point of Sleat and forty-five miles from Isleornsay to Vaternish Point. It is indented with sea lochs including Eishort, Slapin, Scavaig and Brittle on the south; and Bracadale, Dunvegan and Snizort on the west and north. During their Scottish tour of 1773 Dr Samuel Johnson (1709–84) and James Boswell (1740–95) stayed on Skye for a month. At Broadford – called Broadfoot by Boswell in his *Journal of a Tour to the Hebrides* (1785) – they stayed with the Mackinnons at Coire Chatachain (now a farm outbuilding) where (says Boswell in his entry for Monday 6 September 1773) they 'enjoyed the comfort of a table plentifully furnished [and] for the first time had a specimen of the joyous social manners of the inhabitants of the Highlands [who] talked in their own ancient language, with fluent vivacity'. Crossing to Raasay (entry of Wednesday 8 September) they stayed at 'a good family mansion' (Raasay House, an adventure school, stands on the site); on Friday 10 September Boswell left Johnson behind as he explored Raasay, 'passed over not less than four-and-twenty miles of very rugged ground, and had a Highland dance on the top of *Dun Can*, the highest mountain in the island'.

Returning to Skye they resolved to meet (as Boswell described her, entry for Sunday 12 September) 'the celebrated Miss Flora Macdonald, who is married to the present Mr Macdonald of Kingsburgh'; at Kingsburgh (rebuilt) Boswell was impressed by Flora, 'a little woman, of a genteel appearance, and uncommonly mild and well-bred' and that Sunday night Boswell and Johnson slept in the same room, Johnson's bed being one once used by Bonnie Prince Charlie. For ten days Johnson and Boswell stayed at **Dunvegan Castle** (open to the public), seat of the chiefs of Clan Macleod since the twelfth century, the present structure dating mainly from the sixteenth century. Boswell describes Dunvegan in his entry for Monday, 13 September:

> The great size of the castle, which is partly old and partly new, and is built upon a rock close to the sea, while the land around it present nothing but wild, moorish, hilly, and craggy appearances, gave a rude magnificence to the scene.

Before going to Kingsburgh, Johnson and Boswell stopped at Portree. The so-called 'capital' of Skye was originally called Kiltaragleann ('Church at the foot of the glen') and renamed in honour of a state visit from James

V. On 12 September 1773 Johnson and Boswell 'reached the harbour of Portree, in Sky, which is a large and good one'. After thus describing the harbour in his *Journal* Boswell noted: '*Portree* has its name from King James the Fifth having landed there in his tour through the Western Island, *Ree* in Erse being King, as *Re* is in Italian; so it is *Port-Royal*. There was here a tolerable inn.'

Virginia Woolf

On 25 and 26 June 1938 Virginia Woolf stayed at the same inn, then the Flodigarry Hotel now the Royal Hotel. Although Woolf's *To the Lighthouse* (1927) is set on Skye it was not until 1938 that the author visited the island. On 25 June 1938 she wrote to Vanessa Bell:

Well, here we are in Skye, and it feels like the South Seas – completely remote, surrounded by sea, people speaking Gaelic, no railways, no London papers, hardly any inhabitants. Believe it or not, it is (in its way, as people say) so far as I can judge on a level with Italy, Greece or Florence.

In a postcard of 27 June 1938 to Duncan Grant, Virginia Woolf wrote: 'Skye is often raining, but also fine: hardly embodied; semi-transparent; like living in a jelly fish lit up with green light. Remote as Samoa; deserted; prehistoric. No room for more.'

Niall MacLeoid

During the nineteenth century, the people of Skye suffered at the hands of oppressive landlords and there were crofter riots in the 1880s. The Gaelic poet Neil MacLeod of Skye (Niall MacLeoid) confronts the Skye evictions in his poem 'The Skye Crofters' ('Na Croitearan Sgitheanach', translation from Derick Thomson's *An Introduction to Gaelic Poetry*, 1974):

> I find sad the account
> tonight from my country,
> my friends are being scourged
> by Lowland poltroons;
> with sticks at the ready
> being beaten like cattle,
> like slaves quite uncared for
> being shut in a fank.
>
> The folk who were friendly,
> and kindly, warm-hearted,

have now been pressed sore
by landlords' conceit;
their freedom has left them,
their fields are deserted,
sheep have taken the place
of free men in the glen.

That radical tradition in Gaelic poetry has been renewed, in the twentieth century, by the poet Sorley MacLean (see below).

Alexander Smith

South of Loch Harport and Glen Drynoch are the **Cuillin hills**; the Black Cuillin, curved like a horseshoe round Loch Coruisk; and the Red Cuillin, to the east. Although Gaelic tradition derives the name Cuillin from the legendary hero Cuchullin, the plural noun comes from the old Norse Kjöllen, meaning 'keel-shaped ridges'. Made from gabbro and basalt, the Cuillin comprise, for many visitors to Skye, the spectacular essence of the island. For example, one highly imaginative visitor was Alexander Smith (1829–67), the Kilmarnock-born poet who married, in 1857, a Skye girl called Flora Macdonald (related to her celebrated namesake). In *A Summer on Skye* (1865), Smith enthused over the hills which, inevitably, he called the Cuchullins:

> Next morning, in the soft sky was the wild outline of the Cuchillins, with which we were again to make acquaintance. Somehow these hills never weary. I never become familiar with them. Intimacy can no more stale them than it could the beauty of Cleopatra. In Glen Sligachan, although sight of the Cuchullins proper was lost, we were surrounded by their outlying and far-radiating spurs. I had a quickened sense of my own individuality. The enormous bulks, their gradual recedings to invisible crests, their utter movelessness, their austere silence, daunted me. I was conscious of their presence, and I hardly dared speak lest I be overhead. I do not know what effect mountains have on the people who live in them continually, but this stranger they make serious and grave at heart.

Sir Walter Scott

With its surface 26ft above sea-level and ringed by the Cuillin horse-shoe, **Loch Coruisk** measures a mile and a half long by a quarter of a mile wide. On 25 August 1814 Sir Walter Scott (1771–1832) – travelling on a yacht with the Commissioners for the Northern Lighthouse Service – sailed into Loch Scavaig and later made his way to Loch Coruisk. As he noted in his journal of the lighthouse tour, the sight astonished him:

SKYE

The shores [of Loch Coruisk] consisted of huge layers of naked granite, here and there intermixed with bogs and heaps of gravel and sand marking the course of torrents. Vegetation there was little or none and the mountains rose so perpendicularly from the water's edge that Borrowdale is a jest to them. [We were told] the lake was popularly called the Water Kettle.

The proper name is Loch Corrisken, from the deep *corrie* or hollow in the mountains of Cuillin which affords the basin for this wonderful sheet of water. It is as exquisite as a savage scene as Loch Katrine is a scene of stern beauty.

Loch Corrisk reappeared in Scott's narrative poem *The Lord of the Isles* (1815) in which Robert the Bruce is sheltered on 'friendly Skye', a scheme that pleases him. Bruce moors in Scavaig bay and goes on shore to hunt for mountain-deer. When he sees Loch Coruisk he hails it as the most sublimely wild scene he has witnessed in Scotland. Scott (in Canto III, xiv and xv) comments:

>No marvel thus the Monarch spake;
>   For rarely human eye has known
>A scene so stern as that dread lake,
>   With its dark ledge of barren stone.
>Seems that primeval earthquake's sway
>Hath rent a strange and shatter'd way
>   Through the rude bosom of the hill,
>And that each naked precipice,
>Sable ravine, and dark abyss,
>   Tells of the outrage still.
>The wildest glen, but this, can show
>Some touch of Nature's genial glow;
>On high Benmore green mosses grow,
>And heath-bells bud in deep Glencroe,
>   And copse on Cruchan-Ben;
>But here, – above, around, below,
>   On mountain or in glen,
>Nor tree, nor shrub, nor plant, nor flower,
>Nor aught of vegetative power,
>   The weary eye may ken.
>For all is rocks at random thrown,
>Black waves, bare crags, and banks of stone,
>   As if were here denied
>The summer sun, the spring's sweet dew,
>That clothe with many a varied hue
>   The bleakest mountain-side.

And wilder, forward as they wound,
Were the proud cliffs and lake profound.
Huge terraces of granite black
Afforded rude and cumber'd track;
  For from the mountain hoar,
Hurl'd headlong in some night of fear,
When yell'd the wolf and fled the deer,
  Loose crags had toppled o'er;
And some, chance-poised and balanced, lay
So that a stripling arm might sway
  A mass no host could raise,
In Nature's rage at random thrown,
Yet trembling like the Druid's stone
  On its precarious base.

As a result of Scott's dramatic description, Loch Coruisk became an irresistible attraction for landscape painters such as Turner and Horatio McCulloch whose pictures tended to copy Scott's art rather than Skye nature. For despite Scott's vision of an unbelievably bleak and forbidding place, south-facing Loch Coruisk frequently basks in the sun and comes alive with wild flowers and gloriously green grass every summer. During the summer there are boats taking visitors from Elgol (A881) to the loch.

Hugh MacDiarmid

Squrr Alasdair – at 3,251 ft the highest point in the Cuillin – can be conquered without recourse to rock-climbing as there is a walkable approach from Coire Lagain up the Great Stone Shoot. In 1937, while researching his book *The Islands of Scotland* (1939), Hugh MacDiarmid (1892–1978) visited Skye. The third part of his poem 'Dìreadh' (meaning 'the act of surmounting'), which reflects on the Gaelic genius, appropriately invokes the highest point on Skye:

Here near the summit of Sgurr Alasdair
The air is very still and warm,
The Outer Isles look as though
They were cut out of black paper
And stuck on a brilliant silver background. . . .
The Cuillin peaks seem miniature
And nearer than is natural
And they move like liquid ripples
In the molten breath
Of the corries which divide them.
I light my pipe and the match burns steadily
Without the shielding of my hands,

The flame hardly visible in the intensity of light
Which drenches the mountain top

As MacDiarmid embraces his vision of Alba, he reaches out for an apparently impossible peak and cites the Inaccessible Pinnacle, which is at the summit of Sgurr Dearg (3,209 ft) on the Cuillin ridge. Sir Hugh Munro – whose *Table of Heights over 3,000 feet* (1891) led to the name Munro being applied to Scotland's 280 highest mountains – never managed to climb the Inaccessible Pinnacle (though the second highest point on Skye has subsequently been scaled by expert rock climbers). 'Dìreadh' closes:

Let what can be shaken, be shaken,
And the unshakeable remain.
The Inaccessible Pinnacle is not inaccessible.
So does Alba surpass the warriors
As a graceful ash surpasses a thorn,
Or the deer who moves sprinkled with the dewfall
Is far above all other beasts
– Its horns glittering to Heaven itself.

Sorley MacLean

Sorley MacLean (Somhairle MacGill-Eain) was born on 26 October 1911 in Osgaig on the island of Raasay where he first went to school. In 1924 he left Raasay to continue his education at Portree Secondary School (now Portree High School), staying at Portree during the week and going home to Raasay on Saturdays. He was educated at Edinburgh University from 1929 to 1933 and in 1934 returned to Skye to teach English at Portree Secondary School. In 1937 he took a teaching job in Tobermory, Mull, and from January 1939 to September 1940 taught at Boroughmuir School, Edinburgh. During World War Two, McLean served with the Signals Corps in North Africa and was badly wounded at the battle of El Alamein in 1943.

After recovering from his injuries, MacLean returned to teach at Boroughmuir from 1943 until 1956 when he was appointed headmaster of Plockton Secondary School, Wester Ross. He retired in 1972 and when he returned to Skye settled in his great-grandmother's house, 5 Peinnachorrain, Braes. Sorley MacLean is recognised as the greatest Scottish Gaelic poet of the twentieth-century and one of the finest poets ever to emerge from Scotland. His thematic ambitions are large and he has used Gaelic in political as well as lyrical poems. His affirmative attitude to Skye is well conveyed in 'The Island' (translated from his Gaelic original) in *Spring Tide and Neap Tide* (1977):

O great island, island of my love,
many a night of them I fancied
the great ocean itself restless
agitated with love of you
as you lay on the sea,
great beautiful bird of Scotland,
your supremely beautiful wings bent
about many-nooked Loch Bracadale,
your beautiful wings prostrate on the sea
from the Wild Stallion to the Aird of Sleat,
your joyous wings spread
about Loch Snizort and the world.

In 1986, to honour the 75th birthday of Sorley MacLean and the 100th anniversary of the Crofters Act, it was decided to build a cairn at Hallaig, Raasay, and thus mark the setting of his most celebrated poem and the site of a cleared crofting township.

SLAMANNAN, Stirlingshire   (Central)   5m SW of Falkirk on B8022

Joe Corrie

The dramatist Joe Corrie (1894–1968) was born in Slamannan and subsequently worked as a miner in Fife. He contributed to the *Miner* and eventually devoted himself to his writing. After the General Strike of 1926 he wrote a powerful drama, *In Time of Strife* (1929), about the impact of the strike on a coalmining family; the play was successfully revived by the 7:84 Comapany in 1985. Corrie was also an accomplished poet who expressed his political indignation in, for example, 'Miners' Wives' which begins:

We have borne good sons to broken men,
Nurtured them on our hungry breast,
And given them to our masters when
Their day of life was at its best.

SMA' GLEN, Perthshire   (Tayside)   On A822 between Crieff and Amulree

James Macpherson

The Sma' Glen, near Crieff, is popularly supposed to be the place where the legendary Gaelic bard Ossian was buried. Son of Fingal, Ossian flourished in the third century as a warrior-poet. His name was associated with a great literary sensation in the eighteenth century when James Macpherson fabricated his Ossianic volumes *Fragments of Ancient Poetry* (1860), *Fingal* (1761) and *Temora* (1763). These books were acclaimed throughout Europe where the Ossianic craze affected such as Napoleon and Goethe. Dr Samuel Johnson, however, accused Macpherson of literary forgery, observing, as quoted in James Boswell's *Journal of a Tour to the Hebrides* (1774):

> I look upon M'Pherson's *Fingal* to be as gross an imposition as ever the world was troubled with. Had it been really an ancient work, a true specimen of how men thought at that time, it would have been a curiosity of the first rate. As a modern production, it is nothing.

William Wordsworth

William Wordsworth (1770–1850) visited the Sma' Glen in 1803 and wrote, as a tribute to Ossian, his poem 'Glen Almain; or, The Narrow Glen' which begins:

> In this still place, remote from men,
> Sleeps Ossian, in the *Narrow Glen*;
> In this still place, where murmurs on
> But one meek streamlet, only one:
> He sang of battles, and the breath
> Of stormy war, and violent death;
> And should, methinks, when all was past,
> Have rightfully been laid at last
> Where rocks were rudely heaped, and rent
> As by a spirit turbulent;
> Where sights were rough, and sounds were wild,
> And everything unreconciled;
> In some complaining, dim retreat,
> For fear and melancholy meet;
> But this is calm; there cannot be
> A more entire tranquillity.

This should be compared with Wordsworth's opinion of 'Ossian's Hall' on pp. 172–4.

SMAILHOLM, Roxburghshire   (Border)   6m SW of Kelso on B6397

Sir Walter Scott

At the age of eighteen months Sir Walter Scott (1771–1832) lost the power of his right leg due to polio. On the advice of his maternal grandfather

John Rutherford he was sent to get the benefit of fresh country air at paternal grandfather Robert's farmhouse of Sandyknowe, at Smailholm. Thus Scott's 'first consciousness of existence' was the Border country and not his native Edinburgh. The lame child experienced some bizzare folk remedies for his condition such as being wrapped naked inside warm, newly-flayed sheepskins. But, more positively, he heard at Sandyknowe stories of relatives like great-grandfather Beardie who had fought for the Jacobite cause. His, natural in the circumstances, 'very strong prejudice in favour of the Stuart family' was strengthened by horrific tales of the persecution that followed Culloden and he learned to hate the name of Butcher Cumberland. With maiden aunt Janet Scott to read to him, Walter learned by heart passages of prose and poetry at an early age.

At the age of four Scott was taken to Bath, for a year, to see if the waters might improve the use of his right leg. He then returned to Sandyknowe for another two years. A memorial window in Smailholm church commemorates Scott's connection with the village. **Smailholm Tower**, (built 1533) to the south-west of the village, is featured in the third Canto of Scott's *Marmion* (1808). It also appears in the 'The Eve of Saint John' when the Baron of Smaylho'me returns to 'his rocky tower' and asks his foot-page

> Come, tell me all that thou has seen,
> And look though tell me true!
> Since I from Smaylho'me tower have been,
> What did thy lady do?

It is, of course, a leading question that is resolved by supernatural means.

SOUTHEND, Argyllshire   (Strathclyde)   8m SSW of Campbeltown on B842

Angus MacVicar

Angus MacVicar – a minister's son born on 28 October 1908 at Duror, Argyll – came to Southend, at the Mull of Kintyre, aged eighteen months. Except for periods at Glasgow University and in World War Two he has lived at Southend ever since, his bungalow 'Achnamara' being a familiar feature in his autobiographical books. In *Salt in My Porridge* (1971) MacVicar writes:

> As a writer I might have made more money working from a city base. But it has always seemed to me that the advantages of living in the country, particularly in Southend, far outweigh the disadvantages. . . . The scenery is thrilling. The Firth of Clyde fans out to the east,

where Ailsa Craig, nicknamed Paddy's Milestone, stands sentinel. To
the south and west the Mountains of Antrim are like silhouettes in
a Walt Disney cartoon. To the north lie Islay's slate-grey hills and the
improbable Paps of Jura.

SOUTH QUEENSFERRY, West Lothian   (Lothian)

James Hogg

South Queensferry, on the south side of the Firth of Forth (facing Fife),
is now dominated by the Forth road and rail bridges. Formerly travellers
crossed the Forth by ferry, as James Hogg did in 1802. In a letter of 25
July 1802 to Sir Walter Scott – included in Hogg's *Highland Tours* (1981)
– the Ettrick Shepherd describes the burgh:

> In a short time, I arrived at the Royal burgh of Queensferry, most
> advantageously situated on the southern shore of the Firth, in the
> midst of a populous country, from which it must derive considerable
> profit, as well as from its fisheries, coasting trade and the passage of
> the ferry. . . . It seems to be a place where there is a considerable
> stir, a good population and some manufacturers. I think the innkeepers
> on both sides of the ferry should be under proper regulations; the
> passengers, being obliged to wait time and tide, are so entirely in
> their power. When I arrived there was no other wanted to pass and,
> being unwilling to freight a boat, I alighted and ordered my horse a
> feed of oats. In a very little while, three north country gentlemen
> came, on their way home from Leith races. I hasted to join them;
> my horse had not eaten up its corn, yet I had to pay fourpence for
> hay – at which I was very ill pleased and expostulated with the
> hostler, but was told that if it had not eaten, it *might* have eaten! This
> article of forage proved a bone of contention between landlord and
> me the whole day; but I had more reason to complain before I got
> back again.
>
> We had a fine passage across the ferry; I was glad to see the rough
> sailors pay a respect to that holy day. They spoke little and I did not
> hear an oath minced by one of them.

Near the ferry jetty, then as now, stand the **Hawes Inn**, built in the
seventeenth century and extended in the nineteenth century. The Hawes
Pier, built for the ferry, dates from 1809 to 1818.

SOUTH QUEENSFERRY

Sir Walter Scott

In the first chapter of *The Antiquary* (1816) Sir Walter Scott describes the journey – by coach in the company of young Mr Lovel – Jonathan Oldbuck makes from Edinburgh to South Queensferry on his way north:

> when they descended the hill above the Hawes (for so the inn on the southern side of the Queensferry is denominated), the experienced eye of the Antiquary at once discerned, from the extent of wet sand, and the number of black stones and rocks, covered with sea-weed, which were visible along the skirts of the shore, that the hour of tide was past.

Oldbuck the antiquary suggest that they should pass their time until the next tide by having a snack at the Hawes Inn, 'which is a very decent sort of a place'. When Oldbuck and Lovel enter the Hawes there is a good deal of banter between the antiquary and Mackitchinson, landlord of the Hawes:

> 'Hold your tongue, you fool,' said [Oldbuck] the traveller, but in a great good-humour, 'and tell us what you can give this young gentleman and me for dinner.'
> 'Ou, there's fish, nae doubt, – that's sea-trout and caller haddocks,' said Mackitchinson, twisting his napkin; 'and ye'll be for a mutton-chop, and there's cranberry tarts, very well preserved, and – and there's just onything else ye like.'
> 'Which is to say, there is nothing else whatever? Well, well, the fish and the chop, and the tarts, will do very well.'

After more banter, Mackitchinson provides the travellers with a bottle of claret, and Scott notes that 'Mackitchinson's wine was really good'.

Robert Louis Stevenson

Robert Louis Stevenson's *Kidnapped* (1886) which opens in the summer of 1751, is narrated by David Balfour, a schoolmaster's son who is cheated out of his inheritance by his uncle Ebeneezer Balfour of Shaws and kidnapped on a trading brig, the *Covenant*, bound for America. The abduction is arranged at the Hawes Inn to which David Balfour is directed by his uncle Ebeneezer:

> Just then we came to the top of the hill, and looked down on the Ferry and the Hope. The Firth of Forth (as is very well known) narrows at this point to the width of a good-sized river, which makes a convenient ferry going north, and turns the upper reach into a land-locked haven for all manner of ships. Right in the midst of the narrows lies an islet with some ruins; on the south shore they have built a pier

306

for the service of the Ferry; and at the end of the pier, on the other side of the road, and backed against a pretty garden of holly-trees and hawthorns, I could see the building which they call the Hawes Inn.

At the Hawes Inn, Balfour meets Captain Hoseason who carries out the kidnapping, drinks ale with Ransome the cabin-boy, and discusses his uncle with the landlord. When he is enticed out of the Hawes Inn in the company of Hoseason he is kidnapped and his great adventure begins.

STAFFA, Argyllshire (Strathclyde) 8m W of Mull

Sir Walter Scott

There are boat trips to the tiny island of Staffa from Oban and Mull and it is possible to land if the weather permits. In 1814 Sir Walter Scott (1771–1832) made a six-week voyage round Scotland with the Commissioners of the Northern Lights and their Surveyor-Viceroy Robert Stevenson, grandfather of Robert Louis Stevenson. Scott kept a journal of the voyage and his entry for Monday 29 August 1814 explains:

Night squally and rainy – morning ditto – we weigh, however, and return toward Staffa and, very happily, the day clears as we approach the isle. As we ascertained the situation of the cave, I shall only make this memorandum, that when the weather will serve, the best landing is to the lee of Booshala, a little conical islet or rock, composed of basaltic columns placed in an oblique or sloping position. In this way you land at once on the flat causeway, formed by the heads of truncated pillars, which leads to the cave. . . . The stupendous columnar side walls [of the cave] – the depth and strength of the ocean with which the cavern is filled – the variety of tints formed by stalactites dropping and petrifying between the pillars and resembling a sort of chasing of yellow or cream coloured marble filling the interstices of the roof – the corresponding variety below, where the ocean rolls over a red, and in some places a violet-coloured rock, the basis of the basaltic pillars – the dreadful noise of those august billows so well corresponding with the grandeur of the scene – are all circumstances unparalleled.

Fingal's Cave was also celebrated in Felix Mendelssohn's Overture in B minor, Op.26 – *Die Hebriden (Fingals Höhle)*. It is popularly supposed that the composer was inspired to write the principal theme while on a visit to Staffa in 1829. Actually, he had noted the theme in a letter written before he went to the island.

STRICHEN, Aberdeenshire   (Grampian)   8m SW of Fraserburgh on
A981

Lorna Moon

Lorna Moon – the pseudonym of Helen Nora Wilson (1888–1930) – was
born on 16 June 1888 in North Street, Strichen. The daughter of a plas-
terer, she married an American called Hebditch and went to Hollywood
where she became a successful scriptwriter. Her first film, *Don't Tell
Everything* (1921) featured Gloria Swanson who also starred in *Her
Husband's Trademark* (1922). After *Too Much Wife* (1922) Lorna Moon's
Hollywood career was interrupted by illness (tuberculosis) but she produced the stories collected as *Doorways in Drumorty* (1926), a book that
draws on scenes and characters recalled from Strichen.

In 1925 Lorna Moon began to work for MGM and wrote *Upstage* (1926)
and *After Midnight* (1927), both featuring Norma Shearer. *Mr Wu*, starring
Lon Chaney, was released in 1927. Ill again, she entered a sanitorium and
fell in love with Everett Marcy, also tubercular and sixteen years her
junior. Lorna Moon's novel *Dark Star* (1929) was freely adapted by Francis
Marion for the film *Min and Bill* (1930), starring Wallace Beery and Marie
Dresler. On 1 May 1930, two weeks before the film was released, Lorna
Moon died in New Mexico. On 3 June 1930 her ashes were scattered, by
Everett Marcy, on Mormond Hill, near Strichen.

SWANSTON, Midlothian   (Lothian)

Robert Louis Stevenson

Swanston, a wooded hamlet at the north base of Caerketton in the
Pentlands, is six miles south of Edinburgh city centre: it is approached by
Swanston Road (turning on Oxgangs Road). **Swanston Cottage** is clearly
identified by an Interpretation Point on the Robert Louis Stevenson Heritage Trail. Built by the Town Council in 1761 and subsequently altered
and enlarged (now privately occupied), Swanston Cottage was leased by
Thomas Stevenson, father of Robert Louis Stevenson (1850–94), from
1867 to 1880 as a weekend and summer holiday home.

Stevenson often stayed and wrote in the cottage and the surrounding
landscape informs much of his work from the first pamphlet he published
to his unfinished novel *Weir of Hermiston* (1896). Swanston is featured
in *St Ives* (1897, completed by Sir Arthur Quiller-Couch) in which there
is a description of Swanston Cottage as Stevenson romantically recalled
it:

A single gable and chimney of the cottage peered over the shoulder of the hill; not far off, and a trifle higher on the mountain, a tall old white-washed farmhouse stood among the trees, beside a falling brook; beyond were rough hills of pasture. . . . The cottage was a little quaint place of many roughcast gables, and grey roofs. It had something of the air of a rambling infinitesimal cathedral, the body of it rising in the midst two storeys high, with a steep pitched roof, and sending out upon all hands (as it were chapter-houses, chapels, and transepts), one-storeyed and dwarfish projections. To add to this appearance, it was grotesquely decorated with crockets and gargoyles, ravished from some medieval church.

Stevenson's nurse Alison 'Cummy' Cunningham lived for a while in the small house at the entrance gate.

At Swanston, Stevenson found many of the emotional and historical sources that sustained him. Behind the slopes of Caerketton and Allermuir, on the eastern slope of Turnhouse Hill, is the site of the battlefield of Rullion Green where on 28 November 1666 a Covenanting army of 900 horse and foot was destroyed by General Tam Dalyell who commanded 600 horse and more than 2,000 foot. Above the cottage at Rullion Green is the **Martyrs' Monument** erected on 28 September 1738. On the third centenary of the battle, in 1966, a plaque was placed on the railing round the monument.

Stevenson was fascinated by the Covenanters and when he was sixteen published, anonymously, his first work, *The Pentland Rising: a Page of History, 1666.* The seventy-two page pamphlet, dated 28 November 1866, was issued (by Andrew Elliot, 17 Princes Street, Edinburgh) in an edition of 100 copies. In it, Stevenson indulges in some youthful purple prose:

The sun, going down behind the Pentlands, casts golden lights and blue shadows on their snow-clad summits, slanted obliquely into the rich plain before them, bathing with rosy splendour the leafless, snow-sprinkled trees, and fading gradually into shadow in the distance.

Stevenson told Sidney Colvin he would like to be buried 'in the hills, under the heather and a table tombstone like the Martyrs, where the whaups and plovers are crying'. He was, in fact, buried on the summit of Vaea mountain, Samoa, but the Pentlands were in his thoughts until the end of his life. When he received the dedication of S. R. Crockett's *The Stickit Minister* (1893) a year before his death, he wrote a poetic response which invokes the Covenanters and the Pentlands in the first stanza:

Blows the wind today, and the sun and the wind are flying,
    Blows the wind on the moor today and now,
Where about the graves of the martyrs the whaups are crying,
    My heart remembers how!

TANTALLON CASTLE

Edwin Muir

Beyond Swanston Cottage is Swanston Village with its eight single-storey thatched farmworkers' cottages in five whitewashed blocks. At the top of the green is a bench inscribed 'To the memory of Edwin Muir, 1882–1959. Poet, Novelist, Essayist, Teacher. This seat is given by his friends to the village of Swanston where the poet liked to linger and meditate.' In a BBC broadcast of 3 September 1952 Muir explained how he wrote the poem 'In Love for Long':

> I was up at Swanston in the Pentlands one Saturday morning during the War. It was in late summer; a dull, cloudy, windless day, quite warm. I was sitting in the grass, looking at the thatched cottages and the hills, when I realised that I was fond of them, suddenly and without reason, and for themselves, not because the cottages were quaint or the hills romantic. I had an unmistakable warm feeling for the ground I was sitting on, as if I were in love with the earth itself, and the clouds, and the soft subdued light. I had felt these things before, but that afternoon they seemed to crystallise, and the poem came out of them.

'In Love for Long', the last poem in *The Voyage* (1946), has (as the fourth of its six stanzas) the following affirmation:

> This happy, happy love
> Is sieged with crying sorrows,
> Crushed beneath and above
> Between to-days and morrows;
> A little paradise
> Held in the world's vice.

TANTALLON CASTLE, East Lothian (Lothian) 2m E of North Berwick, off A198

The spectacular red ruins of Tantallon Castle (open to the public) date from around 1370 when William, 1st Earl of Douglas, had it built. As a seat of the Douglas family it was besieged by James IV in 1491 and by James V in 1528. In 1639 Tantallon was taken by the Covenanters and in 1651 it was destroyed by General Monk. Sir Hew Dalrymple, Lord President of the Court of Session, bought the castle and barony from the Marquess of Douglas in 1699 and it was given to the Office of Works in 1924.

TANTALLON CASTLE

Gavin Douglas

Tantallon Castle was the birthplace of the poet Gavin Douglas (c
1474–1522) who was subsequently educated at St Andrews University
(1490–4). Thanks to his privileged position as a member of the powerful
Douglas family, he had the benefit of court patronage. After his appointment to the deanery of Dunkeld in 1497 he was styled Rector of Linton (or
Prestonkirk), a village between Tantallon and Dunbar. Douglas became
Provost of the Collegiate Church of St Giles, Edinburgh, in 1503 and in
1515 was appointed Bishop of Dunkeld.

Ezra Pound, in his treatise 'How to Read' (1928), pays tribute to
Douglas's poetic gifts: 'After Chaucer we have Gavin Douglas's *Eneados*,
better than the original, as Douglas had heard the sea.' Indeed he had,
as Tantallon Castle stands on a headland pointing north-east into the
Forth. Douglas's translation of Virgil's *Aeneid* into Middle Scots is a
masterly achievement and Pound's observation is justified by the following
description of a tempest in Book 1:

The aris, hechis and the takillis brast,	*oars, hatches, rigging*
The shippis stevin frawart her went gan wryth,	*prow, waywardly, course*
And turnit her braid side to the wallis swyth.	*waves, swiftly*
Heich as a hill the haw of watir brak	*leaping wave*
And in ane heap cam on them with a swak.	*crash*
Sum hesit hoverand on the wallis hicht	*hoisted, hovering*
And sum the swowchand sea so law gart licht	*sucking, caused, alight*
Them semit the erd openit amid the flude –	*seemed*
The stour up bullerit sand as it were wode.	*turbulence, boiled, mad*

Sir Walter Scott

Sir Walter Scott (1771–1832) mentions Tantallon Castle in *Marmion* – his
narrative poem set in 1513, the year of the battle of Flodden at which
James IV and Marmion are both killed. The passage occurs in Canto V (xvii):

> Displeas'd was James, that stranger view'd
> And tamper'd with his changing mood.
> 'Laugh those that can, weep those that may,'
> Thus did the fiery Monarch say,
> 'Southward I march by break of day;
> And if within Tantallon strong
> The good Lord Marmion tarries long,
> Perchance our meeting next may fall
> At Tamworth, in his castle-hall.'
> The haughty Marmion felt the taunt,
> And answer'd, grave, the royal vaunt.

Robert Louis Stevenson

Robert Louis Stevenson (1850–94), justifying his use of Lowland Scots (Lallan), in his poem 'The Maker to Posterity', from *Underwoods* (1887), used Tantallon to round off his rhyme:

> 'What tongue does your auld bookie speak?'
> He'll spier, an' I, his mou to steik: *ask, mouth, close*
> 'No bein' fit to write in Greek,
>   I wrote in Lallan,
> Dear to my heart as the peat reek,
>   Auld as Tantallon.'

David Balfour – the narrator of Stevenson's *Catriona* (1893), the sequel to *Kidnapped* (1886) – sees 'the three huge towers and broken battlements of Tantallon, that old chief place of the Red Douglasses'.

TARBERT, Argyll   (Strathclyde)   38m N of Campbeltown
on A83

J. MacDougall Hay

Tarbert has been home of the Loch Fyne herring fleet for more than a century and is the setting of *Gillespie* (1914) by J. MacDougall Hay (1881–1919) who was born in Heatherknowe, Tarbert on 23 October 1881. In the novel Tarbert is renamed Brieston and provides the atmospheric background for a tale of human greed and Gothic horror. Gillespie Strang is the merchant who dominates the life of the village and Hay's critical attitude to his native Tarbert is well illustrated by his description of the Back Street:

> This street had once some bigness of life when Bruce of Scotland,
> fleeing to Ireland, had had his boat drawn down the ancient way;
> and returned to build the fortress whose rags yet hang from a height
> over the harbour. The Way of the Boat, once royal, is now cobbled
> and broken; twisted like the precarious lives of its inhabitants,
> squirming among its thatched houses as if ashamed of its holes, and
> at every greater sore scampering round a corner out of sight. It is so
> narrow that the sun rarely comes there, being a sunset street lying
> to the west and the sea.

Gillespie was completed at Elderslie where Hay was minister from 1909 until his death on 10 December 1919. After Hay's death, his son George Campbell Hay (1915–84) moved to Tarbert where he was brought up. His collection *Wind on Loch Fyne* appeared in 1948 and, as the title indicates, celebrates scenes associated with Tarbert. Hay's best-known poem 'The Old Fisherman' ends:

> The sea was good night and morning,
> the winds were friends, the calm was kindly –
> the snow seeks the burn, the brown fronds scatter;
> my dancing days for fishing are over.

In his later years Hay was incapacitated by a depressive illness, the result of a breakdown sustained during World War Two when he attempted unsuccessfully to get out of the army after serving in North Africa. Shortly before he died he returned to Tarbert, living at Breaclarach. However he went back to Edinburgh (6 Maxwell Street) where he died on 25 March 1984.

TARBOLTON, Ayrshire   (Strathclyde)   7½m NE of Ayr, off A758

Robert Burns

The Bachelors' Club (maintained by the National Trust for Scotland: open on request, key with custodian) was a favourite haunt of Robert Burns (1759–96) for eight years, giving him much needed social relief from his work on Lochlea and Mossgiel farms. This two-storey seventeenth-century cottage was renovated and re-thatched in 1971 with the aid of a grant from the Scottish Tourist Board who cite it as an important part of the Burns Heritage Trail.

In 1777 William Burnes, the poet's father, rented the 130 swampy acres of Lochlea farm in the parish of Tarbolton and Robert Burns was well pleased with the move. He was nearing the end of his teens, proud of his reading (which included Sterne's *Tristram Shandy*, Henry Mackenzie's *The Man of Feeling* and English poets such as Pope and Shenstone). Since he wanted to 'give my manners a brush' he went to a country dancing school (in 'absolute defiance' of his father's wishes) and helped found the Tarbolton Bachelors' Club in 1780.

This monthly debating society, which met in the upstairs room of the house (then an inn), was limited to sixteen bachelors each of whom had to be 'a professed lover of one or more of the female sex'. Nor would the club admit any 'mean-spirited, worldly mortal, whose only will is to heap up money'. Obviously Burns drafted the rules of the club and by making himself conspicuous he was breaking the rules of Calvinist Scotland. A Tarbolton teacher recalled that Burns 'wore the only tied hair in the parish; and in the church, his plaid, which was of a particular colour, I think fillemot, he wrapped in a particular manner round his shoulders'.

In July 1781 Burns became a freemason in St David's Lodge, who also used the upper room in the inn (though a dispute later divided the Tarbolton Freemasons into two lodges and Burns and the St James's Lodge met at James Manson's inn nearby, site marked with a stone). Burns's Masonic connections not only put him on intimate terms with men like the Mauchline lawyer, Gavin Hamilton, but made his later entrance into Edinburgh society that much easier.

To the east of Tarbolton is the signposted **Willie's Mill**, commemorated in Burns's epitaph 'On Wm Muir in Tarbolton Mill';

> An honest man here lies at rest,
> As e'er God with His image blest:
> The friend of man, the friend of truth,
> The friend of age, and guide of youth:
> Few hearts like his – with virtue warm'd,
> Few heads with knowledge so inform'd:
> If there's another world, he lives in bliss;
> If there is none, he made the best of this.

Willie Muir, the miller, was one of the poet's closest friends and it was Willie who took in Jean Armour when her father threw her out because of her association with Burns. Willie's Mill is the setting for 'Death and Dr Hornbook':

I was come round about the hill,	
And todlin down on Willie's mill,	
Setting my staff wi' a ' my skill	
To keep me sicker;	*steady*
Tho' leeward whyles, against my will,	*at times*
I took a bicker.	*run*

I there wi' *Something* does forgather,	
That pat me in an eerie swither;	*put, ghostly dread*
An awfu' scythe, out-owre ae shouther,	*across one shoulder*
Clear-dangling, hang;	*hung*
A three-tae'd leister on the ither	*three-pronged fish-spear*
Lay, large an' lang.	

Its stature seem'd lang Scotch ells twa;	
The queerest shape that e'er I saw,	
For fient a wame it had ava	*not a belly, at all*
And then its shanks,	
They were as thin, as sharp an' sma'	
As cheeks o' branks.	

In the poem Burns listens as Death complains he is being put out of business by Jock Hornbook.

A hornbook was sheet of paper, mounted on wood and covered in transparent horn, containing elementary sums and spelling and the Lord's prayer. It was used by schoolteachers like the original of Dr Hornbook, James Wilson, a Tarbolton schoolmaster who lived near the churchyard and augmented his small salary by selling drugs and distributing medical advice – as Burns learned when listening to Wilson give a talk at the Bachelor's Club.

TAYMOUTH CASTLE, Perthshire   (Tayside)   5m SW of Aberfeldy

Fred Urquhart

Standing on the River Tay, near the east end of Loch Tay, the present Taymouth Castle was built by the Breadalbane family from 1801 to 1842. It became a hotel in 1920, was subsequently a school, and is now owned by the Kenmore Hotel. In 1918 novelist and storyteller Fred Urquhart (born 1912) lived at Taymouth Castle when his father became chauffeur to the Marquess of Breadalbane. This background is used in Urquhart's novel *Palace of Green Days* (1979) which begins with Jim Lovat becoming head chauffeur to the Marquis of Bencraigon at Finlochrig Castle:

> They came to Finlochrig Castle in the spring of 1918. It belonged to the old Marquis of Bencraigon and was in Perthshire. Jenny was five and a half, and she'd been at school for six months. Andrew was four, and Tommy was two. . . . Their new home was about a mile from the castle.

In fact the Urquharts lived at Newhall, a small collection of houses a mile from Taymouth Castle, from spring 1918 to spring 1919. Urquhart went to Styx Village School and walked there every day with the other children who lived at Newhall.

TEVIOTHEAD, Roxburghshire   (Border)   9m SW of Hawick on A7

'Johnie Armstrong'

Johnie Armstrong, a heroic figure in the Scottish Border ballads, is buried in Teviothead kirkyard. The historical basis for the ballad of 'Johnie Armstrong' – number 169 in Francis James Child's *The English and Scottish Popular Ballads* (5 vols, 1882–98) – is that in 1530 James V levied an army of some 12,000 men to pacify the Borders where men like

315

Armstrong were laws unto themselves. In this campaign Armstrong was killed. In the ballad (169A) James V summons Johnie to Edinburgh with a promise of safe conduct. When Johnie reaches the capital he is told he is to be hanged. In true Border style he refuses to accept this meekly and fights ferociously for his life before being stabbed in the back. Though long since dead, Johnie is a Border immortal, a man animated by pride and arrogance:

> He had nither lands nor rents coming in,
> Yet he kept eight score men in his hall.

Rev. Henry Scott Riddell

North of Teviothead, on the slopes of Commonside Moor, is the **Riddell Monument**. This commemorates the Rev. Henry Scott Riddell (1798–1870) who ministered in Teviothead where he is buried; and who gained a reputation as the preacher-poet of the village.

TILQUILLIE CASTLE, Kincardineshire (Grampian) 2m SE of
Banchory, off A957

Norman Douglas

Norman Douglas (1868–1952) was born at Tilquillie Castle on 8 December 1868 and was educated at Uppingham School and Karlsruhe, Germany, before becoming a diplomat in the Foreign Office and serving in the diplomatic corps in St Petersburg from 1894 to 1896. He found his spiritual home when he travelled in Italy and eventually settled in Capri (where he came into contact with Compton Mackenzie and D. H. Lawrence). His masterpiece, *South Wind* (1917), is set on the island of Nepenthe, presented as a paradisal place whose inhabitants are hedonistically beyond good and evil. One of the characters, Mr Keith, is a rich Scotsman who visits Nepenthe for a few weeks of each year. His outlook is conditioned by his upbringing:

> Scotland chastened him; its rocks and tawny glinting waters and bleak
> purple uplands rectified his perspective. He called to mind the
> sensuous melancholy of the birches, the foxgloves, the hedgerows
> smothered in dog-roses; he remembered the nights, full of fairy-like
> suggestions and odours of earth and budding leaves

WICK, Caithness   (Highland)   161m NE of Inverness on A9

Wick (from Norse 'Vik' for 'Bay') features in the *Orkneyinga Saga* (written around 1200, translation by Hermann Palsson and Paul Edwards published in 1978): 'While Svein Asleifarson had been in the Hebrides, Earl Rognvald had gone over to Wick in Caithness to attend a feast given by a man called Hroald.'

In the autumn of 1868 Robert Louis Stevenson (1850–94) stayed at Harbour Terrace (where there is a plaque) while his father Thomas Stevenson engineered improvements in the harbour.

WORMIT, Fife   (Fife)   2m W of Newport on B946

George Bruce

From 1940 to 1946 the poet George Bruce (born 1909) lived at 'Bennachie', Newton Park, Wormit. Every day Bruce walked the mile to Wormit station to catch the train to Dundee where he taught English at Dundee High School. The same walk, in the company of his wife and son, on an April holiday in 1945 inspired Bruce's first love poem to his wife. 'Song for Elizabeth' – in *Collected Poems* (1970) – runs:

> Her young son singing
> By her side,
> Blackbird ringing
> His sky-note high and wide –
>
> Laughter over water
> Where, where her heart hides
> There singing sought her
> Singing leaves and airs and tides.

YARROW WATER, Selkirkshire   (Border)

'The Braes of Yarrow'

Yarrow Water rises above St Mary's Loch and flows (via Ettrick Forest) into the Tweed. The river is a melancholy presence in the Border Ballads collected in Francis James Child's *The English and Scottish Popular Ballads* (5 vols, 1882–98). 'The Braes of Yarrow' (214A in Child's collection) begins with an ominous dream as a lady thinks she sees her husband 'come headless hame'. In spite of this the husband goes to meet his brother-in-law on the braes of Yarrow; there he is ambushed and killed from behind. The brother-in-law callously tells his sister that her husband is 'sleeping sound on Yarrow', so she goes to him, combs his hair, ties her own yellow hair around her neck and kills herself on Yarrow. 'Rare Willie Drowned in Yarrow' (215A) is a short lyrical piece in which a lady, looking forward to her wedding, finds her man drowned in the river:

> She sought him east, she sought him west,
>   She sought him brade and narrow;
> Sine, in the clifting of a craig,
>   She found him drowned in Yarrow.

Sir Walter Scott

Sir Walter Scott (1771–1832) introduces the fourth Canto of *Marmion* (1808) by describing the progress of the poem in November:

> That same November gale once more
> Whirls the dry leaves on Yarrow shore.
> Their vex'd boughs streaming to the sky,
> Once more our naked birches sigh.

William Wordsworth

William Wordsworth (1770–1850) was fascinated by the poetic fame of Yarrow. Before he had seen the river, he celebrated it in 'Yarrow Unvisited', a poem written in 1803 after a meeting with Scott:

> Let beeves and home-bred kine partake
> The sweets of Burn-mill meadow;
> The swan on still St Mary's Lake
> Float double, swan and shadow!
> We will not see them; will not go,
> To-day, nor yet to-morrow;
> Enough if in our hearts we know
> There's such a place as Yarrow.

In his second tour of Scotland, in 1814, Wordsworth visited the river, as he explained in 'Yarrow Visited':

> I see – but not by sight alone,
> Loved Yarrow, have I won thee;
> A ray of fancy still survives –
> Her sunshine plays upon thee!
> Thy ever-youthful waters keep
> A course of lively pleasure;
> And gladsome notes my lips can breathe,
> Accordant to the measure.

In 1831 Wordsworth was back in Scotland, and staying with Scott at Abbotsford. His third Yarrow poem, 'Yarrow Revisited', ends:

> Flow on for ever, Yarrow Stream!
>   Fulfil thy pensive duty,
> Well pleased that future Bards should chant
>   For simple hearts thy beauty;
> To dream-light dear while yet unseen,
>   Due to the common sunshine,
> And dearer still, as now I feel!
>   To memory's shadowy moonshine!

BIBLIOGRAPHY

In the course of my research I have, of course, consulted many books, some of them mentioned in the text. The following are noted as being especially useful.

Philip Boardman, *The Worlds of Patrick Geddes* (London: Routledge and Kegan Paul 1978)

Alan Bold, *Modern Scottish Literature* (London: Longman 1983)

Alan Bold, *MacDiarmid: A Critical Biography* (London: John Murray, 1988).

P. H. Butter, *Edwin Muir: Man and Poet* (Edinburgh: Oliver and Boyd 1966)

Laurence Davies and Cedric Watts, *Cunninghame Graham: a Critical Biography* (Cambridge: Cambridge University Press 1979)

Gordon Donaldson and Robert Morpeth, *A Dictionary of Scottish History* (Edinburgh: John Donald 1977)

Dorothy Eagle and Hilary Carnal, *The Oxford Illustrated Guide to Great Britain and Ireland* (Oxford: Oxford University Press 1981)

Andrew Fergus, *Discovering the Burns Country* (Aylesbury: Shire 1976)

John Gifford, Colin McWilliam and David Walker, *Edinburgh* (Harmondsworth: Penguin Books 1984)

Francis Russell Hart, *The Scottish Novel* (London: John Murray 1978)

Francis Russell Hart and John B. Pick, *Neil M. Gunn: a Highland Life* (London: John Murray 1981)

Laurence Hutton, *Literary Landmarks of Edinburgh* (New York: Harper and Brothers 1981)

Maurice Lindsay, *Francis George Scott and the Scottish Renaissance* (Edinburgh: Paul Harris 1980)

Colin McWilliam, *Lothian* (Harmondsworth: Penguin Books 1978)

D. G. Moir, *Pentland Walks* (Edinburgh: Bartholomew 1977)

David Phillips, *No Poets' Corner in the Abbey* (Dundee: David Winter 1971)

Michael Parnell, *Eric Linklater* (London: John Murray 1984)

Trevor Royle, *The Macmillan Companion to Scottish Literature* (London: Macmillan Press 1983)

P. H. Scott, *John Galt* (Edinburgh: Scottish Academic Press 1985)

J. M. Sloan, *The Carlyle Country* (London: Chapman and Hall 1904)

Janet Adam Smith, *John Buchan* (London: Rupert Hart-Davis 1965)

Louis Stott, *Smollett's Scotland* (Dumbarton: Dumbarton District Libraries 1981)

Derick Thomson, *An Introduction to Gaelic Poetry* (London: Victor Gollancz 1974)

BIBLIOGRAPHY

John Tomes, *Blue Guide to Scotland* (London: Ernest Benn, 8th edn 1980)
Charles D. Waterston, *Hugh Miller* (Edinburgh: National Trust for Scotland 1979)
Gordon Wright, *MacDiarmid: An Illustrated Biography* (Edinburgh: Gordon Wright 1977)

INDEX OF AUTHORS